RENEWALS 458-4574.

WITHDRAWN
UTSA Libraries

The Economics of Self-Employment and Entrepreneurship

As self-employment and entrepreneurship become increasingly important in our modern economies, Simon C. Parker provides a timely, definitive and comprehensive overview of the field. In this book he brings together and assesses the large and disparate literature on these subjects and provides an up-to-date overview of new research findings. Key issues addressed include: the impact of ability, risk, personal characteristics and the macroeconomy on entrepreneurship; issues involved in raising finance for entrepreneurial ventures, with an emphasis on the market failures that can arise as a consequence of asymmetric information; the job creation performance of the self-employed; the growth, innovation and exit behaviour of new ventures and small firms; and the appropriate role for governments interested in promoting self-employment and entrepreneurship. This book will serve as an essential reference guide to researchers, students and teachers of entrepreneurship in economics, business and management and other related disciplines.

SIMON C. PARKER is Professor and Head of Economics at the University of Durham. He is also Director of the Centre for Entrepreneurship at Durham Business School. Professor Parker has published widely in economics journals on a variety of issues on self-employment and entrepreneurship.

The Economics of
Self-Employment and
Entrepreneurship

Simon C. Parker

CAMBRIDGE
UNIVERSITY PRESS

PUBLISHED BY THE PRESS SYNDICATE OF THE UNIVERSITY OF CAMBRIDGE
The Pitt Building, Trumpington Street, Cambridge CB2 1RP, United Kingdom

CAMBRIDGE UNIVERSITY PRESS
The Edinburgh Building, Cambridge, CB2 2RU, UK
40 West 20th Street, New York, NY 10011–4211, USA
477 Williamstown Road, Port Melbourne, VIC 3207, Australia
Ruiz de Alarcón 13, 28014 Madrid, Spain
Dock House, The Waterfront, Cape Town 8001, South Africa

http://www.cambridge.org

© Simon C. Parker, 2004

This book is in copyright. Subject to statutory exception
and to the provisions of relevant collective licensing agreements,
no reproduction of any part may take place without
the written permission of Cambridge University Press.

First published 2004

Printed in the United Kingdom at the University Press, Cambridge

Typeface Plantin 10/12 pt.   *System* LᴬTᴇX 2$_\varepsilon$ [TB]

A catalogue record for this book is available from the British Library

Library of Congress Cataloguing in publication data
Parker, Simon C.
The economics of self-employment and entrepreneurship / Simon C. Parker.
   p.   cm.
Includes bibliographical references and index.
ISBN 0-521-82813-9
1. Managerial economics.   2. Entrepreneurship.   3. New business
enterprises–Management.   4. Self-employed.   5. Self-employed–Government
policy–Case studies.   I. Title.
HD30.22.P376 2004
338′.04 – dc22   2003061085

ISBN 0 521 82813 9 hardback

Library
University of Texas
at San Antonio

For Lisa

Contents

Figures

Tables

Preface

Entrepreneurship is a subject that is commonly taught and researched in business schools, but seldom if at all in economics departments. Consequently, most books on entrepreneurship tend to be written from a business and management perspective. Such books often downplay, or ignore altogether, the contribution of modern economics to our understanding of the subject. Indeed, it is common to find them referring to 'the contribution of economics' mainly in terms of the treatises of Frank Knight and Josef Schumpeter – works that were published more than half a century ago! Of modern economics, there is little mention, apart from the occasional disparaging remark that competitive general equilibrium theory leaves little or no room for the entrepreneur, so modern economics has little to offer the study of the subject.

The present book hopes to convince the reader that the foregoing is an unduly negative assessment, by reviewing the many contributions that modern economics has brought, and continues to bring, to our understanding of self-employment and entrepreneurship. These contributions include rigorous analyses of occupational choice ('what economic factors help explain who becomes an entrepreneur?'); the efficiency and economic impact of entrepreneurial ventures ('what is the economic importance and value of entrepreneurship?'); and the appropriate role of governments with respect to entrepreneurship ('what is the rationale for intervening in the market economy to encourage entrepreneurship?'). It is hoped that, by drawing together these contributions in this book, readers who have been trained to ignore or dismiss economics' contributions to the subject will be motivated to think again, and may learn from the many insights that it has generated.

Of course, the book also addresses a target audience of economists, with an agenda of raising the profile of entrepreneurship in that subject. It is unclear why entrepreneurship plays such a marginal role in most economics departments. It is possible that economists are suspicious of a subject with an avowedly mongrel provenance, which reflects a multiplicity of different, and often non-quantitative, perspectives. From a personal standpoint, the multidisciplinary nature of entrepreneurship posed one of the greatest challenges in writing this book. It also offered some of the greatest rewards.

My own view is that the multidisciplinary nature of entrepreneurship is a potential strength, rather than a weakness. But this potential will be achieved only if students and researchers take the trouble to break the boundaries of narrow scholarship, an ideal to which this book is dedicated. Indeed, the book does not confine itself exclusively to one paradigm, despite its predominantly economics-based perspective. The book does attempt to reach out beyond economics in many places, and includes several references to contributions from other disciplines.

The book might never have seen the light of day without the support of Chris Harrison, the Publishing Director of Humanities & Social Sciences at Cambridge University Press. I am also grateful to Alison Powell at Cambridge for the production of this book.

Glossary of commonly used symbols

VARIABLES

a	age or years of experience
A	production function shift variable
$\alpha, \beta, \gamma, \vartheta, \omega$	(vectors of) parameters
b	a 'bad' (risky) entrepreneurial type or venture
B	real current or lifetime wealth of an individual
BAD	a contract term yielding disutility to borrowers
$c, c(\cdot)$	cost, cost function
C	collateral
D	debt repayment an entrepreneur owes a bank
dz	increment of a Wiener process
δ	subjective intertemporal discount rate
e	effort
E	paid-employment
E	the expectations operator
$\phi(\cdot)$	the density function of the standard normal distribution
$\Phi(\cdot)$	the distribution function of the standard normal
$f(\cdot), F(\cdot)$	the density and distribution functions of a random variable
$g(\cdot), G(\cdot)$	the density and distribution functions of another random variable
g	a 'good' (safe) entrepreneurial type or venture
$\Gamma = (\cdot, \ldots)$	a lending contract whose arguments are the contract terms
h_E	employee work-hours
h_S, h	self-employed work-hours
H	total employee labour input
I	non-labour income
IIN	identically and independently normally distributed
k	physical capital input

λ	inverse Mills Ratio
L	size of a bank loan; number of bank loans
$\mathcal{L}$	likelihood function
M, NM	member of a minority (non-minority) ethnic group
n	the number of individuals in a sample
n_j	the number or fraction of individuals in occupation j
Ω	social welfare (function); also state-space/Kuhn–Tucker constraint
p	probability of success of a new enterprise
P	self-employed product price
π	profit from entrepreneurship
π^B	banks' expected profit on a loan
Π	probability a self-employed individual is audited
q	self-employed product output
$q(\cdot, \ldots)$	self-employed production function
Q	aggregate demand for self-employed products
r	interest rate (rental price of capital)
r^A	coefficient of absolute risk aversion
r^R	coefficient of relative risk aversion
R	stochastic return on a risky entrepreneurial venture
R^f	actual return if a risky venture is unsuccessful
R^s	actual return if a risky venture is successful
ρ	the safe (deposit) interest rate = competitive banks' expected return; also used as the correlation coefficient
ϱ	a random variable, a random shock
s	aggregate self-employment rate
sch	years of schooling or some other measure of education
S	self-employment
σ^2	variance of a stochastic regression disturbance term
σ_j	standard deviation of income risk in occupation j
t	time
T	the number of time periods
$T_{ij}, T_{ij}(\cdot)$	tax liability of individual i in occupation j
τ	income tax rate
ς	a subsidy
θ	an entrepreneur's type, a member of Θ
Θ	the set of entrepreneurial types
u, v, ϵ	stochastic (regression) disturbance terms
$U(\cdot)$	a cardinal utility function
$V(\cdot)$	indirect utility, or value, function

v	non-pecuniary utility advantage to self-employment
w, w_E	wage rate received by employees
w_S	'wage rate' received by the self-employed
W, X, M	vectors of explanatory variables
$\psi(\cdot)$, $\varphi(\cdot)$	some continuous function
x	(uni-dimensional) entrepreneurial ability
$\tilde{x}$	the (ability of the) marginal entrepreneur
x_E	ability in paid-employment
ξ	proportion of working time spent in S
y_j	gross (i.e. pre-tax) income received in occupation j
y_j^n	net (after-tax) income received in occupation j
Υ	the state of technology
z_i	a binary observed indicator variable: equal to 1 if individual i is self-employed, else zero
z_i^*	an unobserved binary latent variable: the probability individual i chooses to be self-employed
ζ	consumption

INDEXES

i	(subscript) indexes an individual
j	(subscript) indexes an occupation, usually self-employment (S), paid-employment (E), or unemployment (U); but sometimes also a minority (M) or non-minority (NM) group; or a region; or gender
t	(subscript) indexes a point in time

OTHER SYMBOLS

$\dot{y}$	time derivative of y (say)
$\hat{}$	(when used in a sample) an estimate of a parameter
$*$	optimal value (except for z^*)
$'$ (prime)	vector or matrix transpose
$\tilde{}$	a marginal type

ABBREVIATIONS OF ORGANISATIONS AND DATA-SETS

BHPS	British Household Panel Survey (UK)
CBO	Characteristics of Business Owners (US)
CPS	Current Population Survey (US)
FES	Family Expenditure Survey (UK)
GHS	General Household Survey (UK)

LFS	Labour Force Survey (UK)
NCDS	National Child Development Survey (UK)
NFIB	National Federation of Independent Businesses (US)
NLS	National Longitudinal Survey (US)
NLSY	National Longitudinal Survey of Youth (US)
OECD	Organisation for Economic Co-Operation and Development
PSID	(Michigan) Panel Study of Income Dynamics (US)
SBA	Small Business Administration (US)
SIPP	Survey of Incomes and Program Participation (US)

1 Introduction

The entrepreneur is at the same time one of the most intriguing and one of the most elusive characters ... in economic analysis. He has long been recognised as the apex of the hierarchy that determines the behaviour of the firm and thereby bears a heavy responsibility for the vitality of the free enterprise society. (Baumol, 1968, p. 64)

Self-employment is unquestionably the oldest way by which individuals offer and sell their labour in a market economy. At an earlier time, it was also the primary way. Despite this history, its principal features and the characteristics that differentiate self-employment from wage and salary employment have attracted the attention of only a handful of students of the labour market. (Aronson, 1991, p. ix)

Entrepreneurship is increasingly in the news. Governments all over the world extol its benefits and implement policies designed to promote it. There are several reasons for this interest in, and enthusiasm for, entrepreneurship. Owner-managers of small enterprises run the majority of businesses in most countries. These enterprises are credited with providing specialised goods and services that are ignored by the largest firms. They also intensify competition, thereby increasing economic efficiency. Some entrepreneurs pioneer new markets for innovative products, creating new jobs and enhancing economic growth. In a few cases, today's small owner-managed enterprises grow to become tomorrow's industrial giants. Even those that do not may create positive externalities, like the development of supply chains that help attract inward investment, or greater social inclusion. It is sometimes also claimed that the decentralisation of economic production into a large number of small firms is good for society and democracy, as is the fostering of a self-reliant and hardy 'entrepreneurial spirit'.

Entrepreneurship has only recently come to be regarded as a subject. A complete view of it recognises its multidisciplinary academic underpinnings, drawing as it does from Economics, Finance, Business and Management, Sociology, Psychology, Economic Geography, Economic History, Law, Politics and Anthropology. This heterogeneous provenance reflects the multidimensional nature of entrepreneurship, which partly contributes to the elusiveness of the entrepreneur alluded to by William Baumol.

1.1   Aims, motivation and scope of the book

There is general agreement that entrepreneurship is sadly neglected in most economics textbooks (see, e.g. Rosen, 1997; Kent and Rushing, 1999). Some commentators have attributed this neglect to an inherent unsuitability of economics for studying entrepreneurship. These commentators allege that economics is concerned only with equilibrium outcomes in competitive markets with perfectly informed agents, whereas entrepreneurship embodies imperfect information and unexpected innovations that disrupt equilibria (Barreto, 1989; Kirchhoff, 1991; Harper, 1996; Rosen, 1997). While it is true that economists usually take the state of technology as given, this point should not be pushed too far. For a start, there is much more to entrepreneurship than just innovation. This book makes the case that the tools of modern economics are invaluable for understanding the determinants of, and constraints on, entrepreneurship, the behaviour of entrepreneurs, the contribution of entrepreneurs to the broader economy and the impact of government policies on entrepreneurship. It is hoped that the book will go some way towards correcting mistaken and prejudiced impressions about the contribution of economics to this field, and will convince the reader that it is not an oxymoron to talk about the 'economics of entrepreneurship'.

One aspect of entrepreneurship that economists have researched quite thoroughly is occupational choice. Despite the limitations of employing such a narrow definition – an issue we shall discuss further below – many applied labour economists have equated self-employment with entrepreneurship, and have analysed behavioural choice between paid- and self-employment. Unfortunately, here too the economics textbooks have been guilty of neglect: the above quotation from Richard Aronson about self-employment remains as true today as it did over a decade ago. To appreciate the economic importance of self-employment, consider the following facts:

1. Around 10 per cent of the workforces in most OECD economies are self-employed. The figure climbs to about 20 per cent when individuals who work for the self-employed are also included (Haber, Lamas and Lichtenstein, 1987). Two-thirds of people in the US labour force have some linkage to self-employment, by having experienced self-employment, by coming from a background in which the household head was self-employed, or by having a close friend who is self-employed (Steinmetz and Wright, 1989). And by the end of

their working lives, about two-fifths of the American workforce will have had at least one spell of self-employment (Reynolds and White, 1997).

2. Between 80 and 90 per cent of businesses are operated by self-employed individuals (Acs, Audretsch and Evans, 1994; Selden, 1999).

3. Many employees in industrialised countries claim that they would like to be self-employed. For example, according to Blanchflower (2000), 63 per cent of Americans, 48 per cent of Britons and 49 per cent of Germans stated a preference for self-employment over paid-employment.[1]

Why have the economics textbooks so conspicuously neglected self-employment and entrepreneurship? The answer is unclear, but might involve a lingering mistrust of entrepreneurship among economists, and an inability to pigeon-hole this multifaceted subject. There is certainly no lack of research on self-employment and entrepreneurship by economists. Indeed, we hope that one of the contributions of this book is to organise and assess the current state of this branching, acquisitive and rapidly growing literature. The book is intended to serve as a comprehensive overview and guide to researchers and students of entrepreneurship in a variety of disciplines, not just in Economics. The book can also be used to support teaching in modules such as Small Business Economics and Entrepreneurship. Readers with a working knowledge of basic undergraduate calculus, statistics and economics should cope easily with the book's modest technical demands. Readers without this technical background will still be able to read the majority of the book without difficulty, and understand the gist of the remainder by 'reading between the Greek'.

For brevity and focus, some topics will be excluded. These include entrepreneurship in education; 'social entrepreneurship' and 'intrapreneurship';[2] organisational, strategic and managerial decision making by entrepreneurs; network and organisational ecology approaches to entrepreneurship; 'evolutionary economics'; and practical advice (including 'how to' information) to entrepreneurs. Nor will we provide descriptive case studies either of individual entrepreneurs, or of small firms or the industries in which they operate. These topics are ably covered in numerous texts in the Business/Management literature, and will not be repeated here.

1.2   Structure of the book

The remainder of this chapter is organised as follows. Section 1.3 discusses issues in the definition and measurement of entrepreneurship and self-employment. The distinction between these two concepts explains their joint presence in the title of this book. Sections 1.4 and 1.5 introduce the reader to some stylised facts about the self-employed, including their number, incomes and income inequality. Section 1.6 describes some useful econometric models of occupational choice referred to extensively in the book.

Part I deals with theories of entrepreneurship and the characteristics of entrepreneurs. Chapter 2 outlines economic theories of the entrepreneur and entrepreneurship, both 'early' (Section 2.1) and 'modern' (Section 2.2). The former tend to paint a broad-brush picture of entrepreneurship, whereas the latter apply the tools of microeconomics to the problem of entrepreneurship as an occupational choice. Chapter 3 fills out some detail by considering the roles of pecuniary factors, individual characteristics, family background and environmental variables for explaining the decision to become an entrepreneur. Chapter 4 considers separately issues of race, gender and immigration as they relate to entrepreneurship.

Part II treats the important problem of raising finance for entrepreneurial ventures. Chapter 5 analyses the economic issues arising from bank finance of new start-ups, bank loans being the largest and most frequently used source of outside funds by entrepreneurs. Although we will touch on such 'practical' issues as collateral and bank–borrower relationships, the focus of this chapter will be on the market failures that can arise as a consequence of asymmetric information, including credit rationing, under-investment and over-investment. These issues carry important policy implications about whether governments should encourage or discourage entrepreneurship. Chapter 6 considers other sources of funds, including equity finance, trade credit, group lending schemes and borrowing from family and friends. Chapter 7 summarises evidence on whether, and to what extent, entrepreneurs face credit rationing.

Part III investigates what happens to new ventures after they are launched. Chapter 8 discusses theory and evidence about job creation by entrepreneurs, and their labour supply and retirement behaviour. Chapter 9 analyses the growth, innovation and exit behaviour of new ventures and small firms. With all of this apparatus in place, it is possible to explore systematically the scope for governments to intervene in the market to promote entrepreneurship. This is the subject of part IV (chapter 10). Government policies can take several forms, including credit market interventions, taxation and direct assistance and regulation. Chapter 11 concludes, and draws together some suggestions for future research where our understanding of particular issues is especially incomplete.

1.3   Definition and measurement issues

The problem of defining the word 'entrepreneur' and establishing the boundaries of the field of entrepreneurship still has not been solved. (Bruyat and Julien, 2001, p. 166)

Our first and most pressing task is to define entrepreneurs and entrepreneurship. Unfortunately, this happens to be one of the most difficult and intractable tasks faced by researchers working in the field. There is a proliferation of theories, definitions and taxonomies of entrepreneurship which often conflict and overlap, resulting in confusion and disagreement among researchers and practitioners about precisely what entrepreneurship is (see Parker, 2002a). For example, consider the following illustrative and abbreviated set of viewpoints. In applied work, labour economists often equate entrepreneurs with the self-employed, on the grounds that the self-employed fulfil the entrepreneurial function of being risk-bearing residual claimants. However, others think this definition is too broad, claiming that only business owners who co-ordinate factors of production (in particular, those who employ workers) are really entrepreneurs. Still others think that the economist's definition is too narrow, because it excludes entrepreneurship in the corporate and social spheres. Then there are those steeped in the Schumpeterian tradition who argue that entrepreneurship is identified primarily with the introduction of new paradigm-shifting innovations. Others again have emphasised psychological traits and attitudes supposedly peculiar to entrepreneurship. And so the list goes on.

It is easier to define the terms 'self-employed' and 'self-employment', though even here there are measurement problems and disagreements, which we discuss below. Given the widespread availability of data on the self-employed in government and private surveys world wide, it is also an easier entity to operationalise in empirical research (Katz, 1990). To cut through a paralysing and ultimately fruitless debate, and to achieve consistency, we will adopt the following convention in this book. At the conceptual level, the terms 'entrepreneur' and 'entrepreneurship' will be used; at the practical level, where issues of measurement, estimation and policy are involved, we will use the closest approximation to the manifestation of entrepreneurship that appears to be suitable. That will usually be 'self-employment', though occasionally the term 'small firm' will be more relevant. Note that the problems of defining 'small' firms are also non-trivial. Firm-size definitions are arbitrary and industry-specific, and are not obviously congruent with entrepreneurship. Not all entrepreneurs run small firms, and not every small firm is run by an entrepreneur (Brock and Evans, 1986; Holtz-Eakin, 2000).

The self-employed are often taken to be individuals who earn no wage or salary but who derive their income by exercising their profession or business on their own account and at their own risk. Likewise, partners of an unincorporated business are usually classified as self-employed. It is sometimes helpful to partition the self-employed into employers and own-account workers (the latter of which work alone), or into owners of incorporated or unincorporated businesses. In most countries, incorporation of a business renders it susceptible to company law, which requires the owner to publicise stipulated data about the business. In the UK and USA, for example, these include audited accounts if business turnover exceeds a specified level. Despite the costs and inconvenience involved, there are several advantages to incorporation. They include: protection from creditors via limited liability; favourable pension contribution rules; greater credibility with customers (Storey, 1994b); and payment of corporation tax on company profits, which at high owner incomes may be substantially lower than personal income tax rates (Fuest, Huber and Nielsen, 2002). Incorporated business owners can either receive an *employee* salary as a director of their company, or they can pay themselves dividends – so escaping payroll taxes in some jurisdictions, including the UK. Most self-employed people in most countries own unincorporated businesses,[3] which renders their incomes liable to personal income tax.

The first definitional problem is that in many countries (including the UK and USA), owners of incorporated businesses are defined as employees rather than self-employed. This is despite them resembling in all other respects (e.g. residual claimant status) the 'self-employed'. This is sometimes an important distinction in applied self-employment research.

Second, for some individuals, the legal and tax-based definitions of self-employment are at variance with each other. In law, the issue comes down to whether there is a contract *of* service or a contract *for* services. The first indicates paid-employment, the second self-employment.[4] In contrast, different criteria are often used for determining who is self-employed for the purposes of income taxation and social security eligibility. There is no shortage of examples where the legal and tax definitions fail to coincide (Harvey, 1995; Dennis, 1996).

Third, in many government surveys used in empirical research, self-employment status is self-assessed by the survey respondents. This can lead to further differences in the classification of workers, compared with legal and tax-based definitions (Casey and Creigh, 1988; Boden and Nucci, 1997). Partly for this reason, some surveys (e.g. the UK Labour Force Survey (LFS) and the US Characteristics of Business Owners (CBO)) use tax-based definitions of self-employment.

Fourth, there appears to be a 'grey area' between paid-employment and self-employment. Some workers classified as self-employed with apparent autonomy over their work hours are effectively employees, being 'peripheral' workers subordinated to the demands of one client firm (Pollert, 1988; Harvey, 1995). For example, Harvey (1995) contends that, in the construction industry, most self-employed workers are to all intents and purposes direct employees, working exclusively for one contractor, and providing independently only their labour.[5] Employers provide the materials, capital and plant and set the terms of work and pay. This is a potential matter of concern to policy makers to the extent that self-employed workers are engaged on worse terms than employees, lacking job security, entitlement to holidays, sick pay, employment protection, or trades union rights. It is sometimes argued that employers actively seek to organise their workforce in self-employment contracts, to cut costs and to avoid their social obligations.[6]

This debate is related to one on contracting-out of labour by large firms, a phenomenon that was thought to have been particularly pronounced in the 1980s, a decade when self-employment rates in several countries increased dramatically. Hakim (1988) pointed to some evidence that UK firms made some limited moves during the 1980s to outsource work to self-employed contractors. However, according to Blackburn (1992) subcontracting has always existed and the increase in the UK in the 1980s was relatively slight. Also, case study evidence from Leighton (1982) suggested that many employers prefer hiring employees to self-employed contractors even in industries where self-employment is relatively common. Benefits of hiring employees directly include greater control, discipline and stability. If this argument is valid, it suggests that the amount of 'grey' self-employment in the form of outsourced labour has not grown dramatically in the recent past, and is presumably likely to remain stable in the near future.

Other examples of workers in the 'grey area' between employment and self-employment include commission salespersons, freelancers, homeworkers and tele-workers,[7] workers contracted through temporary employment agencies and franchise holders. Regarding the latter, it is often difficult to determine whether a franchise is an independent small business or part of a large firm. Felstead (1992) argued that many 'self-employed' franchisees are effectively directed by their franchisor, who holds most of the ownership rights and has a senior claim on profits. With relatively little discretion about the format of their business, one could certainly claim that some franchisees resemble branch managers more than independent entrepreneurs. On the other hand, one could argue that a self-employed retailer who is pressurised into stocking the goods of mainly one goods manufacturer also has limited discretion about the nature of his or her business. And like other self-employed workers, franchisees face uncertainty. In their case, not only is their income uncertain, but there is also a possibility that the franchisor will either go out of business, or refuse to renew the franchise agreement at the expiration of its term.[8]

Two other 'grey' categories include unpaid family workers who work in a business run by a self-employed person; and members of worker co-operatives, who are not obviously either employees or self-employed workers in the conventional sense of the term. Both groups tend to be more numerous in developing than in developed countries, and in rural than in urban areas. According to Bregger (1996, p. 5), 'Unpaid family workers are persons who work on a family farm or in a family business for at least 15 hours a week and who receive no earnings or share of the profits of the enterprise'. Blanchflower (2000) detected substantial variation within developed countries in the proportion of self-employed workers who are unpaid family workers, being as high as 33 per cent in Japan, compared with 14 per cent in Italy and just 1.7 per cent in the USA. As Blanchflower points out, it may not make sense just to discard unpaid family workers from the self-employment count, since they often share indirectly (e.g. via consuming household goods) the proceeds generated by the business. Worker co-operatives are also relatively uncommon in the UK, and tend to be larger and better established in European countries, such as France, Italy and Spain (Spear, 1992).

Section 1.4 documents some international evidence on levels of, and trends in, aggregate self-employment rates. At the aggregate level, it is likely that alternative measures of self-employment are highly correlated with each other, allowing trends within a given country to be identified fairly reliably (Blau, 1987). However, to the extent that different countries use different definitions of self-employment, cross-country comparisons of levels have to be treated with caution.

1.4   International evidence on self-employment rates and trends

There is great diversity in the level and time-series pattern of self-employment rates across countries. This is evident from tables 1.1, 1.2 and 1.3, which summarise data for a selection of OECD countries, Eastern European transition economies and developing countries, respectively.[9]

Two additional features of these tables stand out. One is that self-employment rates are higher on average in developing than developed countries. A second is that the treatment of agricultural workers makes

Table 1.1 *Aggregate self-employment rates in some selected OECD countries, 1960–2000[a] (per cent)*

	1960	1970	1980	1990	2000
A All workers					
USA	13.83	8.94	8.70	8.50	7.33
Canada[b]	18.81	13.20	9.74	9.52	10.66
Japan	22.68	19.18	17.18	14.05	11.34
Mexico	34.25	31.29	21.67	25.64	28.53
Australia	15.86[c]	14.09	16.16	15.05	13.49
France[b]	30.51	22.17	16.79	13.26	10.56
Italy	25.93	23.59	23.26	24.53	24.48
Netherlands[b]	21.87	16.65	12.23	9.64	10.46[d]
Norway	21.79	17.90	10.03	9.24	7.03
Spain[b]	38.97	35.59	30.47	26.27	20.49
UK	7.28	7.36	8.05	13.32	11.34
B Non-agricultural workers					
USA	10.45	6.94	7.26	7.51	6.55
Canada[b]	10.17	8.33	7.05	7.40	9.46
Japan	17.38	14.44	13.75	11.50	9.35
Mexico	23.01	25.20	14.33	19.89	25.48
Australia	11.01[c]	10.00	12.73	12.34	11.72
France[b]	16.90	12.71	10.71	9.32	8.06
Italy	20.60	18.97	19.20	22.24	23.21
Netherlands[b]	15.08	12.02	9.06	7.84	9.25[d]
Norway	10.14	8.61	6.53	6.12	4.83
Spain[b]	23.60	21.55	20.63	20.69	17.69
UK	5.89	6.27	7.11	12.41	10.83

Notes: [a]Self-employment rates defined as employers plus persons working on their own account, as a proportion of the total workforce.
[b]Includes unpaid family workers [c] 1964 not 1960 [d] 1999 not 2000.
Source: OECD *Labour Force Statistics*, issues 1980–2000, 1970–81 and 1960–71.

a substantial difference to measured self-employment rates in most (but not all) countries.

1.4.1 The OECD countries

Consider the USA first. According to table 1.1,[10] if agricultural workers are included, the US self-employment rate has been in continual decline since at least 1960. According to Steinmetz and Wright (1989), this decline can actually be traced back to the 1870s, when the self-employment rate stood at just over 40 per cent of the labour force, and it underwent an especially steep decline between 1950 and 1970 (see also table 1.1).[11]

Table 1.2 *Aggregate self-employment rates in some selected transition economies, 1980–1998/1999[a] (per cent)*

	1980	1990	1992	1994	1998/99[b]
Poland (all workers)	25.44	27.17			22.44
(non-agricultural)	3.37	9.16			11.70
Russian Federation			0.76		5.29
Czech Rep. (all workers)				10.18	14.59
(non-agricultural)				10.25	14.50
Hungary (all workers)				16.93	14.56
(non-agricultural)				16.94	12.81
Slovak Rep. (all workers)				6.21	7.80
(non-agricultural)				6.49	8.00

Notes: [a] Self-employment rates defined as employers plus persons working on their own account, as a proportion of the total workforce.
[b] '1998/99' is 1998 for Poland and 1999 for the Russian Federation.
Source: UN *Yearbook of Labour Statistics*, various issues.

Table 1.3 *Aggregate self-employment rates in developing countries, 1960s–1990s[a] (per cent)*

	1960s[b]	1970s[b]	1980s[b]	1990s[b]
Africa				
Mauritius	13.03	10.30	n.a.	16.72
Egypt	29.19	26.14	28.20	27.19
Americas				
Bolivia	n.a.	48.86	40.27	34.81
Costa Rica	20.78	17.10	21.80	24.70
Dominican Rep.	44.79	29.44	36.46	37.11
Ecuador	42.97	37.81	37.27	37.03
Asia				
Bangladesh	7.33	45.56	38.83	29.59
Korean Rep.	44.04	33.92	33.07	28.02
Pakistan	21.94	46.90	55.95	48.18
Sri Lanka	26.94	22.90	24.74	26.68
Thailand	29.83	29.65	29.75	28.45

Notes: [a] Self-employment rates defined as employers plus persons working on their own account, as a proportion of the total workforce. Includes agricultural workers.
[b] '1960s' is either 1960, 1961, 1962 or 1963 for all countries; '1970s' is some year between 1970 and 1976; '1980s' is 1980 or 1981 except Ecuador (1982), Costa Rica (1984) and Bolivia (1989); '1990s' is some year between 1990 and 1996.
Source: UN *Yearbook of Labour Statistics*, various issues.

However, if agricultural workers are excluded, table 1.1 shows that a revival in US self-employment occurred during the 1970s and 1980s, a finding that has also been observed by some other authors.[12] But unlike these other authors, table 1.1 reveals that this revival in non-agricultural US self-employment has apparently come to an end: by 2000 the non-agricultural self-employment rate had fallen back to below its 1970 level.

The US experience is mirrored by France, which has also seen its overall self-employment rate decline steadily since the start of the twentieth century (Steinmetz and Wright, 1989).[13] However, this trend is not observed in every OECD country. For example, table 1.1 shows that both Canadian self-employment rates exhibited U-shaped patterns, increasing particularly strongly in the 1990s.[14] In contrast, both measures of the UK self-employment rate increased dramatically in the 1980s, a finding that attracted substantial research interest when it was first discovered (Hakim, 1988; Campbell and Daly, 1992). It declined in the 1990s, especially among males (Moralee, 1998). According to Storey (1994a), the UK historical trend in self-employment was one of steady decline between 1910 and 1960, followed by increase from 1960 to 1990, with the rate in 1990 being similar to that in 1910.

Most researchers tend to exclude agricultural workers from their definitions of self-employment, on the grounds that farm businesses have very different characteristics to non-farm businesses. It has been known at least since Kuznets (1966) that the agricultural sector tends to decline as an economy develops – and that this may distort self-employment trends (Blanchflower, 2000). Consequently, to analyse trends we focus henceforth on panel B of table 1.1. These data indicate a striking variety of patterns over 1960–2000. Four countries (Japan, France, Norway and Spain) had steadily declining self-employment rates. Six witnessed a revival in self-employment at some point within the period (USA, Canada, Mexico, Italy, the UK and the Netherlands); and one (Australia) had a relatively stable self-employment rate.

Finally, we will say a word about the relative importance of *small firms* in the economy. The overwhelming majority of US businesses employ fewer than five individuals (see, e.g. White, 1984; Brock and Evans, 1986, chapter 2, for details). There are high rates of business formation and dissolution among small firms, especially in industries like retailing, where low capital requirements make entry easy and keep profits modest. The aggregate number of small businesses grew in the USA in the post-war period, but their relative economic importance (measured in terms of their employment share or share of gross domestic product (GDP)) declined somewhat over that period. The most recent evidence suggests that the share of private non-farm GDP accounted for by small businesses in the USA has now stabilised, at around 50 per cent over the last two decades (SBA, 2002a). That the earlier decline was not greater is mainly attributable to the growth of the service sector, in which small firms are disproportionately concentrated. We will return to the issue of changing industrial structure later in the book.

1.4.2   The transition economies of Eastern Europe

Of special interest are the so-called 'transition economies' of Eastern Europe, which underwent a switch from communist central planning to a more market-based system at the end of the 1980s. In the words of Earle and Sakova (2000, p. 583): 'it is difficult to imagine a regime more hostile towards self-employment and entrepreneurship than the centrally planned economies of Eastern Europe.' These regimes fixed prices and wages, placed restrictions on hiring workers and acquiring capital and levied confiscatory taxes on entrepreneurs. This is reflected in the low non-agricultural self-employment rates observed in Poland in 1980, and in Russia in 1992 (see table 1.2).[15]

Part of the interest in studying the transition economies is that they serve as a test-bed for the strength of dormant entrepreneurial vigour that could be released after market liberalisation.[16] Real opportunities emerged for entrepreneurs to exploit market gaps left by the previous communist regimes, especially in the provision of services and the production of consumer goods. The incentive to become self-employed was no doubt enhanced by declining opportunities in wage employment and growing unemployment as the sprawling former state-run companies began to contract in the 1990s. But although legal barriers to private enterprise and self-employment came down after 1989, bureaucracy and the limited rule of law has continued to stifle productive entrepreneurship in many of these countries (Baumol, 1990, 1993; Dutz, Ordover and Willig, 2000). For example, Baumol contended that, although the supply of entrepreneurs varies from country to country, probably a greater source of variation in entrepreneurs' social productivity is the scope to engage in privately profitable but socially unproductive rent-seeking and organised crime. If payoffs to such activities are sufficiently high, entrepreneurs will rationally divert effort from productive innovation to exploit them. It remains to be seen what will happen to productive entrepreneurship in the transition economies as we move further into the twenty-first century.[17]

1.4.3   Developing countries

In the early post-war period, researchers attached great importance to fostering entrepreneurship in developing countries. In the words of

W. Arthur Lewis (1955, p. 182): 'Economic growth is bound to slow unless there is an adequate supply of entrepreneurs looking out for new ideas, and willing to take the risk of introducing them.' According to Leff (1979), interest in the issue had dwindled by the 1970s. Leff asserted that this was because of a perception that the entrepreneurial problem had been 'solved', with high rates of real output growth serving as evidence of entrepreneurial vigour. Subsequently, slower growth, high rates of population growth, widespread failures of state-owned enterprises (SOEs), constraints on public sector employment and the spread of free-market beliefs reactivated interest in promoting entrepreneurship in developing economies.

Table 1.3 shows that, on average, developing countries have markedly higher self-employment rates than developed countries. Nevertheless, table 1.3 also reveals considerable variation in these rates. It has been noted elsewhere that Asian countries often have very high self-employment rates, sometimes exceeding half the workforce.[18] However, in contrast to claims by some previous researchers that the trend in developing countries is away from self-employment (Blau, 1987; Schultz, 1990), the evidence in table 1.3 reveals that no such trend can be generally established.

Why are self-employment rates so high in developing countries? We will return to the broad issue of economic development and entrepreneurship later in the book; here we consider just two specific factors. First, the data in table 1.3 (and those used in most other studies of these countries) include agriculture. Agriculture plays a prominent role in the economies of many developing countries, in which high self-employment rates are traditionally found. Second, high self-employment rates may reflect limited development of formal economic and financial markets. For example, Leibenstein (1968) argued that entrepreneurship in developing countries often simply involves overcoming constraints caused by poor economic and financial infrastructure, and is quite basic in nature. This viewpoint is related to the long-standing dual labour market model of development, comprising a formal urban sector in which employees earn premium wages, and an informal rural sector in which entrepreneurs receive below-average incomes (Lewis, 1955; Harris and Todaro, 1970). The model predicts that as poor economies develop, labour will move from the informal to the formal sector, with a decline in self-employment. However, evidence from the field refutes both the prediction of higher income in paid-employment in developing countries, and the prediction of workers shifting from self- to paid-employment as they age.[19] Arguably, more recent economic theories offer greater scope for explaining high self-employment rates in developing countries. We return to this topic in chapter 3, section 3.3.

1.5   Self-employment incomes and income inequality

This section attempts three tasks. First, we discuss issues relating to the definition and measurement of self-employment incomes, and review evidence about the levels of and trends in average self-employment incomes relative to average paid-employment incomes. Second, we analyse the inequality of self-employment incomes. Third, we review evidence from earnings functions on the determinants of self-employment incomes.

1.5.1   Incomes and relative incomes

Measurement issues

Self-employment income can be measured in several different ways. Consider the following identity:

$$\text{Net profit} \equiv \text{Revenue} - \text{Costs} \equiv \text{Draw} + \text{Retained earnings.}$$

Net profit from running an enterprise is a widely used measure of self-employment income. An alternative is Draw, the amount of money drawn from the business on a regular basis by the owner. This represents the consumption-generating value of the business and as such may be less prone to income under-reporting. A less frequently used third measure is Draw augmented by the growth in business equity (Hamilton, 2000).

It should be stressed at the outset that any analysis of self-employment income data should be performed with the utmost caution. There are several reasons for this:

1. *Income under-reporting by the self-employed.* This is possibly the most serious problem with using self-employment data. It is partly attributable to self-employed respondents who over-claim business tax deductions, or under-report gross incomes to the tax authorities, mistrusting interviewers' claims that they are truly independent of the tax inspectorate. Ways of estimating self-employment income under-reporting rates are discussed in chapter 10, subsection 10.4.1.

2. *Different ways of treating owners of incorporated businesses.* Incorporated self-employed individuals are usually treated as employees of their company. Because they are richer on average, their exclusion from the self-employed sample may bias downwards the average income of the self-employed.[20] On the other hand, including the incorporated self-employed is not without its problems, since it is not clear how to interpret the salary that an incorporated self-employed business owner chooses to pay her/himself.

3. *Relatively high non-response rates to survey income questions by the self-employed.* This problem can be quite pervasive and can substantially bias estimates of absolute and relative returns to self-employment

(Devine, 1995).[21] There are several possible reasons for survey non-response. One is mistrust of survey interviewers by self-employed respondents, for the reasons given above. A second is that richer people (of whom a disproportionate number are self-employed – see below) have a higher marginal valuation of time, so participate less in surveys. Third, many self-employed do not accurately know their incomes, which according to Meager, Court and Moralee (1994) accounted for two-thirds of missing British income cases in the 1991 British Household Panel Survey (BHPS) – rather than refusal to co-operate with the survey.

4. *A failure to deal properly with negative incomes and 'top-coding'* can introduce biases (Devine, 1995). Many researchers either drop negative income observations or round them up to a small positive number before applying logarithmic transformations; both practices impart an upward bias to average self-employment income. Top-coding on the other hand, which is a procedure of truncating very high earnings values to a maximum level, imparts a downward bias.

5. *Ignoring employee fringe benefits that are unavailable in self-employment* biases upwards any relative income advantage to self-employment. Some of these benefits can be substantial, especially employer contributions to health care and occupational pension schemes (Holtz-Eakin, Penrod and Rosen 1996; Wellington, 2001).

6. *Self-employment incomes include returns to capital as well as returns to labour.* National Accounts' experts have long argued about how best to disentangle these returns, which might explain why few researchers choose to separate them in practice.[22] Headen (1990) proposed an especially straightforward approach, which works as follows. Let h_j, y_j and w_j denote an individual's work hours, total 'labour' income and wage rate respectively in sector $j = \{E, S\}$, where E is paid-employment and S is self-employment. Also, let y_k denote returns to capital in self-employment. While h_j and y_j values are observed in most data sets, w_js are not and must be calculated (in E) or estimated (in S). We have $y_E = w_E h_E$ and $y_S = w_S h_S + y_k$. To estimate y_k, first calculate $w_E = y_E / h_E$ and estimate an 'earnings function' like $\ln w_E = \beta' X + u$, where X is a vector of personal characteristics, β is a vector of coefficients and u is a random disturbance (see chapter 1, subsection 1.5.3). This yields parameter estimates $\hat{\beta}$. Second, predict $\hat{w}_S$ for the self-employed from $\widehat{\ln w_S} = \hat{\beta}' X$. This can be taken as the return to self-employed labour assuming (i) that employee incomes are purely returns to labour, and (ii) that the self-employed have the same rates of return to personal characteristics as employees do (see subsection 1.5.3 for a critical assessment of this assumption). Finally,

denoting sample mean values by overbars, calculate

$$\overline{y_k/h_S} = \overline{y_S/h_S} - \overline{w}_S.$$

Using this approach Headen (1990) estimated the returns to labour and capital as, respectively, 84 and 16 per cent for a sample of US self-employed physicians in 1984.

In practice, few researchers have addressed any of the above six problems in much depth. Only the first two have attracted any real attention, but even here the coverage has been uneven. This caveat should be borne in mind when interpreting the following evidence.

International evidence on relative average self-employment incomes and trends

Standard economic theory predicts that workers move between occupations until incomes in each occupation are equalised. However, that prediction must be qualified when one takes into account the heterogeneity of individual abilities and job characteristics, including non-pecuniary compensating differentials, risk and over-optimism among individuals choosing risky occupations. As will be seen below, few studies have found equality between average incomes in self-employment and paid-employment.

In the USA, the evidence on the relative income position of the self-employed is mixed. This is no doubt partly attributable to the different income definitions and sampling frames used in different data-sets. However, there is a tentative emerging consensus that the self-employed earn less on average than employees do.[23] Hamilton (2000) conducted an especially thorough study of relative self-employment incomes. Because of the pronounced income inequality of self-employment incomes (see below), Hamilton analysed median rather than mean incomes. Hamilton controlled for experience when comparing incomes in self-employment and paid-employment, and utilised all three different measures of self-employment income described at the start of this section. Using 1984 Survey of Incomes and Program Participation (SIPP) data on personal characteristics, Hamilton estimated that on average all individuals except those in the upper quartile of the self-employment income distribution would have earned more, and enjoyed higher future income growth rates, if they had quit self-employment and become employees. For example, for individuals in business for ten years the median earnings differential was 35 per cent in favour of paid-employment. This finding, which was found to be robust to different definitions of self-employment income, may under-state the true differential since it does not take account of employee fringe benefits such as employer-subsidised health insurance.

Conversely, however, Hamilton may have over-stated the income differential by ignoring the possibility of income under-reporting and business tax deduction opportunities for the self-employed.

There is also evidence that US median incomes in self-employment have lagged behind median employee incomes for several decades (Carrington, McCue and Pierce, 1996: Current Population Survey (CPS) data, 1967–92).[24] Aronson (1991: US Social Security data, 1951–88) showed that a 48 per cent income advantage to the self-employed in 1951–4 had dwindled to a 23 per cent advantage by 1975–9. This became a 10 per cent disadvantage by 1980–4, widening to a 20 per cent disadvantage by 1985–8. It appears that a similar story holds irrespective of occupation and education (SBA, 1986); and adjusting for the longer average work hours of the self-employed reduced further their relative income position – by around 70 per cent according to Aronson (1991).

The UK has also witnessed a downward trend in relative average self-employment incomes since the 1970s (Robson, 1997; Clark and Drinkwater, 1998).[25] In contrast to the USA, the UK evidence points to a relative income advantage to self-employment. Disagreement centres on how large this advantage is. General Household Survey (GHS) microdata point suggests a small premium to self-employment of 7 per cent over 1983–95, according to Clark and Drinkwater (1998) (see also Meager, Court and Moralee, 1996). In contrast, aggregate UK National Accounts data suggest a greater difference, of 35 per cent in terms of pre-tax gross income in 1993 according to Robson (1997). It may be relevant that the latter, unlike the former estimate, includes an adjustment for income under-reporting by the self-employed.

Evidence from eleven OECD countries supports the notion that in many countries the self-employed are not well remunerated relative to employees. According to OECD (1986), only in West Germany did the ratio of median self-employment to paid-employment incomes exceed unity. In Finland, Sweden and Japan the ratios were below that of the USA. Similar evidence was also found independently by Covick (1983) and Kidd (1993) for Australia; and Covick noted the same downward trend in relative self-employment incomes as observed in the USA and the UK.

The special circumstances prevailing in the transition economies of Eastern Europe may help explain why opposite findings have been found there. Earle and Sakova (2000) studied self-employment choices and incomes in six Eastern European countries between 1988 and 1993: Poland, Russia, Slovakia, Bulgaria, Hungary and the Czech Republic. They found that, in all countries apart from Poland, the mean income of employees was less than that of own-account self-employed individuals, which in turn was less than the mean income of self-employed employers.

We conclude this section with three puzzles. One is why, if the self-employed in the USA earn less on average than employees do, and if they are only moderately older on average than employees are, they nevertheless possess substantially greater savings and asset holdings (Quadrini, 1999; Gentry and Hubbard, 2001). A second puzzle is why individuals remain in self-employment despite apparently earning less and working longer hours (see chapter 8, section 8.2) than employees do. Third, why do entrepreneurs invest in undiversified and hence risky private businesses, when they could obtain similar rates of return from less risky publicly traded equity (Moskowitz and Vissing-Jørgensen, 2002)? A possible answer to the first puzzle is income (but not asset) under-reporting by the self-employed, reflecting the greater taxation of income than wealth. A tentative answer to the second puzzle is proposed in section 8.2. Possible answers to the third include non-pecuniary benefits to entrepreneurship, a preference for skewed returns and systematic over-estimation by entrepreneurs of the probability of survival and success in entrepreneurship.

1.5.2   Income inequality

It is now well established that in most countries the incomes of the self-employed are more unequal than employees' are. This fact usually becomes immediately obvious when histograms of incomes are graphed separately for the two groups.[26] Relatively large numbers of the self-employed are concentrated in the lower and upper tails of their income distribution, compared with employees. Consequently, when data from the two occupations are combined, the self-employed are invariably observed to be disproportionately concentrated in both the upper and lower tails of the overall income distribution. In their British analysis based on 1991 BHPS data, Meager, Court and Moralee (1996) showed that this result is not an artefact of sampling error, and remained after controlling for observable characteristics such as gender, work status, work hours, age, education, industry and occupation.[27]

The same story of pronounced self-employment income inequality is observed when sample data are mapped into scalar inequality measures, such as the Gini coefficient or the mean log deviation.[28] Typical results were obtained by Parker (1999b), who computed a range of inequality measures from UK Family Expenditure Survey (FES) data over 1979–1994/5. Parker reported that self-employment income inequality indices were between two and five times as great as those for employees, depending on the year and the particular inequality index chosen.[29] Arguably the UK context is particularly interesting because self-employment income inequality grew especially rapidly in the 1980s, the same decade when self-employment itself expanded substantially (see subsection 1.4.1). The increased self-employment income inequality in the 1980s was large enough for Jenkins (1995) to cite it as the primary reason for the growth of overall UK income inequality in the 1980s, exacerbated by a greater self-employment population share. Subsequently, Parker (1999b) reported that by the mid-1990s UK self-employment income inequality had fallen back from its 1991 peak.

Why does self-employment income inequality tend to be so high? More generally, what are the underlying factors generating self-employment income inequality? There is little theoretical guidance at present to help us answer these questions. While Rosen's (1981) theory of 'superstars' explains why the most talented individuals command salaries that are disproportionately higher than those of their nearest rivals, this theory cannot explain income dispersion among the bulk of the self-employed, who earn much more modest incomes. Likewise, while it follows that if idiosyncratic ability augments the returns of entrepreneurs but not of employees then the upper tail of the income distribution will be disproportionately full of entrepreneurs (Lazear, 2002), this assumption about ability is demanding and may not be warranted. And Parker's (1997b) parametric model of the self-employment income distribution, which combines several stylised facts about income dynamics and firm size growth processes, does not really reveal the *underlying* causes of income dispersion.[30]

Unfortunately, empirical work has not improved our understanding of the causes of self-employment income inequality much either. Using income inequality decomposition techniques, Parker (1999b) found that none of age, gender, marital status, region, occupation, work status, or educational qualification explained more than a small fraction of UK self-employment income inequality levels or trends. In contrast, these variables helped explain a sizeable share of employee income inequality. Parker concluded that these results reflect the marked heterogeneity of the self-employed, heterogeneity that increased in Britain in the 1980s along some unmeasured dimensions. It will be seen below how attempts to explain average self-employment incomes themselves (rather than their inequality) have also met with only limited success.

Another issue is the extent to which self-employment facilitates earnings and social mobility. Holtz-Eakin, Rosen and Weathers (2000) reported that becoming self-employed increases upward earnings mobility for low-income Americans, relative to remaining as employees. But the opposite was found for high-income Americans, for whom self-employment entailed downward mobility. Regarding social mobility, measured in terms of social class, the sociological literature reports mixed results (e.g. compare Mayer, 1975 with Bland, Elliott and Bechhofer, 1978).

Finally, we mention for completeness that even less is known about the wealth distribution of entrepreneurs. Although there are models of entrepreneuria wealth transfers and accumulation (Shorrocks, 1988; Banerjee and Newman, 1993; Parker, 2000), none explains why wealth distribution takes its observed shape. According to estimates compiled by Parker (2003b), older self-employed Britons enjoy above-average wealth holdings, yet only moderate wealth inequality.

1.5.3   Earnings functions

Methods

In this subsection we ask whether it is possible to explain individuals' self-employment incomes in terms of a few personal and economic variables. The most popular method for attempting this is estimation of a so-called 'earnings function'. Earnings functions were originally developed by human capital theorists to explain the determinants of employment earnings. An earnings function typically regresses log earnings, $\ln y$, on a set of explanatory variables that includes age or experience, a, years of education, sch and a vector of other personal and family characteristics, X. Let u be a stochastic disturbance term, and index individuals by i in a sample of size n. Employee earnings functions typically take the form

$$\ln y_i = \beta_0 + \beta_1 a_i + \beta_2 a_i^2 + \beta_3 sch_i + \gamma' X_i + u_i \qquad i = 1, \dots, n,$$

(1.1)

where the βs and γ are coefficients. The β_3 coefficient measures the rate of return to an extra year of education, and for this reason is of particular interest to human capital theorists.

In principle, it is a straightforward matter to estimate (1.1) using a sample of self-employed individuals. However, there are several reasons why one would expect the coefficients of (1.1), and their interpretation, to differ from those obtained using employee samples.

First, the self-employed rate of return to schooling may differ from employees' rate of return. On one hand, entrepreneurial success is likely to depend on numerous factors other than formal education, implying that the self-employed β_3 will be low relative to its value for employees (Brown and Sessions, 1998, 1999). Indeed, formal education might even inculcate attitudes that are antithetical to entrepreneurship (Casson, 2003). On the other hand, if employers demand education from their workers primarily as an otherwise unproductive screening device (the 'screening hypothesis'), then the self-employed who do not face this requirement can be expected to quit education before its rate of return falls as low as that of employees'. This implies that, if screening occurs, the self-employed β_3 will be relatively high (Riley, 1979).[31]

Second, the self-employed earnings–age profile may differ from that of employees. In terms of (1.1), a steeper profile implies a larger β_1 and/or a smaller β_2 coefficient. There are at least three reasons why the self-employed earnings–age profile may be steeper than that of employees. First, the self-employed do not share the returns of their human (or physical) capital investments with employers, who might smooth out their costs and returns over employees' lifetimes. Second, if the self-employed learn about their abilities over time with the ablest surviving (Jovanovic, 1982), then one might expect to see any self-employed cohort's average returns increase over time. Third, investment in physical capital reduces earnings of the young self-employed, while the returns of that investment accrue to the older self-employed – again implying a steep earnings-age profile. On the other hand, if employees can shirk on the job, then employers may respond by steepening employees' earnings profiles in order to elicit appropriate worker effort (Lazear and Moore, 1984). Naturally, no such agency problem arises in self-employment where the principal *is* the agent.[32]

These considerations suggest that earnings functions should be estimated separately for employees and the self-employed. It is not advisable to estimate an earnings function that pools data on the two occupations, such as

$$\ln y_i = \beta' X_i + \delta z_i + u_i \tag{1.2}$$

(as in, e.g. Amit, Muller and Cockburn, 1995), where z_i is an indicator (dummy) variable for self-employment/paid-employment status. While (1.2) looks attractive by providing a direct estimate of relative occupational earnings advantage, it imposes the strong restrictions of identical rates of return to all of the explanatory variables for both occupations, which, for the reasons given above, are unlikely to hold.

When estimating earnings functions, it is necessary to avoid *selection bias*. Incomes are observed only in the occupation that individuals choose to participate in; and those who participate in self-employment might not be a random sample from the population. Rather, they might possess characteristics that make them particularly favourably disposed to self-employment. Without correcting for this, the estimated coefficients of (1.1) will be susceptible to bias. By correcting for this bias, it becomes possible to ask whether self-employed people (and employees) could improve their lot by switching into the other occupation. A popular practical way of removing selection bias is Heckman's (1979) method.

Heckman's method comprises two steps. The first step estimates the participation equation

$$z_i = \omega' W_i + v_i,$$ (1.3)

where z_i is an indicator variable equalling 1 if individual i is self-employed and 0 otherwise; W_i is a set of explanatory variables, ω is a vector of coefficients and v_i is a disturbance term, with unit variance. Second, having computed fitted values $\hat{z}_i$ from this regression, the 'Inverse Mills Ratio' $\lambda_i = -\phi(\hat{z}_i)/\Phi(\hat{z}_i)$ is added to the right-hand side of (1.1), where $\phi(\cdot)$ and $\Phi(\cdot)$ are the density and cumulative distribution functions of the standard normal distribution. Thus one estimates the augmented earnings function

$$\ln y_i = \beta_0 + \beta_1 a_i + \beta_2 a_i^2 + \beta_3 sch_i + \gamma' X_i + \alpha \lambda_i + u_i,$$ (1.4)

where $\alpha > 0$ implies positive self-selection into self-employment.

Results

Various estimates of earnings functions of type (1.4) have been performed, using a variety of data sources and explanatory variables.[33] Even more studies have estimated (1.1), i.e. without correcting for self-selection. Despite the heterogeneity of the studies to date, several empirical regularities are detectable. First, rates of return to schooling tend to be lower for the self-employed than for employees, and not consistently positive and significant. For example, in their overview of the literature, Van der Sluis, Van Praag and Vijverberg (2003) documented an average rate of return of 6.1 per cent for self-employed Americans, compared with 7–9 per cent for American employees. In other countries, self-employed rates of return are usually lower still. These findings are consistent with the idea that entrepreneurial skills are non-academic in nature. They also do not support the screening hypothesis.[34] Indeed, the screening hypothesis is thrown into further doubt by additional findings that the self-employed acquire as much – and sometimes even more – formal education and vocational training as employees (Wolpin, 1977; Fredland and Little, 1981; Parker, 1999b).

Second, the evidence consistently points to flatter earnings–age profiles for the self-employed than for employees. While this finding is in line with the agency cost model of Lazear and Moore (1984) mentioned above, several caveats to this interpretation can be mentioned. They include mismeasurement of self-employment experience, and a failure to control for parental managerial experience, which is known to be very important for the self-employed (Lentz and Laband, 1990).

Third, few explanatory variables possess much explanatory power in self-employed earnings functions, resulting in poor goodness-of-fit: it is common to find R^2 values of 10 per cent and less. This is consistent with the poor performance of univariate decompositions of self-employed income inequality measures described earlier. In contrast, employee earnings functions tend to provide much better fits.[35] Subsequently, researchers have tried including a range of non-human capital variables in an effort to improve the explanatory power of self-employment earnings functions. These include dummies for industries, disabilities, ill-health and immigration status. But few have improved matters noticeably in this respect.

Fourth, on the sample selection issue, there is general disagreement among the studies that have estimated (1.4) about the direction and significance of sample selection effects. There is therefore no clear-cut evidence that the self-employed select into self-employment because they enjoy a comparative earnings advantage there. In contrast, many studies find positive selection effects for wage employment, implying that the self-employed would earn more if they became employees.[36] This may reflect greater human capital (skills and experience) possessed by the self-employed, which commands a higher return in paid-employment than in self-employment.

Extensions

Williams (2001) extended the analysis of earnings comparisons to ask whether self-employed workers would earn more by becoming a franchisee (F) or an independent business owner (I). Williams estimated selectivity-corrected profit functions in both F and I using data on 14,550 firms taken from the 1987 CBO data set. Selectivity effects were found to be important, with individuals in F earning less than those in I, after controlling for personal characteristics. Furthermore, franchisees were estimated to be substantially worse off if they became independent owners. These findings suggest that franchisees have relatively low average ability, whereas independent business owners have relatively high average ability. A policy implication is that legal restrictions on franchising activities may therefore have deleterious effects on the material wellbeing of this group of self-employed people.

It is also possible that individuals mix their work hours between self-employment, S, and paid-employment, E. Work mixing appears to be more widespread in developing than in developed countries (Sumner, 1981; Vijverberg, 1986).[37] If work mixing occurs, then (1.3) and (1.4) are inappropriate, and one should estimate a composite earnings function of combined individual wages w_i:

$$\ln w_i = (1 - \xi_i)\beta'_E X_{Ei} + \xi_i \beta'_S X_{Si} + u_i, \tag{1.5}$$

where ξ_i is the proportion of work hours i devotes to S; the βs are vectors of coefficients; and the Xs are matrices of observations on personal and occupation-relevant characteristics. Because ξ_i may be endogenously chosen, (1.5) can be estimated only after an equation for ξ_i is specified on a set of exogenous variables. This permits direct comparison of the two occupations' $\hat{\beta}$ coefficients.

1.6   Some useful econometric models

This section describes several econometric models that have become widely used for explaining individuals' decisions to participate in, to enter and to exit from, self-employment. The non-technical reader may skip this section, though at the risk of missing some of the subtleties of the empirical results discussed later in the book.

1.6.1   Occupational choice and probit/logit models

Consider a cross-section of data on n individuals, indexed by i: $i = 1, \ldots, n$. There are two occupations denoted by j: self-employment, S, and paid-employment, E. Each individual has a vector of observed characteristics W_i and derives utility $U_{ij} = U(W_i; j) + u_{ij}$ if they work in occupation j, where $U(\cdot; \cdot)$ is observable utility and u_{ij} is idiosyncratic unobserved utility. Define the 'latent' variable (i.e. the relative advantage to S) as

$$z_i^* = U(W_i; S) - U(W_i; E) - u_{iE} + u_{iS}. \tag{1.6}$$

If we assume that $U(\cdot; \cdot)$ is linear, taking the form $U(W_i; j) = \beta_j' W_i$, where β_j are vectors of coefficients, then we can write

$$z_i^* = \alpha + \beta' W_i + v_i, \tag{1.7}$$

where $\beta' := \beta_S' - \beta_E'$ is a vector of coefficients, $\alpha := \mathsf{E}[u_{iS} - u_{iE}]$ is an intercept, and where $v_i := u_{iS} - u_{iE} - \alpha \sim IID(0, \sigma^2)$ is a disturbance term. Henceforth we shall incorporate the intercept term in W_i as a set of ones, so β will be treated as the complete set of coefficients.

Individual i chooses self-employment over paid-employment if $z_i^* \geq 0$. Hence define the *observable* occupational indicator variable

$$z_i := \begin{cases} 1 & \text{if individual } i \text{ is observed in } S, \text{ i.e. if } z_i^* \geq 0 \\ 0 & \text{if individual } i \text{ is observed in } E, \text{ i.e. if } z_i^* < 0 \end{cases}$$

Therefore the probability that an individual with characteristic vector W_i is drawn from the population and appears in the sample is

$$\Pr(z_i = 1) = \Pr(z_i^* \geq 0). \tag{1.8}$$

The *probit* model assumes that the distribution of the disturbance term v_i is normal. Hence $\Pr(z_i = 1) = \Phi(\beta' W_i / \sigma)$ and $\Pr(z_i = 0) = 1 - \Phi(\beta' W_i / \sigma)$, where $\Phi(\cdot)$ is the (cumulative) distribution function of the normal distribution. The likelihood function is

$$\mathcal{L} = \prod_{i=1}^{n} \Phi(\beta' W_i / \sigma)^{z_i} [1 - \Phi(\beta' W_i / \sigma)]^{1-z_i}. \tag{1.9}$$

Non-linear methods are needed to maximise (1.9) to estimate the β parameters (up to a scalar transformation since σ is unknown). It is standard to normalise σ^2 to unity without loss of generality.

The *logit* model arises if the distribution function of v_i is assumed to be that of the logistic distribution, in which case (1.8) becomes

$$\Pr(z_i = 1) = \frac{\exp\{\beta' W_i\}}{1 + \exp\{\beta' W_i\}}. \tag{1.10}$$

The likelihood function can be formed in a similar way as above and β' estimated in a like manner.

In practice, estimates of β' tend to be insensitive to whether the probit or logit assumption is made. Both estimators are widely implemented on computer software packages. Both dominate ordinary least squares (OLS) estimation of $z_i = \beta' W_i + v_i$ (called the linear probability model), since OLS is an inefficient and heteroscedastic estimator in this context, and problematically can predict probabilities outside the unit interval (see, e.g. Maddala, 1983).

It is often of interest to calculate the effects of changes in the kth explanatory variable of W_i, i.e. W_{ik}, on the probability of self-employment. These effects are given by

$$\frac{\partial \Pr(z_i = 1)}{\partial W_{ik}} := \begin{cases} \beta_k & \text{for the linear probability model} \\ \beta_k \Pr(z_i = 1)[1 - \Pr(z_i = 1)] & \text{for the logit model} \\ \beta_k \phi(\beta' W_i) & \text{for the probit model,} \end{cases} \tag{1.11}$$

where $\phi(\cdot)$ is the density function of the standard normal distribution. In practice, these calculations are usually evaluated at sample means of the variables.

There are at least three distinct applications of the probit/logit model to occupational choice. One (I) focuses on the probability that individuals are self-employed rather than employees. A second (II) asks the different question of what factors affect the decision to *become* self-employed, as opposed to remaining in paid-employment. A third (III) investigates the decision to leave self-employment, as opposed to continuing in it. All of these applications can be handled by the probit/logit model: they merely require different definitions of the dependent variable, z_i. However, it is possible to dispute the relative merits of each. For example, Evans and Leighton (1989b) argued that II is preferable to I, on the grounds that the latter confounds entry and survival effects. This is because the probability of *being* self-employed at time t depends on the probability of switching into self-employment at some previous time *and then* surviving until t. On the other hand, as Wellington (2001) has pointed out, application II excludes people who are already successfully self-employed, which is evidently a group of some interest. Low annual switching rates from paid-employment to self-employment (see chapter 2, section 2.2) also means that II sometimes suffers from having small numbers of self-employed observations; and the characteristics of switchers may well be different from those of non-switchers. There is less disagreement about the importance of application III, which we discuss separately in chapter 9. We would simply assert that all three applications generate useful information and play an important role in applied research.

1.6.2   The structural probit model

Microeconomic theory teaches us that relative prices often affect individual choices. If this precept is true for occupational choice, then one of the explanatory variables in the matrix W above should be relative income, or its logarithm: $(\ln y_{iS} - \ln y_{iE})$. However, we know from subsection 1.5.3 that occupational incomes are endogenous, and prone to selection effects, so this information needs to be incorporated into the probit model to obtain efficient and unbiased estimates of the parameters of interest. The structural probit model is a popular method that accomplishes this.

The first stage of the structural probit model is to estimate selectivity-corrected earnings functions separately for the self-employed and employees. Extending the discussion in subsection 1.5.3, and letting M denote the vector of explanatory variables used in the earnings functions, one estimates the equations

$$z_i = \beta' W_i + v_i \qquad i \in \{S, E\} \tag{1.12}$$

$$[\ln y_{iS} | z_i = 1] = \gamma'_S M_i + \vartheta_S \lambda_{iS} + u_{iS} \qquad i \in S \tag{1.13}$$

$$[\ln y_{iE} | z_i = 0] = \gamma'_E M_i + \vartheta_E \lambda_{iE} + u_{iE} \qquad i \in E, \tag{1.14}$$

where $\lambda_{iS} = -\phi(\hat{z}_i)/\Phi(\hat{z}_i)$ and $\lambda_{iE} = \phi(\hat{z}_i)/[1 - \Phi(\hat{z}_i)]$ are the Inverse Mills Ratios to correct for selectivity into each occupation. Equation (1.12) is called the 'reduced form probit' and is not of direct interest: its principal role is to correct for selection bias in the earnings functions (1.13) and (1.14).

The second stage of the structural probit model generates the predicted log incomes from both occupations derived from (1.13) and (1.14), namely $\ln \widehat{y_{iS}}$ and $\ln \widehat{y_{iE}}$. The third stage estimates the 'structural probit' model

$$z_i = \alpha[\ln \widehat{y_{iS}} - \ln \widehat{y_{iE}}] + \omega' X_i + \tilde{v}_i, \tag{1.15}$$

where $X \neq M$ is a further vector of explanatory variables such that $W = X \cup M$, and where $\tilde{v}_i$, u_{iS}, u_{iE} and v_i are all assumed to be normally distributed disturbance terms. If occupational choice depends on relative financial returns in each occupation, then $\alpha > 0$. Standard t-statistics can be used to test the hypothesis that an individual is more likely to be self-employed the greater is their relative income in self-employment.

Estimation at each stage is easily accomplished using standard econometric software, taking note of the following three points. First, because the relative income variable in (1.15) has been generated from previous regressions (i.e. it is a 'generated regressor'), Newey–West corrected standard errors should be used. Second, income under-reporting by the self-employed may bias y_{iS} and hence the coefficients in (1.15). This problem should be overcome by applying income under-reporting corrections (if available) to the data at the outset. Third, one should ensure that the disturbances of the earnings equations are normally distributed (Bernhardt, 1994). This can be achieved by suitable transformations of the earnings variables in (1.13) and (1.14) (Parker, 2003a). Unfortunately, many previous applications of the structural probit model have ignored these points, leading to biases of unknown magnitude.[38]

1.6.3 Extensions to cross-section models of occupational choice

While the models described above are widely used and appropriate for most applications, it is sometimes necessary to extend them. We describe three extensions below.

First, although individuals may wish to become self-employed, they may not have the opportunity to do so. This motivates the use of the bivariate probit (BVP) model, which separates individuals' *opportunities* to become self-employed from their *willingness* to do so. Let z_{1i}^* be a latent variable representing the former effect and let z_{2i}^* represent the latter effect. Potentially different factors impinge on willingness and opportunity, suggesting the specifications

$$z_{1i}^* = \beta_1' W_{1i} + v_{1i} \tag{1.16}$$

$$z_{2i}^* = \beta_2' W_{2i} + v_{2i}, \tag{1.17}$$

where (v_{1i}, v_{2i}) are distributed as bivariate normal variates with correlation coefficient ρ: the joint distribution function is $\Phi(\cdot, \cdot; \rho)$. As before, define z_i as an indicator variable, equal to 1 if individual i becomes self-employed, and 0 otherwise. Evidently

$$\Pr(z_i = 1) = \Pr[\min(z^*_{1i}, z^*_{2i}) \geq 0] = \Phi(\beta'_1 W_{1i}, \beta'_2 W_{2i}; \rho),$$

and analogous to (1.9), the likelihood function is

$$\mathcal{L} = \prod_{i=1}^{n} \Phi(\beta'_1 W_{1i}, \beta'_2 W_{2i}; \rho)^{z_i} [1 - \Phi(\beta'_1 W_{1i}, \beta'_2 W_{2i}; \rho)]^{1-z_i}.$$

To identify this model, it is necessary that $W_1 \neq W_2$. The researcher must impose identifying restrictions on the basis of *a priori* reasoning.

A second extension recognises that there may be more than two occupations to choose from. For example, Earle and Sakova (2000) studied the problem of choosing between employer self-employment, own-account self-employment, paid-employment, or unemployment. Multiple occupational choices can be handled by using multinomial choice models. Perhaps the most popular model within this class is the *multinomial logit* (MNL) model, which can be regarded as an extension to the simple logit model described above. In this model, individual i must choose between $j = 1, \ldots, \mathcal{J}$ alternatives. Define z_{ij} as equal to 1 if i chooses j, and 0 otherwise. Then the MNL model proposes that the probability that i chooses j is

$$\Pr(z_{ij} = 1 | W_i, X_j) = \frac{\exp\{\beta'_j W_i + \gamma' X_j\}}{\sum_j \exp\{\beta'_j W_i + \gamma' X_j\}}. \tag{1.18}$$

Here W_i is a vector of variables whose values vary across individuals, whereas X_j is a vector of variables whose values vary across occupations. The β_j coefficients must vary across occupations or else they cannot be identified. Analogous to the genesis of the simple probit/logit model discussed in subsection 1.6.1, (1.18) is the probability that results from a choice problem in which individuals maximise utility across each alternative, where the utilities are given by $U_{ij} = \beta'_j W_i + \gamma' X_j + u_{ij}$. Also as there, the β_j and γ coefficients can be estimated by maximum likelihood, a procedure that has now been incorporated in many standard econometric software packages.

All of the models discussed so far have assumed that individuals choose to spend *all of their time* either in self-employment or in paid-employment. As noted in subsection 1.5.3, some individuals mix their work time between multiple occupations. A third extension is needed to handle work mixing. Let h_E denote the proportion of total available work hours that an individual is observed to spend in paid-employment, and let h^*_E be a latent variable relating the *desired proportion* of work hours in paid-employment to the regressors X. Consider the model

$$h_{iE} = \begin{cases} 1 & \text{if } h^*_{iE} \geq 1 \\ h^*_{iE} & \text{if } 0 < h^*_{iE} < 1 \\ 0 & \text{if } h^*_{iE} \leq 0 \end{cases} \tag{1.19}$$

$$h^*_{iE} = \beta' X_i + u_i.$$

This model can be estimated by double-limit tobit maximum likelihood (see Vijverberg, 1986, for details). However, in the light of the discussion in subsection 1.6.2, a limitation of this model is its omission of relative occupational returns from the set of explanatory variables, X. Incorporating this extension into (1.19) can be expected to complicate the estimation substantially – which may account for its absence from the applied entrepreneurship literature to date.

1.6.4 Issues arising from the use of time-series and panel data

Time-series applications take a set of T time-series observations on the self-employment rate, s_t, and regress them against a set of explanatory variables X_t, as follows:

$$s_t = \gamma' X_t + v_t \qquad t = 1, \ldots, T, \tag{1.20}$$

where γ is a vector of regression coefficients and v_t is a disturbance term.

One rationale for estimating a time-series model is that, unlike cross-section studies, it becomes possible to analyse *trends* in self-employment. Also, the time-series approach can identify determinants of self-employment rates that are uniform for all or most members of a cross-section at a given point in time, e.g. income tax variables, interest rates and other macroeconomic variables.

Prior to the 1990s, the preferred technique for estimating (1.20) was ordinary or generalised least squares (OLS or GLS: see, e.g., Blau, 1987, Steinmetz and Wright, 1989). Since then, however, it has become known that least squares estimators are inappropriate when any of the regressors in (1.20) are non-stationary.[39] The application of least squares estimators to non-stationary data is known to generate spurious regressions and renders classical inference invalid (Phillips, 1986). The R^2 goodness-of-fit measure is no longer informative and t and F statistics can no longer be used for hypothesis testing. The importance of this point is underlined by the fact that self-employment rates in the USA, UK, and most other

OECD countries appear to be non-stationary in practice (Parker, 1996; Parker and Robson, 2000). Hence this point appears to be of considerable practical importance. When time-series variables are non-stationary, it is necessary to check whether they *cointegrate*, i.e. whether there exists at least one linear combination of the variables (called a *cointegrating vector*) that is stationary. If so, there is said to be a long-run (non-spurious) relationship between the variables. It is then possible to obtain consistent estimates of the coefficients of that relationship, and to perform appropriate hypothesis tests on the coefficients. It is also possible to examine a dynamic ('short-run') error-correction model that describes how agents behave out of equilibrium.[40]

Following Parker (1996), we set out below a 'working guide' for estimating and performing inference on the parameters of (1.20) using cointegration methods:

1. Check that each variable in (1.20) is non-stationary using unit root tests.
2. If at least two variables are non-stationary, use a multivariate cointegration estimator to identify the number of cointegration vectors.
3. If there is a unique cointegration vector, test if s_t is weakly exogenous. If so, perform significance tests on each element of γ.
4. Estimate an error-correction model using the cointegrating residuals $\hat{v}_t$ in order to determine the short-run determinants of aggregate self-employment.

If time-series data are available for the *same* set of individuals (or firms or countries) then a 'panel' of data is available. Panel data combines the case-specific variation of cross-section data with the temporal variation of time-series data, and enables the researcher to control for cohort and person-specific effects that are absent from a pool of repeated cross-sections.

There is now a large literature on panel data estimation; below, we describe only the most widely used ones in applied self-employment research. Suppose that the panel comprises N individuals i observed over T time periods t. A simple *pooled* regression model corresponding to (1.20) is

$$s_{it} = \gamma' X_{it} + \alpha + v_{it}, \tag{1.21}$$

where α is an intercept common to all individuals. A more general specification allows the intercept to vary across individuals, giving rise to the *fixed-effects* model:

$$s_{it} = \gamma' X_{it} + \alpha_i + v_{it}. \tag{1.22}$$

The *random-effects* model is similar to (1.22), except it assumes that the intercepts are drawn from a common distribution with mean α and variance σ_α^2.

Some applications of pooled and fixed- /random-effects models of self-employment have taken the cross-section units to be countries rather than individuals. For example, Robson and Wren (1999) and OECD (2000a) both estimated the following dynamic specification:

$$\Delta \ln s_{it} = \alpha_i + \beta' \Delta X_{it} - \gamma \ln s_{i\,t-1} + \omega' X_{i\,t-1} + \vartheta_t + v_{it}, \quad (1.23)$$

where X is a matrix of explanatory variables; α_i is a country-specific intercept term; and ϑ_t is a set of time dummies. The β coefficients capture short-run effects of variables on self-employment whereas the ω coefficients pick up long-run effects. However, as in the time-series case, least squares estimates of panel models will be biased if any of the variables in the model is non-stationary. Cointegrated panel techniques are appropriate in this case (see Parker and Robson, 2000, for details).

NOTES

1. Of course, these types of surveys can be severely criticised for asking hypothetical questions, without forcing individuals to bear the constraints of self-employment as they would if they acted upon their declared preferences. Indeed, much lower rates of serious entrepreneurial intention emerge from longitudinal analysis of wage and salary workers (Katz, 1990). For this reason, we will often adopt in this book the standard economic practice of ignoring studies that report interviewees' declared preferences, focusing instead on revealed preferences.
2. Intrapreneurship – the practice of entrepreneurship within corporations – is an emerging field in economics. For an important recent contribution, see Gromb and Scharfstein (2002).
3. According to CPS data compiled by Bregger (1996), 38 per cent of self-employed Americans run incorporated businesses. These tend to be businesses that employ others, which might explain why incorporation rates among new (and typically small) entrants to self-employment are about half this rate (Evans and Jovanovic, 1989).
4. Harvey (1995) cites the UK legal case of *Young and Woods* v. *West*, whereby the criteria for a worker being under a contract of service includes the worker not determining their own hours, not supplying their own materials and equipment, not allocating or designating their own work, not being able to nominate a substitute to work in their place and not setting their rate of pay (see also Leighton, 1983).
5. See also Marsh, Heady and Matheson (1981), Casey and Creigh (1988) and Hakim (1988).

6. Firms certainly appear to exercise some discretion about the mode of employment contract they offer. For example, in her exploration of new laws penalising companies that misclassify employees as self-employed to avoid tax payments, Moralee (1998) found that in response to the new laws the number of 'employees' in the construction industry increased sharply while the number of 'self-employed' workers decreased sharply.

7. According to Moralee (1998), 13 per cent of the UK self-employed in 1997 were home-workers, with little change in self-employed home-working taking place over the 1990s. Moralee also observed that 61 per cent of teleworkers were self-employed.

8. Williams (2001) argued that franchisees take *less* risk than independent self-employed business owners, because of profit sharing arrangements with franchisors and lower demand uncertainty resulting from selling a known product. Williams also observed a lower variance of self-employment incomes among franchisees than non-franchisees in his 1987 CBO sample of full-time self-employed workers. However, he appears to over-state the case, not least because exit rates are higher among franchisees than independent business owners (Bates, 1994).

9. Data limitations can be quite severe, especially for developing and transition economies. They largely determined the countries selected, and account for the exclusion of Germany in particular.

10. The primary source for the US entries in table 1.1 is the CPS Monthly Household Labour Force Survey.

11. In his historical study, Phillips (1962) characterised US self-employment as a 'shrinking world within a growing economy'. Phillips predicted that self-employment would eventually serve as a refuge only for older, handicapped or unproductive workers as a safeguard against unemployment.

12. See Blau (1987), Steinmetz and Wright (1989), Aronson (1991), Bregger (1996) and Williams (2000).

13. See also Kuznets (1966, table 4.2) who documented declining self-employment shares between the mid-nineteenth and mid-twentieth century in Germany, Switzerland, Canada and the UK, as well as in the USA and France.

14. See also Lin, Picot and Compton (2000), Manser and Picot (2000), Kuhn and Schuetze (2001) and Moore and Mueller (2002). Self-employment accounted for most overall job growth in Canada in the 1990s, which was concentrated among own-account workers.

15. Agriculture was never fully collectivised in Poland, which accounts for its high rate of self-employment for all workers inclusive of agriculture.

16. According to Blanchflower, Oswald and Stutzer (2001), Poles topped the list of respondents to a survey of 25,000 people in twenty-three countries asking whether they would prefer to be self-employed to being a wage worker: 80 per cent responded in the affirmative. Blanchflower, Oswald and Stutzer concluded that there is no shortage of potential entrepreneurs in the transition economies.

17. For further discussion about the state of entrepreneurship in Eastern Europe, see OECD (1998, ch. XIII) and Smallbone and Welter (2001). Tyson, Petrin and Rogers (1994) and Luthans, Stajkovic and Ibrayeva (2000) describe the

environmental and psychological challenges facing entrepreneurial development in transition economies.

18. This includes the Philippines and Indonesia (Le, 1999) and Nepal (Acs, Audretsch and Evans, 1994). According to Acs, Audretsch and Evans, the self-employment rate in Nepal in the 1980s reached over 85 per cent, compared with only 3.1 per cent in Botswana.

19. See, e.g., Blau (1985, 1986) and Teilhet-Waldorf and Waldorf (1983). Other studies reporting higher self-employment than paid-employment incomes in developing countries include Chiswick (1976) and Bertrand and Squire (1980) for Thailand; Mazumdar (1981) for Kuala Lumpar; and House, Ikiara, and McCormick (1993) for Kenya.

20. For example, SBA (1986) estimated that incorporated business owners earned over twice as much on average as the unincorporated self-employed.

21. Devine (1995) calculated self-employed non-response rates of about 30 per cent (CPS data, 1976–91), compared with 17–19 per cent for wage and salary workers. In related work, Devine (1994a) estimated non-response rates of 25 per cent for the incorporated and 40 per cent for the unincorporated self-employed.

22. Early efforts to separate factor returns from self-employment incomes include Kravis (1959), Denison (1967), Christiansen (1971) and Chiswick (1976). See Carrington, McCue and Pierce (1996) for a discussion of the issue with regard to two US data sets: the CPS and the (Michigan) Panel Study of Income Dynamics (PSID).

23. Studies finding higher average incomes in paid-employment include Fain (1980), Becker (1984), SBA (1986), Haber, Lamas and Lichtenstein (1987), Carrington, McCue and Pierce (1996) and Hamilton (2000). In contrast, Form (1985), Borjas (1986), Evans and Jovanovic (1989), Ferber and Waldfogel (1998) and Quadrini (1999) reported an income advantage to self-employment on average, while Borjas and Bronars (1989, table 1) reported similar average incomes. For early work see Johnson (1954) and Lebergott (1964).

24. Carrington, McCue and Pierce (1996) also reported that median hourly wages and annual incomes in self-employment were substantially and significantly more volatile and pro-cyclical than those of employees; and that while economic downturns were associated with lower wages for all workers, the decline for the self-employed was some three or four times greater than that for employees.

25. Robson (1997) attempted to explain the trend in terms of macroeconomic and fiscal variables and the aggregate self-employment rate. However, causality can run both ways between average self-employment incomes and the aggregate self-employment rate.

26. To our knowledge, most applications have been based on UK data. See, e.g., Curran, Burrows and Evandrou (1987), Hakim (1989a), Rubery, Earnshaw and Burchell (1993), Goodman and Webb (1994), Meager, Court and Moralee (1994, 1996) and Storey (1994a).

27. However, part-timers and females are especially likely to be found in the poorest self-employment groups in Britain (Hakim, 1989a). Of course, it is possible that the preponderance of self-employed in the lower tail might be

partly explained by individuals choosing to reinvest profits directly in the business rather than consuming them as income.

28. For British evidence, see Rees and Shah (1986), Pissarides and Weber (1989), Dolton and Makepeace (1990), Jenkins (1995), Meager, Court and Moralee (1994, 1996) and Parker (1997b, 1999b). For a Dutch example, see Nisjen (1988).

29. Parker corrected for self-employment income under-reporting and deployed inequality measures that are robust to mean-preserving measurement error. However, he did not attempt to separate returns to labour from returns to capital.

30. Parker's model ultimately gave rise to the Pearson Type VI distribution as a parametric form for the density function of the self-employment income distribution. This is a unimodal and positively skewed distribution, which seems to fit self-employment income data quite well. It also has the advantage of being able to handle zero and negative incomes, an important property given that over 6 per cent of UK self-employees had zero or negative incomes in 1991.

31. There are caveats to this hypothesis, however. The self-employed may invest in education as a hedge, or in order to work for others before commencing a spell of self-employment. Customers, suppliers of credit and government agencies may also screen self-employed workers. See Fredland and Little (1981) for further discussion of these points.

32. Flat self-employment earnings–age profiles can also emerge if the self-employed optimally do little investment in human capital on the job. This and other possible explanations of flat profiles are explored by Kawaguchi (2003).

33. UK studies include Rees and Shah (1986), Dolton and Makepeace (1990), Taylor (1996), Burke, Fitz-Roy and Nolan (2000), Clark and Drinkwater (2000) and Parker (2003a). US studies include Brock and Evans (1986), Gill (1988), Borjas and Bronars (1989), Evans and Jovanovic (1989), Fujii and Hawley (1991), Fairlie and Meyer (1996) and Hamilton (2000). Kidd (1993) is an Australian study; Maxim (1992) and Bernhardt (1994) are Canadian studies; and de Wit (1993) and de Wit and van Winden (1989, 1990, 1991) provide evidence for the Netherlands. Earle and Sakova (2000) used Eastern European data; and Blau (1985) used Malaysian data. For a detailed meta-analysis, see van der Sluis, Praag and Vijverberg (2003). The latter highlighted several limitations in the estimation methods used in previous studies, including failure to control for ability, endogeneity of schooling, and measurement error.

34. Fredland and Little (1981) showed that estimates of self-employed rates of return can be sensitive to the inclusion or exclusion of professionals in the sample – an important practical point that should be borne in mind when estimating (1.1) or (1.4) using data on the self-employed.

35. Fredland and Little (1981) suggested that relatively low self-employed earnings function R^2s can be taken to support the screening hypothesis. However, low self-employed R^2s could be caused by a variety of factors, including unobserved heterogeneity among the self-employed.

36. These findings are consistent with those of Evans and Leighton (1989b), Headen (1990), Maxim (1992) and Hamilton (2000). Of these studies, Hamilton provides the most detailed evidence of the gains to the self-employed from switching to paid-employment.

37. For example, Vijverberg (1986) reported that some 20 per cent of respondents in a 1976 Malaysian survey data set performed work mixing. The author's calculations using 1994/5 FES data revealed that only 1.4 per cent of UK workers mixed paid-employment and self-employment. The proportion of self-employed people doing work mixing (3.3 per cent) exceeded the proportion of employees doing so (1.1 per cent).

38. An alternative to the three-step approach is structural estimation of the parameters of an underlying utility maximisation model (Brock and Evans, 1986). However, this approach is complicated, not obviously superior and has not been widely used.

39. In simple terms, a non-stationary process is one in which there is no mechanism forcing values of the series to revert to the mean.

40. See, e.g., Harris and Sollis (2003) for an introduction to cointegration analysis.

Part I

Entrepreneurship: theories,
characteristics and evidence

2   Theories of entrepreneurship

Numerous thinkers have speculated on the origin and function of the entrepreneur, and on the nature of entrepreneurship. A large body of economic research now exists on these topics. Section 2.1 briefly surveys 'early' (chiefly pre-1975) views about entrepreneurship. These are mainly concerned with defining and identifying salient aspects of entrepreneurship in a fairly general way. Section 2.2 treats 'modern' (post-1975) contributions to the economic literature on entrepreneurship. These are typically framed in terms of optimising choices between entrepreneurship and paid-employment, and essentially belong to the tradition of neoclassical microeconomics. They tend to be less concerned with definitional issues, usually implicitly taking entrepreneurship to be any activity where individuals work for themselves and trade off risk and returns. Section 2.3 draws some conclusions.

2.1   'Early' views about entrepreneurship

Our treatment of early views about entrepreneurship will be brief, since much of this literature has been summarised before.[1] We will group these views by theme rather than chronologically:

1. *Arbitrage and the bearing of uncertainty* Richard Cantillon (1755) stressed the importance of the entrepreneur as an arbitrageur or speculator, who conducts all exchanges and bears risk as a result of buying at certain prices and selling at uncertain ones. Cantillon's is a risk theory of profit: anyone who receives an uncertain income can essentially be regarded as an entrepreneur. According to Cantillon, successful entrepreneurs perform a key role in the economy by relieving the paralysis engendered by uncertainty, allowing production and exchange to occur and market equilibrium to be attained. Unsuccessful entrepreneurs go out of business: only the 'fittest' survive. Entrants appear when profits persist. Cantillon's entrepreneur is not an innovator, nor does he change supply or demand. Instead, he is perceptive, intelligent and

willing to take risks: his role is to bring the two sides of the market together, bearing all the risks involved in this process.

Subsequent researchers have developed Cantillon's thoughts in two separate directions. Kirzner (1973, 1985) emphasised the importance of the entrepreneur as a middleman or arbitrageur, who is alert to profitable opportunities that are in principle available to all. Successful entrepreneurs merely notice what others have overlooked and profit from their exceptional alertness. Kirzner did not explain where alertness comes from, nor whether individuals or government can deliberately cultivate it.[2]

Following Knight (1921), the second line of research highlights the importance of uncertainty. According to Knight, entrepreneurs face uncertainty from the unknown availability of natural resources, technological change and fluctuating prices. Although factor prices are contractible and certain, output prices (and hence profits) are not.[3] Hence entrepreneurs need to possess particular characteristics such as self-confidence, judgement, a venturesome nature, foresight – and luck. One of Knight's key contributions was to recognise that the decision to become a worker or an entrepreneur depends on the risk-adjusted relative rewards in each sector. In his own words:

The labourer asks what he thinks the entrepreneur will be able to pay, and in any case will not accept less than he can get from some other entrepreneur, or by turning entrepreneur himself. In the same way the entrepreneur offers to any labourer what he thinks he must in order to secure his services. (Knight, 1921, p. 273)

Thus Knight viewed individuals not as born entrepreneurs or non-entrepreneurs, but opportunists, who can turn their hand to entrepreneurship when the risk-adjusted returns there are relatively favourable or alternatively to paid-employment when they are not. It will be seen in section 2.2 how modern economic research has followed directly in this tradition, making explicit the risk-adjusted returns Knight referred to.[4]

2. *Co-ordination of factors of production* According to Jean-Baptiste Say (1828), the chief contribution of the entrepreneur is to combine and co-ordinate factors of production. The entrepreneur stands at the centre of the economic system, directing and rewarding the various factors of production, and taking the residual as profit. Personal characteristics such as judgement, perseverance and experience required for successful entrepreneurship would be in scarce supply, providing high profits to these entrepreneurs. Furthermore, all of these characteristics would have to be present simultaneously in order for an entrepreneur

to be successful. Entrepreneurs need to be resourceful, knowing how to overcome unexpected problems and to exploit (although not develop) existing knowledge. Although some have criticised Say's view of the entrepreneur as just a superior kind of worker with managerial duties (e.g. Hébert and Link, 1988), others have offered modern re-statements of Say's perspective (e.g. Casson, 2003, 1999).[5]

3. *Innovation* According to Josef Schumpeter (1934, 1939), entrepreneurship entails innovation. The entrepreneur does not operate within conventional technological constraints, making small gradual changes to existing production methods; instead, he develops new technologies or products that make discrete discontinuous changes that shift the paradigm altogether. In Schumpeter's words, the entrepreneur as innovator is responsible for 'the doing of new things or the doing of things that are already being done in a new way' (1947, p. 151). This could involve (i) the creation of a new product; (ii) a new method of production; (iii) the opening of a new market; (iv) the capture of a new source of supply; or (v) a new organisation of industry. Similar to Say, the entrepreneur is an exploiter rather than an inventor of new knowledge. Schumpeter regarded entrepreneurial actions as the principal cause of business cycles and economic development. In his grand vision of 'creative destruction', a wave of entrepreneurial innovation would hit the economy, displacing old products and production processes, followed by rapid imitation by new competitors. Ultimately stability would be restored and entrepreneurship would reach a temporary cessation before the next wave occurred. Both entrepreneurial activity and the ensuing profits would be temporary, unless the entrepreneur continued to innovate.[6]

Schumpeter viewed the entrepreneur not as a calculating utility maximiser but as a rare, unusual creature driven by instinctive motives. He regarded profit as a residual, not a return to the entrepreneur as a 'factor of production', and claimed that 'the entrepreneur is never a risk bearer' (1934, p. 137; and see also Schultz, 1980). However, the view that only capitalists and not entrepreneurs bear risks has been roundly criticised by several subsequent writers (e.g. Kanbur, 1980), for imposing an arbitrary distinction between 'capitalists' and 'entrepreneurs', and for ignoring entrepreneurs' actual and opportunity costs in operating ventures that can (and often do) fail.

4. *Leadership and motivation* In contrast to Schumpeter, others have claimed that a defining feature of entrepreneurs is that they bring about changes of a gradual nature to existing products and processes, through a combination of leadership, motivation, the ability to resolve crises and risk-taking (Leibenstein, 1968).

5. *Personal or psychological traits* This line of thought relates entrepreneurship to the possession of personal characteristics. It is discussed in chapter 3, section 3.2.

While not exhaustive, the above list includes many of the most influential 'traditional' views about entrepreneurs. The brevity of our overview was deliberate. Much of this material has been discussed extensively before and, as others have noted, 'A tome could be written on the connections and contradictions between these theories' (Barreto, 1989, p. 43). We close our discussion by drawing three conclusions. First, we contend that there is a broad dichotomy underlying these theories. The dichotomy is between those in the neoclassical tradition (such as Knight, 1921, Marshall, 1930 and Schultz, 1980) who believe that entrepreneurs lead markets into equilibrium, and those in the Austrian tradition (such as Kirzner, 1973) who see entrepreneurs as part of an ongoing disequilibrium process. Rosen (1997) has attempted to find some common ground between the two schools of thought.

Second, we would argue that none of the above theories is complete. That is, none of them provides necessary or sufficient conditions for identifying entrepreneurship. For example, farmers can face uncertainty and corporate employees can contribute to the development of an innovation, without either being in any sense an 'entrepreneur'. This is what makes entrepreneurship an elusive, and almost certainly multidimensional, concept (Parker, 2002a).

Third, some writers have claimed that modern economics ignores the entrepreneur (Baumol, 1968; Barreto, 1989; Kirchhoff, 1991; Rosen, 1997; Casson, 2003). For example, according to Baumol, 'the theoretical firm is entrepreneur-less – the Prince of Denmark has been expunged from the discussion of Hamlet' (1968, p. 66). Such writers give the impression that modern economic theory is concerned purely with establishing general equilibrium, and that in contrast entrepreneurship is all about disrupting that equilibrium, for example by innovation. They also claim that ability (e.g. superior judgement) and other distinctive traits of entrepreneurs are missing from the modern economist's models. In fact, each of these criticisms misses the mark. First, economics is about much more than Arrow–Debreu general equilibrium theory, which occupies only a small area within the subject. Second, economists are well aware that market adjustment takes time: equilibrium is merely a useful way of thinking about the long-term effects of change. And modern economics *can* analyse innovations that change production technologies, for example establishing the conditions under which such innovations are likely to be adopted in preference to continuation with existing technology (see, e.g., King and Levine, 1993). Third, as will be seen in section 2.2, economists have long been aware of the special nature of entrepreneurs, and now routinely build into their models heterogeneous entrepreneurial abilities. It is probably true that in modern economic theory 'one hears of no ... brilliant innovations, of no charisma or any of the other stuff of which entrepreneurship is made' (Baumol, 1968, p. 67). But that does not mean that the theoretical firm is 'entrepreneur-less', as we go on to show in section 2.2. If the non-economist's criticism is that economics has lost the grand sweep of broad conjecture and prose eloquence, then few would disagree; but for their part few economists lament the passing of a manner of writing that lacks a tight structural framework, clear testable predictions and ready application to rigorous empirical testing.

2.2   'Modern' economic theories

2.2.1   Introduction and some definitions

Modern economic theories of entrepreneurship differ in at least two important respects from those described above. Perhaps the most important distinction relates to the dominance of the utility maximising paradigm in the modern literature. Modern theories take as their starting point the Knightian premise that individuals do not have to be entrepreneurs. They can choose between entrepreneurship and some outside option (usually taken to be paid-employment); and they choose the occupation that offers them the greatest expected utility. Most theories treat occupational choice as a discrete, rather than a continuous, decision. This follows Kanbur (1981), who noted the difficulty of viewing occupational choice as an adjustment at the margin of a continuous process, such as 'engaging a 'little bit' more in entrepreneurial activity' (p. 163). However, some researchers have also analysed how individuals mix their time between different occupations, which resembles more a continuous than a discrete choice.

A second distinctive feature of modern economic theories of entrepreneurship is that they often assume that product markets are perfectly competitive, that technology is given and that individual workers and entrepreneurs are price takers. These assumptions are primarily simplifying, and are sometimes relaxed where this does not complicate the analysis too much. To fix ideas, consider an economy without uncertainty, where a firm's average costs of production $c(q)$ are increasing in output q. Suppose there are n_S firms, each of which is run by one entrepreneur. Firms are identical and each produces q units of output. Total supply is $n_S q = Q(P)$, where product demand $Q(P)$ is decreasing in the output price P. Each entrepreneur is a price taker in P, i.e. cannot influence P

by their actions, and each entrepreneur produces at minimum cost. Each entrepreneur earns a profit of

$$\pi = Pq - c(q). \tag{2.1}$$

The number of firms, and hence aggregate output and price, is determined where demand equals supply.

In this scenario occupational choice is straightforward. Individuals can either operate a firm and earn profits or take some outside wage $w > 0$ offered by an employer. In the absence of compensating differentials, such as pleasant or unpleasant working conditions, and absent switching costs, it must be the case that $\pi = w$, otherwise individuals would have an incentive to switch to the occupation with the highest return. For example, suppose $\pi > w$. This cannot be an equilibrium because workers would then switch into entrepreneurship, increasing n_S and therefore Q and so reducing P and profit by (2.1) until equality between π and w was restored. A similar argument can be used to rule out an equilibrium with $\pi < w$.

This simple model can be used to determine the equilibrium number of firms, or equivalently the total number (or share, if the workforce is normalised to size unity) of entrepreneurs. It can also be used to establish simple 'comparative static' results – for example that an exogenous increase in the outside wage w results in fewer entrepreneurs, n_S (de Wit, 1993). It can also be extended to analyse, among other things, the effect of uncertainty on entrepreneurship (see subsection 2.2.2 below for further details).

This simple model of identical competitive firms evidently suffers from several serious drawbacks. It assumes that all firms are of equal sizes, and so cannot explain why large and small enterprises coexist in actual markets. It also rules out interesting questions such as 'who becomes an entrepreneur?'. For these reasons, richer models have been developed, which are reviewed below.

Before proceeding, it might be helpful to define some of the terms that will be used extensively in what follows. While they can be found in many standard economics texts, it is convenient to group them together and establish a common notation.

To commence, consider a utility function $U(\cdot)$ whose argument is income, y. This utility function is assumed to be *concave*, having a positive first derivative with respect to y, i.e. $U_y(y) > 0$, and a negative second derivative, i.e. $U_{yy}(y) < 0$. Viewed graphically, utility is strictly increasing in income, but extra units of income increase utility by progressively smaller amounts. This utility function is also said to embody *risk aversion*, something that is implied by its negative second derivative. If $U_{yy}(y) = 0$, individuals would be *risk neutral*; and if $U_{yy}(y) > 0$ (a case where the utility function is *convex*), individuals would be *risk lovers*.[7] Only the risk-averse case is of much practical interest (see below). The following definitions propose some useful ways of quantifying risk aversion.

Definition 1. *Given a twice-differentiable utility function $U(y)$, the Arrow–Pratt coefficient of absolute risk aversion at income y is defined as $r^A(y) = -U_{yy}(y)/U_y(y)$.*

Definition 2. *The utility function $U(y)$ exhibits decreasing absolute risk aversion if $r^A(y)$ is a decreasing function of y.*

Definition 3. *Given a twice-differentiable utility function $U(y)$, the coefficient of relative risk aversion at income y is defined as $r^R(y) = -yU_{yy}(y)/U_y(y)$.*

The concept of absolute risk aversion is useful for describing preferences over risky outcomes that involve absolute gains or losses of income. In contrast, relative risk aversion is more appropriate for risky situations where outcomes are percentage gains or losses of income. Individuals whose preferences are described by decreasing absolute risk aversion (Definition 2) take more risks as they become better off. While this often yields economically reasonable results about risk taking behaviour, it is sometimes too weak and is complemented by the stronger assumption of *non-increasing relative risk aversion*. This assumption states that individuals become more willing to risk fractions of their income as their income increases. It is a stronger assumption than decreasing absolute risk aversion because, by $r^R(y) = yr^A(y)$, decreasing relative risk aversion implies decreasing absolute risk aversion, but the converse does not necessarily follow. It will be convenient in several places in this book to consider the case where both apply, encapsulated in the following assumption.

Assumption 1. *The utility function $U(y)$ exhibits decreasing absolute risk aversion and non-increasing relative risk aversion.*

Assumption 1 has received theoretical and empirical support from many sources (see, e.g., Stiglitz, 1970). In view of the popular belief that entrepreneurs are gamblers, it might appear odd that we assume entrepreneurs at the outset to be risk averse rather than risk lovers. But evidence shows that entrepreneurs' behaviour seems to be better described by moderate and calculated risk taking than outright gambling (Meredith, Nelson and Neck, 1982).[8]

It is also helpful to have a precise definition of 'an increase in risk'. Two useful and general definitions are second-order stochastic dominance (SOSD) and mean-preserving spread (MPS). Both definitions rank two return distributions, with distribution functions $F(y)$ and $G(y)$. Consider the following ranking:

$$\int U(y)\,dF(y) \geq \int U(y)\,dG(y), \tag{2.2}$$

where $U(\cdot)$ does not necessarily have to be (though often is) the utility function defined earlier.

Definition 4 (Second-order stochastic dominance). *For any distributions $F(\cdot)$ and $G(\cdot)$ with the same mean, $F(\cdot)$ second-order stochastically dominates (is less risky than) $G(\cdot)$ if, for every non-decreasing function $U(\cdot)$, (2.2) holds.*

Definition 5 (Mean preserving spread). *For any distributions $F(\cdot)$ and $G(\cdot)$ with the same mean, $G(\cdot)$ is a mean preserving spread of (i.e. is in this sense riskier than) $F(\cdot)$ if, for $U(\cdot)$ some concave function, (2.2) holds.*

SOSD evidently places less structure on $U(\cdot)$ than MPS, which is in turn a more general measure of 'increase in risk' than an increase in variance because it implies (but is not implied by) the latter. Under both definitions, every risk averter prefers $F(\cdot)$ to $G(\cdot)$.

Definition 6 (First-order stochastic dominance). *The distribution $F(\cdot)$ first-order stochastically dominates $G(\cdot)$ if, for every non-decreasing function $U(\cdot)$, (2.2) holds.*

Definition 6 implies that every expected utility maximiser who prefers more to less prefers $F(\cdot)$ to $G(\cdot)$. Equivalently, for any amount of money income y, the probability of getting at least y is higher under $F(\cdot)$ than under $G(\cdot)$.

2.2.2   Homogeneous individuals

Static models of risk, risk aversion and the equilibrium number of entrepreneurs

Several researchers have analysed the effects of uncertainty on the equilibrium number of firms in an industry. As above, we will treat the number of firms as equivalent to the number of entrepreneurs.

Uncertainty can emanate from various sources. Entrepreneurs may be unsure about the demand for their good, their ability to produce, or future costs of production. On the other hand, employees may be uncertain about whether they will retain their job if the economic outlook for their firm worsens. Casual observation, together with the evidence of highly dispersed self-employment incomes reviewed in chapter 1, subsection 1.5.2, suggests that entrepreneurs face greater uncertainty than employees do. In this section we initially assume that entrepreneurs face some form of idiosyncratic risk to their profits, whereas employees all face a certain wage, w. The assumption of perfect certainty in paid-employment may appear extreme, but it is usually possible to relax it without changing the essential results. It will also be assumed that entrepreneurs cannot completely diversify or sell their risk. This appears to be a reasonable assumption. Markets for private unemployment, accident and sickness insurance are limited and prone to moral hazard problems; few entrepreneurs have access to stock markets to share risk; and real-world capital markets are imperfect, undermining entrepreneurs' efforts to smooth consumption in the face of income uncertainty.

It might be thought that, given risk aversion among entrepreneurs, an increase in risk in entrepreneurship would necessarily decrease the equilibrium number of entrepreneurs. In fact, this does not automatically follow, as we now demonstrate.

A pertinent early result was derived by Sheshinski and Drèze (1976), who considered a set of identical firms that face an uncertain demand for their products, $q = q(\varrho)$, where ϱ is a random variable, and a convex total cost function $c(q)$ (where $c_q > 0$, $c_{qq} > 0$: subscripts denote derivatives). The decision to operate a firm is made before the outcome of ϱ is known, but individuals who become entrepreneurs can choose their output after ϱ is known. Although Sheshinski and Drèze did not analyse occupational choice, this is easily accomplished by positing an outside wage of $w > 0$. Suppose for the moment that all individuals are risk neutral. Then we have the following result.

Proposition 1. *With demand uncertainty and convex marginal costs, a mean-preserving spread in the distribution of ϱ increases the equilibrium number of entrepreneurs.*

Proof. Profit maximisation under competition forces firms to equate price to marginal cost: $P = c_q$. Hence profit is $\pi(q) = c_q q - c(q)$. Differentiate this twice to obtain $\pi_q(q) = c_{qq} q > 0$ and $\pi_{qq}(q) = c_{qqq} q + c_{qq} > 0$. Therefore if marginal cost c_{qq} is convex in q (i.e. if $c_{qqq} > 0$), then so is $\pi(q)$. Finally, invoking the converse of Definition 5, a MPS in the distribution of ϱ must increase expected profits $E\pi(q)$ above its initial equilibrium level of w, prompting entry into entrepreneurship which reduces P and so restores the occupational equilibrium $w = \pi$. ∎

The prediction that greater uncertainty attracts risk-averse individuals to entrepreneurship is a surprising one, especially since the assumption of convex marginal costs seems innocuous. The result also holds if individuals are risk averse. However, it is *not* robust to the case where risk-averse entrepreneurs face price rather than demand uncertainty, i.e. $P = P(\varrho)$, as stated in the following proposition.

Proposition 2 (Appelbaum and Katz, 1986). *With risk-averse individuals and price uncertainty, a mean-preserving spread in the distribution of ϱ has ambiguous effects on the equilibrium number of entrepreneurs.*

Proof. Entrepreneurs maximise expected utility from profits $\mathsf{E}U(\pi) \equiv \mathsf{E}U[P(\varrho)q - c(q)]$, where $P = P(\varrho)$, E is the expectations operator, and $U(\cdot)$ is concave. Initial occupational equilibrium occurs with $\mathsf{E}U(\pi) = U(w)$. There are two offsetting effects from a MPS in the distribution of ϱ on entrepreneurs' expected utilities. (1) By Definition 5, a MPS reduces $\mathsf{E}U(\pi)$. (2) Writing $P(\varrho) = \mu + \gamma\varrho$, where $\mu := \mathsf{E}(P)$, $\mathsf{E}\varrho = 0$, and a MPS $\Leftrightarrow$ an increase in the positive parameter γ, the occupational equilibrium condition can be written as

$$\mathcal{H}(q,\mu) := \mathsf{E}\{U[(\mu + \gamma\varrho)q - c(q)]\} - U(w) = 0.$$

Then

$$\frac{\partial\mu}{\partial\gamma} = -\frac{\mathcal{H}_\gamma}{\mathcal{H}_\mu} = -\frac{\mathsf{E}[U_\pi\varrho]}{\mathsf{E}[U_\pi]} > 0.$$

Hence a MPS causes an increase in industry price which increases $\mathsf{E}(\pi)$. Hence together with (1), the total effect of the MPS on expected profits and hence the inducement to enter entrepreneurship is ambiguous *a priori*.[9] ∎

It is not possible to obtain more definitive results for the case of price uncertainty even if the additional structure of Assumption 1 is imposed on the problem. However, Assumption 1 does clarify that a higher w definitely decreases the equilibrium number of entrepreneurs (Appelbaum and Katz, 1986).

The studies considered so far investigated the consequences of greater risk in the economy, perhaps caused by more volatile trading conditions. But what if there is a general increase in *risk aversion* among individuals? This might reflect a change in tastes within an economy; alternatively it can be thought of as a device to analyse the implications of cross-country differences in risk attitudes.[10] Kanbur (1979) studied the effects of greater risk aversion on the equilibrium number of entrepreneurs. Suppose that all individuals have a common index of absolute risk aversion, r^A; normalise the size of the workforce and the output price to unity without loss of generality. Letting E denote the expectations operator, an individual is indifferent between hiring H workers in entrepreneurship and taking the safe wage w when

$$V(w; r^A) := \max_H EU[q(H, \varrho) - wH; r^A] = U(w; r^A), \qquad (2.3)$$

where r^A appears explicitly in the utility function as a parameter (*not* as an argument) to adumbrate later results. As usual, both the utility function $U(\cdot; r^A)$ and the production function $q(\cdot, \cdot)$ are assumed to be concave in their arguments. Because all employees are hired by entrepreneurs, labour markets clear only when $n_S H^* = 1 - n_S$, where n_S is the aggregate number of entrepreneurs, and where $H^* = \text{argmax } V(w; r^A) = H(w; r^A)$. Hence the market-clearing condition can also be written as

$$n_S = n_S(w; r^A) = \frac{1}{1 + H(w; r^A)}. \qquad (2.4)$$

Kanbur showed that the effects of a generic change in r^A depend crucially on whether entrepreneurs hire employees *before* or *after* the outcome of the random shock ϱ is revealed.

Proposition 3 (Kanbur, 1979). *(i) If labour is hired after the realisation of ϱ is known, then an increase in risk aversion r^A decreases the equilibrium number of entrepreneurs. (ii) If labour is hired before the realisation of ϱ is known, then even invoking Assumption 1, an increase in risk aversion r^A has an ambiguous effect on the number of entrepreneurs, since expected returns in both occupations decrease.*

Proof. (i) In this case, entrepreneurs face no risk when choosing H to maximise $V(w; r^A)$, so the first-order condition is simply $q_H(H, \varrho) - w = 0$, where a subscript again denotes a derivative. Thus a change in r^A has no effect on the H^* implied by this condition. But for any degree of risk an increase in r^A clearly decreases expected utility in the risky occupation, namely entrepreneurship, and thereby n_S. Equilibrium is restored because the reduction in aggregate labour demand needed to satisfy (2.4) reduces the equilibrium wage until (2.3) holds again.
(ii) Differentiate both sides of (2.3) to obtain

$$dw/dr^A = (V_{r^A} - U_{r^A}) / (U_w - V_w),$$

where V_{r^A} and U_{r^A} are the marginal indirect utilities in entrepreneurship and paid-employment, respectively. Now π is a MPS of w, so $V_{r^A} - U_{r^A} < 0$. Hence as r^A increases, there is less incentive to become an entrepreneur. But differentiation of the LHS of (2.3) yields $V_w = -HEU_\pi < 0$, which together with $V_{r^A} - U_{r^A} < 0$ implies $dw/dr^A < 0$, implying less incentive to become an employee. Since both occupations are less attractive, the effects of an increase in r^A on the equilibrium

number of entrepreneurs, employees per firm and returns in entrepreneurship and paid-employment are all ambiguous in general.   ∎

Proposition 3 is of interest partly because of what it says – and does not
say – about cross-country comparisons of entrepreneurship. For example,
it is sometime asserted that Europeans are more risk averse than Americans (see chapter 3, subsection 3.2.4). Case (i) of Proposition 3, where
entrepreneurs hire workers only once uncertainty has been resolved, appears to provide some theoretical backing to this view. However, there are
at least two reasons to treat this argument with scepticism. First, most
entrepreneurs who hire workers in practice do so continuously and therefore in the presence of uncertainty, so making case (ii) the relevant one.
But as we have seen, it is not possible to establish a clear link between
risk aversion and the amount of entrepreneurship in this case. Second,
the Kanbur model assumes that every individual is identical, and that
all entrepreneurs hire workers – two unrealistic assumptions. These assumptions are relaxed in some of the models discussed below.

Dynamic models of risky entrepreneurship with costly switching
The models discussed so far and in all other sections apart from this one
assume costless switching between occupations. Thus if entrepreneurship
becomes attractive relative to paid-employment, workers are assumed to
move immediately into entrepreneurship; the converse also applies. However, in some cases it seems reasonable to suppose that individuals incur
costs of switching occupation. These costs could be economic in nature
involving, for example, lost sector-specific experience, costs of raising
start-up capital (if entering entrepreneurship), or re-training costs (if entering paid-employment). Or they could be non-pecuniary involving, for
example, the sudden loss of a pleasant compensating differential, disruption to an accustomed lifestyle, or a feeling of rootlessness or failure.

One consequence of assuming costless switching is that it is possible
to analyse occupational choice in a static framework. If individuals can
switch effortlessly in the next period, one need be concerned only with
comparing payoffs in different occupations in the current period. This
greatly simplifies the analysis of occupational choice, which is no doubt
one reason why zero switching costs are so commonly assumed. Allowing
for switching costs necessitates a more comprehensive forward-looking,
dynamic modelling framework. We now explore two models of this type.[11]

In the first model, Dixit and Rob (1994) assumed the existence of two
occupations, which while not labelled as such by those authors, can be
thought of fairly naturally as 'paid-employment', E, and 'entrepreneurship', S. Each entrepreneur in S produces output q whose evolution

through time t follows a *Geometric Brownian Motion*:

$$dq = \alpha q.dt + \sigma q.dz, \tag{2.5}$$

where $\alpha > 0$ is the mean growth rate of output; $\sigma q > 0$ is the standard deviation of stochastic shocks to output; and dz is the increment of a Wiener process, which can be thought of as a continuous representation of random draws from a standard normal distribution. Equation (2.5) is a representation of a dynamic output process that contains both deterministic and stochastic components.

The size of the workforce is normalised to unity. The two goods sell at potentially different output prices: it is possible to use them to define a price index and hence a measure of real income, y. Aggregate output in S at time t is $n_S(t)q(t)$, where $n_S(t)$ is the number of individuals who choose to be entrepreneurs at t. Each employee produces a single unit of output with certainty, so aggregate output in E is $1 - n_S(t)$.

All individuals are risk averse and forward-looking, possessing rational expectations about the stochastic process underlying the shocks and the economy's responses to them. The shocks in S represent genuine uncertainty, and if especially favourable or unfavourable may create incentives to switch occupation. However, each switch costs $c > 0$ in utility, and the future gains from switching are uncertain because the output price in S (and hence income) is uncertain. The key point of the Dixit–Rob model is that uncertainty generates an 'option value' to remain in the present occupation and to defer a costly switch.

Individuals are infinitely lived. Letting $y(t)$ denote real income at t, $\delta > 0$ the rate at which individuals discount future returns,[12] and t_i the dates of each switch ($i = 1, \ldots, n$), individuals seek to maximise the objective

$$\mathsf{E}\left\{\int_0^\infty U[y(t)]\,e^{-\delta t}\,dt - \sum_i ce^{-\delta t_i}\right\}. \tag{2.6}$$

This objective functional is simply the expected value of total discounted utility net of all switching costs.

The key results from the model are as follows. First, it can be shown that individuals switch from E to S when output in S – which evolves with a stochastic component by (2.5) – reaches some upper threshold. Conversely, entrepreneurs switch into E when output in S reaches some lower threshold. If output varies between these two thresholds, individuals will remain in their current occupation: the switching cost effectively deters them from moving. Second, a decrease in risk aversion or an increase in δ (i.e. greater impatience) moves the thresholds closer together, and so makes switching more likely. This is because less risk-averse workers (or those who heavily discount the future) are more willing to bear a switching cost in order to realise certain current gains despite future uncertainty. Third, the thresholds diverge as the switching cost c increases: individuals will tend to stick with their current occupation, even if it is relatively unsatisfactory, because the cost of switching to the other more favourable occupation deters movement.

In short, Dixit and Rob showed that there may be *hysteresis* in occupational choice. Individuals may remain in entrepreneurship even if the returns there *at a given instant* are less than those available in an alternative occupation. It is rational to remain in the occupation not only because of the switching cost, but also because there is an option value to wait and see if conditions in the currently unfavourable occupation improve. Only if output changes such that this option value becomes sufficiently small will switching become worthwhile.[13]

Although Dixit and Rob did not discuss this implication of their work, the hysteresis result is useful because it goes some way to explaining why there is relatively little voluntary switching between self- and paid-employment from year to year, despite the apparent income differential between them. US estimates of the proportion switching from E to S in any given year are only 2–3.5 per cent.[14] The figures for switching out of self-employment into paid-employment are higher: for example, using PSID data on non-agricultural males over 1966–89, Fairlie (1999) reported one-year exit rates of 18.5 per cent for whites and 36.6 per cent for blacks. This primarily reflects the high failure rates of small businesses, especially newly established ones (see chapter 9, section 9.3).

It was seen above that the higher the switching cost, the less switching takes place. In the limit, these costs may be so high that no individual ever anticipates switching. In this case, and if utility embodies constant relative risk aversion so that $U(y) = y^{1-r^R}/\left(1 - r^R\right)$, for $r^R \geq 0$ (see Definition 3), then individuals have an objective that is a special case of (2.6), namely

$$\mathsf{E}\left\{ \int_0^\infty \frac{[y(t)]^{1-r^R}}{1 - r^R} e^{-\delta t}\, dt \right\}, \tag{2.7}$$

where $y(t)$ is an individual's total personal income, defined below. It is worth exploring occupational choice using this simplified model for two reasons. First, we can easily investigate the effects of introducing uncertainty into the hitherto safe sector, E, as well as in S. Second, it is possible to allow for mixing of work hours between the occupations, enabling occupational choice to be analysed as a continuous, rather than just a discrete, choice.

To this end, Parker (1996, 1997a) assumed that incomes in both occupations, y_j for $j = \{S, E\}$, follow potentially different but uncorrelated Brownian motions:

$$dy_j = \alpha_j y_j.dt + \sigma_j y_j.dz, \tag{2.8}$$

where α_j are occupation-specific average income growth rates, and $\sigma_j^2 y_j^2$ are variance terms capturing occupation-specific risk. If individuals can freely choose the fraction of their time spent working in each occupation, then total income is

$$y(t) = \xi y_S(t) + (1 - \xi) y_E(t),$$

where $\xi \in [0, 1]$ is the proportion of time allocated to S. If an interior solution to the problem of maximising (2.7) subject to (2.8) exists, it can be shown to take the form

$$\xi^* = \frac{(\dot{y}_S/y) - (\dot{y}_E/y)}{r^R(\sigma_S - \sigma_E)^2} - \frac{\sigma_E}{\sigma_S - \sigma_E} \qquad \text{for } 0 \leq \xi^* \leq 1, \tag{2.9}$$

where $\dot{y}_j = \frac{dy_j}{dt}$ is the rate of change of income in occupation j.

Suppose, as is commonly believed, that there is greater risk in S than in E. Treating the variance of innovations to income as a measure of risk, this implies that $\sigma_S^2 > \sigma_E^2$. Then from inspection of (2.9), an interior solution requires entrepreneurs to be compensated with a higher expected income growth rate, i.e. $\dot{y}_S/y > \dot{y}_E/y$. If this holds, then the next proposition follows directly from (2.9).

Proposition 4 (Parker, 1997a). *If $\dot{y}_S/y > \dot{y}_E/y$ and if there is no income uncertainty in paid-employment (i.e. $\sigma_E^2 = 0$) then greater income risk in entrepreneurship unambiguously reduces the fraction of chosen time spent in entrepreneurship. But if $\dot{y}_S/y > \dot{y}_E/y$ and if there is uncertainty in paid-employment (i.e. $\sigma_E^2 > 0$), then greater income risk in entrepreneurship has ambiguous effects on the fraction of chosen time in entrepreneurship.*

Proof. Differentiate (2.9) with respect to σ_S to obtain

$$\frac{d\xi^*}{d\sigma_S} = -2 \frac{\dot{y}_S/y - \dot{y}_E/y}{r^R(\sigma_S - \sigma_E)^3} + \frac{\sigma_E}{(\sigma_S - \sigma_E)^2}.$$

By inspection, this derivative is negative if $\sigma_E = 0$, but takes an ambiguous sign if $\sigma_E > 0$. ∎

At first sight, it might appear surprising that risk-averse individuals could respond to an increase in risk in entrepreneurship by choosing to spend even more time in it. But the logic is analogous to that applying in the two-asset portfolio problem in finance, where the risk of the overall portfolio is a convex combination of the risk of each asset. *Overall* portfolio risk can sometimes be reduced by increasing the portfolio share of the riskiest asset.[15]

Parker's assumption of no switching is a strong one, but can be relaxed in the following way. Parker (1997a) analysed the case where individuals cannot mix their time between occupations, and are trapped in an occupation for $T > 0$ periods, where T may be made arbitrarily small. The optimal solution is that individuals choose the occupation j that maximises their risk-adjusted return:

$$\max_{j \in \{S, E\}} \left\{ 2\alpha_j - \sigma_j^2 r^R \right\} . \tag{2.10}$$

That is, higher expected income growth in an occupation increases the likelihood that an individual chooses to participate in it; but greater risk in the occupation decreases that likelihood to the extent that individuals are risk averse (measured by r^R). Notice the property that the optimal occupational choice given by (2.10) is invariant to the no-switching duration, T. The reason is that the same underlying taste and technology parameters are taken to apply in all periods.

2.2.3   Heterogeneous entrepreneurial ability

In practice, it is likely that entrepreneurs differ from employees and among themselves in terms of innate 'entrepreneurial ability'. For now, it is not necessary to elaborate on the nature of ability in entrepreneurship: it might reflect, for example, leadership qualities (Leibenstein, 1968) or judgement (Casson, 2003). Suppose that entrepreneurial ability can be represented by a unidimensional variable, x, with support $[\underline{x}, \overline{x}]$ and distribution function $F(x)$, with $F(\underline{x}) = 0$ and $F(\overline{x}) = 1$. It is assumed that x either enters the entrepreneur's production function in a positive manner, or his cost function in a negative manner. Ability ultimately determines which individuals become entrepreneurs and which become employees. It is also commonly assumed that abilities are fixed and known with certainty by each individual.[16]

A highly influential paper that analysed the implications of heterogeneous ability for occupational choice and entrepreneurship is Lucas (1978). We first outline Lucas' static model of occupational choice, then explain and critically assess the dynamic version of that model, before considering variants and extensions of it.

The static Lucas model

Lucas considered a closed economy with a homogeneous capital stock of a given size, and a workforce of a given size that is homogeneous with respect to productivity in paid-employment, but heterogeneous with respect to managerial ability in entrepreneurship. Price taking risk-neutral individuals freely choose whether to become a worker in a firm managed by an entrepreneur, earning the wage w, or to set up their own firm as an entrepreneur, employing capital k and labour H. Entrepreneurs use a given constant-returns-to-scale technology to produce output (sold at unit price) of $x.q[H.\psi(\kappa)]$, where $\kappa := k/H$ is the capital–labour ratio used by the firm, $\psi(\cdot)$ is an increasing and concave function and $q[\cdot]$ is the production function, also assumed to be increasing and concave. Thus higher ability translates directly into higher output, for any k and H.

Entrepreneurs maximise profits, given by revenue less factor input costs:

$$\max_{k,H} \pi(x) = x.q[H.\psi(\kappa)] - wh - rk, \tag{2.11}$$

where r is the rental price of capital, i.e. the interest rate. Using subscripts to denote derivatives, the first-order conditions for this problem, in k and H, respectively, are

$$xq_{H.\psi(\kappa)}[H.\psi(\kappa)]\psi_\kappa(\kappa) - r = 0 \quad \text{for} \quad x \geq \tilde{x} \quad \text{(2.12)}$$

$$xq_{H.\psi(\kappa)}[H.\psi(\kappa)]\{\psi(\kappa) - \kappa\psi_\kappa(\kappa)\} - w = 0 \quad \text{for} \quad x \geq \tilde{x}, \quad \text{(2.13)}$$

from which we can derive demand functions for labour $H(x, w, r)$ and capital $k(x, w, r)$; where $\tilde{x}$ denotes the *marginal entrepreneur*, defined implicitly by $\pi(\tilde{x}) = w$. The marginal entrepreneur is the individual who is indifferent between entrepreneurship and paid-employment. Both demand functions are increasing functions of ability x. This implies that more able entrepreneurs run larger firms (irrespective of whether size is defined in terms of employment or capital assets), even though the capital–labour ratio is invariant to ability (to see the latter, take the ratio of (2.12) and (2.13)). Individuals with ability $x \geq \tilde{x}$ enter entrepreneurship and the rest become workers. Hence the proportion of entrepreneurs is $1 - F(\tilde{x})$, implying a mix of workers between the occupations if $\underline{x} < \tilde{x} < \overline{x}$. To close the model, the equilibrium factor prices w and r are determined by equating the demands for and supplies of each factor.

The dynamic Lucas model

To place greater structure on the model, and to relate entrepreneurship to economic growth, Lucas invoked Gibrat's Law. This 'Law' (which is explained in greater detail in chapter 9, section 9.2) takes firm growth rates to be independent of firm size. In the context of Lucas' model, the Law not only ensures that there is a uniquely determined marginal entrepreneur $\tilde{x}$, but also that the following proposition holds.[17]

Proposition 5. *If the elasticity of substitution is less than (greater than) (equal to) unity, then increases in* per capita *capital in the economy decrease (increase) (leave unchanged) the equilibrium number of entrepreneurs, and increase (decrease) (leave unchanged) the average firm size.*

To see the intuition behind Proposition 5, note that extra capital increases κ, and hence both the profits of entrepreneurs and the real wage. Members of both occupations gain; but the group that gains the most depends on the elasticity of substitution. If the latter is less than unity, then the returns in paid-employment increase by more than the returns in entrepreneurship, because a low substitution elasticity implies that factor usage does not respond much following the change in their relative prices. This induces marginal entrepreneurs to become employees, which increases $\tilde{x}$ and thereby also the average size of firms.

It is interesting to interpret the result stated in Proposition 5 in terms of a prediction about future trends in the fraction of the workforce who are entrepreneurs. Empirical estimates consistently point to an elasticity of substitution of less than unity (Hamermesh, 1993, pp. 92–104). Given also that capital per head tends to grow over time (Maddison, 1991), Proposition 5 implies that the fraction of entrepreneurs will decline inexorably over time, while the average firm size and industrial concentration will inexorably increase.

How accurate are these predictions? Lucas obtained some evidence that average firm size is positively related to the *per capita* capital stock. He regressed employees per firm (as a proxy for average firm size) against *per capita* gross national product (as a proxy for the stock of capital per head). He estimated that a 1 per cent increase in GNP is significantly associated with a 1 per cent increase in the number of employees per firm.

However, Lucas' other prediction receives somewhat less support – at least if the aggregate self-employment rate is used as a proxy for the size of the entrepreneurship sector. As chapter 1, section 1.4 showed, while the self-employment rate decreased steadily in the last part of the nineteenth and early part of the twentieth centuries in most developed economies, in some economies the trend reversed in the last quarter of the twentieth century. This leads one to ask whether something is amiss in Lucas' model, or whether other factors are at work, overwhelming the mechanism proposed there.

Consider the limitations of the Lucas model. One objection is the assumption of Gibrat's Law. Recent studies have cast doubt on the applicability of this Law, finding that firm growth rates are actually not invariant to firm size (see chapter 9, section 9.2). Another problem is that Lucas' model is highly aggregated and simplified, glossing over industry composition effects that may be important given the concentration of self-employed workers in particular sectors (see chapter 3, subsection 3.3.1).[18] Among possible omitted factors is technological change, which may be a more important cause of macroeconomic growth than changes in the capital stock analysed by Lucas. For example, if technological change occurs in ways that disproportionately benefit smaller firms, then more rather than less entrepreneurship may result. The growth of the service sector may also be relevant. Rising levels of prosperity often translate into greater demand for services that entrepreneurs may be particularly efficient at supplying. Finally, it may be inappropriate to treat entrepreneurial managerial ability as exogenous, especially if entrepreneurs learn over time (Otani, 1996).

Variants and extensions to the Lucas model
Several variants of Lucas's model have been proposed (e.g. Calvo and Wellisz, 1980; Oi, 1983; Blau, 1985; Bond, 1986; Brock and Evans, 1986; de Wit and van Winden, 1991). In each of these models, the ablest individuals select into entrepreneurship. In the model of Calvo and Wellisz (1980), for example, x describes the ability to learn about productivity-enhancing technological information. An individual's output, $q(x)$, is assumed to grow through time t according to the differential equation $\dot{q}(x, t) = x[\overline{q}(t) - q(x, t)]$, where the dot indicates a time derivative and the term in square brackets measures the gap between the individual's output and the maximum available given the stock of knowledge at time t, i.e. $\overline{q}(t)$. Thus the greater the individual's learning ability x, or the greater the gap to be made up, the faster the individual learns and the more she produces. Calvo and Wellisz showed that in steady-state equilibrium, the greater the growth rate in the total stock of knowledge and therefore potential output $\overline{q}(t)$, the more able is the marginal entrepreneur $\tilde{x}$. Hence, given a fixed distribution of ability, the smaller is the number of entrepreneurs and the larger the average firm size.[19] This result is interesting because it provides another rationale for Lucas's prediction of ever-declining entrepreneurship and an ever-increasing average firm size. However, the Calvo–Wellisz model is ad hoc and partial equilibrium in nature: ideally a general equilibrium analysis of both occupations with optimising behaviour is needed to fully understand the impact of technological change on entrepreneurship.

These models all assume that heterogeneous abilities generate heterogeneous returns only in entrepreneurship: returns in paid-employment are assumed to be invariant to ability. A couple of papers have relaxed this assumption. Suppose each individual possesses a pair of abilities (x, x_E)

that are productive in both occupations, the former being ability in entrepreneurship and the latter being ability in paid-employment. Jovanovic (1994) assumed that returns in paid-employment are given by $w.x_E$, where $w > 0$ is a constant. An individual becomes an entrepreneur if

$$\pi(x, w) := \max_H \{xq(H) - wh\} \geq wx_E, \qquad (2.14)$$

where $q(\cdot)$ is an increasing and concave function of hired labour, H. If the condition in (2.14) is not satisfied for an individual characterised by (x, x_E), then that individual becomes an employee. Firms derive their optimal labour demand function $H^* = H(x, w)$, with $H_x > 0$. By the envelope theorem, $\pi_x = q[H(x, w)] > 0$ and $\pi_{xx} = q_H[H(x, w)]H_x > 0$. Thus entrepreneurs' returns are a convex function of their ability.

The main contribution of Jovanovic's paper is to show that those with the greatest entrepreneurial abilities x do not necessarily become entrepreneurs. To see this, suppose that x and x_E are positively related: $x_E = \psi(x)$, where $\psi(\cdot)$ is a strictly increasing function of x_E. For example, more educated individuals might earn more in both occupations – a possibility which receives some support from our discussion of earnings functions in chapter 1, subsection 1.5.3. For the marginal entrepreneur $\tilde{x}$,

$$\pi(\tilde{x}, w) = w.\psi(\tilde{x}),$$

so the ablest (resp., least able) individuals enter paid-employment if

$$\pi(x; w) < (\text{resp.,} >) w.\psi(x) \quad \text{for } x > \tilde{x}.$$

Thus it is possible for individuals with the lowest managerial abilities to become entrepreneurs (as illustrated in figure 2.1(a)), depending on the shape of the $\psi(x)$ function.

Another possibility is that x and x_E are negatively correlated, i.e. $\psi(\cdot)$ is a decreasing function of x_E. This might be, for example, if x measures productive rebelliousness, which pays off in entrepreneurship but is penalised in team-based paid-employment. In this case, figure 2.1(b) is applicable and, as in Lucas' model, only the highest-ability types become entrepreneurs.

One criticism of Jovanovic's model is its inconsistent treatment of heterogeneous employee ability. If employees have heterogeneous x_Es, why is this not reflected in the employer's production function $q(\cdot)$? After all, in a competitive economy, workers must be paid different wages to reward their different productivities. While it might be possible in principle to circumvent this problem by assuming that no entrepreneur hires any workers, it is then unclear how employees' wages are determined.

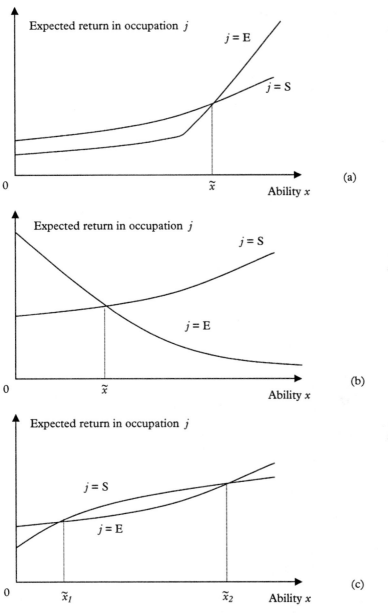

Figure 2.1 Occupational choice with two occupations, entrepreneurship (S) and paid-employment (E)
(a) E attracts the ablest entrepreneurs: $x > \tilde{x}$ enter E
(b) S attracts the ablest entrepreneurs: $x > \tilde{x}$ enter S
(c) Multiple marginal entrepreneurs, $\tilde{x}_1$, and $\tilde{x}_2$

This issue is treated explicitly in a second paper, by the author (Parker, 2003d). Individuals are assumed to have heterogeneous abilities which are private information and cannot be credibly revealed to outside agents. Individuals can choose freely between producing a good using a safe or a risky technology. In the case of the former, an individual with ability x produces output $w(x)$ with certainty; with the latter, the individual has a probability $p(x)$ of generating positive output R^s, and $1 - p(x)$ of producing zero. Suppose that both $w(\cdot)$ and $p(\cdot)$ are increasing functions of x, possibly for the reasons explained above. Both technologies require a single indivisible unit of capital that no individual possesses initially. Two contracts are available. One contract is offered by a competitive employer, which supplies the unit of capital, owns the rights to the output produced and rewards the individual with a wage. The other is issued by a competitive bank, which lends the required capital, takes an agreed debt repayment $D < R^s$, and leaves the individual to take the surplus output. In general, all individuals, banks and employers have incentives to perform monitoring to reveal hidden abilities.

Several equilibria are possible in this model. One equilibrium of particular interest has banks optimally monitoring only borrowers who fail, in order to deter opportunistic defaults, whereas employers optimally monitor all employees to reveal their hidden abilities. Employees optimally choose safe production and are paid a type-specific wage of $w(x) - c$, where c is the monitoring cost. Banks issue a debt contract that pools heterogeneous borrowers together, who optimally choose the risky technology. An individual with x chooses the bank contract ('entrepreneurship') if expected returns there exceed $w(x) - c$, otherwise they take the employer ('paid-employment') contract. Individual $\tilde{x}$ is indifferent between the two occupations:

$$p(\tilde{x})[R^s - D] = w(\tilde{x}) - c . \tag{2.15}$$

This model not only shows how the different occupations can coexist in equilibrium (rather than just assuming that this is so, as was previously the case), but also generates a rich variety of potential occupational choice outcomes. These include the single crossings of expected returns depicted in figure 2.1(a) and (b), and also multiple crossings (multiple marginal entrepreneurs) as in figure 2.1(c). This model also has some implications for the efficiency of bank financing of entrepreneurial investments – as we will explain in chapter 5.

A distinct but related contribution by Barzel (1987) identified the residual claimant feature of entrepreneurship stressed by Knight as a means of resolving imperfect information and hidden action problems, and enabling mutually beneficial productive collaborations to take place. As an illustrative case, Barzel considered two individuals in separate jobs, one of which (A, say) makes output that is intrinsically easy to monitor, while the other (B) makes a productive contribution that is intrinsically difficult to monitor. For example, A could be the producer of widgets, whereas B is the coordinator of contracts to supply clients, the keeper of accounts and records and the searcher for new clients and cheaper raw materials. Barzel argued that B would become the entrepreneur, being the residual claimant and employer of A via a wage contract. The reason is simply that, by the nature of his job, B finds it easier to shirk. But B has fewer incentives to shirk if he is given residual claimant status rather than a wage contract, since as a residual claimant he bears directly the costs of his own forgone effort. Hence this arrangement maximises the joint product from collaboration and the individual returns for the two agents.

There are two other interesting implications of Barzel's model. One is that the infusion of B's capital into production endows the fixed wage contract with credibility in the eyes of A – capital effectively serves as a bond. This implies that capital makes a secondary contribution to output, in addition to its primary role as a factor of production. The second is that the identity of the entrepreneur is not fixed, but depends on the relative wages of the two collaborators. In particular, if A's productivity (and hence wage) increases relative to B's, then A could eventually replace B as the entrepreneur. The reason is that the loss from shirking by A under a fixed wage contract may eventually become so great that it becomes imperative to eliminate it – which is achieved by shifting the residual claimant status from B to A.

2.2.4   Heterogeneous risk aversion

What if individuals can choose freely between entrepreneurship and paid-employment, as in the models just discussed, but face uncertainty in entrepreneurship and have *heterogeneous aversion to risk* rather than heterogeneous entrepreneurial ability? The economic implications of this scenario have been analysed by Kihlstrom and Laffont (1979) (henceforth KL79). In Kihlstrom and Laffont's own words, their model is 'a formalisation, for a special case, of Knight's discussion of the entrepreneur' (1979, p. 745). This is because entrepreneurs exercise control over the production process, bear the risks associated with production, and freely choose whether to become entrepreneurs or workers – as in Knight – but in the special case where all individuals possess identical managerial abilities.

Below, let θ identify individuals from a continuum defined on the unit interval. Suppose without loss of generality that higher values of θ indicate greater aversion to risk, as measured by $r^A(\pi)$. Individuals have quasi-concave utility functions $U(y; \theta)$, where y is income. All individuals start with common exogenous non-labour income $I > 0$, which is sufficiently great to rule out the possibility of bankruptcy. Individuals in paid-employment all receive the safe wage w, where $w > 0$ equates aggregate labour demand and supply; but entrepreneurs face uncertain profits because of random shocks ϱ to their production function $q = q(H, \varrho)$, where H is the number of hired workers. Unlike the Lucas model there is no explicit treatment of capital. Higher values of ϱ correspond to greater output. The value of ϱ is revealed to individuals only after they have made their occupational choices, labour hiring and production decisions. Let $H(w, \theta)$ be θ's optimal labour demand, i.e. the H that maximises $EU(I + \pi; \theta)$. With a unit output price, entrepreneurs' stochastic profits are

$$\pi(w, \theta) = q\ (H(w, \theta), \varrho) - wH(w, \theta).$$

In the usual way, individual θ chooses to become an entrepreneur if

$$EU(I + \pi(w, \theta); \theta) \geq U(I + w; \theta), \tag{2.16}$$

otherwise he chooses paid-employment; the marginal entrepreneur is denoted by $\tilde{\theta}$.

After showing that their model possesses a unique equilibrium, KL79 established the following results:[20]

KL79.1 More (resp., less) risk-averse individuals than the marginal entrepreneur $\tilde{\theta}$ become employees (resp., entrepreneurs).

KL79.2 More risk-averse entrepreneurs operate smaller firms, i.e. use less labour than less risk-averse entrepreneurs, provided that the total product $q(H, \varrho)$ and marginal product $q_H(H, \varrho)$ are either both monotonically increasing or both monotonically decreasing functions of ϱ (an example of a production technology for which this holds is $q(H, \varrho) = \varrho q(H)$).

KL79.3 A general increase in individual risk aversion reduces the equilibrium wage.[21] This is because greater risk aversion increases the equilibrium number of employees by result KL79.1, and decreases the demand for labour by each entrepreneur by result KL79.2. Both changes reduce the aggregate demand for labour and hence w.

KL79.4 Industry equilibrium would be Pareto efficient (i.e. efficient in the sense that there exist no allocations that could make one individual better off without making another individual worse off) if all individuals were risk neutral; but it is inefficient when some individuals are risk averse. There are three different manifestations of inefficiency. First, maximisation of aggregate output requires all firms to produce the same output when the production function is concave. However, entrepreneurs with heterogeneous risk aversion operate differently sized firms by result KL79.2. Second, individuals could be made better off if risks were shared, but there is no mechanism for facilitating this. Third, in general the wrong number of individuals become entrepreneurs. On the one hand risk aversion causes too few individuals to become entrepreneurs (from the standpoint of efficiency), but on the other hand risk aversion causes too small a demand for labour by result KL79.2, and hence w is too low, causing too many individuals to choose entrepreneurship. In general, the two effects will offset each other and the net effect cannot be predicted without further information about tastes and technology.[22]

KL79.5 Apart from the problems described in KL79.4 and caused by the maldistribution of risks across individuals, the equilibrium is in other respects efficient. One way of achieving full efficiency would be to introduce a risk-sharing mechanism such as a stock market (Kihlstrom and Laffont, 1983a).

Perhaps the most widely cited of the above results is the first one, KL79.1. The prediction that individuals who are relatively less risk averse are more likely to become entrepreneurs is intuitive, and has also motivated empirical tests (see chapter 3, subsection 3.2.4). However, KL79's other results are also thought-provoking, and shed further light on the interaction between risk and entrepreneurship.

For example, result KL79.3 can be compared with part (ii) of Proposition 3 stated earlier, due to Kanbur (1979). Both models predict the employee wage to decline in response to an increase in risk aversion; but they generate different predictions about the equilibrium number of entrepreneurs. This is attributable to differences in the structure of the two models, in particular the heterogeneity of risk aversion in KL79 compared with homogeneity in Kanbur (1979).

Regarding result KL79.5, others have echoed KL79's recommendation of introducing risk sharing mechanisms. For example, Grossman (1984) proposed a similar model to Kanbur (1979) in which the absence of markets for risk sharing causes an inefficiently small number of entrepreneurs. Grossman showed how allowing free trade with foreigners who have a comparative advantage in entrepreneurship-rich goods reduces the supply of domestic entrepreneurs even further. Yet he concluded that the provision of risk sharing mechanisms to stimulate domestic entrepreneurship would be a better solution than imposing welfare-reducing tariffs or other trade restrictions. Of course, an obvious problem with the specific solution of a stock market to share risks is that it is likely to be impractical for small firms. The high fixed costs incurred by a stock market listing are known to deter small firms from diversifying their risks in this way (see chapter 6, section 6.2 for more on this).

Before we conclude, it is appropriate to pinpoint one important contribution made by both the KL79 and the Lucas (1978) models. It relates to a fundamental question about why it is that, when large firms have scale economies in production, small firms exist at all. Both KL79 and Lucas propose explanations based on exogenous heterogeneous entrepreneurial characteristics which, in conjunction with concave production functions, rule out an equilibrium in which one firm produces all the output. Of course, this is not the only reason why small entrepreneurial firms can coexist with large ones. Small entrepreneurial firms might be able to avoid agency problems, diseconomies of scale and diluted incentives to innovate that can hinder the economic performance of large firms (Williamson, 1985; Reid and Jacobsen, 1988). Also, small entrepreneurial ventures might be more efficient at supplying small batches of goods or customised goods and services than their larger rivals, who might have a comparative advantage at producing standardised products in large production runs. Part of the interest of the KL79 and Lucas models is therefore that they can explain the coexistence of small entrepreneurial and large corporate firms even in the absence of these special factors.

2.3   Conclusion

This chapter reviewed early and modern economic theories of entrepreneurship. While the early theories tended to treat issues in a general and discursive manner, modern economic analysis asks more precisely targeted questions focused on occupational choice. Its approach is therefore narrower, but it arguably obtains sharper results. For example, modern theories predict what types of individuals are likely to become entrepreneurs, and why they do so, as well as tracing out the implications for economic efficiency. Being tightly focused, this approach also has the advantage of generating hypotheses that can be tested and falsified in the accepted scientific tradition. An example is Kihlstrom and Laffont's (1979) prediction that the least risk-averse individuals are more likely to become entrepreneurs, and run larger firms.

Another strength of the modern theories is that they clarify what can, and cannot, be said about the determinants of entrepreneurship. For example, we saw that greater risk in entrepreneurship does not necessarily reduce the equilibrium number of entrepreneurs. The reason is that greater risk in entrepreneurship also affects employees indirectly by decreasing the equilibrium wage. We also showed why rational individuals might not switch between entrepreneurship and paid-employment despite apparently being able to make clear-cut gains from doing so; and how imperfect information enables the entrepreneurial function to be endogenised. Regarding the latter, an especially interesting hypothesis is that, within firms, the individual who becomes the entrepreneur (i.e. the residual claimant) is the one with the greatest freedom to undertake hidden actions such as shirking.

One criticism sometimes made of the modern economic approach by non-economists is that it adopts an inappropriately narrow perspective of entrepreneurship. Specifically, it does not define entrepreneurship above and beyond the receipt of residual profits and the bearing of financial risk. Chapter 3 goes some way towards addressing that criticism by filling out our picture of entrepreneurs and entrepreneurship. We do this by synthesising theoretical and empirical work on specific personal characteristics and the broader environmental factors associated with entrepreneurship.

NOTES

1. See, for example, Hébert and Link (1988), Barreto (1989), Binks and Vale (1990), Chell, Haworth and Brearley (1991) and van Praag (1999). Hébert and Link's monograph provides a particularly thorough account of the entrepreneur in the history of economic thought, from 'the prehistory of entrepreneurship' through to the modern era. Van Praag provides an illuminating comparison between competing views of entrepreneurship.
2. More recently Gifford (1998) endogenised alertness in a model of limited entrepreneurial attention. Entrepreneurs endowed with high levels of managerial ability optimally spend their time operating numerous projects: they therefore face a high opportunity cost of perceiving new innovative opportunities, which renders them less 'alert'.
3. Knight viewed profits as a fluctuating residual, not as a return to the entrepreneurial factor of production. In contrast, Frederick Hawley (1907) regarded profit as a reward to risk-taking. According to Hawley, what sets the entrepreneur apart is his willingness to be the ultimately responsible agent in the productive process, liable for ownership of output but also for loss. This willingness entitles him to direct and guide production.
4. One aspect of Knight's writing that has arguably generated more heat than light is the distinction between risk and uncertainty – or, more accurately, informed and uninformed uncertainty. Informed uncertainty occurs when an individual does not know in advance the (random) outcome of a draw from a given probability distribution, but does know the form and parameters of the underlying probability distribution. Then individuals can form expectations of events. In contrast, uninformed uncertainty occurs when individuals are not only ignorant of the outcomes of the random draw, but also do not know the form of the probability distribution. Some authors have claimed that the latter kind of uncertainty precludes systematic optimising choice. However, quite apart from the fact that a careful reading of Knight's treatise points to his apparent belief in informed rather than uninformed uncertainty (LeRoy and Singell, 1987), the whole distinction between informed and uninformed uncertainty

is actually irrelevant from a Bayesian viewpoint. Bayesians characterise (posterior) beliefs as the product of initial prior beliefs ('priors') and the likelihood of observed subsequent events having occurred. The case of informed uncertainty corresponds to one with sharp priors; uninformed uncertainty merely corresponds to one with diffuse priors, where there is no concentration of probability mass in any particular outcome. In either case, entrepreneurs can form expectations and therefore *can* make meaningful decisions. In our view the distinction between informed and uninformed uncertainty is therefore empty and is ignored in the remainder of the book.

5. For example, 'an entrepreneur is someone who specialises in taking judgemental decisions about the co-ordination of scarce resources' (Casson, 2003, p. 20).

6. 'Everyone is an entrepreneur only when he actually carries out new combinations and loses that character as soon as he has built up his business, when he settles down to running it as other people run their business' (Schumpeter, 1934, p. 78). Schumpeter predicted the eventual demise of the entrepreneur because of the rise of large monopolistic firms, which have advantages at co-ordinating teams of workers to perform R&D. However, this prediction has not come to pass, partly because small firms continue to innovate (see chapter 9), and partly because the majority of US basic research is funded not by large firms but by the Federal government (Schultz, 1980). Findings of a positive correlation between the number of businesses and the aggregate number of patents issued (Shane, 1996) are also of interest in this light.

7. Individuals with these utility functions would maximise their expected utility by avoiding gambles, being indifferent to gambles, and seeking gambles, respectively. See any standard microeconomics text for proofs.

8. 'They enjoy the excitement of a challenge, but they don't gamble. Entrepreneurs avoid low-risk situations because there is a lack of challenge and avoid high-risk situations because they want to succeed. They like achievable challenges' (Meredith, Nelson and Neck, 1982, p. 25).

9. Appelbaum and Lim (1982) appeared to overlook effect (2), and hence incorrectly concluded that greater price uncertainty unambiguously reduces expected profits and hence decreases the equilibrium number of entrepreneurs.

10. See chapter 3, subsection 3.2.4 for some evidence about cross-country differences in attitudes to risk.

11. An influential dynamic model by Jovanovic (1982) analyses learning under uncertainty but ignores switching costs. This model is discussed in chapter 9, section 9.1.

12. Thus $\delta > 0$ implies that individuals value utility available tomorrow less than they value the same level of utility available today. This is commonly taken to reflect 'impatience': the greater is δ, the more impatient an individual is.

13. Dixit and Rob (1994) also showed that a socially suboptimal amount of switching takes place in equilibrium. Greater labour mobility decreases the variability of output prices, which benefits the imperfectly insured risk-averse population. There is therefore a role in principle for government to improve on the free-market equilibrium by speeding up the re-allocation of labour between occupations.

14. The estimates are: circa 2 per cent (Meyer, 1990; van Praag and van Ophem, 1995: National Longitudinal Survey (NLS)); 2.5 per cent (Evans and Leighton, 1989b: CPS); 3 per cent (Boden, 1996: CPS; Dunn and Holtz-Eakin, 2000: NLS); and 3.4 per cent (Fairlie, 1999: PSID). Boden calculated that the female switching rate was about 1 per cent lower than that of males. According to Evans and Leighton (1989b), switching into self-employment by Americans occurs steadily up to age forty and then levels off. See Taylor (2001, p. 546) for British evidence on switching rates.

15. Parker (1996) obtained some time-series evidence suggesting that greater risk in entrepreneurship, proxied by the number of strikes, was significantly associated with a lower aggregate self-employment rate in the UK in the post-war period. However, he did not control for risk in paid-employment. While Foti and Vivarelli (1994) proposed the number of involuntary job losses as a measure of wage uncertainty, this measure also carries alternative interpretations, and confounds the impact of unemployment on new-firm creation.

16. This assumption has been relaxed in a model by Jovanovic (1982), where entrepreneurs learn about their x by observing their performance in entrepreneurship. Discussion of the Jovanovic model is deferred until chapter 9, section 9.1.

17. The proof is straightforward but technical: the interested reader is referred to Lucas' (1978) original article.

18. Brock and Evans (1986) went so far as to dismiss the empirical relevance of this model, and another by Kihlstrom and Laffont (1979), discussed below, concluding that they 'were developed primarily to study general equilibrium issues and have limited empirical content' (1986, n. 39, p. 204).

19. If young entrepreneurs learn fastest then it can be shown that the age of the youngest entrepreneur and the average firm size are both decreasing functions of the rate of technological progress. Making ability two-dimensional, so individuals are characterised by youth and ability, Calvo and Wellisz (1980) showed that faster technological progress leads to an equilibrium outcome where older, inherently less able entrepreneurs are replaced by younger and inherently more able entrepreneurs. See Gifford (1998) for another two-dimensional model of ability, comprising 'managerial ability' (for operating existing projects) and 'entrepreneurial ability' (for innovating new projects).

20. Proofs are omitted for brevity: the interested reader is referred to the original KL79 article.

21. Strictly speaking, this result requires either the utility or the production function to be strictly concave.

22. For example, in the special case where all individuals are equally risk averse, it can be shown that there will be too many entrepreneurs in equilibrium. Another special case is constant returns to scale technology, under which only one firm is optimal, compared to the greater number that would emerge in the competitive equilibrium.

3 Characteristics of entrepreneurs and the environment for entrepreneurship

Chapter 2 discussed several theories of entrepreneurship, the role of entrepreneurs and the factors influencing individuals to participate in entrepreneurship. The purpose of this chapter is to fill out the picture of entrepreneurship that has been sketched so far. Complementing the theoretical analysis of chapter 2, section 2.2, section 3.1 reviews the evidence about the impact of financial rewards on entrepreneurial behaviour. It also explores the role of specific aspects of entrepreneurial ability embodied in human and social capital. Section 3.2 focuses on linkages between entrepreneurship, family circumstances and personal characteristics. Section 3.3 summarises theory and evidence about the broader macroeconomic factors that affect entrepreneurship, including economic development, changes in industrial structure, unemployment, regional effects and government policy variables. Throughout, the self-employed are invariably used as a working empirical definition of entrepreneurs. Section 3.4 briefly summarises the main results of the chapter and concludes.

3.1 Relative earnings, human and social capital

3.1.1 Earnings differentials

The most widely used tool for estimating the effects of earnings differentials on participation in entrepreneurship is the structural probit model described in chapter 1, subsection 1.6.2. Recall from (1.15) that only if $\hat{\alpha}$, the estimated coefficient on the earnings differential term in the probit model, is positive and significant does a relative earnings advantage in entrepreneurship increase the likelihood of participation in entrepreneurship.

Taking self-employment to be a working definition of entrepreneurship, (1.15) has been estimated by several British researchers, most of whom have reported positive α estimates. Estimates include 0.365 (Rees and Shah, 1986); 0.036 (Dolton and Makepeace, 1990); 0.09–0.13 (Clark and Drinkwater, 2000); and 0.597 (Taylor, 1996). The first two estimates are insignificantly different from zero; the latter two are statistically significant. Parker (2003a) obtained mixed results ($\hat{\alpha}$ took varying signs) using several British data-sets from different years; the estimate of α was positive but marginally insignificant for switchers between paid-employment and self-employment. Gill (1988) and Fujii and Hawley (1991) obtained estimates based on US data. This evidence is also mixed, the former reporting significant negative and the latter significant positive α estimates. For other countries, Bernhardt (1994) estimated α to be positive and significant for a sample of Canadian white, full-time non-agricultural males. De Wit (1993) and de Wit and van Winden (1989, 1990, 1991) reported insignificant positive α estimates using Dutch data; and Earle and Sakova (2000) reported negative α estimates using household data from six Eastern European transition economies.[1]

In short, relative earnings do not play a clear-cut role in explaining cross-section self-employment choice. One might attribute the mixed empirical results to the variety of different data-sets and specifications used by researchers. However, one could just as easily conclude that the failure to obtain a clear positive effect from relative earnings *despite* the variety of specifications and data-sets indicates non-robustness in the relative earnings motive for self-employment. Several explanations for this inconclusive result can be proposed. First, it is not clear that previous researchers have successfully isolated variables that affect earnings in the two sectors but not occupational choice itself – as required to identify the structural probit model (see subsection 1.6.2). Second, the poor quality of self-employment data may also be partly responsible for the conflicting results.[2] Third, in developing and transition economies market imperfections might undermine neoclassical occupational choices (Earle and Sakova, 2000), although this explanation is less convincing for developed economies.

Alternatively, these results may simply be telling us that pecuniary rewards are not the primary motive for choosing self-employment. For example, participation in self-employment might be motivated by lifestyle considerations, for instance as a means of being one's own boss. Another possibility is that the self-employed suffer from unrealistic optimism and remain in a low-return occupation because they anticipate high future profits. While there might be some truth in these hypotheses, there is so much economic evidence that human beings adjust their behaviour in response to changes in relative prices that it would be puzzling if the same calculus ceased to apply entirely in the realm of occupational choice.

At a more aggregate level, two time-series studies have found that the difference between average aggregate income in self-employment and paid-employment is a significant determinant of post-war trends in the

UK aggregate self-employment rate (Parker, 1996; Cowling and Mitchell, 1997). However, these findings should be treated with caution, for at least two reasons. First, average occupational incomes are endogenous, depending also on the number of individuals engaged in the occupation. It is known, for example, that the increase in UK self-employment in the 1980s was accompanied by a reduction in average self-employment incomes (Robson, 1997). Second, time-series studies usually define average self-employment income as aggregate self-employment income divided by the total number of self-employed, n_S. If aggregate self-employment income is subject to measurement error, then the presence of n_S on both sides of the regression equation can suggest an apparent relationship between the aggregate self-employment rate and average (relative) self-employment income where none really exists.

3.1.2 Human capital

Age and experience

One might expect older and/or more experienced people to become entrepreneurs, for the following reasons:

1. The human and physical capital requirements of entrepreneurship are often unavailable to younger workers. Older people are more likely to have received inheritances and to have accumulated capital which can be used to set up a business more cheaply, or to overcome borrowing constraints (see chapter 7). There might also exist a particular type of human capital which is productive both in managing and in working for others, and which can be acquired most effectively by working initially as an employee (Lucas, 1978).
2. Older individuals might choose self-employment to avoid mandatory retirement provisions sometimes found in paid-employment.
3. Older people have had time to build better networks, and to have identified valuable opportunities in entrepreneurship, possibly through learning about the business environment (Calvo and Wellisz, 1980).
4. As their own masters, entrepreneurs often possess greater control over the amount and pace of their work, making it sometimes better suited to older people who have lost their physical stamina, or to workers in poor health or with skills that are obsolete in paid-employment.

Offsetting these factors, the old may be more risk averse than the young, and less capable of working the long hours often undertaken by entrepreneurs. Also, Miller's (1984) 'job-shopping' theory predicts that workers try riskier occupations (like entrepreneurship) when they are younger, since these occupations provide the richest information about workers' personal job-matching opportunities. It is noteworthy that this prediction does not rest on ad hoc assumptions such as the young having an innate taste for risk, or irrational expectations such as youthful over-optimism.

Descriptive studies tend to find that self-employment is concentrated among individuals in mid-career, i.e. between thirty-five and forty-four years of age (see, e.g., Cowling, 2000 and Reynolds *et al.*, 2002, for international evidence). Aronson (1991) demonstrated that self-employed Americans of both sexes were older on average than their employee counterparts throughout the entire post-second World War period. Numerous other descriptive studies from a variety of countries confirm these findings.

Before we turn to the econometric evidence, we mention two important caveats to the use of age as a measure of experience. Age and experience are not synonymous, yet a common practice (often dictated by data limitations) is to measure 'experience' as current age minus school-leaving age. This measure is imperfect because it takes no account of breaks from labour force participation in individuals' work histories. This may be a particularly salient consideration when analysing female entrepreneurship. Second, it is important to separate cohort effects from experience effects. To see this, consider using a cross-section of data to cross-tabulate self-employment rates by age. Suppose that there has been a secular decline in self-employment over time. Then older cohorts will be observed to have higher self-employment rates than younger cohorts, irrespective of any experience effects. To separate cohort effects from genuine experience effects, either longitudinal (panel) data or accurate measures of years of actual work experience are required. It might also be helpful to distinguish between experience in paid-employment and experience in self-employment, since different types of experience might generate different returns and so impact differently on occupational choice. Several empirical studies make this distinction, as discussed below.

Despite these caveats, most econometric investigations have explored the effects of age on self-employment using cross-section data. Most of these studies have found a significant positive relationship between these two variables, while a minority report insignificant effects.[3]

Age may have different effects on the willingness and opportunity to *become* self-employed. For example, using the bivariate probit estimation approach described in chapter 1, subsection 1.6.3, van Praag and van Ophem (1995) found that the opportunity to become self-employed was significantly higher for older than for younger Americans. However, older workers were significantly less willing to become self-employed than younger workers were. These findings receive some support from international survey evidence reported by Blanchflower, Oswald and Stutzer

(2001), that individuals' reported interest in self-employment decreases with age, while the actual number choosing self-employment increases with age.

As noted above, it is often informative to distinguish between different types of labour market experience. The results here are scant but interesting. Evans and Leighton (1989b) estimated that previous self-employment experience had a positive and significant impact on the probability of white male Americans entering self-employment, whereas previous employment experience (and age) had no effect (see also Carroll and Mosakowski, 1987; van Praag and van Ophem, 1995; Quadrini, 1999; Lin, Picot and Compton, 2000). This result is consistent with Jovanovic's (1982) theory that entrepreneurs learn about their abilities over time, which they can do only from having engaged in entrepreneurship (see chapter 9, section 9.1). Also, Boden (1996) reported that employees of small firms (defined as having fewer than 100 employees) were more likely to switch to self-employment *ceteris paribus* than employees of large firms – which may be indicative of (indirect) entrepreneurial learning.

Does self-employment experience have long-term effects on what an individual can earn if they later switch to paid-employment? Four studies have explored this question, all using US data: Evans and Leighton (1989b), Ferber and Waldfogel (1998), Holtz-Eakin, Rosen and Weathers (2000) and Williams (2000). They all found weak long-term effects of self-employment experience on future paid-employment incomes, though perhaps unsurprisingly employees who had been self-employed in the past tend to be much less likely to have health benefits or pensions than were those who had always been employees (Ferber and Waldfogel, 1998).

Using Stanford graduate alumni data, Lazear (2002) estimated that more varied labour market experience (measured by the number of different work roles in previous jobs) was significantly associated with business formation. Lazear took this as supportive evidence for his theory that entrepreneurs are jacks of all trades, unlike employees who invest in a small number of specialist skills.

In summary, it is important to distinguish between age and experience when trying to explain why individuals choose self-employment. While both variables are usually found to be positively associated with self-employment, experience captures most accurately the impact of human capital.

Finally, the perceptive reader will have noticed that we have not yet discussed the topic of entrepreneurship in old age. This is a subject in its own right, treated separately in chapter 8, subsection 8.2.2.

Education

As with age, one can advance arguments to propose either a negative or a positive relationship between entrepreneurship and education. On one hand, more educated workers might select themselves into occupations in which entrepreneurship is more common, such as managerial occupations for professionals (Evans and Leighton, 1989b) and skilled craft jobs for manual workers (Form, 1985). As Keeble, Walker and Robson (1993) showed, there are many opportunities for self-employment in knowledge-based industries. Also, greater levels of education may promote entrepreneurship because more educated people are better informed about business opportunities.

On the other hand, the skills that make good entrepreneurs are unlikely to be the same as those embodied in formal qualifications (Casson, 2003). In particular, one hesitates to suggest education as a proxy for managerial ability in entrepreneurship *à là* Lucas (1978) (see chapter 2, section 2.2). As noted in chapter 1, subsection 1.5.3, entrepreneurs may also have fewer incentives to acquire formal educational qualifications than employees if education is an unproductive screening device used chiefly by employers to sort hidden worker types. Additional grounds for doubting the impact of education on the decision to be an entrepreneur rests on the result that rates of return to education appear to be greater for employees than for the self-employed (see chapter 1, subsection 1.5.3).

Most econometric studies of the effects of education on self-employment are cross-sectional. In these studies, educational attainment is usually measured either as years of education completed, or as a set of dummy variables registering whether survey respondents hold particular qualifications. As with age, the evidence generally points to a positive relationship between educational attainment and the probability of being or becoming self-employed.[4] However, many other studies have found insignificant effects of education on self-employment;[5] and several have detected negative effects.[6]

It is possible that the divergent results in this branch of the literature can be attributed to the use of different econometric specifications, in particular whether controls for financial variables and occupational status are included (Le, 1999). One might expect an individual's specific occupation to be related to education, imparting possible upward bias to education coefficients in earnings functions that omit detailed occupational controls. Also, effects of education on self-employment appear to be sensitive to the industry in which self-employment is performed. For example, Bates (1995, 1997) reported positive and significant effects of education on the probability of entering self-employment in skilled services; negative and significant effects on the probability of entering self-employment in construction; and insignificant effects on the probability of entering self-employment in manufacturing and wholesaling. Bates concluded that the overall impact of education on self-employment is obscured by aggregation across dissimilar industries. Another potentially important factor is different cultural traditions. Borooah and Hart (1999) presented some British evidence that higher education is associated with a greater probability of self-employment among whites, but a lower probability of self-employment among Indians.

3.1.3   Social capital

'Social capital' is the name given to social relations that facilitate individual actions. It may exist at the country level, for example in the degree of trust in government and other institutions; at the community level, such as the quality of connections within communities; and at the individual level, in the form of confidence or motivation (Glaeser, Laibson and Sacerdote, 2000). Sanders and Nee (1996) suggested that social relations may increase entrepreneurial success by providing instrumental support, such as cheap labour and capital; productive information, such as knowledge about customers, suppliers, and competitors; and psychological aid, such as helping the entrepreneur to weather emotional stress and to keep their business afloat. In principle, social capital might be used to compensate for limited financial or human capital.

Gomez and Santor (2001) tested whether social capital affects success in entrepreneurship. They did this by augmenting a self-employed earnings function with two proxy variables: whether respondents belonged to any community organisation ('club') that meets regularly, and self-reported estimates of the value of one's own social contacts and how well one knows one's neighbours. Using data on borrowers from a Toronto microfinance organisation from the 1990s, Gomez and Santor found that self-employed club members earned significantly and substantially more than self-employed non-members. It is not yet clear, however, whether social capital increases entry into self-employment.[7]

3.2   Personal characteristics and family circumstances

3.2.1   Marital status

One might expect a disproportionate number of married people to be entrepreneurs compared with single people, for the following reasons:
1. A spouse can help provide start-up capital.
2. Once in business, a spouse can provide labour at below-market rates, or they can use their income as insurance against risky income in

entrepreneurship.[8] Spouses may also be more trustworthy workers, being less likely to shirk (Borjas, 1986). And spouses can offer valuable emotional support.

3. Having a spouse may offer tax advantages. These include income sharing to exploit personal tax allowances; introducing the spouse as a 'sleeping partner' and allocating them a share of the enterprise's profits; and, if trading through a limited company, providing them with benefits (such as a company car or private medical insurance), or making payments into the spouse's pension scheme.

4. Entrepreneurs are older on average, and older people are more likely to be married.

On the other hand, married people with children may be unwilling to take the risks associated with entrepreneurship; and to the extent that non-married people are 'displaced' or dissatisfied, they are arguably more likely to be entrepreneurs (see subsection 3.2.3).

Cross-section econometric evidence from probit models tells a consistent story: self-employed people are significantly more likely to be, or to have been, married, with dependent children.[9] This finding appears to hold quite generally, with the possible exception of black Americans (Borjas, 1986) and ethnic minority English (Clark and Drinkwater, 2000). The evidence on the effects of marital status on the probability of switching into self-employment is similar, if a little weaker;[10] and the evidence about the effects on entrepreneurship of having a working spouse is mixed.[11]

In summary, there is general but not unanimous agreement that self-employment status is positively associated with marital status. Because most of the findings reported above control for individuals' ages, these findings are probably capturing some kind of co-operative factor as in points 1–3 above rather than indirect effects from age itself. This conclusion is consistent with direct evidence from Brüderl and Preisendörfer (1998) that emotional support from a spouse improves the survival and profitability prospects of new German business ventures.

3.2.2 Ill-health and disability

Entrepreneurship is often believed to offer greater flexibility than paid-employment in terms of the individual's discretion over the length, location and scheduling of their work time (Quinn, 1980). To the extent that people with poor health or disabilities need such flexibility, it might be expected that, all else equal, they are more likely to be self-employed. In addition, self-employment may offer a route out of employer discrimination against the disabled. However, self-employment may be a poor choice for individuals in poor health. Some jobs with high self-employment concentrations such as construction are intrinsically less suited to those with disabilities – not to mention more dangerous, implying that self-employment can also cause disability and ill-health. Work hours and stress are also greater on average in self-employment (see chapter 8, section 8.2). And whereas many employees receive health cover from their employers, the self-employed must provide their own.[12]

Survey evidence from the UK suggests that self-employed men actually have slightly better (self-reported) health than male employees do, whereas self-employed females are slightly less healthy than their employee counterparts (Curran and Burrows, 1989). In contrast, Fredland and Little (1981) reported that mature American self-employed workers were in significantly poorer health than employees. Probit estimates reflect mixed effects of ill-health on self-employment status.[13]

In summary, the association between self-employment and ill-health and disability is ambiguous. It is unclear at present what underlies the lack of agreement between the various empirical studies; but it would seem that there is ample scope for further research on this topic.

3.2.3   Psychological factors

Entrepreneurial traits

A large psychological literature has developed which claims that entrepreneurs possess special traits that predispose them to entrepreneurship. Economists are now catching on to this idea, by including psychological variables in cross-section probit models of self-employment choice.

In their review of the role of psychological factors in entrepreneurship research, Amit, Glosten and Muller (1993) identified four traits that have attracted substantial research interest:

1. *Need for achievement.* One of the first systematic attempts to provide a psychological profile of entrepreneurs was McClelland (1961). McClelland highlighted the constructive role of 'business heroes' who promote the importance of entrepreneurial achievement to subsequent generations. According to McClelland, the key characteristic of successful entrepreneurs is the 'need for achievement' (n-Ach), rather than a desire for money (1961, pp. 233–7). In McClelland's words: 'a society with a generally high level of n-Ach will produce more energetic entrepreneurs who, in turn, produce rapid economic development' (p. 205). McClelland's conclusions were drawn from results of applying Thematic Apperception Tests (see Brockhaus, 1982, for a description and a critique). As well as having n-Ach,

McClelland also argued that entrepreneurs are proactive and committed to others; like to take personal responsibility for their decisions; prefer decisions involving a moderate amount of risk; desire feedback on their performance; and dislike repetitive, routine work. A corollary of McClelland's thesis is that the achievement motive can be deliberately inculcated through socialisation and training, although results from such efforts have drawn a mixed response (Chell, Haworth and Brearley 1991). It is not clear that n-Ach can be 'coached', as has been claimed; and it is questionable whether entrepreneurship is the only vocation in which n-Ach can be expressed (Sexton and Bowman, 1985).[14]

2. *Internal locus of control.* Another psychological trait is a person's innate belief that their performance depends largely on their own actions, rather than external factors. Psychologists call this 'having a high internal locus of control'. Since self-employment often offers greater scope for individuals to exercise their own discretion at work than does paid-employment, it follows that those with a high internal locus of control might have a greater probability of being self-employed. A psychological metric known as the Rotter Scale (Rotter, 1982) provides the basis for empirical tests of this hypothesis. The more a survey respondent believes a range of factors to be under her control, as opposed to outside her control, the lower her Rotter score in any given test. While Evans and Leighton (1989b) and Schiller and Crewson (1997) obtained evidence from probit regressions supporting the locus of control hypothesis, van Praag and van Ophem (1995) obtained contrary results. The mixed findings may reflect the fact that having a high locus of control is not unique to entrepreneurs, since it has also been identified among successful business managers (Sexton and Bowman, 1985).

3. *Above-average risk taking propensity.* As chapter 2, subsection 2.2.4 showed, Kihlstrom and Laffont's (1979) model of entrepreneurship predicts that entrepreneurs are less risk averse than employees are. Evidence on this issue will be discussed in subsection 3.2.4.

4. *A tolerance of ambiguity* (Timmons, 1976; Schere, 1982). It is proposed that entrepreneurs have a greater capacity than employees for dealing with environments where the overall framework is ill defined.

The above list is by no means exhaustive. Others have claimed that entrepreneurs exhibit 'Type A' behaviour, which is characterised by competitiveness, aggression, a striving for achievement and impatience (Boyd, 1984). Another trait is claimed to be over-optimism (see below). Still others have argued that entrepreneurs are misfits or displaced persons who live outside the mainstream of society, and are possibly prone to deviant and criminal behaviour (Shapero, 1975; Kets de Vries, 1977). Kets de

Vries argued that childhood disruption makes it harder for individuals to accept authority or to work closely with others, rendering them insecure and lacking in self-esteem and confidence. Consequently they establish new enterprises in an act of 'innovative rebelliousness' to boost their self-esteem and to acquire external approbation. This view, which finds echoes in Schumpeter (1934), has received empirical backing. Light and Rosenstein (1995) reported that at-risk youth and prisoners demonstrate a keen interest in business ownership and evince disdain for available jobs in paid-employment. In an econometric study based on British National Child Development Survey (NCDS) data, Burke, Fitz-Roy and Nolan (2000) found that those who were anxious to be accepted by others early in life were significantly more likely to be self-employed later in life, perhaps as a means of generating respect. But van Praag and van Ophem (1995) reported that more outgoing American children were significantly more willing to become self-employed in later life.

If obsessive, inner-directed and non-conformist traits are deep-rooted, and only entrepreneurship can satisfy the individuals who possess them, then we might expect to see these individuals persisting in entrepreneurship despite a lack of reward. In this light it is interesting that Shapero (1975) reported that 72 per cent of the entrepreneurs he surveyed would still want to start a new company if their present one failed. In a similar vein, it appears that some individuals are deeply attached to 'making it' in entrepreneurship, perhaps for deep personal reasons, drifting from one entrepreneurial venture to another before hitting success (Copulsky and McNulty, 1974).

However, this view of the 'entrepreneur as misfit' or 'deviant' is vulnerable to the usual charge that occupations other than self-employment may also appeal to individuals with the proposed psychological trait. The hypothesis has also been disputed by Reynolds and White (1997), whose US survey data responses indicated that new business founders tend to be people belonging to the centre rather than the periphery of the economy, with stable work and family circumstances (see also Blanchflower and Oswald, 1998). This may reflect the fact that many start-ups have a co-operative character, in contrast to the notion implicit in much of the foregoing of the 'solo entrepreneur'.

Broader objections have also been registered against the whole psychological traits approach. It is still not known whether there is an essential set of entrepreneurial characteristics, and if so what they are. Partly this reflects the small sizes and non-comparability of the samples used in previous research, and the conflicting results obtained from them.[15] But it also seems unlikely that such a diverse group of individuals as entrepreneurs are amenable to glib generalisations in terms of their psychological characteristics. Traits are unlikely to be unique to entrepreneurs, raising a demarcation problem; and being unobservable *ex ante*, they are virtually impossible to separate *ex post* from luck and other extraneous factors (Amit, Glosten and Muller, 1993). There is also, as Kaufmann and Dant have pointed out, 'a tendency in this literature to personify entrepreneurs as embodiments of all that may be desirable in a business person, and almost deify entrepreneurs in the process' (1998, pp. 7–8). The conclusion reached by several authors, including this one, is that psychological factors are neither necessary nor sufficient conditions for entrepreneurs or entrepreneurship.

Love of independence and job satisfaction
It is commonly suggested that an attractive feature of entrepreneurship is independence in the workplace, something that is variously referred to as a love of autonomy or 'being one's own boss'. This idea can be traced back to Knight (1921), and has been emphasised by non-economists (Scase and Goffee, 1982; Cromie, 1987; Dennis, 1996), as well as by economists seeking explanations of why individuals remain self-employed despite apparently earning less than employees do (Aronson, 1991; Hamilton, 2000).

This subsection reviews evidence about the love of independence in entrepreneurship, before asking whether it feeds through into greater happiness among entrepreneurs relative to employees, in terms of both job satisfaction and life–work balance.

Based on an analysis of 466 male self-employed Britons from the 1991 wave of the BHPS, Taylor (1996) found that fewer self-employees than paid-employees regarded pay and security as important job aspects. The proportions were 37 and 32 per cent compared with 48 and 57 per cent, respectively. However, greater proportions of self-employed workers felt that initiative (51 per cent) and the enjoyment of work itself (57 per cent) were important job aspects, compared with 21 and 41 per cent of employees, respectively. This bears out the idea that the self-employed enjoy relative freedom from managerial constraints and working for themselves. These non-pecuniary factors were significantly associated with being self-employed, even after controlling for personal characteristics (see also Burke, Fitz-Roy and Nolan, 2000; and Hundley, 2001b).[16]

Table 3.1 summarises reasons for being self-employed cited by respondents of the UK's spring 2000 LFS. These responses bear out the importance of independence, the single most important reason cited by

Table 3.1 *Reasons given for becoming self-employed in the UK (per cent)*

Reason	All	Men	Women
To be independent	31	33	25
Wanted more money	13	15	7
Better conditions of work	5	6	3
Family commitments	7	2	21
Capital, space, equipment			
opportunities	12	12	11
Saw the demand	8	9	8
Joined the family business	6	6	7
Nature of occupation	22	21	23
No jobs available locally	3	3	2
Made redundant	9	11	3
Other reasons	15	14	18
No reason given	3	4	3
No. valid responses (000) [a]	2,960	2,156	804

Note: Columns do not sum to 100 per cent because respondents can give up to four reasons.
[a] Imputed percentages based on all those who gave a valid response to the 'reasons for becoming self-employed' questions.
Source: LFS (2000).

the LFS respondents. The next most important reason is the nature of the occupation, perhaps reflecting the fact that self-employment is the chief or only mode of employment in some locations or occupations (e.g. forestry or construction). Both men and women have similar responses, although women stress independence a little less than men, and family commitments substantially more (see also Hakim, 1989a).

It should be remembered, however, that not all people enter self-employment in order to gain independence. Nor is it clear that people always obtain much actual independence from being self-employed, especially those who work long hours (see chapter 8, section 8.2) or who work in one the 'grey areas' between paid-employment and self-employment.[17]

Numerous studies show that the self-employed consistently claim to enjoy greater job satisfaction than employees do, even after controlling for job and personal characteristics such as income gained and hours worked. For example, using British NCDS data from 1981 and 1991, Blanchflower and Oswald (1998) reported that approximately 46 per cent of the self-employed claimed they were 'very satisfied' with their job, compared with only 29 per cent for employees. Blanchflower and Freeman

(1994), Blanchflower (2000), Blanchflower, Oswald and Stutzer (2001) and Frey and Benz (2002) have since confirmed these findings for several OECD countries. Frey and Benz explicitly traced individuals' greater job satisfaction to the use of initiative and actual work itself, and to the weakness of hierarchy in which they worked.

It might be thought that job satisfaction would spill over into overall satisfaction with life, including work–family balance. Several authors have suggested that the flexibility of self-employment may make that occupation more conducive to balancing work and family role responsibilities, leading to enhanced psychological wellbeing (Eden, 1975; Cromie, 1987; Loscocco, 1997). Set against this, however, is the fact that self-employed people work longer hours on average than employees do, while bearing direct responsibility for the success and survival of a business. This may result in *greater* work–family conflict for self-employed individuals than for employees. This is precisely what Parasuraman and Simmers (2001) found from their survey of 386 American graduate students. The self-employed respondents in this sample enjoyed greater flexibility and autonomy at work, and reported higher levels of job involvement and job satisfaction than their employee counterparts; but they also experienced higher levels of work–family conflict and lower levels of family satisfaction than employees. Longer work hours and greater parental responsibilities appear to be chiefly responsible. These drawbacks to self-employment were more pronounced for men than for women.

Thus while entrepreneurs may indeed enjoy greater job satisfaction, they may also bear greater stress in relation to their family lives, a source of life conflict that might deter some individuals from contemplating entrepreneurship altogether.

Over-optimism

A vast psychological literature has established a systematic tendency among human beings to be over-optimistic, especially about events that are only partially under their control. De Meza and Southey (1996) reviewed some of this literature, and argued that entrepreneurs are especially vulnerable to systematic over-optimism (see also Camerer and Lovallo, 1999).[18]

Certainly the interview responses obtained by Cooper, Woo and Dunkelberg (1988) point to high levels of entrepreneurial optimism – or even 'entrepreneurial euphoria' in the words of those authors. 68 per cent of their entrepreneur respondents thought that the odds of their business succeeding were better than for others in the same sector while only 5 per cent thought that they were worse. However, while interesting, these findings are no more than suggestive. While the interviewees displayed greater confidence than is merited by statistics about business failure rates, Cooper, Woo and Dunkelberg did not compare their expectations with outcomes or establish whether entrepreneurs are more optimistic than non-entrepreneurs. Both tasks were attempted by Arabsheibani *et al.* (2000). Using BHPS panel data over 1990–6 to compare expectations of future prosperity with actual outcomes, these authors found that employees and self-employed Britons were both systematically over-optimistic; and that the self-employed were consistently and substantially the most over-optimistic. For example, 4.6 times as many self-employed people forecast an improvement in their prosperity but experienced deterioration as forecast a deterioration but experienced an improvement. For employees the ratio was 2.9. This result was robust to the inclusion of controls for other personal characteristics.

An obvious question is how over-optimism, which is inconsistent with rational maximising behaviour, can persist in the market. As Friedman (1953) pointed out, in the long run one might expect sober-minded profit maximising realists to drive over-optimists out of competitive markets. In fact, one can propose several reasons why over-optimism could persist in, and even come to dominate, a market. First, de Meza and Southey (1996) argued that, if individuals enter entrepreneurship until expected returns there are driven down to equality with the paid-employment wage, then the optimists (who over-estimate entrepreneurial profits) crowd out realists (who correctly estimate profits) from entrepreneurship, the latter choosing to congregate in paid-employment. Second, Manove (2000) argued that over-optimistic entrepreneurs can hold their own against (and, under some conditions, drive out of the market) realists by working and saving extra hard to compensate for mistakes caused by their over-optimism. Third, Bernardo and Welch (2001) claimed that over-optimistic entrepreneurs are less likely to imitate their peers and more likely to explore their environment. This generates valuable informational benefits to the entrepreneurial group, which enables that group to thrive in spite of the costs incurred by the individuals who obtain the information. Fourth, over-optimism might confer an advantage by signalling high ability to outsiders, such as customers or financiers.

De Meza and Southey (1996) claimed that unrealistic optimism explains several well-known features of entrepreneurship. One is entrepreneurs choosing to remain in entrepreneurship, despite earning less and bearing greater risk than employees. Another is purely self-financed entrepreneurs facing higher business failure rates than debt-financed entrepreneurs. By over-estimating their prospects of success, optimists prefer maximum self-finance of their projects – unlike realists, who prefer debt finance. But also unlike realists, optimists make negative expected returns net of opportunity costs, leading to higher exit rates. There may also be policy implications. Most of the models cited above find that over-optimistic behaviour causes distortions in the economy as a whole. In a practical vein, Cooper, Woo and Dunkelberg (1988) recommended that entrepreneurs be encouraged to form relationships with outsiders, such as non-executive board members and professional advisors. Outsiders have the objectivity and detachment to counteract unrealistic optimism – hopefully without extinguishing the essential fire of entrepreneurial zeal.

3.2.4   Risk attitudes and risk

Chapter 2, subsections 2.2.2 and 2.2.4 distinguished between risk attitudes (e.g. individual risk aversion embodied in the utility function) and the actual or perceived level of risk itself. Below, we continue with this distinction, first summarising empirical work on risk attitudes, followed by empirical work on levels of risk.

There are various ways of measuring risk attitudes. One is to ask people how they would choose between risky hypothetical situations. Examples include Brockhaus' (1980) Choice Dilemma Questionnaire, and van Praag and Cramer's (2001) interview questions about gambling. The results are mixed. Whereas Brockhaus found insignificant differences in responses between entrepreneurs and non-entrepreneurs, van Praag and Cramer claimed that entrepreneurs were significantly more willing to gamble than employees were. Van Praag et al. (2002) also claimed that risk aversion significantly decreased the probability that given individuals would choose to be entrepreneurs – consistent with the theory of Kihlstrom and Laffont (1979) outlined in chapter 2, subsection 2.2.4. But, while Uusitalo (2001) reported similar findings, Tucker (1988) detected insignificant effects from risk attitudes on self-employment choice using a specially framed survey question from the PSID. And direct evidence indicates that self-employed people are *less* likely to participate in lotteries than employees – at least in Scandinavia (Lindh and Ohlsson, 1996; Uusitalo, 2001).

It is also unclear what these findings really tell us. It is all too easy to conflate genuine risk attitudes with optimism, since there is evidence that entrepreneurs interpret the same business stimuli more favourably than non-entrepreneurs do (Palich and Bagby, 1995; Norton and Moore, 2002). Thus researchers could misconstrue adventurous actions based on over-optimistic expectations of outcomes as evidence of greater risk tolerance. There are also likely to be inherent reporting biases in individuals' responses to hypothetical, as opposed to actual, business stimuli. The problem is compounded by the *ex post* nature of the questions and the possible reverse causality from entrepreneurship to risk attitude. Thus Taylor's (1996) finding from the 1991 BHPS that self-employed respondents are significantly less likely than employees to regard job security as an important job aspect could simply reflect self-employees' familiarity with working in uncertain conditions, and/or *ex post* rationalisation at their prior choices.

Fairlie (2002) suggested that former drug dealers might be less risk averse than the average. Therefore his finding that former drug dealers are 11–21 per cent more likely to subsequently choose legitimate self-employment than non-drug dealers, all else equal, might be interpreted as supportive of Kihlstrom and Laffont's (1979) hypothesis. However, as Fairlie pointed out, characteristics other than risk attitudes might also be responsible, including entrepreneurial ability and a love of autonomy.

Arguably, the gap between theory and empirical application is particularly wide when it comes to measuring the *level* of risk. If one had panel data, one could calculate the variance of individuals' previous incomes: an *ex post* measure of risk. In time-series applications, several proxies for business risk have been proposed, including the number of strikes, the inflation rate and fixed capital formation as an inverse measure.[19] The rationale is that economic uncertainty is greater at times of domestic macroeconomic turbulence when strike activity and the inflation rate are high, while firms presumably invest less under conditions of uncertainty. The UK time-series applications cited in n. 19 all found these measures of risk to be significantly and substantially negatively related to the aggregate self-employment rate.

Williams (2001) proposed a cross-section measure of risk: the standard deviation (or coefficient of variation) of sales within the four-digit industry of the business owner. Williams explored the effect of this measure of risk on decisions among respondents of the 1987 CBO survey to become a franchisee rather than an independent self-employed business owner. Probit estimates indicated that franchisee status was positively associated with risk. Williams interpreted this finding as evidence that franchising is a relatively less risky option than independent self-employment. However, a problem with this risk measure is that it might be conflated with industry effects.

3.2.5   Family background

It has been widely recognised that self-employment tends to run in families. There are several reasons why having a self-employed parent might increase the probability that a given individual turns to self-employment himself. Self-employed parents might offer their offspring informal induction in business methods, transfer business experience and provide access to capital and equipment, business networks, consultancy and reputation. Also, children may be motivated to become entrepreneurs if this eventually entitles them to inherit the family business. This transmission process could be especially important in some sectors, such as agriculture, where parents often pass on farms to their children.

In contrast, sociologists have stressed the role of the family as a channel through which cultural values can be passed on to individuals. Hence family backgrounds in which entrepreneurship is prominent can be expected to foster similar favourable attitudes in the family's offspring. The self-employed certainly seem to have more pro-business attitudes on average than employees do[20] – though the extent to which this is attributable to the inculcation of family values is questionable. Households with self-employed heads might also furnish role models – although of course they could also convey some of the less savoury aspects of self-employment, such as long hours and family stress (see above). Role models are also suggested by findings of a negative relationship between the size of a worker's employer and the propensity of workers to opt for self-employment (Storey, 1994a): presumably larger firms offer fewer entrepreneurial role models. But this negative relationship might also reflect more favourable working conditions in larger firms, since it is known that larger firms offer wage premiums, which may deter switching into self-employment.

The direct evidence points clearly to strong intergenerational links between parents and children. In work based on 1979 US NFIB survey data, Lentz and Laband (1990) observed that around half of all US self-employed proprietors were second-generation business people; while sons of self-employed fathers were three times more likely to be 'occupational followers' than the average worker (Laband and Lentz, 1983). Parental self-employment both increases the fraction of time that offspring spend in self-employment and reduces the age at which they enter it (Dunn and Holtz-Eakin, 2000). Followers also earn higher self-employment incomes than non-followers in self-employment (Lentz and Laband, 1990). These effects are robust to the inclusion of observable characteristics in probit models of self-employment choice, which invariably identify significant positive and substantial effects from dummy variables representing *father's* self-employment status.[21] The US evidence is mixed on whether blacks as well as whites have positive self-employment fatherhood effects (c.f. Fairlie, 1999; Hout and Rosen, 2000). For white Americans, the likelihood of self-employment increases if the father is a manager, and decreases if the father is unskilled (Evans and Leighton, 1989b). De Wit and van Winden (1989, 1990) noted that if a father who was previously self-employed stopped being self-employed, father's work history no longer had a significant impact on the offspring's self-employment decision. Finally, there is mixed evidence from probit studies about the impact of *mother's* self-employment status on the probability of self-employment of her offspring.[22] According to Dunn and Holtz-Eakin (2000), while fathers' self-employment experience had a stronger effect on the probability that sons became self-employed than mothers' self-employment experience, the latter was more important for daughters. Having two self-employed parents had the greatest overall effect.

It is necessary to dig deeper to find the precise channels through which this observed intergenerational transmission process takes place. Dunn and Holtz-Eakin (2000) identified two: parental self-employment experience and business success, where the latter was measured in several ways, including by self-employment income. Effects from parental experience and success proved to be strikingly prominent and significant, almost doubling the probability of a son entering self-employment even after controlling for the individual's and parent's financial capital and the individual's human capital. It suggests that parents primarily transfer managerial skills to their offspring, rather than merely familiarity with or a taste for self-employment.[23] Second, parental business and non-business wealth also had a large positive effect on the probability that an individual made a transition to self-employment. This might reflect the value of family finance (see chapter 6, section 6.1).

3.3   Entrepreneurship and macroeconomic factors

3.3.1   Economic development and changing industrial structure

Economic development

This section asks how economic development affects the nature and extent of entrepreneurship, from both a theoretical and an empirical perspective. Economic development can occur in a number of ways, that have potentially different impacts on entrepreneurship. Leading on from the seminal work of Lucas (1978), one form of economic development involves exogenous increases in the capital stock, capital being one of the inputs to entrepreneurs' production functions. A second form of development is technological progress, which can either be exogenous (shifting entrepreneurs' production functions) or endogenous (e.g. knowledge grows as a result of efforts to exploit it). A third form of development is driven by endogenous increases in personal wealth stocks, enabling individuals to engage in risky investments that they were unable to afford before. All three forms of development can be analysed as special cases of the following entrepreneurial production function:

$$q(t) = A(t).q[k(t), H(t), \Upsilon(t)],$$
(3.1)

where $q(t)$ is output; $q[\cdot, \cdot, \cdot]$ is a continuous production function that is increasing in all of its arguments: capital k, hired labour H and technological knowledge, Υ; and A is a technology shift variable. All of these are potentially functions of time, t.

Growth in the capital stock. As we saw in chapter 2, subsection 2.2.3, Lucas (1978) traced out the implications of an increasing capital stock in a model where entrepreneurs have heterogeneous abilities and operate firms of different sizes. In terms of (3.1), $A(t) \equiv A$ can be interpreted as the ability of a given entrepreneur and $\Upsilon(t) \equiv 0$. As shown in subsection 2.2.3, if $q[\cdot, \cdot]$ is such that the elasticity of substitution between k and H is less than unity, then increases in the capital stock are predicted to increase the number of workers and decrease the number of entrepreneurs. As discussed in subsection 2.2.3, this prediction has met with mixed empirical success.

Technological progress. Exogenous technological progress can be represented by growth in the $\Upsilon(t)$ of (3.1), or by growth in $A(t)$. The former could occur if technological progress is embodied in knowledge; the latter if, for example, more efficient production techniques become available, or if improvements in infrastructure enable existing techniques to be deployed more effectively. Naturally, to the extent that entrepreneurs operate small firms, the implications of technological progress for entrepreneurs depend on whether it impacts on firm sizes neutrally, or whether there are systematic differences that are related to firm size. Some authors, from at least the time of Schumpeter, have apparently believed that technological progress will be biased in favour of large firms, making the latter's economies of scale increasingly dominant over time, thereby squeezing out smaller producers (and hence, by implication, entrepreneurs). Another mechanism may also be at work in one particular sector in which self-employment has been traditionally concentrated, namely agriculture. Engel curve estimates indicate that the demand for agricultural produce increases only slowly in response to greater income, whereas the demand for manufactured goods in which economies of scale may be more important increases more rapidly. Thus one can expect the relative derived demand for self-employed labour (especially in agriculture) to decrease as an economy grows. Historical and cross-country evidence has generally been supportive of this view, finding a negative correlation between the size of the agricultural self-employment sector and *per capita* GNP (Kuznets, 1966; Schultz, 1990).

More recently, however, it has been suggested that technological change has begun to operate the other way, in favour of smaller rather than larger businesses. Arguably, the advent of more flexible manufacturing techniques has begun to make scale economies less important, reducing minimum efficient scale and facilitating competition from smaller firms (Piore and Sabel, 1984; Dosi, 1988; Carlsson, 1989, 1992; Carlsson et al., 1994; Wennekers and Thurik, 1999). These changes might also have endowed small firms with a comparative advantage in supplying markets with low or fluctuating levels of demand. The emergence of new technologies, including IT and telecommunications, and the growing demand for labour-intensive services and 'niche' customised products might also have favoured smaller firms, by requiring less physical capital and more human capital. However, little detailed evidence is available at present about the extent to which technological change of this sort has impacted on entrepreneurship.

Calvo and Wellisz (1980) and Schaffner (1993) have proposed economic models of size neutral exogenous technological progress. As discussed in subsection 2.2.3, Calvo and Wellisz combined the assumptions of growing technological knowledge $\Upsilon(t)$ and heterogeneous abilities. A Lucas-type result emerged – continually increasing numbers of workers, and decreasing number of entrepreneurs. A similar result follows from Schaffner's model, in which there are two modes of production: by firms hiring workers, and by entrepreneurs producing on their own account without any workers. Both types of production are subject to uncertainty. Unlike firms, which can smooth workers' incomes and diversify risk in the presence of aggregate productivity shocks, entrepreneurs are unable to smooth their own incomes. To see the implications of this, suppose that technology $A(t)$ increases equally for both types of producer, increasing expected returns and risk to both entrepreneurs and firms (in terms of (3.1), Υ is absent). Firms can increase the employee wage by less than the increase in entrepreneurs' incomes because workers value income smoothing. This wage saving makes it profitable for firms with previously uneconomic organisational and monitoring costs to set up, drawing individuals out of entrepreneurship and into paid-employment. The implication is again that paid-employment will continually grow as the economy develops, and entrepreneurship will decline.[24]

Schmitz (1989) proposed a model of endogenous technological progress and entrepreneurship. Schmitz's model explains how entrepreneurs can contribute to practical technological knowledge and thereby change the conditions under which entrepreneurship is attractive. Like Say and Schumpeter, Schmitz argued that successful, growth-inducing entrepreneurship is not principally about developing new knowledge, but instead involves imitation, transfer and application of technologies in the marketplace. In terms of (3.1), there is no managerial ability or capital input, and the workforce is normalised to unity. The basic structure of the model consists of the following modification of (3.1), and three equations describing the structure and evolution of technological knowledge:

$$q(t) = q\left[\frac{1 - n_S(t)}{n_S(t)}, \Upsilon(t)\right] = \Upsilon(t).\varphi\left[\frac{1 - n_S(t)}{n_S(t)\Upsilon(t)}\right] \quad (3.2)$$

$$\frac{d\Upsilon(t)}{dt} = \Upsilon_0(t).\psi\left[\frac{\tilde{\Upsilon}(t)}{\Upsilon_0(t)}\right] \quad (3.3)$$

$$\Upsilon_0(t) = n_S(t)\Upsilon(t) \quad (3.4)$$

$$\tilde{\Upsilon}(t) = \gamma n_S(t)\Upsilon(t), \quad (3.5)$$

where $q[\cdot, \cdot]$, $\psi(\cdot)$ and $\varphi(\cdot)$ are concave increasing functions that are homogeneous of degree one. Equation (3.2) modifies (3.1) by ignoring exogenous technological change, and writing employee labour input $[1 - n_S(t)]$ as a proportion of the number of entrepreneurs, $n_S(t)$. Equation (3.3) states that the evolution of the stock of practical knowledge $\Upsilon(t)$ is an increasing function of both 'own-industry' knowledge, denoted by $\Upsilon_0(t)$, and a knowledge spillover (to other industries), denoted by $\tilde{\Upsilon}(t)$. Equation (3.4) states that own-industry knowledge is given by the product of the total knowledge stock and the number of entrepreneurs using it. Equation (3.5) states that the spillover effect is modified by imperfect communications infrastructure, $\gamma < 1$. The greater is γ, the greater the spillover to neighbouring industries and hence the greater the impact on total knowledge accumulation.

A competitive equilibrium for this economy is characterised similarly to Lucas (1978): $n_S(t)$ adjusts until all individuals are indifferent between the two occupations. Schmitz compared the competitive equilibrium with the outcome that would maximise social welfare. The competitive equilibrium is characterised by a steady-state entrepreneurship and knowledge pair $\{n_S^*, \Upsilon^*\}$ that is the steady-state solution of the problem

$$\max \int_0^\infty e^{-\delta t} U[\zeta(t)]\, dt \quad \text{subject to} \quad \zeta(t) = n_S(t)q(t) \quad \text{and} \quad (3.3)$$

$$(3.6)$$

(with $\Upsilon(0) > 0$ given), where $\zeta(t)$ is aggregate consumption (= output) at time t and $\delta > 0$ is the discount rate. In contradistinction, the social welfare optimum is characterised by the steady-state pair $\{n_S^\Omega, \Upsilon^\Omega\}$ that is the steady state solution of the problem (3.6) subject also to (3.4) and

(3.5) – i.e. which unlike the competitive equilibrium takes account of the aggregate knowledge spillover.

Proposition 6 (Schmitz, 1989). *The steady-state competitive equilibrium characterised by* $\{n_S^*, \Upsilon^*\}$ *does not maximise social welfare; and* $n_S^* < n_S^\Omega$, *implying there are too few entrepreneurs in equilibrium relative to the social optimum.*

The competitive equilibrium is not welfare maximising because atomistic individuals do not take account of the effects of their own behaviour on the aggregate knowledge spillover. The free-market economy is predicted to generate too little entrepreneurship. More entrepreneurship is desirable because it increases the aggregate value of the spillover by (3.3) and (3.5). One policy implication is to encourage technology-based entrepreneurship in order to increase economic growth.

Endogenous growth of personal wealth   Banerjee and Newman (1993) proposed a model in which banks make only secured loans. The greater the loan size, the greater the temptation for borrowers to 'take the money and run' and forfeit their collateral. Anticipating this, banks limit the scale of loans (and therefore also the size of investment projects) according to individuals' wealth. Thus the initial distribution of wealth determines who becomes an entrepreneur with workers (an 'employer'), who becomes an entrepreneur without workers ('self-employed'), and who becomes a 'worker' in one of the firms run by the employers. Each individual lives for a single period: they choose how much of their wealth to bequeath to their offspring. This imparts path dependence to capital $k(t)$ and, because of the above capital market imperfection, also to aggregate wealth and the occupational structure of the economy. (In terms of the production function (3.1), A is fixed and $\Upsilon = 0$; and there are two versions of $q[\cdot, \cdot]$, one for 'employers' and one for the 'self-employed'.)

Various development paths can arise in Banerjee and Newman's model; two are of particular interest. In one, an economy 'F' starts with a small fraction of workers, so wages are relatively high and plenty of individuals possess the collateral to become self-employed. Although some successful self-employed people in 'F' have sufficient wealth to become employers, they cannot find cheap workers, and so choose to remain self-employed. This becomes a self-perpetuating outcome via the bequest mechanism, and it characterises the economy's equilibrium. A second case is an economy 'E', say, starting with a large fraction of poor workers, so wages are low. If individuals choose to bequeath little to their offspring, workers remain poor and face binding borrowing constraints in all subsequent generations. This economy converges to an equilibrium in which there are many employers and workers, and only a small number of self-employed workers. A key point is that differences between these two hypothetical economies can become entrenched. In a rich economy, subsequent generations of 'poor' workers are able to rise up the wealth and social scales, becoming self-employed and employers. This economy becomes increasingly prosperous and 'entrepreneurial'. Although a poor economy can switch over to the more favourable state if it does not start too far away from the rich one, if it starts sufficiently poor it will remain so, and entrepreneurship will never be able to flourish.

On the face of it the Banerjee and Newman model does not receive clear empirical support from cross-country data on self-employment rates outlined in tables 1.1 and 1.3 in chapter 1. It was seen there that the poorest countries had the highest self-employment rates and the richest countries had the lowest ones. Hence the applicability of Banerjee and Newman's model is probably confined to the evolution of developed countries over long time spans, as those authors themselves implied by their discussion of the different paths taken by England ('E') and France ('F') at the time of the Industrial Revolution.[25]

This concludes our outline of theoretical models of entrepreneurship and economic development. We now turn to evidence on the issue. Applied researchers have proposed several ways of gauging the effects of economic development on entrepreneurship, although it is fair to say that for the most part the linkages between theory and empirical implementation are rather weak. Empirical studies have either devised proxies for technological progress, or they have discussed development in terms of growing national income. With the exception of Lucas' findings, which have already been discussed in chapter 2, section 2.2, we briefly review the evidence below:

1. Using published data on total factor productivity (TFP) for ten broad industry groups in the USA, Blau (1987) calculated indices of weighted sums of TFP for both the self-employed and employees. The ratio of the self-employed TFP index to the employee TFP index was proposed as a measure of relative self-employment technological advantage. Blau's regression results indicated that changes in the TFP ratio favouring industries in which self-employment is common was one of the causes of rising US self-employment between 1972 and 1982. He went on to suggest that the spread of computers might have been the source of the technological advantage. However, there is a problem with this explanation, because self-employment rates have declined steadily in France and Japan, despite these countries experiencing similar productivity improvements. Also, personal computers were not widespread even by 1982, the last year of Blau's sample. And Devine

and Mlakar (1993) found that an index of the price of computing power over 1975–90 did not explain probabilities of self-employment across a range of US industries.[26]

2. Acs, Audretsch and Evans (1994) suggested that the relationship between aggregate self-employment and exogenous technological change $A(t)$ is U-shaped. They argued that at early stages of a country's development $A(t)$ changes such that output shifts away from agriculture and small-scale manufacturing towards large-scale manufacturing, with a consequent reduction in self-employment. At later stages of development, $A(t)$ changes such that manufacturing gives way to services, and self-employment recovers. Acs, Audretsch and Evans adduced some support for this hypothesis from pooled time-series/cross-section regressions in which technological change was proxied by measures of value added in manufacturing and services as a proportion of GNP. However, applying a more appropriate panel cointegration estimator and a richer set of explanatory variables to similar data, Parker and Robson (2000) found that Acs, Audretsch and Evans, 'value added' variables were generally insignificant as determinants of self-employment rates.

3. Interpreting *per capita* GNP as a general measure of development, scatter-plots of this variable against aggregate self-employment rates for a range of countries at varying stages of development seem to indicate a negative relationship. The bulk of evidence from multivariate analyses appear to confirm this finding (Acs, Audretsch and Evans, 1994; Schultz, 1990; Fölster, 2002; an exception is Parker and Robson, 2000). While this is broadly consistent with the predictions of Lucas, Schaffner, and Calvo and Wellisz that self-employment rates decline with economic development, GNP *per capita* is a crude measure of development and does not distinguish its underlying sources. These empirical findings certainly do not give explicit support to any of the particular theories outlined above.

It is hard to reach any definitive conclusions from this empirical work. Also, among developed countries there has been, and continues to be, enormous diversity of self-employment rates and trends (see chapter 1, section 1.4). This is despite the fact that technological change has been pervasive and broadly similar in these countries. It therefore seems unlikely that technological change alone can explain the observed variations and trends in aggregate self-employment rates.

Changing industrial structure

Some jobs lend themselves more naturally to self-employment than others. These include labour-intensive 'one to one' personal services, seasonal jobs and jobs with erratic demand that would be too costly for large firms to organise, and which can be filled more cheaply by independent self-employed workers. Another consideration is the mix of skills required in particular industries. For example, if entrepreneurs are 'jacks of all trades' with balanced skills sets, then industries like art (which requires disparate skills in artistic talent and business management) are less likely to be populated by entrepreneurs than insurance, say, where the required skills are more similar to each other (Lazear, 2002).

Capital requirements in different industries may also play a role. It is unlikely that individuals will opt for self-employment in industries dominated by large, capital-intensive firms, since the latter often have a comparative and absolute advantage in raising capital. The evidence seems to bear this conjecture out. White (1982) found that there were fewer small US manufacturing firms in industries with high capital intensities; and Acs and Audretsch (1989) reported that high capital–labour ratios were associated with lower rates of US small business entry in 247 manufacturing industries.

No doubt reflecting the combined effects of these factors, most countries exhibit high concentrations of self-employed workers in particular sectors and industries. The available evidence comprises both simple tabulations and results from self-employment probit models that include occupation and industry dummy variables. The latter have the advantage that industry effects can be separated from other factors, such as skill requirements, that also bear on occupational choice.[27]

In North America, male self-employed workers tend to be concentrated in construction, services and retail trades; and in the sales, agriculture, hotels, repairs, craft, managerial and professional occupations. The lowest self-employment rates by sector are observed in manufacturing. The predominance of service sector self-employment has a long history. For example, Aronson (1991) reported that about three-quarters of pre-first World War non-farm US self-employment was in service-sector industries. The service sector has of course grown relative to manufacturing since that time, although shifts have also occurred within the service sector especially since the 1950s, towards finance, insurance and personal and business services. The role of self-employment in each of the transportation, communications and retail sectors has steadily declined. Similar patterns of industry and occupation self-employment are observed in the UK, with high concentrations in construction, distribution, hotel and repairs, banking and financial services. According to 1991 LFS data, these sectors accounted for 62 per cent of all UK self-employment.[28] The broad sectoral composition of self-employment appears to be fairly similar to this in other OECD countries (Loufti, 1992).

The professions provide an important core of self-employed people in many countries, especially law, medicine and architecture. In an historical overview, Aronson (1991) noted little change in the pattern of US self-employment in the professions since the end of the Second World War, except for some declines in the legal and health occupations. Aronson believed that four factors might explain the trend away from self-employment in these two occupations: (i) changing demographics, since older professionals are more likely to be self-employed; (ii) greater specialisation (especially in health); (iii) economies of scale since, for example, more expensive medical technologies make larger units cheaper; and (iv) a reduction in occupational licensing that previously protected self-employed incumbents from competition. However, he did not test these hypotheses.

To discover whether secular shifts in industrial structure explain changes in aggregate self-employment rates, Steinmetz and Wright (1989) performed a shift-share analysis of US self-employment rates between 1940 and 1980. They claimed that changes in the sectoral distribution of the self-employed labour force accounted for 80 per cent of the decline in the self-employment rate between 1940 and 1950, but only 20 per cent in the 1970s. Much of the explanatory power of the shift-share analysis was accounted for by the secular decline in agricultural self-employment. Steinmetz and Wright also found that the expansion of new 'post-industrial' sectors such as banking and personal services, and also increased self-employment *within* traditional industrial sectors, largely accounted for the resurgence of US self-employment from the early 1970s onwards. However, the deep factors underlying all of these sectoral changes remain unexplained. It is certainly incorrect to claim that these changing patterns reflect a sudden shift towards the service sector, since the latter pre-dates the increases in self-employment rates in many countries in the 1970s and 1980s (Aronson, 1991). Furthermore, there has also been a trend towards larger-scale business organisations in sectors in which the self-employed are concentrated–for example, banking, retail, and restaurants–which would have been expected to reduce the aggregate self-employment rate. Clearly, much more research is needed to improve our understanding of the interface between entrepreneurship and changes in industrial structure.

3.3.2   Unemployment

There is now an extensive literature on the relationship between self-employment and unemployment. One of the motivations for studying this topic is the policy interest about promoting self-employment as a way of reducing unemployment. There are two channels through which this could occur. First, there is the direct effect of removing a newly self-employed individual from the official unemployment register. Second, there is the indirect effect of eventual job creation by entrepreneurs who succeed in running enterprises that require outside labour.

According to conventional wisdom, unemployment affects self-employment in two ways: via 'recession-push' and 'prosperity-pull' effects. According to the 'recession-push' hypothesis, unemployment reduces the opportunities of gaining paid-employment and the expected gains from job search, which 'pushes' people into self-employment. A secondary and complementary effect is that, as firms close down in recessions, the availability and affordability of second-hand capital equipment increases, reducing barriers to entry (Binks and Jennings, 1986). Both effects are suggestive of a positive relationship between self-employment and unemployment.

According to the 'prosperity-pull' hypothesis, at times of high unemployment the products and services of the self-employed face a lower market demand. This reduces self-employment incomes and possibly also the availability of capital, while increasing the risk of bankruptcy. Thus individuals are 'pulled' out of self-employment. At the same time, self-employment may become riskier because if the venture fails, it is less likely that the self-employed worker can fall back on a job in paid-employment. In contrast to the recession-push hypothesis, these factors suggest a negative relationship between self-employment and unemployment.

Empirical estimates of the self-employment/unemployment relationship invariably confound the above two effects, capturing a 'net' effect. Nevertheless, the size and direction of the net effect is still of policy interest. It is helpful to sort the large number of results on this topic by empirical method, since the results tend to reflect the method employed. Results obtained using cross-section probit models are reviewed first, followed by results from time-series and panel data models.

Cross-section evidence

Most cross-section econometric studies have found a negative relationship between the probability that an individual is self-employed and the local unemployment rate.[29] Furthermore, a number of British studies have established that between 20 and 50 per cent of new entrants to self-employment were directly or recently unemployed (Storey, 1982; Hakim, 1988, 1989b; Meager, 1992b), with the majority switching from paid-employment. A similar pattern also seems to hold in other OECD countries (Evans and Leighton, 1989b; Blanchflower and Meyer, 1994;

Kuhn and Schuetze, 2001). For example, Evans and Leighton (1989b) concluded that between 1968 and 1986 unemployed workers were about twice as likely to start businesses as employees were; and almost three times as many individuals enter self-employment from outside the labour force as from unemployment (Dennis, 1996). To put this in perspective, from one year to the next most unemployed people either remain unemployed or become employees; only a small minority become self-employed (Cowling and Taylor, 2001). But these results all appear to support the 'prosperity-pull' hypothesis. The state of the business cycle also seems to matter. According to Carrasco (1999), unemployed male Spaniards are more likely to enter self-employment in boom times, i.e. when the unemployment rate is low.

It has also been shown that, of the unemployed, those with more unstable work histories (including periods of past unemployment) are significantly more likely to enter self-employment and to be self-employed (Evans and Leighton, 1989b; Carrasco, 1999; Knight and McKay, 2000; Uusitalo, 2001). Evans and Leighton construed this as evidence that the self-employed may be 'misfits' who are driven into entrepreneurship. But, the evidence on this point is not clear-cut. A closer analysis of the data reveals that a history of *job changes*, rather than unemployment *per se*, significantly increases the willingness of workers to become self-employed (van Praag and van Ophem, 1995). Furthermore, Farber (1999) reported that US employees who had lost their jobs in the previous three years ('job-losers') were significantly *less* likely to be self-employed (by 3 percentage points) than 'non-losers'. That remained the case even after controlling for other personal characteristics of the survey respondents. This evidence suggests that self-employment in the USA is not a transitional process following job loss – unlike temporary and part-time work.[30]

It may be important to distinguish between men and women when measuring the inflow to self-employment from non-employment states. Kuhn and Schuetze (2001) found that most of the increase in female Canadian self-employment in the 1980s and 1990s was attributable to an increase in retention rates in self-employment, whereas for men, most of the increase was attributable to a decrease in stability in paid-employment and inflows from unemployment (for similar British findings, see Blanchflower and Freeman, 1994).[31] It is also possible that the effects of unemployment on self-employment may vary from occupation to occupation. For example, some professional occupations may be protected against unlicensed new entrants, making the number of self-employed professionals less cyclical than the number of self-employed non-professionals (Meager, 1992a). In principle, interacting local unemployment rates in cross-section regressions with occupational dummy variables could allow this possibility to be tested.

Time-series and panel data evidence

In contrast to the cross-section studies, the overwhelming majority of time-series studies report significant *positive* effects of national unemployment rates on national self-employment and new firm formation rates. This appears to support the 'recession-push' hypothesis. Most of this work has been conducted using UK and US data.[32] Estimation has generally assumed a linear relationship between self-employment and unemployment rates, despite the possibility, suggested by Hamilton (1989), of non-linearity.[33] Evidence of a positive and significant cointegrating relationship (see chapter 1, subsection 1.6.4) between aggregate self-employment and unemployment rates is especially well documented for the UK.[34]

One channel through which unemployment can feed into self-employment is through job layoffs. Storey and Jones (1987) and Foti and Vivarelli (1994) both uncovered significant positive effects from local job layoffs on new firm formation rates (n. 30 notwithstanding). Also, time-series evidence from Robson (1991) identified a significant positive impact on self-employment from redundancy payments.

In view of the differences between empirical results obtained from the cross-section and time-series approaches, it is perhaps unsurprising that panel data studies that combine cross-section and time-series elements have generated mixed results. Two types of panel study can be distinguished: (a) one utilising a relatively large cross-section dimension and (b) one utilising a relatively large time-series dimension. Recent studies under (a) include Blanchflower (2000) and Schuetze (2000). Pooling individual-level data from nineteen OECD countries and interacting unemployment variables with country dummies, Blanchflower found that some countries exhibited significant negative, some significant positive, and some insignificant relationships between self-employment and unemployment rates.[35] In contrast, Schuetze (2000) pooled individual-level data on American and Canadian working-age males over 1983–94, and found strong positive relationships between self-employment and state/provincial unemployment rates.

Under (b), Acs, Audretsch and Evans (1994) reported a significant positive correlation between aggregate OECD self-employment and unemployment rates; but this disappeared when additional variables (including GDP) were controlled for (see also Parker and Robson, 2000). One reason for these results might be that controlling for GDP takes account of prosperity-pull effects and so enables a (weak or non-existent) recession-push effect to be identified. What complicates the story, however, is findings of positive correlations between aggregate self-employment and GDP growth rates (Audretsch and Acs, 1994; Dennis, 1996; Robson, 1996, 1998b; Reynolds *et al.*, 2002). Unemployment rates tend to be highest when GDP growth rates are lowest, complicating any relationship between the state of the business cycle and self-employment. Notably there is mixed evidence about how aggregate self-employment rates vary over the business cycle (c.f. Becker, 1984; OECD, 1986; Evans and Leighton, 1989a; Bögenhold and Staber, 1991).

Conclusion: reconciling the results
Clearly there is considerable disagreement in the literature about how un-employment affects self-employment. Time-series studies tend to find a positive relationship between self-employment and unemployment rates, n_S and n_U, whereas cross-section studies tend to find a negative relation-ship. While it is possible to propose *ad hoc* explanations to fit these facts,[36] the following argument might be more plausible. Consider again the rea-soning behind the push and pull influences. The former is supposed to capture a positive effect from higher unemployment, increasing expected incomes in self-employment relative to those in paid-employment; the latter is supposed to capture a negative effect from higher unemploy-ment, decreasing self-employment incomes via lower product demand. Arguably, time-series studies have used data that are too aggregated to measure accurately local demand conditions, so biasing in an upward di-rection the predicted effect of n_U on n_S. For their part, the cross-section studies may have failed to measure accurately *expected* incomes in self-employment relative to paid-employment or unemployment, so biasing downwards the predicted effect of n_U on n_S.

In any case, the unemployment rate is only an imperfect proxy for the underlying factors inducing workers to enter, or leave, self-employment. Undergraduate economics students know that exogenous technological change need not cause unemployment if workers are sufficiently flexi-ble and skilled to switch from contracting sectors into those benefiting from technological change. Thus if technological change is the cause of labour-saving changes to production, unemployment is only the symp-tom of slow adjustments in the labour market. Likewise if costs or tech-nology change so that self-employment becomes a more efficient and attractive form of productive organisation, then we would expect to see transitions between paid-employment and self-employment without nec-essarily observing much of an impact on unemployment. Therefore there is really is no economic reason why unemployment and self-employment have to be related at all. The extent to which they are may in any case

Table 3.2 *Self-employment rates in the British regions, 1970 and 2000*

Region	1970 rate (%)	2000 rate (%)	Rank in 1970	Rank in 2000
North	6.02	7.96	8	10
Yorkshire & Humberside	6.45	10.42	7	6
East Midlands	7.00	10.71	5	5
East Anglia	10.11	13.35	3	3
South East	7.28	13.47	4	2
South West	11.71	14.98	1	1
West Midlands	5.74	10.29	9	7
North West	6.54	9.87	6	8
Wales	10.37	12.43	2	4
Scotland	5.68	9.31	10	9

Note: The self-employment rate is defined as the number of self-employed jobs (male plus female) in the region divided by the region's labour force.
Source: Abstract of Regional Statistics, 1974 (HMSO, London, table 39) and *Regional Trends, 2001* (The Stationery Office, London, tables 5.1, 5.5).

vary over time as governments alter the tax-benefit system and their stance on labour market intervention – and thereby the flexibility of the economy.

To conclude, the 'true' impact of unemployment on self-employment probably lies somewhere between the strong positive and strong negative estimates recorded in the present literature. Modest positive or negative effects look like the safest bet, though on balance, it seems to the author that the cross-section studies are likely to be the least misleading. This is because several of the cross-section studies include some measure of relative incomes, in addition to variables capturing localised demand conditions. In contrast, the problems of omitted variable and aggregation bias are likely to be more pronounced in the time-series studies.

3.3.3 Regional factors

Previous research has identified substantial and persistent regional variations in self-employment and business start-up rates, in a variety of countries, including the UK and the US (Georgellis and Wall, 2000). Regional variations have been observed within neighbourhoods and cities, and across broader administrative regions. Table 3.2 contains some illustrative British data that point to pronounced regional differences in self-employment rates. These differences have been fairly persistent over the last thirty years. For example, the Spearman correlation coefficient for table 3.2's rank orderings in 1970 compared with 2000 is 0.87.

Why do regional differences exist and persist? Possible answers include the following. Regions that suffer from low levels of demand, that have poorly educated workers, or that have high concentrations of capital-intensive industries that sustain effective barriers to entry, might be less likely to witness high rates of entrepreneurial participation. Role models may also be important: regions with strong traditions of entrepreneurship may be able to perpetuate them over time and across generations, in contrast to less favoured regions that lack them.

The problem with these stories is that none of them explains why firms and individuals fail to seize profitable opportunities and equalise outcomes across regions. For example, if factors of production are mobile, why do entrepreneurs not relocate to areas with less competition from other entrepreneurs – and possibly also lower wages – increasing entrepreneurial activity in those regions? Also, just because heavy industries have traditionally dominated employment in particular regions in the past should not prevent new industries from starting up, especially if profitable opportunities (such as a low cost base) are there for the taking.

It seems that a more satisfactory story is needed to explain why some regions (e.g. the South West of England) sustain relatively high levels of entrepreneurship, and why others (e.g. the North of England and Scotland) are stuck with persistently low levels of entrepreneurial activity. One story might go as follows. Adapting Banerjee and Newman's (1993) model, suppose that some workers in all regions are unable to become entrepreneurs owing to borrowing constraints. At the same time, they cannot migrate as workers from 'poor' to 'rich' regions because (endogenously determined) house prices are too high in the rich region to make this desirable (or even feasible). And a production externality or knowledge spillover might induce entrepreneurs to cluster in the rich region where a large number of other entrepreneurs are concentrated, despite facing higher wage costs (and therefore higher house prices) there. Taken together, these forces could all entrench different regional living standards, house prices, wages and levels of entrepreneurship as equilibrium outcomes. Indeed, in this story regional differences could even grow over time. Any migration to the rich region might increase house prices there sufficiently that it becomes even easier for workers in the rich region to muster the required collateral, leading to still higher levels of entrepreneurship there – while the opposite occurs in the poor region. While this is only the sketch of a story, it seems to possess enough frictions to frustrate geographic equalisation of entrepreneurial talent – and it seems broadly consistent with the data.

Furthermore, evidence from Robson (1998a) supports the notion that, in Britain at least, regional house prices are positively related to regional rates of entrepreneurship. Robson investigated the determinants of regional variations in UK male regional self-employment rates using pooled time-series cross-section data from the eleven standard regions of the UK (comprising the ten in table 3.2 plus Northern Ireland) over 1973–93. Robson regressed regional male self-employment rates on several regional explanatory variables, including net housing wealth, nhw_j; income shares accounted for by agriculture, $agric_j$, and Construction, Distribution, Hotels and Catering, $cdhc_j$; GDP *per capita*; real average earnings; the unemployment–vacancy ratio; the long-term unemployment rate; and proxies for average regional age and education profiles. Strikingly, Robson found that, of all these variables, only the first three were statistically significant in a long-run model of the log male self-employment rate, n_{Sj}, where j denotes a region:

$$\widehat{\ln n_{Sj}} = \hat{k}_j + 0.031\,agric_j + 0.047\,cdhc_j + 0.207\,\ln nhw_j\,, \quad (3.7)$$

and where the $\hat{k}_j$ are regional fixed effects. Thus a 10 per cent increase in a region's real net housing wealth is predicted to increase that region's male self-employment rate by over 2 per cent. Clearly housing wealth – whose values closely reflect house prices – plays a central role in explaining regional variations self-employment rates, as suggested above. However, taken together the last three variables on the RHS of (3.7) explained only 35 per cent of the differential in the self-employment ratio between the highest- and lowest-ranked regions for male self-employment, namely the North and the South-West of England.[37] The regional dummies $\hat{k}_j$ accounted for 23 per cent of the North–South self-employment differential. These presumably capture the effects of unobserved variables, perhaps historical and cultural factors (Reynolds, Storey and Westhead, 1994; Spilling, 1996; Georgellis and Wall, 2000).

Turning from self-employment rates to new-firm creation rates as a measure of entrepreneurship, we note that there is a large 'economic geography' literature on spatial variations in small-firm formation rates. That literature will not be exhaustively surveyed here: Reynolds, Storey and Westhead (1994) supply an overview. Using data from six OECD countries, Reynolds, Storey and Westhead found that firm birth rates were highest in regions with high proportions of employment in small firms, as well as high rates of in-migration, demand growth, employment specialisation, and population densities (see also Spilling, 1996). However, many of these explanatory variables are likely to be endogenous. Interestingly, local government expenditures and assistance programmes were found to have only limited effects on regional firm birth rates.

Another dimension of regional variation is the distinction between urban and rural locations. Arguments can be made both for and against the relative advantages for entrepreneurship in urban relative to rural locations. On one hand, urban markets tend to be larger and enjoy higher average disposable incomes. On the other hand, inputs such as rent and labour can be more expensive in urban areas; and there are often fewer paid-employment opportunities in rural areas, increasing the relative attractiveness of new-firm creation and self-employment there. The evidence from self-employment probit regressions with an urban dummy variable is mixed.[38]

There might also be systematic variation in entrepreneurial activity within a given urban area. A range of neighbourhood characteristics can potentially affect the returns to self-employment relative to paid-employment. For example, higher average neighbourhood incomes, population densities and commercial concentrations can generate higher levels of demand for the services of small-scale entrepreneurs. Particular neighbourhoods may also facilitate information exchange and the formation of social capital. Levels of education, home ownership, urban design and community spirit may also vary across neighbourhoods, and in some cases there may be an important ethnic dimension to urban composition (see chapter 4 for more on the latter).

In summary, the economic literature on regional dimensions of entrepreneurship looks to be ripe for further investigation and extension. This is especially true of the theory side, though our understanding of the empirical structure of regional variations in entrepreneurship is also incomplete. The available evidence suggests that many hard-to-observe region-specific and individual-specific factors affect regional levels of entrepreneurship. To separate individual from regional factors it will almost certainly be necessary to deploy detailed micro-level cross-section data, rather than aggregate data, which by their nature omit too many individual-level variables to distinguish sharply between the different influences.

3.3.4   Government policy variables

Minimum wages and employment protection

Minimum wages and employment protection tend to be directed towards employees and employers rather than on own-account self-employed workers. It is possible that wage rigidities caused by these forms of government intervention ration workers out of paid-employment, thereby increasing the numbers entering own-account self-employment. On the other hand, a binding minimum wage increases labour costs to self-employed employers, and may hit small firms disproportionately hard because they tend to be more labour-intensive than large firms are. In a time-series study based on aggregate US data over 1948–82, Blau (1987) found little evidence that the minimum wage had any net effect on the aggregate US self-employment rate.

The OECD (1998) asserted that employment protection may be a strong barrier to entrepreneurship in countries where it is prominent, such as Sweden and Spain. As with government regulation more generally, there can also be disincentives for the growth of enterprises if small-firm exemptions are withdrawn once a given size is attained. This issue will be explored further in chapter 10, section 10.5.

Government benefits

Retirement benefits may increase the attractiveness to employees of switching to self-employment as a form of partial retirement, especially if social security earnings tests penalise full-time paid-work. Blau (1987) and Robson (1998b) found some evidence to support the notion that higher state retirement benefits promote self-employment. Carrasco (1999) reported that unemployment benefits significantly and substantially decrease the probability of transitions from unemployment to self-employment in Spain, with a smaller impact on transitions from unemployment to paid-employment.

More generally, the replacement rate is defined as the ratio of average out-of-work benefits (including unemployment benefits) to average earnings. A higher replacement ratio will decrease self-employment if benefits discourage unemployed workers from turning to self-employment – or if employees value these benefits which are unavailable to, or restricted for, the self-employed. Parker and Robson (2000) showed that the replacement ratio had significant negative effects on aggregate self-employment rates in an OECD panel over 1972–93.

Even more generally, a larger welfare state may discourage entrepreneurship by crowding out private savings required to leverage start-up finance, especially if borrowing constraints exist (Fölster, 2002). Public-sector employment might also crowd out self-employment: see Boyd (1990) for evidence that this may have occurred among American blacks.

Interest rates

Higher interest rates increase the cost of financing a business. This includes direct costs (debt repayments) and indirect, or opportunity, costs such as tying up one's funds in a firm. Higher interest rates may therefore be expected to decrease firm births and increase firm deaths, and so have a negative effect on self-employment. However, if banks offer long-term loans at fixed interest rates, then new-firm starts measured at

Table 3.3 *Summary of determinants of entrepreneurship*

Explanatory variable	No. +	No. −	No. 0	Ref.
1. Income differential[a]	6	2	4	[d]
2. Age	36	1	8	n. 3
3. Labour market experience	7	1	0	[e]
4. Education[a]	25	11	14	nn. 4–6
5. Married/working spouse	20	4	3	nn. 9–11
6. Ill health/disability	4	2	0	n. 13
7. Risk	0	3	0	n. 19
8. Self-employed parent	17	2	0	[f]
9. Technological progress	2	4	2	[g]
10. Unemployment				
Cross-section	3	10	6	[h]
Time-series	21	5	2	[i]
11. Urban location	5	0	3	n. 38
12. Government benefits	2	2	0	[j]
13. Interest rates	0	7	2	n. 39
14. Personal wealth[b]	18	0	2	[k]
15. Personal income tax rates[c]	10	3	1	[l]

Note: +, − and 0 denote significantly positive, significantly negative and zero (insignificant) coefficients, respectively. Only multivariate studies (i.e. those including controls for other explanatory variables) are included; descriptive studies are excluded. 'Ref' gives sources of individual studies as footnotes ('n.') in chapter 3, or in the following notes, where semicolons separate the three groups of outcomes.

[a] Counting all the de Wit and de Wit and van Winden studies as one.

[b] Based on results summarised in chapter 7, section 7.1.

[c] Based on results summarised in chapter 10, section 10.4.

[d] Fujii and Hawley (1991), Bernhardt (1994), Parker (1996), Taylor (1996), Cowling and Mitchell (1997), Clark and Drinkwater (2000), Gill (1988), Earle and Sakova (2000), Rees and Shah (1986), Dolton and Makepeace (1990); de Wit and van Winden (various), Parker (2003).

[e] Carroll and Mosakowski (1987), Tucker (1988), Evans and Leighton (1989b), van Praag and van Ophem (1995), Bates (1997), Schiller and Crewson (1997), Quadrini (1999); Tucker (1990: for professionals).

[f] See n.n 21 and 22. Additional positive effects found by Laband and Lentz (1983), Lentz and Laband (1990), Dunn and Holtz-Eakin (2000), Lin, Picot and Compton (2000), Cramer *et al.* (2002).

[g] Blau (1987), Acs, Audretsch and Evans (1994); Kuznets (1966), Schultz (1990), Acs, Audretsch and Evans (1994), Fölster (2002); Devine and Mlakar (1993), Parker and Robson (2000).

[h] Evans and Leighton (1989b), Carrasco (1999), Schuetze (2000); Hamilton (1989), Laferrère and McEntee (1995), van Praag and van Ophem (1995), Lindh and Ohlsson (1996), Taylor (1996), Blanchflower and Oswald (1998), Farber (1999), Clark and Drinkwater (1998, 2000), Bruce (2000); Pickles and O'Farrell (1987), Reynolds, Storey and Westhead (1994), van Praag and van Ophem (1995), Blanchflower (2000), Lin, Picot and Compton (2000), Moore and Mueller (2002).

time t might be relatively insensitive to interest rates also measured at time t, depending instead on lagged interest rates. This point ought to be borne in mind when weighing the evidence, since many studies link start-up/self-employment rates with contemporaneous interest rates.

UK and US time-series evidence suggests that interest rates have a significant negative effect on self-employment rates, although its effects on new-firm formation rates are less clear-cut.[39] We discuss further the impact of interest rates on small firm exit behaviour in chapter 9, section 9.3.

The 'enterprise culture': a British myth?

Some commentators have claimed that reforms to the UK labour market and welfare system in the 1980s created an 'entrepreneurial culture' in which self-employment and entrepreneurship were allowed to flourish. In the 1980s, the British government not only deregulated markets and introduced means-tested welfare benefits, but also initiated loan guarantee and enterprise allowance schemes; small business advice centres, grants, and training programmes; tax deductions; and higher value added tax (VAT) (sales tax) registration thresholds, in a concerted attempt to encourage enterprise. At the same time, the UK witnessed a dramatic increase in the self-employment rate (see chapter 1, subsection 1.4.1), increases in business registrations and deregistrations and strong growth of unlisted securities markets and venture capital activity (Bannock and Peacock, 1989).

More detailed and careful analysis tends to rebut the view that the 1980s witnessed a renaissance in the British entrepreneurial spirit. According to the British Social Attitudes Survey, the proportion of employee respondents thinking about becoming self-employed did not change between 1983 and 1989 – a time when the renaissance of an enterprise culture was presumed to have occurred (Blanchflower and Oswald, 1990).

---

[i] For positive effects see nn. 32 and 34, plus Storey and Jones (1987), Foti and Vivarelli (1994), Georgellis and Wall (2000); Robson (1996, 1998a, 1998b), Lin, Picot and Compton (2000), Cullen and Gordon (2002); Acs, Audretesch and Evans (1994), Parker and Robson (2000).

[j] Blau (1987), Robson (1998b); Carrasco (1999), Parker and Robson (2000).

[k] For positive effects, see n. 2 of chapter 7. For insignificant effects, see Taylor (2001) and Uusitalo (2001).

[l] Long (1982a), Moore (1983a), Blau (1987), Evans and Leighton (1989a), Parker (1996), Robson (1998b), Robson and Wren (1999), Bruce (2000), Parker and Robson (2000), Schuetze (2000); Robson and Wren (1999), Parker and Robson (2000), Fölster (2002); Cowling and Mitchell (1997).

Instead, Blanchflower and Oswald claimed that a combination of changing personal characteristics and favourable developments in the macroeconomic environment were able to explain the rise in the UK self-employment rate, without any need to rely on (unmeasured) factors like 'entrepreneurial spirit'. Blanchflower and Freeman (1994) were also sceptical about an 'enterprise culture' effect, noting that although transitions from unemployment and non-labour force status to self-employment increased over the 1980s, transition rates from paid-employment to self-employment did not. Blanchflower and Freeman declared that 'it is hard to believe claims that an 'enterprise culture' has been established without some significant increase in this flow'.

3.4   Conclusion

Table 3.3 summarises the balance of evidence relating to the effects on entrepreneurship of most of the explanatory variables discussed in this chapter. In the present context we define 'entrepreneurship' broadly, to include both self-employment and new-firm creation. We have omitted results on psychological factors (including risk attitudes), since their diversity makes them difficult to summarise in this way. We have summarised only published research results based on multivariate analysis, excluding studies citing simple bivariate correlations, since these are vulnerable to the most severe form of omitted variable bias. Positive and negative entries refer to measured effects on entrepreneurship that are significantly positive or negative; the zero entries refer to effects that are too imprecisely estimated to reach standard levels of statistical significance (usually 5 per cent).

Table 3.3 shows that a broad consensus has now been reached on the impact of many – though not all – of these variables. The clearest influences on measures of entrepreneurship (usually the likelihood or extent of self-employment) are age, labour market experience, marital status, having a self-employed parent and average rates of income tax (all with positive effects). Greater levels of risk and higher interest rates generally have negative effects, although to date only a handful of studies have satisfactorily investigated the former. Further research is needed on these topics specifically, and also more generally on the linkages between the theoretical models of entrepreneurship discussed in chapter 2 and empirical implementations. In many cases, data limitations have forced researchers to use proxies in the place of variables suggested by the theory. Better data are needed to consolidate and extend our knowledge about the individual and environmental determinants of entrepreneurship.

NOTES

1. See also Clark, Drinkwater and Leslie (1998) for British evidence of effects that differ across ethnic groups. In contrast, aggregate studies of new business starts usually report positive effects from business profits relative to wages (Creedy and Johnson, 1983; Foti and Vivarelli, 1994; Audretsch and Vivarelli, 1997; Goedhuys and Sleuwaegen, 2000; Lofstrom, 2002).

2. Income under-reporting is one possibility, although adjustments made by the author to cope with this (Parker, 2003a) made little practical difference. Note also that the exclusion of health insurance benefits from measured incomes appears to have little effect on self-employment participation either (Bruce, Holtz-Eakin and Quinn, 2000).

3. The following studies have reported positive (usually quadratic, i.e. increasing with age, but with diminishing returns at higher ages) and significant effects from age on the probability of being or becoming self-employed. For the UK: Rees and Shah (1986), Taylor (1996), Clark and Drinkwater (1998, 2002), Clark, Drinkwater and Leslie (1998) and Borooah and Hart (1999). For the USA: Moore (1983a), Borjas (1986), Brock and Evans (1986), Borjas and Bronars (1989), Evans and Leighton (1989a), Boyd (1990), Fujii and Hawley (1991), Holtz-Eakin, Joulfaian and Rosen (1994a, 1994b), Blanchflower and Meyer (1994), Robinson and Sexton (1994), Carr (1996), Bates (1995, 1997), Boden (1996), Schiller and Crewson (1997), Schuetze (2000), Flota and Mora (2001), Fairlie (2002) and Lofstrom (2002). For other countries: Maxim (1992), Schuetze (2000) and Moore and Mueller (2002) for Canada; Kidd (1993) and Blanchflower and Meyer (1994) for Australia; Laferrère and McEntee (1995) for France; Goedhuys and Sleuwaegen (2000) for Côte d'Ivoire; Uusitalo (2001) for Finland; and Blanchflower (2000), Cowling (2000) and Blanchflower, Oswald and Stutzes (2001) using international data. Studies finding no significant effects of age on self-employment include Taylor (1996) and Robson (1998a) for the UK; Blau (1987), Gill (1988), Evans and Leighton (1989b), Evans and Jovanovic (1989) and Dunn and Holtz-Eakin (2000) for the USA; and Bernhardt (1994) for Canada. Lin, Picot and Compton (2000) reported significant negative effects for Canada.

4. For the UK: Rees and Shah (1986), Dolton and Makepeace (1990), Taylor (1996), and Clark and Drinkwater (1998). For the USA: Borjas (1986), Gill (1988), Borjas and Bronars (1989), Evans and Leighton (1989a), Boyd (1990: for blacks), Tucker (1990: for non-professionals), Fujii and Hawley (1991), Blanchflower and Meyer (1994), Robinson and Sexton (1994), Carr (1996), Bates (1995, 1997), Boden (1996), Schuetze (2000), Flota and Mora (2001) and Lofstrom (2002). For other countries: Carrasco (1999) for Spain, Blanchflower (2000) for nineteen OECD countries, Goedhuys and Sleuwaegen (2000) for Côte d'Ivoire, Cramer et al. (2002) for the Netherlands and Moore and Mueller (2002) for Canada.

5. For the UK: Robson (1998a), Taylor (2001) and Clark and Drinkwater (2002). For the USA: Brock and Evans (1986), Evans and Leighon (1989b), Evans and Jovanovic (1989), Boyd (1990: for Asians), van Praag and van Ophem (1995), Schiller and Crewson (1997), and Dunn and Holtz-Eakin (2000).

See also Maxim (1992), Lin, Picot and Compton (2000) and Schuetze (2000) for Canada; and de Wit and van Winden (1990, 1991) and de Wit (1993) for the Netherlands.

6. See, e.g., Clark, Drinkwater and Leslie (1998), Burke, Fitz-Roy and Nolan (2000) and Georgellis and Wall (2000) for the UK; Pickles and O'Farrell (1987) for Ireland; Laferrère and McEntee (1995) for France; Tucker (1988), Bruce (2000) and Fairlie (2002) for the USA; Johansson (2000) and Uusitalo (2001) for Finland; and Blanchflower, Oswald and Stutzer (2001) for evidence from a pool of twenty-three countries. Most of these authors studied switching into self-employment, rather than being self-employed. Interestingly, there is evidence that vocational qualifications and apprenticeship training rather than academic qualifications bear on self-employment choice (Burke, Holz-Eakin and Quinn, 2000; Knight and McKay, 2000; Cramer *et al.*, 2002). International evidence on the role of education is mixed (Cowling, 2000), as are results obtained using data on particular educational qualifications (Meager, 1992b).

7. See also Brüderl and Preisendörfer (1998) for evidence that social network support is positively and significantly associated with the survival and profitability of new German business ventures.

8. See, e.g., Scase and Goffee (1982) for case studies citing the importance to self-employed males of their wives' unpaid labour, for example, self-employed tradesmen relying on their wives to take telephone bookings for work while they are out on jobs.

9. For UK evidence, see Taylor (1996), Clark and Drinkwater (1998), Clark, Drinkwater and Leslie (1998), Borooah and Hart (1999), and Knight and McKay (2000). US evidence includes Long (1982a), Borjas and Bronars (1989), Holtz-Eakin, Joulfaian and Rosen (1994a), Robinson and Sexton (1994), Fairlie and Meyer (1996), Schuetze (2000), and Edwards and Field-Hendrey (2002). See also Maxim (1992), Laferrère and McEntee (1995) and Moore and Mueller (2002). Exceptions are Gill (1988), who detected negative effects, and Brock and Evans (1986), Boyd (1990) and Cowling (2000), who detected no significant effects.

10. While Blanchflower and Meyer (1994), Bates (1995) and Johansson (2000) reported positive effects from marital status on the probability of entry into self-employment, opposite results were obtained by Laferrère and McEntee (1995) and Carrasco (1999).

11. Positive effects were reported by Bernhardt (1994) and Laferrère and McEntee (1995), whereas Fujii and Hawley (1991) reported negative effects. Lin, Picot and Compton (2000) reported Canadian evidence that having a self-employed spouse significantly increased the likelihood of the other spouse becoming self-employed.

12. For US evidence that the self-employed are less likely than employees to have health insurance, see Gruber and Poterba (1994), Hamilton (2000) and Wellington (2001).

13. Positive effects were detected by Cowling and Taylor (2001) in the UK and Quinn (1980), Fuchs (1982) and Borjas (1986) in the USA; but negative effects were cited by Rees and Shah (1986) and Gill (1988).

14. But Tucker (1988) offers some evidence from a probit model suggesting that achievement motivation significantly affects the choice of self-employment.

15. Brock and Evans (1986) argued that many of the sociologists' and psychologists' studies are based on questionable sampling methods: 'The scientific validity of these studies, which are seldom based on random samples and often use ambiguous or overly inclusive definitions of an entrepreneur, is open to question' (Brock and Evans, 1986, n. 9, p. 190). A salient bias could be towards sampling only successful entrepreneurs, leading to the danger that observed traits are confused with entrepreneurial experience (Amit, Glosten and Muller, 1993).

16. KPMG (1999) observed that these 'lifestyle' motives for self-employment were strongest among founding entrepreneurs and weakest for those operating growing and innovating firms, who were more likely to stress rapid further growth as an objective.

17. See Scase and Goffee (1982) and MacDonald and Coffield (1991), whose (rather unenthusiastic) survey respondents appeared to be more concerned with making a living ('getting by') than with being autonomous. Also, in Lee's (1985) survey of redundant British steelworkers who subsequently became self-employed, one-third claimed they did so because they 'had no other choice'. A similar proportion claim to be 'necessity entrepreneurs' in the international GEM study (Reynolds et al., 2002), with higher proportions in developing than in developed countries. In the USA, for example, only 8 per cent of the self-employed ascribed their mode of employment to a lack of alternatives (Dennis, 1996). Of course, these responses are all based on declared rather than revealed preferences, so should be treated with commensurate caution.

18. C.f. Adam Smith (1937): 'The chance of gain is by every man more or less overvalued, and the chance of loss is by most men undervalued.'

19. See Parker (1996), Robson (1996), and Cowling and Mitchell (1997), respectively.

20. According to Blanchflower and Oswald (1990), higher proportions of British self-employed people than employees believe that welfare benefits should be reduced to increase self-reliance, and that people on unemployment benefit were 'on the fiddle'. Also, substantially more self-employed people described themselves as Conservative voters, compared to employees; and fewer self-employed people favoured redistribution from the rich to the poor than employees did.

21. For UK evidence see Taylor (1996, 2001), Blanchflower and Oswald (1998), and Burke et al. (2000). For US evidence see Evans and Leighton (1989b), Fairlie (1999) and Hout and Rosen (2000). See also de Wit and van Winden (1989, 1990), Laferrère and McEntee (1995), Lindh and Ohlsson (1996) and Uusitalo (2001) for evidence from the Netherlands, France, Sweden and Finland, respectively.

22. Negative effects were reported by Laferrère and McEntee (1995) and Lindh and Ohlsson (1996); positive effects appear in the North American studies of Borjas and Bronars (1989) and Bernhardt (1994).

23. See also Lentz and Laband (1990), who split 'followers' into heirs and non-heirs to identify the role of managerial experience from mere goodwill/network/brand-loyalty effects, since heirs have the latter but non-heirs do not. Lentz and Laband found that the importance of being a follower for relative self-employment earnings was similar for both groups, suggesting that the common factor was parental managerial experience. In any case, only a minority of followers had inherited or purchased their parents' business.

24. See also Iyigun and Owen (1999), who argued that technological progress generates greater income but also greater absolute risk in entrepreneurship, such that the net incentive to become an entrepreneur decreases as economies develop. However, this result is not general, since one can imagine many kinds of technological change which in conjunction with particular preferences (e.g. decreasing absolute risk aversion) lead to the opposite result. On a different tack, Lazear (2002) argued that if entrepreneurs are 'jacks of all trades' who have to deploy a mix of skills in production, then technological progress that demands additional skills requirements will decrease the number of suitably equipped individuals and therefore also the number of entrepreneurs.

25. By relaxing the borrowing constraint in Banerjee and Newman's (1993) model, financial development might also boost entrepreneurship. It should be borne in mind, however, that economic and financial development often go together. So financial development of itself is unlikely to be a practical panacea for slow economic development.

26. See Fairlie and Meyer (2000) for further evidence against the ability of TFP to explain trends in US self-employment.

27. Examples of the probit approach with industry and/or occupation dummies include Long (1982a), Moore (1983a), Brock and Evans (1986), Evans and Leighton (1989a) and Schuetze (2000) (all US studies); and Georgellis and Wall (2000) for the UK.

28. According to Harvey (1995), self-employment accounted for 45 per cent of the workforce in the UK construction industry in 1993; the next highest proportion was 14 per cent in Distribution, Hotels and Catering. Curran and Burrows (1991) calculated that the highest self-employment growth rates over 1984–9 were in manufacturing rather than in services, especially in construction and engineering, with business and finance being the fastest growing self-employment service sectors.

29. See, e.g., Hamilton (1989), Taylor (1996), Blanchflower and Oswald (1998) and Clark and Drinkwater (1998, 2000) for the UK; van Praag and van Ophem (1995) and Bruce (2000) for the USA; and Lindh and Ohlsson (1996) for Sweden. Simple regional cross-tabulations bear out this finding (Whittington, 1984), though the international cross-section evidence presents a more mixed picture (Reynolds, Storey and Westhead, 1994).

30. For supporting evidence, see Gordus, Jarley and Ferman (1981), Laferrère and McEntee (1995) and Carroll and Mosakowski (1987). Moore and Mueller (2002) observed that Canadians collecting unemployment benefit were less likely to enter self-employment, but that those with longer unemployment spells were more likely to enter it. Although layoffs and redundancy

windfalls appear to significantly and substantially increase the probability of transitions into self-employment (Taylor, 2001; Moore and Mueller, 2002), typically only a small minority of redundant employees subsequently set up their own business (Johnson, 1981). Of those that do, only very limited amounts of job creation ultimately follow, at least in Britain (Johnson and Rodger, 1983).

31. Kuhn and Schuetze claimed that opportunities for women improved in self-employment in terms of increased income and full-time work. In contrast, they asserted that opportunities deteriorated for men both in self-employment and paid-employment – though it is unclear why.

32. UK examples include Harrison and Hart (1983), Foreman-Peck (1985), Binks and Jennings (1986), Hudson (1987a) and Hamilton (1989). US examples include Highfield and Smiley (1987) (for new business incorporations), Ray (1975) and Steinmetz and Wright (1989) (for US self-employment) and Hudson (1989) and Audretsch and Acs (1994) (for new firm start-ups). See Bögenhold and Staber (1991) and Meager (1994) for evidence from other countries, and Storey (1991, 1994a) for a partial overview.

33. Hamilton proposed a positive relationship at low levels of unemployment, when there are plentiful opportunities to start a new business. But at higher unemployment rates (in excess of 20 per cent), the supply of new business opportunities and entrepreneurs to exploit them decline. Supporting evidence of a concave quadratic relationship appears in Georgellis and Wall (2000).

34. See Robson (1991), Black, de Meza and Jeffreys (1996), Parker (1996) and Cowling and Mitchell (1997). Cowling and Mitchell argued that the 'long-term' unemployment rate has a positive effect, and the 'short-term' unemployment rate a negative effect, on the aggregate self-employment rate. This is because the short-term unemployed may return to paid-employment rapidly whereas the long-term unemployed eventually become discouraged by fruitlessly seeking paid-employment, turning to self-employment as a last resort.

Meager (1992a, 1994) highlights a potential problem with regressing the aggregate self-employment rate, n_S, on the unemployment rate. n_S is commonly defined as the number of self-employed people as a proportion of the total workforce. The latter includes the number of unemployed people, so imparting bias to estimates of the self-employment–unemployment rate relationship. In principle it is possible to bypass this problem by defining the workforce to exclude the unemployed. This implicitly treats the labour force participation decision separately from occupation choice. However, it does not address Meager's other critique, which is that inflow data to self-employment allow more accurate tests of the push and pull hypotheses than stock data.

35. This is reflected in scatter plots of self-employment and unemployment rates for individual countries. As Meager (1992a) observed, no general pattern emerges.

36. For example, Hamilton (1989) hypothesised a negatively sloped cross-section schedule in (n_S, n_U) space that shifts upwards north-easterly over time. Clearly, however, it is possible to have north-westerly as well as the north-easterly shifts that Hamilton envisaged, rendering the time-series relationship ambiguous *a priori*.

37. Georgellis and Wall (2000) discovered a greater role for economic variables to explain regional variations in self-employment rates, especially average levels of human capital. They also found that the North of Britain is an outlier in the sense that, unlike any other region, unexplained fixed effects explain virtually all of the variation in those data.

38. Long (1982a), Brock and Evans (1986), Boyd (1990: for blacks but not Asians), Laferrère and McEntee (1995) and Lindh and Ohlsson (1996) found significant positive effects from urban dummies, but Reynolds, Storey West-head (1994) and Carrasco (1999) did not.

39. For self-employment studies reporting negative effects, see Evans and Leighton (1989a), Black, de Meza and Jeffreys (1996), Parker (1996), Robson (1996, 1998b) and Cullen and Gordon (2002). For new-firm foundation studies, contrast Audretsch and Acs (1994), who found a negative effect, with Highfield and Smiley (1987) and Hudson (1989), who did not.

4   Ethnic minority and female entrepreneurship

In many developed countries, ethnic groups comprise a growing minority of the labour force, and females are no longer a minority of employees. Yet ethnic groups exhibit pronounced differences in their propensities to be self-employed, while females remain a minority of the self-employed workforce in all developed economies. Why?

'Minority entrepreneurship' – defined here to encompass ethnic minorities and females – is attracting growing research interest. One reason might be the belief that entrepreneurship offers a route out of poverty and into economic advancement and assimilation for ethnic groups, especially immigrants (Sanders and Nee, 1996). Another is the concern that minorities may face discrimination that hinders their ability to practice entrepreneurship. And there is growing interest in promoting flexible labour markets, enabling females in particular to participate more effectively in the workforce.

It might be helpful to commence with several 'stylised facts' about ethnic minority entrepreneurship; females are treated later in the chapter. First, in the UK and the USA, it is pretty well established that blacks have self-employment rates that are substantially and persistently below average.[1] For example, Clark and Drinkwater (1998) observed from 1991 British Census data that whites had self-employment rates twice that of black Caribbeans; according to Fairlie (1999), the white self-employment rate in the USA was three times that of blacks. According to Fairlie and Meyer (2000), this differential has persisted since at least 1910, suggesting that little has changed since Myrdal (1944) bemoaned the dearth of black-owned businesses in America.

Second, many non-black ethnic groups have above-average self-employment rates, so much so that some authors have concluded that members of the broad 'non-white' group have a higher probability of self-employment in the UK and the USA than 'whites' do. For example, Clark and Drinkwater (1998) reported that Chinese, Pakistanis, Bangladeshis and Indians in Britain had substantially higher self-employment rates (of 26.6, 22.8, 17.8 and 19.6 per cent, respectively) than whites did

113

(12.3 per cent). And using 1990 US Census data, Fairlie and Meyer (1996) found that non-rural male self-employment rates varied substantially across 60 ethnic and racial groups, both before and after controlling for age, education, immigrant status and length of time spent in the USA. For example, only 4.4 per cent of black males worked for themselves, compared with 27.9 per cent of Korean-American men, while European-Americans had self-employment rates close to the US average. Members of ethnic groups from the Middle East and neighbouring countries such as Armenia, Israel and Turkey also had high self-employment rates; but Hispanics (other than Cubans) had low self-employment rates. Fairlie and Meyer (1996) also noted some diversity within the 'black' ethnic group, with black Africans and Caribbeans having slightly higher self-employment rates than other black Americans (but still below the US average). This and similar evidence from the UK cautions against treating ethnic minorities as a single homogeneous group.

Third, self-employed minority workers tend to earn less on average than their white self-employed counterparts. According to Borjas and Bronars (1989), mean self-employment income among black males in 1980 was about half that of self-employed white males, while the mean income of male Hispanics was nearly 30 per cent less than that of whites (see also Flota and Mora, 2001). In contrast, self-employed Asians receive very similar returns to whites. Blacks also have lower average business receipts than members of other minority groups (Borjas and Bronars, 1989).

Exploring the factors underlying these 'stylised' facts is the aim of section 4.1, which focuses on ethnic minority entrepreneurship. Both theoretical models and empirical evidence are discussed. Section 4.2 treats female entrepreneurship, and section 4.3 discusses particular issues relating to immigration.

4.1   Ethnic minority entrepreneurship

Two hypotheses have been advanced to explain the observed variations in rates of entrepreneurship between ethnic groups. The first is discrimination, perpetrated either by employers in the labour market, banks in the capital market, or consumers in the product market. The second is a positive set of factors that can help make entrepreneurship attractive to members of particular minority groups. In the remainder of the chapter, M and NM will be used to denote 'minority' and 'non-minority' values of the variables to which they are attached. In particular, w_M and w_{NM} denote minority and non-minority wage rates in paid-employment, respectively; while π_M and π_{NM} denote minority and non-minority profits in entrepreneurship, respectively.

4.1.1 Discrimination

Employer discrimination

If employers have an exogenous taste for discriminating against members of ethnic minorities, M, what are the implications for ethnic entrepreneurship, and entrepreneurial profits of minority members? Previous researchers have proposed two outcomes from employer discrimination (Sowell, 1981; Moore, 1983b; and Metcalf, Modood and Virdee 1996):

1. By preventing members of minorities from obtaining jobs in paid-employment or by restricting them to relatively low-paid jobs, discrimination increases the attractiveness to them of entrepreneurship. In other words, entrepreneurship can act as an 'escape route' from employer discrimination, implying greater participation in entrepreneurship for these individuals.
2. Discrimination reduces the minority employment wage below that of non-minority members, i.e. it reduces w_M/w_{NM}, so the ratio of minority to non-minority average entrepreneurial profits, π_M/π_{NM}, exceeds the ratio of minority to non-minority wages, w_M/w_{NM} (Moore, 1983b).

However, if we equate entrepreneurship with self-employment, point 2 is not borne out by the evidence (see Moore, 1983b; Borjas and Bronars, 1989; Fujii and Hawley, 1991; Clark and Drinkwater, 1998). One reason is that crowding of Ms into entrepreneurship competes down their output price and hence their profits, π_M, until $\pi_M/\pi_{NM} = w_M/w_{NM}$. Alternatively, even if the distribution of ability within each ethnic group is identical, there are circumstances under which employer discrimination might indirectly reduce π_M relative to π_{NM}. This could occur if entrepreneurs' profits are an increasing function of entrepreneurial ability x: $\pi_j = \pi(x_j)$ ($j = \{M, NM\}$), with $\partial\pi_j/\partial x > 0\ \forall j$. To see this, let the distribution function of x, $G(x)$, be the same for each group. Recall that $w_{NM} > w_M$ because of employer discrimination. Denote the marginal entrepreneur in each ethnic group, i.e. who is indifferent between paid-employment and entrepreneurship, by $\tilde{x}_{NM}$ and $\tilde{x}_M$, respectively. These individuals are defined by the equalities

$$w_{NM} = \pi(\tilde{x}_{NM}) \quad \text{and} \quad w_M = \pi(\tilde{x}_M).$$

Then it follows that $w_{NM} > w_M \Rightarrow \pi(\tilde{x}_{NM}) > \pi(\tilde{x}_M)$, i.e. the minority marginal entrepreneur is less able, and less well remunerated, than the non-minority marginal entrepreneur. There are also more M than NM entrepreneurs in equilibrium, since $1 - G(\tilde{x}_M) > 1 - G(\tilde{x}_{NM})$.

Another problem with the employer discrimination hypothesis is that point 1 above is inconsistent with the facts about American and British blacks, who have lower self-employment rates than whites. Although some ethnic minorities (such as Korean-Americans or British Asians) have above-average self-employment rates, this is an unsatisfactory defence of the employer discrimination hypothesis because it fails to explain why employers discriminate against some ethnic groups but not others.[2]

Discrimination in the capital markets

If lenders discriminate against ethnic minorities, then members of these minorities may find it harder to borrow and become entrepreneurs. The stylised facts are stark. Blanchflower and Oswald (1998) reported that more than 60 per cent of black Americans are turned down for loans by US banks, compared with just 30 per cent for whites. Knight and Dorsey (1976), and more recently, Bates (1997), reported that blacks are granted smaller loans for start-ups than whites – even after controlling for characteristics such as education and financial assets. Similar outcomes have been observed in the venture capital market (Bates and Bradford, 1992). An implication is that blacks are both less likely to be able to start businesses and more likely to be under-capitalised and therefore vulnerable to failure than whites. A striking finding from Bates' (1991) analysis of 1982 CBO data is that, controlling for a range of human capital, physical capital and demographic traits, blacks' failure rates would have been no different from those of whites if they had received the same amounts of external finance.

The UK evidence paints a somewhat different picture. There, the main financing difference appears not to be between whites and blacks, but between Asians and Afro-Caribbeans. According to Jones McEroy and Barrett (1994), Asians have a higher probability of obtaining a bank loan than Afro-Caribbeans and whites, and leverage more funds from banks. These facts cast doubt on the proposition that UK banks are guilty of blanket discrimination, though it does beg the question about why Afro-Caribbeans have greater difficulties in raising bank loans than whites do (Bank of England, 1999).

One possible answer is *statistical discrimination*. This describes the situation where an ethnic group has different characteristics *on average* from others, which are then used to adversely screen all members of that group. For example, UK minority-owned businesses tend to establish themselves in sectors such as retailing, transportation and catering, that have above-average failure rates (Bank of England, 1999). Also, blacks tend to have lower wealth levels on average and hence less collateral than whites do. Even if banks do not discriminate on the basis of ethnicity, bank competition may generate bank lending rules that reward high-collateral and safe-sector start-ups with larger loans – resulting in outcomes that resemble discrimination, since blacks will be observed to obtain smaller loans on average.

Coate and Tennyson (1992) demonstrated how employer discrimination can spill over into statistical discrimination in the credit market. Entrepreneurs must borrow a unit of capital to operate an investment project whose return is uncertain. Let p_i be the (heterogeneous) probability that individual i's enterprise succeeds – which is private information to the individual. Let $R^s > 0$ (respectively, $R^f = 0$) be the return if a project is successful (respectively, unsuccessful); and r_i be the interest rate charged to i. With an outside wage of $w_i = w_{NM}$ if i belongs to the non-minority group and $w_i = w_M$ otherwise, the individual with success probability $\tilde{p}_i = \tilde{p}_i(w_i, r_i)$ is indifferent between entrepreneurship and paid-employment:

$$\tilde{p}_i(w_i, r_i) = w_i / [R^s - (1 + r_i)].$$

Employer discrimination implies that $w_{NM} > w_M$. Hence

$$\tilde{p}_i(w_M, r_M) < \tilde{p}_i(w_{NM}, r_{NM}),$$

i.e. the marginal entrepreneur in M is of lower ability compared with his NM counterpart. Consequently, statistical discrimination occurs: ethnicity is an observable characteristic, and in a competitive credit market every loan applicant from M must be charged a higher interest rate than their NM counterpart to reflect their lower average probability of success. Thus $r_M > r_{NM}$, which for any ability type reduces an M entrepreneur's expected profits (net of interest payments) below that of the corresponding NM entrepreneur.

As it stands, a higher proportion of Ms than NMs is predicted to enter entrepreneurship in this model – which is contradicted by evidence about black self-employment rates. Coate and Tennyson (1992) showed that this prediction can be overturned if entrepreneurial ability is partly determined by human capital investment since, facing employer discrimination, it is rational for Ms to acquire less human capital than NMs. If this reduced M entrepreneurs' returns π_M by more than it reduced w_M, then fewer Ms might choose entrepreneurship than NMs. However, it was seen in chapter 3, section 3.1 that human capital has a greater impact on returns in paid-employment than in self-employment. Hence Coate and Tennyson's model has real difficulties explaining why black self-employment rates are so relatively low.

If for whatever reason minorities encounter difficulties with raising bank loans, then they presumably have an incentive to raise capital within their own ranks. There is a small but growing literature (see also chapter 6, subsection 6.1.3), on minority-owned banks and Rotating Savings and

Credit Associations (Roscas), which have proven especially popular among Chinese, Japanese and Korean immigrant groups in the USA. Several researchers have suggested that Roscas have enabled impecunious immigrants to bootstrap their way to business success (Light and Bonacich, 1988; Aldrich and Waldinger, 1990; Yoon, 1991). For example, in Yoon's (1991) survey of 199 Korean merchants in minority neighbourhoods in Chicago, 27.6 per cent used loans from Korean Roscas, 27.1 per cent used loans from banks, and 34.7 used loans from kin. However, this coverage does not seem to extend to national data sets such as the CBO, where Rosca lending appears to be of marginal importance and is associated with smaller and more failure-prone businesses (Bates, 1997). Involvement in Roscas in the USA seems to have been strongest in the early part of the twentieth century, becoming less important over time as ethnic groups gained greater access to formal credit markets (Besley, 1995).

Another problem with the proposition that minority-owned banks can solve capital market discrimination problems is that many ethnic groups (including blacks) have not emulated Asian Roscas – which might have been expected to occur if they were so effective. Closer inspection reveals that Roscas' value is actually rather dubious. Much Rosca finance is short-term and at high interest rates that can exceed 30 per cent per annum – which presumably makes a Rosca a lender of last resort to many borrowers. It is also pertinent that many Roscas are designed primarily to encourage savings rather than business investment by members.

Consumer discrimination

Another possibility is that NM consumers dislike buying goods and services from M entrepreneurs. This can be expected to reduce the latter's returns in entrepreneurship, and hence the number of M entrepreneurs.[3] Borjas and Bronars (1989) studied a model with this feature, in which NM consumers are assumed to have a taste for discrimination against M sellers, while M consumers are indifferent to the race of the seller.[4] Thus if M sellers charge price P, NM buyers perceive it as $P/(1 - \alpha)$, where $\alpha < 1$ measures the strength of the taste for discrimination. There is imperfect information about prices of goods and the race of sellers. Therefore all consumers are prepared to search for goods. There are four reservation prices $P(j, j')$, from sellers of race j to buyers of race j': $j \times j' = \{M, NM\} \times \{M, NM\}$. These are the highest prices that a buyer is prepared to pay rather than continuing to search. Reservation prices are ordered as follows:

$$P(NM, NM) \geq P(NM, M) = P(M, M) > P(M, NM)$$
$$= (1 - \alpha)P(NM, NM) . \qquad (4.1)$$

The strict inequality in (4.1) reflects the possibility that a NM buyer encounters a M seller in the future, which reduces the former's value of search and raises the reservation price $P(NM, NM)$ above $P(M, NM)$.

Sellers maximise the utility function $U = \pi - (h^\beta/\beta)$, where π is entrepreneurial profit, h is hours worked, and $\beta > 1$ is a parameter. Individuals choose optimal work hours h^* and the set of buyers that they are prepared to sell to ('segregation policy'). To trade, offer prices must be below the reservation prices of the targeted buyers. It is assumed that within each ethnic group sellers have heterogeneous abilities at producing goods, and that the distribution of ability within the two groups is identical. Let $\Theta = \{b, g\}$ denote the set of different abilities, 'bad' (or unskilled) and 'good' (skilled) respectively. There are four offer prices indexed by $P_{j,\Theta}$. In equilibrium, the more able can produce more output and so have higher opportunity costs of not selling. This reduces their offer price within their racial group. This, together with (4.1), yields the ranking

$$P_{NM,b} \geq P_{NM,g} \geq P_{M,b} \geq P_{M,g}. \qquad (4.2)$$

Borjas and Bronars' two key results then follow directly: (i) In equilibrium the mean income of M sellers will be lower than that of NM sellers. Skilled Ms have greater incentives to enter paid-employment than skilled NMs. (ii) NM sellers have a higher return to ability than M sellers. These predictions contrast with those of the employer discrimination model and accord with the third 'stylised fact' listed in the introduction to this chapter. Using a sample of 1980 US Census data, Borjas and Bronars found some support for their predictions, observing significant positive selection into self-employment among whites, significant negative selection among Hispanics and Asians (see also Flota and Mora, 2001), but zero selection among blacks.

While Borjas and Bronars' model appears useful for understanding ethnic differences in self-employment rates, it seems less suitable for explaining gender differences. As Aronson (1991) pointed out, women are commonly employed in sales jobs, which would not be optimal if profit maximising firms knew that consumers discriminated against them. Another problem with the consumer discrimination hypothesis is that black businesses are relatively common in industries patronised by white customers (Meyer, 1990). One reason could be franchising, since franchisors often discourage attempts by franchisees to differentiate their units (Kaufmann and Lafontaine, 1994) – so reducing consumers' ability to discriminate. Indeed, Williams (2001) found that black entrepreneurs were more likely than any other racial group to become franchisees. Williams also estimated that blacks earned more as franchisees than they would as independent business owners, a finding that is also consistent with Borjas and Bronar' discrimination model. If Williams' findings are true more generally, they suggest that franchising could be a successful way of increasing the level of entrepreneurial activity among blacks.

4.1.2 Positive factors

Discrimination can be regarded as a factor that 'pushes' members of ethnic minorities into the escape route of entrepreneurship. Another possibility is that 'pull' factors make entrepreneurship positively attractive to members of minority groups. The following pull factors have been proposed:

1. *Positive expected relative returns in entrepreneurship* Positive rewards in entrepreneurship, rather than discrimination in paid-employment, may explain high rates of entrepreneurship among some ethnic groups (Bearse, 1984). For example, using US and British data, respectively, and implementing the structural probit model outlined in chapter 1. subsection 1.6.2, Fairlie and Meyer (1996) and Clark and Drinkwater (2000) found that relative income differences helped explain differences in self-employment rates across ethnic groups.
2. *Ethnic enclaves* 'Enclaves' are geographical clusters of ethnic group members who form self-supporting economic communities. Enclaves can offer information networks, sources of credit, 'niche' markets for the output of ethnic entrepreneurs and a steady supply of workers, possibly drawn from close-knit extended families (Light and Bonacich, 1988). For example, ethnic minority entrepreneurs may know more about the tastes of ethnic consumers, in such 'protected markets' as clothing, foodstuffs, religious goods and services (Aldrich *et al.*, 1985). These factors, and the absence of consumer discrimination by co-ethnics, presumably increase the opportunities and ease with which minority group members can operate a business. Set against this argument, however, is the possibility that the scope for expanding operations into broader markets is more difficult for enclave producers. Also, enclaves can foster intense competition among ethnic entrepreneurs, so limiting entrepreneurial opportunities (Aldrich and Waldinger, 1990) and reducing survival prospects (Bates and Bradford, 1992). Furthermore, employment incomes may be relatively high in enclaves since ethnic employers presumably do not discriminate against members of their own group. And opportunities for profitable entrepreneurship in enclaves may be limited if ethnic disposable incomes and hence consumer demand are low.

The available evidence from a range of countries certainly points to a concentration of self-employed immigrants and minorities in particular industrial sectors. For example, US Census data from 1980 revealed that 27 per cent of self-employed immigrants were working in the retail sector, compared with 17 per cent of the native-born self-employed (Borjas, 1986). Becker (1984) reported that white self-employed individuals were concentrated in managerial, technical and professional occupations, whereas their black counterparts were concentrated in manual jobs. Similar evidence comes from the 1991 British Census, with 90 per cent of Asian self-employed people working in services, and only a tiny minority working in the construction sector (Clark and Drinkwater, 1998). Clark and Drinkwater also reported that 50 per cent of Indian, Pakistani and Bangladeshi self-employed individuals worked in retail distribution, restaurants and taxi driving, while 80 per cent of the Chinese self-employed worked in the restaurant industry.

A direct empirical test of the ethnic enclave hypothesis examines whether the proportion of an area's population belonging to one ethnic group positively affects that group's self-employment incidence in the area. Borjas (1986) pioneered this approach by including as an explanatory variable in a logit model of self-employment participation the proportion of individuals' local populations who were Hispanic. Borjas estimated that male Hispanics aged 18–64 were significantly and substantially more likely to be self-employed in areas with a large Hispanic population, whereas no such effect was detectable for whites. Subsequent evidence on the issue has been mixed, with some studies offering support (Boyd, 1990: for blacks; Le, 2000; Flota and Mora, 2001; Lofstrom, 2002) and others failing to find significant effects (Borjas and Bronars, 1989; Boyd, 1990: for Asians; Yuengert, 1995; Razin and Langlois, 1996; Clark and Drinkwater, 1998, 2000, 2002).

The enclave hypothesis also has problems explaining low black self-employment rates, especially since there is evidence in the USA and the UK of strong black networks, including a loyal black customer base and a practice of blacks hiring of other blacks (Aronson, 1991; Jones McEvoy and Barrett 1993). In contrast, members of other self-employed minority groups (especially Asians) often predominantly hire workers from outside their ethnic group (Aldrich and Waldinger, 1990). Nor is the use of family labour confined to ethnic minorities: it appears to be a common practice among all racial groups (Jones McEvoy and Barrett 1993).

Bates (1997) argued that enclaves are not a route to entrepreneurial success, and primarily serve as a fallback for marginal ethnic entrepreneurs. Bates demonstrated that successful Asian-American entrepreneurs predominantly serve non-minority clients, raise finance from conventional lenders and employ non-minority employees. Their success appeared to be attributable not to ethnic resources but to heavy physical and human capital investments.[5] in contrast, the least successful Asian-owned firms relied on social support networks in enclaves; and those with a predominantly minority clientele and located in areas with large minority populations had significantly lower survival and profitability rates than the average.

3. *Culture* Building on Weber's (1930) 'Protestant Ethic' thesis, it is possible that attitudes to entrepreneurship are determined by the religion of particular ethnic groups (Rafiq, 1992). Some prominent figures in Islam and the Sikh religion were businessmen; and some Hindu castes specialise in business activities. In Britain, Clark and Drinkwater (2000) found that, all else equal, Muslims, Hindus and Sikhs had significantly higher probabilities of being self-employed than Christians from ethnic minorities were. Related to this, some Asian cultures stress self-sufficiency, thrift and hard work, which may help to explain high Britain Asian self-employment rates (Borooah and Hart, 1999). However, most empirical studies have found religion variables to be insignificant (Pickles and O'Farrell, 1987; O'Farrell and Pickles, 1989; de Wit and Winden, 1989; de Wit, 1993), though there are exceptions (Carroll and Mosakowski, 1987; Clark and Drinkwater, 2000).

Poor command of the host country's language might increase the likelihood of ethnic self-employment, by restricting employment opportunities in the formal employment market without affecting trading opportunities among members of one's own language group (Bates, 1997). The evidence on the issue derived from probit models is mixed, with some studies finding that poor English-language skills increase self-employment participation (Boyd, 1990; among Asians but not blacks; Fairlie and Meyer, 1996; Portes and Zhou, 1996; Clark and Drinkwater, 2002), and others finding the opposite (Evans, 1989; Flota and Mora, 2001; Lofstrom, 2002). Flota and Mora (2001) claimed that poor English fluency was associated not only with lower self-employment propensities, but also with lower self-employment incomes. Another possibility is that belonging to a minority group may create a feeling of insecurity that encourages a drive for entrepreneurial success (Kilby, 1983; Elkan, 1988).[6]

4. *Role models* Applying quantile regression techniques to 1984 SIPP data, Hamilton (2000) found that black self-employment incomes are similar to those of whites at the three lower quartiles but are significantly lower than whites' incomes at the upper quartile. An absence of black entrepreneurial 'superstars' may contribute to the lower self-employment rates of blacks generally – as well as accounting for their lower *average* self-employment incomes. A lack of black role models within and outside the immediate family might also explain why Hout and Rosen (2000) found intergenerational links in self-employment to be strong for every American ethnic group except blacks.

4.1.3   Conclusion

The literature has identified both negative and positive factors that impinge on ethnic entrepreneurship. Most of the negative factors are based on some kind of discrimination. As we saw, however, the role of discrimination has been questioned on both theoretical and empirical grounds. In the USA, for example, Bates (1997) concluded that the substantial human and physical capital inputs by Asian-American entrepreneurs relative to blacks help explain the former's substantially higher self-employment rates.

Is it different personal characteristics, or is it different returns given the same personal characteristics, that account for the observed differences in self-employment rates between ethnic groups? In an attempt to answer this question, Borjas and Bronars (1989) estimated what average minority self-employment rates would have been if the coefficients from a self-employment probit regression based on a white subsample (i.e. imposing the same returns to characteristics) were applied to non-whites. To make this precise, consider the probit regression equation (1.7), and (suppressing the intercept purely for notational clarity) let $\hat{\beta}_{NM}$ denote the estimated coefficients of that equation obtained using a purely non-minority data sample. Then if only M members' characteristics were different, the predicted probability of M self-employment would be

$$\hat{p}_M = \sum_{i \in M} \frac{\Phi(\hat{\beta}'_{NM} W_i)}{n}, \qquad (4.3)$$

where n is the sample size, $\Phi(\cdot)$ is the cumulative distribution function of the normal distribution and where the summation takes place over all persons in the minority group, M. Using this method, Borjas and Bronars (1989) found that blacks and Hispanics would have had the same self-employment rates as whites, and that Asians would have had a higher self-employment rate than whites. This implies that unobserved differences in rates of return, rather than differences in observable characteristics, account for the ethnic variation in self-employment rates.[7] Unfortunately, it is unclear whether discrimination, cultural factors, or unobserved characteristics are responsible for these different rates of return.

Self-employment rates themselves conflate entry decisions and survival outcomes. Fairlie (1999) demonstrated the importance of separating these effects to identify more precisely the causes of the relatively low US black self-employment rate. Using PSID data over 1968–89, Fairlie found that black entry rates into self-employment were about half those of whites, while black exit rates were about twice those of whites. Using a decomposition analysis, Fairlie found that although some variables helped explain lower black entry rates (notably lower assets and a lower incidence of self-employed fathers), they did not help explain higher black exit rates.[8] According to Fairlie, education was not a significant factor for either entry or exit. Fairlie concluded that the scope for policy intervention to increase black self-employment rates is limited. Even quadrupling current black asset levels was estimated to reduce the ethnic gap in self-employment entry rates by only 13 per cent. Bates (1984) also expressed doubts about the potential for government policies (such as the SBA's Equal Opportunities Loan Programme and US Federal government procurement policies) to stimulate business ownership among ethnic minorities.

4.2   Female entrepreneurship

4.2.1   Explaining female self-employment rates

Females are a minority of the self-employed workforce in all developed countries, and within all ethnic groups (see, e.g. Fairlie and Meyer, 1996). American female self-employment in particular grew especially rapidly in the 1970s and 1980s, doubling in number while growth in male self-employment was much more modest (Becker, 1984; Evans and Leighton, 1989a). Female self-employment grew from about one-quarter of the US non-agricultural self-employed workforce in 1975 to about one-third by 1990 (Devine, 1994a). According to Aronson (1991) this represents a continuation of a trend increase since at least 1955, when the female share of the US self-employed workforce was about 12 per cent. Female self-employment rates in the EU vary considerably, from just over 20 per cent in the UK, Ireland and Sweden to 40 per cent in Belgium and Portugal (Cowling, 2000).

Self-employed women in the USA tend to be older than their female employee counterparts, though this difference has narrowed since 1975 (Devine, 1994a). Between 1975 and 1990, the increase in US female self-employment was accompanied by few changes in occupational or industrial concentration. Self-employed females remain over-represented in a few sectors like 'sales' and 'other services' (which include financial, insurance and real estate; professional services; and business services: Bates, 1995). Few self-employed females are found in the construction industry, which remains dominated by males. The concentration of self-employed females in service industries is particularly pronounced, being greater than that of either female employees or either category of males. But as Aronson (1991) pointed out, the secular growth in services predated the growth in female self-employment and hence cannot explain it.

According to Devine (1994a, 1994b), self-employed American females are more likely than their employee counterparts to be married with a spouse present, to be covered by somebody else's health insurance and to work either a relatively small or a relatively large number of hours. Being married and having infants or school-age children in the household appear to be strongly associated with female self-employment.[9] The cost of child-care may be one reason underlying these results, since self-employment often offers greater flexibility for arranging child-care around a work schedule. It is noteworthy that several authors have observed that family variables have little impact on male self-employment participation (Boden, 1996; Carr, 1996).

In line with the flexibility hypothesis, Carr (1996) found from 1980 US Census data that 20 per cent of female self-employed individuals worked from home, compared with just 6 per cent of men. Edwards and Field-Hendrey (2002) investigated this issue in further detail, finding that home-based work is an attractive option for women with high fixed costs of work, associated with such factors as the presence of small children, disability and rural location. Naturally, home-workers can engage more easily than on-site workers in joint market and household production. Edwards and Field-Hendrey also reported that home-based workers were more likely to choose self-employment (63 per cent) than on-site workers were (33 per cent). Apart from joint production, home-based self-employment enjoys several advantages over on-site employment, including the absence of employer monitoring and office rental costs. For the UK, further evidence in support of the flexibility hypothesis comes from Hakim (1989a), who showed that while the desire for independence and monetary rewards were important for both genders in the UK, females valued the freedom of choosing when to work more than men did.

Until recently, a neglected issue in research on female self-employment was the husband's role in the household. This gap is now being filled. For example, Caputo and Dolinsky (1998) found that the incomes, self-employment experience and child-care provision of husbands all significantly increased the probability that an American woman was self-employed. The strongest effects came from simply having a self-employed husband in the household. Bruce (1999) confirmed this result, finding that the presence of a self-employed husband doubled the probability of an American female switching into self-employment.[10] According to Devine (1994a), 40 per cent of all self-employed American women in husband–wife households had self-employed spouses in 1990. Husbands may enable women to overcome capital constraints; provide role models, business skills and valuable advice; and free up the woman's time to enable her to run her business.

The following stylised facts about labour supply patterns emerged from Devine's (1994a) study of American self-employed females. First, self-employed females were likelier than female employees or males in either employment category to be part-time workers.[11] Second, part-time female self-employment was commonest among those who were married with a spouse present. Third, work hours of part-time and full-time self-employed women were more dispersed than female employees' work hours. Devine concluded that self-employed females faced greater choice than males did in terms of the hours of work they supplied. That may partly explain Lee and Rendall's (2001) finding that white American women had shorter spells in self-employment on average than men did, despite having worked similar numbers of spells.

Education has also been identified as an important aspect of female self-employment. Cowling and Taylor (2001) showed that on average British self-employed females possessed more advanced educational qualifications than self-employed own-account (but not employer) males. Advanced education also appears to be associated with female self-employment in the USA.[12] This finding might be explained by the concentration of female employees in clerical and administrative jobs which require less advanced qualifications and that yield work experience that is ill-suited to switching into self-employment (Boden, 1996).

A drawback of several of the above studies is that they ignore relative earnings as a determinant of female self-employment. This has been partially dealt with by Devine (1994b), who used CPS data over 1975–87 to estimate the earnings function (1.1), in order to compare potential female incomes by occupation. The predicted employment earnings of self-employed females exceeded those of females who were employees.[13] Devine also reported that female self-employment participation rates did not vary systematically by job skill level. This is inconsistent with the hypothesis that skilled women choose self-employment to avoid a 'glass ceiling' of limited earnings in self-employment; and also with the notion that women use employment skills as a launching pad for entry into self-employment.

To the author's knowledge there has not yet been an application of the structural probit model (described in chapter 1, subsection 1.6.2) to female self-employment. Such an exercise would be valuable provided that a sufficiently large data sample could be obtained.

4.2.2   Female self-employed earnings

It is now well established that self-employed females earn less on average than self-employed men or employees of either gender. For example, the US SBA (1986) estimated that the ratio of female to male self-employment incomes remained roughly constant at around 0.50 between 1974 and 1984, at the same time as the ratio of female to male employment incomes increased from 0.46 to 0.53. These numbers include both part-time and full-time workers. Using 1983 SIPP data, Haber, Lamas and Lichtenstein (1987) estimated that the ratio of US median *full-time* female to male self-employment incomes was only 0.30, compared to a ratio of 0.60 in paid-employment. Self-employed females also suffer a 30 per cent median earnings disadvantage relative to female employees (Becker, 1984; Devine, 1994a). Female self-employed workers do better on average in some other countries, with female/male earnings ratios reaching 87 per cent in the case of Australia (OECD, 1986).

Aronson (1991) offered an interesting historical perspective on female relative self-employment incomes. He cited evidence that, in the inter-war and early post-war periods, self-employed females earned more than female employees did – although the comprehensiveness of these data is limited. What is clear is that between 1955 and 1984 the relative earnings position of self-employed females declined steadily relative to their employee counterparts and also to self-employed males. It is less clear whether this decline reflects greater part-time participation by self-employed females or a relative worsening of the human capital of females choosing self-employment. While the inclusion of incorporated self-employed workers in sample data tends to close the income gap of male self-employed relative to male employees, it makes relatively little difference to the female self-employed–employee income gap (Aronson, 1991). That presumably reflects the small number of incorporated self-employed females.

For the self-employed generally, it should be borne in mind that self-employment incomes usually omit important additional dimensions of job remuneration, such as health care coverage. Female self-employed workers have relatively scant job-related health care coverage compared with female employees, male employees and male self-employees (Devine, 1994a).

Why are female self-employment incomes relatively low? One reason is that female self-employed workers have fewer years of experience than female employees or males (Aronson, 1991; Lee and Rendall, 2001). Also, female self-employees tend to have more diverse backgrounds than their male counterparts: women are more likely than men to set up a business without having a track record of achievement, vocational training, or experience (Watkins and Watkins, 1984). Second, women have greater opportunities or preferences for potentially less remunerative home working, as noted above. Third, females tend to operate a smaller scale of business, utilising less capital and finance from banks and other lenders than males do (Aronson, 1991). This might reflect a preference for smaller enterprises since these minimise the disruptions to a family that could result from operating a larger enterprise. Of course, a lower capital base can be expected to reduce future entrepreneurial incomes and increase the probability of business failure. Carter, Williams and Reynolds (1997) confirmed that female-owned businesses start on a smaller scale than male-owned ones, and have higher discontinuance rates – although they stressed that this did not seem to be attributable to females being disadvantaged with respect to access to credit.[14]

A study by Hundley (2001a) sought to test these competing explanations against each other by applying an Oaxaca decomposition to gender-specific earnings functions. To see how this works, write (1.1) of chapter 1, subsection 1.5.3 in the form $\ln y_{ij} = \beta_j' X_{ij} + u_{ij}$, where the j subscript denotes gender: $j = f$ indexes females and $j = m$ indexes males. Consider a particular explanatory variable X_{ijk}. Letting an overbar denote sample means and a hat denote a regression estimate, we can write

$$\overline{\ln y_m} - \overline{\ln y_f} = \hat{\beta}_m' \left(\overline{X_{mk}} - \overline{X_{fk}} \right) + \left(\hat{\beta}_m - \hat{\beta}_f \right)' \overline{X_{fk}}, \qquad (4.4)$$

where y denotes annual earnings. The first term on the RHS of (4.4) is the part of the average earnings difference attributable to characteristic X_{ijk}. The other term is the part of the earnings difference that is unexplained by X_{ijk}.[15] Hundley (2001a) found that, in terms of (4.4), the most important explanatory variables were housework, work hours and the number of young children, which together accounted for between 30 per cent and 50 per cent of the American annual self-employment earnings' gender differential. This suggests that women earn less than men do because they spend less time managing and developing their businesses. The next most important factor found by Hundley (2001a) was industrial sector, which accounted for between 9 and 14 per cent of the gender self-employment earnings' differential. This captures the concentration of women in the relatively unrewarding personal services sector, and their under-representation in the more remunerative professional services and construction industries. Physical capital explained only between 3 and 7 per cent of the differential, and other variables (including experience) were even less important.

It is not just the case that female self-employees under-perform relative to males in terms of their income. The same appears to be true of their output, employment and turnover, according to overviews of US and UK evidence conducted by Brusch (1992) and Rosa, Carter and Hamilton (1996). As Du Rietz and Henrekson (2000) show, controlling for other factors such as industrial sector attenuates, but does not eliminate, this finding.

Finally, the inequality of female self-employment incomes also appears to be substantially higher than that of female employees or males of either occupation (Meager, Court and Moralee, 1996). This is likely to reflect, in part, the greater incidence of part-time self-employment among females than males. And self-employment appears to be a less fruitful vehicle for upward earnings mobility for American females than males (Holtz-Eakin, Rosen and Weathers, 2000).

4.2.3 Conclusion

Despite its intrinsic interest and importance, the subject of female entrepreneurship has arguably not commanded the degree of research effort that it deserves. Little is known about precisely why there is less female than male entrepreneurship, why it is growing in popularity and why self-employed females earn so much less on average than either females in paid-employment or males in self- and paid-employment. Aronson (1991) concluded that female self-employed and employed workers have similar characteristics, and conjectured that they differ in their attitudes to 'independence' and in their taste for leisure relative to income. This may partly explain the evidence that being married and having children are such important determinants of female self-employment. However, because tastes and attitudes are difficult if not impossible to observe and quantify, it looks as though sharp tests of this conjecture will be hard to devise.

4.3 Immigration and entrepreneurship

It has been suggested that immigrants are likelier than native-born workers ('natives' henceforth) to be entrepreneurs, for the following reasons.
1. On average, immigrants are better educated and motivated than natives.
2. Immigrants have access to 'ethnic resources' and social capital (Light, 1984), including a tradition of trading, access to low-paid and trusted workers from the same ethnic group and access to a ready market of niche products within an ethnic enclave.
3. Some immigrants are 'sojourners', who wish to immigrate temporarily in order to accumulate wealth before returning to their homeland. Entrepreneurship may be the most effective means to this end.
4. Immigrants turn to entrepreneurship because of 'blocked mobility' in paid-employment, owing to language difficulties, discrimination, or possession of non-validated foreign qualifications.
5. Immigrants are self-selected risk takers by virtue of their willingness to leave their homeland to make their way in a foreign country.

6. Among illegal immigrants, entrepreneurship in the form of self-employment may be a means of escaping detection by the authorities.
7. Immigrants enter industries and occupations that have high rates of entrepreneurship.

Empirical studies, which invariably measure entrepreneurship as self-employment, have generated diverse findings about the role of immigration. Borjas (1986) and Lofstrom (2002) claimed to find higher self-employment rates among immigrants than natives in the USA, while Brock and Evans (1986) found no such pattern. All of these studies used US Census data. Part of the problem may be one of classification: Light (1984) emphasised the diversity of self-employment experience among immigrants by 'home' country, which he attributed to different traditions of commerce. This theme was taken up by Yuengert (1995), whose analysis of 1980 US Census data indicated that immigrants from countries with relatively high self-employment rates are likelier to become self-employed in the US.[16]

The roles of some of the factors listed above have also been challenged. Regarding 2 above, Bates (1997) showed that most immigrant business owners obtained most of their finance from their personal wealth and from mainstream lenders, rather than from social resources. Immigrant businesses depending on the latter tended to be 'marginal' and more prone to failure. Regarding 3, it does not necessarily follow that entrepreneurship is a better way of getting rich than paid-employment. While some studies have claimed that immigrants do better in self-employment than in paid-employment (Borjas, 1986; Lofstrom, 2002), the income experiences of immigrants can vary considerably, and sometimes entail disadvantage (Borjas and Bronars, 1989; Portes and Zhou, 1996). An important aspect to this debate appears to be duration of residence in the host country. Both Brock and Evans (1986) and Lofstrom (2002) found that longer self-employment spells in the host country by immigrants eventually reverse initial earnings disadvantage relative to natives – in contrast to immigrant employees whose relative earnings disadvantage tends to persist throughout their lifetimes.

Another problem for the sojourner theory is that many immigrants ultimately choose to remain in the host country, whatever their original intentions were. Fairlie and Meyer (1996) found that immigrants who had been in the USA for over thirty years had higher self-employment rates than immigrants who had been in the USA for less than ten years and who were presumably more likely to be sojourners (see also Lofstrom, 2002). Immigrant self-employment rates that increase with length of residence might reflect not only the positive income-duration relationship mentioned above, but also other factors. These might include (i) greater knowledge of labour markets, tastes of ethnic groups and institutions within the host country; (ii) accumulation of wealth required for entry into entrepreneurship; and (iii) greater access to factors of production.

When studying length of residence effects it appears important to distinguish between 'assimilation effects', which capture the extent to which individuals within a given cohort assimilate into the host country, and 'cohort effects', which capture the possibility that cohorts differ in quality. To disentangle the two effects, Borjas (1986) suggested the following decomposition. Let $\hat{p}_{t,j}$ denote the predicted probability of entrepreneurship for a representative member of cohort j at time t, and let $\hat{p}_{t,j+10}$ be the probability of entrepreneurship at t for a representative member of a cohort who arrived ten years later (say) than members of j. Then

$$\hat{p}_{t,j} - \hat{p}_{t,j+10} = \left(\hat{p}_{t,j} - \hat{p}_{t-10,j}\right) + \left(\hat{p}_{t-10,j} - \hat{p}_{t,j+10}\right) \qquad (4.5)$$

measures the cross-section difference between members of different cohorts at t. The first term on the RHS of (4.5) measures the 'within cohort j' change in entrepreneurship probability since year $t - 10$ ('the assimilation effect'). The second term measures the change in entrepreneurship probability for immigrants with the same number of years' experience since immigration (the 'cross-cohort effect').

Borjas recognised that (4.5) could be biased if changing aggregate labour market conditions altered the attractiveness of entrepreneurship for everyone. To control for secular changes in broader labour market conditions, Borjas suggested decomposing changes in immigrant entrepreneurship *relative to native-born entrepreneurs*, the latter being denoted by subscript j':

$$\hat{p}_{t,j} - \hat{p}_{t,j+10} = \left[\left(\hat{p}_{t,j} - \hat{p}_{t-10,j}\right) - \left(\hat{p}_{t,j'} - \hat{p}_{t-10,j'}\right)\right]$$
$$+ \left[\left(\hat{p}_{t-10,j} - \hat{p}_{t,j+10}\right) - \left(\hat{p}_{t-10,j'} - \hat{p}_{t,j'}\right)\right] . \qquad (4.6)$$

The first term in square brackets is a refined measure of the assimilation effect. It measures the change in entrepreneurship propensities of a given cohort net of the change experienced by a similar native-born cohort. Likewise, the second term measures the cross-cohort effect on entrepreneurship propensities net of economy-wide changes experienced by native-born workers between $t - 10$ and t.

Using a sample of US Census data on male workers, and selecting $t = 1980$, Borjas reported substantial variation in the magnitude of the two terms of (4.5) and (4.6) across ethnic groups. Yet two common features held for almost all groups. First, the first term on the RHS of (4.6) indicated a strong assimilation effect, suggesting that the relative attractiveness of self-employment increases the longer the individual has been living in the USA. Second, the cross-cohort effect (the second term) usually indicated a greater propensity for more recent immigrant cohorts to choose self-employment relative to earlier cohorts. This is reflected in the higher self-employment rates among more recent immigrants, which is consistent with the notion that more recent immigrants to the USA have been of lower average quality, at least in terms of their employment opportunities in the 'formal' labour market.[17]

An advantage of Borjas' decomposition technique is that it separates two important and distinct aspects of immigrant self-employment propensities. But it has yet to be widely adopted by researchers in the field.

NOTES

1. Most of the available evidence pertains to these two countries. Evidence is of two sorts: tabulations from micro data, and estimations of self-employment probit regressions in which ethnicity is represented by dummy variables while other personal characteristics are controlled for. Examples of the latter include Rees and Shah (1986), Dolton and Makepeace (1990), Taylor (1996) and Clark and Drinkwater (1998, 2000) for the UK; Long (1982a), Gill (1988), Tucker (1988) and Hout and Rosen (2000) for the USA; and Blau (1985) and Vijverberg (1986) for Malaysia.

2. In contrast, employers do appear to discriminate against individuals of all races with previous criminal convictions, who are significantly associated with greater self-employment propensities: see Fairlie (2002) for evidence from the National Logitudinal Survey of Youth (NLSY).

3. See, e.g., Myrdal (1944) for an account of the proliferation of black personal service companies that catered specifically for black Americans in response to white consumer discrimination in the first half of the twentieth century.

4. This second assumption, which can be relaxed, implies that $P(NM, M) = P(M, M)$ in (4.1) below.

5. For example, of Asian-immigrant entrepreneurs operating young firms in 1987, 58 per cent were college graduates (compared with 38 per cent of non-minority business owners), with an average start-up capital of $53,550 compared with just $31,939 for non-minority business owners. Bates (1985) also observed that the most successful minority entrepreneurs were located outside the 'traditional' personal service and retail sectors.

6. Cultural factors might deter female ethnic self-employment in particular. Clark and Drinkwater (2000) found that in Britain, ethnic female self-employment rates were substantially below those of males, except among Chinese people.

7. See also Fairlie and Meyer (2000), who found that relatively low black self-employment rates in the USA could not be explained by a concentration of blacks in low self-employment industries. In a similar way, Hout and Rosen (2000) were unable to explain black–white self-employment rate differentials in terms of family background. Different decompositions to (4.3) have been suggested by Clark and Drinkwater (1998), Clark, Drinkwater and Leslie (1998) and Borooah and Hart (1999), but with similar qualitative findings.

8. But see Bates (1997), who had greater success in explaining high black business exit rates, especially in terms of low levels of capital inputs.

9. As well as Devine (1994a, 1994b), see also Robinson and Sexton (1994), Carr (1996) and Cowling and Taylor (2001). Some rare contrary evidence that marital status is unimportant comes from a study by Caputo and Dolinsky (1998), who controlled for many household level variables – see below. On the importance of the presence of children, see Macpherson (1988), Evans and Leighton (1989a), Connelly (1992), Boden (1996), Carr (1996), Caputo and Dolinsky (1998) and Wellington (2001).

10. See also Macpherson (1988), who reported a significant positive effect on the probability of self-employment among married American women from husbands' incomes.

11. Calculations made from the BHPS data-set by the present author revealed that females comprise only 16 per cent of the full-time, but 70 per cent of the part-time self-employed workforce in Britain.

12. See Macpherson (1988), Evans and Leighton (1989a), Devine (1994a), Bates (1995) and Carr (1996).

13. See also Macpherson (1988), who estimated (1.4) and reported negative selectivity for female employees, implying that their average earnings were less than what self-employed females could have obtained in paid-employment.

14. For contrary evidence that gender has an insignificant effect on business survival rates, see Kalleberg and Leicht (1991) and Brüderl and Preisendorfer (1998).

15. Note that we can alternatively write an analogous expression using $\hat{\beta}'_f$ in the first term of the RHS of (4.4). Since the choice is arbitrary, results based on this decomposition method should be quoted for both calculations.

16. Yuengert estimated that 55 per cent of the immigrant–native self-employment rate differential was attributable to immigrants having above-average home-country self-employment rates than the USA. However, other researchers have obtained contrary evidence. Evans (1989) found that immigrant Australian business owners who were employers were significantly more likely to have obtained labour market experience in the host country, and significantly less likely to have obtained it their home country. See also Fairlie and Meyer (1996).

17. It has been suggested that shifts in US immigration policy that have prioritised family issues have been responsible for a decline in immigrant 'quality', at least when measured in terms of employment earnings.

Part II

Financing entrepreneurial ventures

5   Debt finance for entrepreneurial ventures

Part I treated the factors that bear on the willingness of individuals to try entrepreneurship. In part II, we recognise that sometimes individuals have limited opportunities to become entrepreneurs, because of difficulties raising sufficient finance to purchase the working capital, marketing services, initial living expenses and other miscellaneous requirements needed to establish a business.

Most start-up finance in developed countries tends to be personal equity ('self-finance'), i.e. finance supplied by the entrepreneurs themselves. For example, according to the Bank of England (2001), 60 per cent of start-up businesses in Britain use self-finance. The remaining funds are raised from external sources. According to the Bank, about 60 per cent of external finance is raised through debt-finance contracts (comprising overdrafts and term loans) followed by asset-based finance (e.g. leasing: around 20 per cent). A similar picture applies in the USA, where banks also issue most debt finance. Also important is family finance, at around 10 per cent of external finance on average, whereas venture capital (equity finance) tends to play only a very minor role for most entrepreneurs (between 1 and 3 per cent). This chapter focuses on the implications for entrepreneurship of raising debt finance. Chapter 6 deals with various other sources of finance.

If lenders and entrepreneurs were both perfectly informed about all aspects of new entrepreneurial ventures, and if financial markets were flexible and competitive, then all ventures with positive net present value (npv) would be funded. Also, it would not matter if lenders or entrepreneurs undertook the ventures. However, this idealised scenario rarely obtains in practice. Many entrepreneurs complain that they are unable to obtain enough funding, or sometimes any funding at all, for what they believe are viable ventures. (These groups claim to be 'credit rationed'.) Another possibility is that imperfections in the capital market cause there to be too few, or too many, entrepreneurs in equilibrium, judged in terms of efficiency or social welfare.

The present chapter investigates these issues. Along the way, the role of collateral, loan sizes, lender–borrower relationships and group lending will also be discussed. We will leave aside topics such as what lenders and borrowers think about each other, what induces entrepreneurs to apply for loans and how entrepreneurs can write business plans to improve their chances of successfully obtaining a loan. These issues are covered in any number of texts within the Business and Management literature. For notational brevity, lenders will be referred to simply as 'banks' henceforth, and any new entrepreneurial investments, whether undertaken by incumbent entrepreneurs or new entrants, will be called 'ventures'.

This chapter emphasises the importance of asymmetric information for the debt finance of new ventures. Information is often asymmetric because while entrepreneurs may have accurate information about the quality of their risky proposed ventures and their ability and commitment to expedite them, banks often cannot perfectly distinguish the quality of loan applications from each other. Reasons include the lack of a track record for new ventures and prohibitive costs of acquiring reliable information about them. There is no equivalent institution to a credit rating agency for entrepreneurs; banks have to rely on their own imperfect screening devices. It will be assumed below that although banks can screen entrepreneurs into groups defined by some observable characteristics, there is invariably also some residual imperfect information that forces them to pool, at least initially, heterogeneous risk types together within each group.

There is now an extensive economic literature on the efficiency of debt financed ventures in general, and on credit rationing of entrepreneurs in particular. Credit rationing has also received considerable attention in policy circles, at least since the publication of influential reports by the Federal Reserve System (1958) in the USA, and the 'Bolton' and 'Wilson' reports (HMSO 1971, 1979) in the UK. These reports contended that there was a general shortage of financial capital to fund new start-ups and expand existing small businesses. The reports prompted the creation of government-backed loan guarantee schemes for small firms, described and evaluated in chapter 10, subsection 10.1.1. It is hard to assess the extent to which the views of these reports reflected rather old-fashioned conditions in banking and credit prior to the financial de-regulation of the 1980s and 1990s. For example, a subsequent UK government report (HMSO, 1991) concluded that 'small firms in Great Britain currently face few difficulties in raising finance for their innovation and investment proposals in the private sector' (1991, p. 17). In contrast, the SBA (1996) reiterated its concern that private capital markets still do not provide adequate start-up finance.

Credit rationing and under-investment are the subjects of section 5.1. We analyse the possible causes of these two phenomena, their effects on efficiency and the equilibrium number of entrepreneurs and the scope for corrective action by governments. We then present arguments against the phenomena, showing how agents can in principle write contracts to reveal the hidden information and so eliminate the market imperfection. We conclude the section by evaluating the theoretical case for credit rationing.[1] Section 5.2 discusses the possibility of over-investment, and section 5.3 treats the class of general models that generate multiple sources of inefficiency. Section 5.4 concludes.

5.1 Models of credit rationing and under-investment

We commence with definitions of the salient concepts discussed in this chapter.

Definition 7 (Type I credit rationing). *Type I credit rationing occurs when some or all loan applicants receive a smaller loan than they desire at the quoted interest rate.*

Definition 8 (Type II credit rationing). *Type II credit rationing occurs when some randomly selected loan applicants are denied a loan altogether despite being observationally identical to applicants who receive one, and despite being willing to borrow on precisely the same terms; and when banks have such rationing as an equilibrium and optimal policy.*

Definition 9 (Redlining). *Redlining occurs when a bank refuses to lend to a loan applicant because the bank cannot obtain its required return at any interest rate.*

Definition 10 (Under-investment). *Under-investment occurs when some socially efficient ventures (i.e. ventures whose expected value is no less than that obtained from employing its resources in their best alternative use) are not undertaken.*

Definition 11 (Over-investment). *Over-investment occurs when some socially inefficient ventures are undertaken.*

The credit rationing typology above follows Keeton (1979). In the case of Type II rationing, a rationed borrower might offer to pay a higher interest rate in order to obtain funds; but the last clause of the definition indicates that this cannot break the rationing outcome.[2] For both Types, the interesting manifestations analysed below are 'equilibrium' rationing outcomes. In contrast, 'temporary' credit rationing is caused by transient imbalances between the demand for and supply of loans. This case is

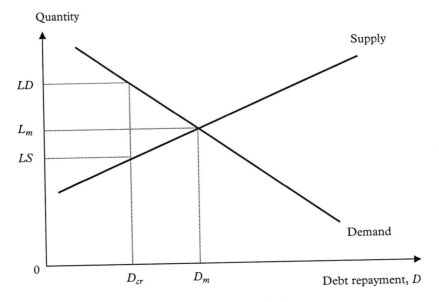

Figure 5.1   The supply of and demand for loans

of less interest because such imbalances will eventually be eliminated as markets adjust towards equilibrium. Neither temporary credit rationing, nor equilibrium credit rationing caused by governments fixing interest rates below market-clearing levels by diktat (e.g. usury laws), will be discussed below. The latter 'beg the question of what basic forces lead to observed loan market institutions' (Jaffee and Russell, 1976, p. 651); and they are also of limited relevance in most deregulated modern economies.

Figure 5.1 illustrates both types of credit rationing. The interest repayment D_m would clear the market for credit, but the actual interest rate is stuck at $D_{cr} < D_m$, with an excess demand for funds of $LD - LS$. In the case of Type I rationing, LS is the offered loan size *for an individual*: LD is the desired loan size. In the case of Type II rationing, LS is the *number of entrepreneurs* who obtain a loan: LD is the number of loan applicants. Reasons why the interest rate may not rise above D_{cr} to D_m to eliminate rationing are explored for each of the two cases below.

5.1.1   Type I credit rationing

Models of Type I credit rationing have a long pedigree (see Baltensperger, 1978, for a survey of the early literature). We briefly summarise and critique some of the best-known ones:

1. Banks charge a single interest rate to heterogeneous borrowers (Jaffee and Modigliani, 1969). Then entrepreneurs with ventures embodying above-average risk must receive smaller loans than they desire (see also Cukierman, 1978). However, it is unclear what constrains banks to charge only one interest rate. If banks were free to charge any interest rate, then competition would force them to charge different rates for different entrepreneurial types, to reflect their different risk profiles. Even if for some reason they were unable to charge different rates, presumably non-interest loan terms would be a cheap alternative way of separating heterogeneous borrower types (Baltensperger, 1978).

2. Bankruptcy costs (Barro, 1976; Jaffee and Russell, 1976). In Barro's model, entrepreneurs post collateral, which they are willing to forfeit in default states if it is less than the value of their debt repayments. But bankruptcy costs mean that banks can recover only a fraction of defaulting entrepreneurs' collateral. Higher loan sizes increase the incentive for entrepreneurs to 'take the money and run', which eventually generates such high bankruptcy costs that banks have to place a ceiling on loan sizes to break even (see also Keeton, 1979; Koskela, 1983; and Gale and Hellwig, 1985).

   In Jaffee and Russell's (1976) model, entrepreneurs do not post collateral but suffer some fixed personal penalty (guilt, perhaps) of defaulting opportunistically. An entrepreneur defaults if the debt repayment exceeds their default penalty. Because greater loan sizes involve greater mandated repayments they are also associated with more defaults. Competition among banks forces the loan size below entrepreneurs' desired levels, since this reduces the interest rate they must charge to break even, while reducing the number of defaults. Hence the competitive equilibrium is characterised by Type I rationing of all borrowers – which, moreover, is sufficiently severe that in equilibrium no-one defaults.[3] This no-default outcome appears unrealistic. Also, it is troubling that a stable market equilibrium does not actually exist in this model (Besanko and Thakor, 1987a). Furthermore, Milde and Riley (1988) pointed out that the term 'rationing' might be a misnomer in the Jaffee–Russell model. Rationing occurs when the demand for a product *of given quality* exceeds supply; that is not the case in Jaffee–Russell, where the risk characteristics of ventures vary with the loan size.[4]

3. An implicit contract under which risk-neutral banks effectively insure risk-averse entrepreneurs by replacing an exogenously fluctuating (and hence risky) spot interest rate with a fixed rate that is higher than the average spot rate (Fried and Howitt, 1980). The absence of market clearing can result in some entrepreneurs not obtaining their desired loan, a

result that is robust to the case where banks as well as entrepreneurs are risk averse (Olekalns and Sibly, 1992). However, as in other implicit contract models there is always an incentive for one party to break the contract, ruling out implicit contracts in competitive equilibrium.

4. Uncertainty (Clemenz, 1986, sec. 5.3). If venture returns are an increasing function of loan size then entrepreneurs' profit is a convex function of loan size, since debt repayments are fixed and entrepreneurs' losses are bounded in bad states of nature. Greater uncertainty increases the requested loan size, as entrepreneurs seek to gain from the upside of managing larger ventures without taking account of the increase in downside risk borne by the banks. Anticipating this, banks limit their losses by capping loan sizes (see also de Meza and Webb, 1992; Bernhardt, 2000).

5. Type I credit rationing can facilitate efficient contracting under asymmetric information (Besanko and Thakor, 1987b; Milde and Riley, 1988). This idea is explained in subsection 5.1.3.

6. Monitoring costs (Gray and Wu, 1995). The logic here is the same as for the Barro (1976) model described above.

There are several reasons why Type I rationing has received less attention in the literature and among policy makers than Type II rationing. First, Type I rationing arguably does not capture the sharpest form of credit rationing. That is given by Type II rationing, where loans are refused altogether. Second, in most models of Type I rationing all borrowers obtain an efficient amount of funds and can still set up in business – so it is not clear that it is in any sense a 'problem' to be addressed. Third, the Type I rationing outcome is not robust. It is straightforward to create models in which borrowers receive *larger* loans than they would like – the opposite of Type I rationing. This could occur, for example, if banks' administrative costs depend on the number of loans made rather than the size of loans. Then cost minimisation under competitive conditions obliges banks to make a few large loans rather than many small ones, yielding the required result.

5.1.2   Type II credit rationing and under-investment

Several rather unconvincing reasons have been proposed purporting to explain why banks might practice Type II credit rationing. First, banks might be too risk averse to find risky lending worthwhile (Jaffee and Stiglitz, 1990). However, this argument is implausible because banks can usually spread their risks over numerous customers, so that risk neutrality is probably a better assumption about banks' preferences. Second, banks might ration some loan applicants in order to economise on information processing costs that might occur, for example, if applicants can approach more than one bank (Thakor and Calloway, 1983; Thakor, 1996). Third, banks might identify particular loan applicants as inherently dishonest and almost certain to 'take the money and run'. Banks would then deny credit outright to these borrowers. Fourth, starry-eyed entrepreneurs might be over-optimistic about the prospects of their venture (see chapter 3, subsection 3.2.3), and claim to be rationed by objective banks that refuse a loan because they would not expect to break even on these ventures at any interest rate.[5] But these last two outcomes resemble redlining more than credit rationing.

More interesting, and arguably more plausible, models of Type II credit rationing are based on asymmetric information about the value of new ventures. These models assume that individuals with new investment ventures are heterogeneous in a manner which (a) impacts on banks' expected returns, and (b) is private information to themselves and hidden from banks. Individuals who are 'good risks' from the banks' viewpoint cannot credibly signal their 'type' because 'bad risks' always possess the incentive to untruthfully emulate them. As stated in the introduction to the chapter, it is assumed below that the imperfect information is residual in the sense that bank screening has already been performed. It is important to be clear about this point, since its oversight has sometimes generated confusion (see, e.g., Stiglitz and Weiss', 1987, response to Riley, 1987).

It is helpful to set out the assumptions used in most of these models. Exceptions will be noted in the text below as and when they arise.

A1. Entrepreneurs are heterogeneous; banks do not observe individual entrepreneurs' types but do observe the frequency distribution of types.

A2. All banks and entrepreneurs are risk neutral, i.e. each maximises expected profits.[6]

A3. All banks are identical and competitive, making zero profits. This is a convenient simplification because it ensures that there is neither entry into nor exit from the capital market. Notice that this assumption does not necessitate a countable infinity of banks: Bertrand duopolists who compete on price (i.e. the interest rate) also generate the competitive outcome.

A4. Entrepreneurs undertake only one venture, into which they plough all their wealth B, and which requires a single unit of capital that is borrowed from a bank.

A5. There is a single period and a stochastic venture return R, which can take one of two outcomes at the end of the period: R^s in the success state, or R^f in the failure state. $R^s > D > R^f \geq 0$, where $D = 1 + r$ is the mandated debt repayment, and r is the risky interest rate.

A6. Banks obtain funds from depositors, who are rewarded with a safe (and endogenously determined) gross deposit rate, ρ, where $1 < \rho < D$. The supply of deposits (from outside investors) is an increasing function of ρ. Banks therefore compete in both the deposit and loans markets.

A7. There is a standard debt contract, which specifies a fixed repayment (henceforth called the gross interest rate, or simply the interest rate) of D in non-bankruptcy states and requires the entrepreneur to declare bankruptcy if this payment cannot be met. Banks seize R^f in its entirety in the bankruptcy state. Banks observe venture outcomes perfectly if they monitor *ex post* returns. Banks optimally monitor all and only defaulters, so there is no incentive for entrepreneurs to default ('take the money and run') unless the outcome is R^f.[7]

A8. Entrepreneurs get:[8]

$$\max\{R - D, -B\}. \tag{5.1}$$

A9. Individuals can choose between entrepreneurship (in which they obtain the uncertain return (5.1)), and safe investment.

A10. All prices are perfectly flexible and all agents optimise.

The Stiglitz–Weiss model

The most influential model of Type II credit rationing is that of Stiglitz and Weiss (1981) (hereafter, SW). SW considered a set of ventures with the same *expected* return, but heterogeneous risk, described by a parameter θ. Denote the density and distribution functions of returns by $f(R, \theta)$ and $F(R, \theta)$, respectively, where a greater θ corresponds to greater risk in the sense that this distribution is a mean-preserving spread of one with a lower θ (see Definition 5 in chapter 2). Each entrepreneur operates a venture with a unique θ, which they know but banks do not. Denote the density and distribution functions of $\theta \in \Theta$ by $g(\theta)$ and $G(\theta)$, respectively, defined on the support $[0, \infty)$, where Θ is the set of entrepreneur (venture) types. Assume $R^f = 0$ for simplicity. Banks are unable to separate heterogeneous borrowers into type-specific contracts, so they are obliged to pool them together.

Given some interest rate D, define $\tilde{\theta} = \tilde{\theta}(D)$ as the marginal venture, in the sense that it makes zero expected profits for entrepreneurs:

$$\pi(D, \tilde{\theta}) := \int_0^\infty \max\{R - D, -B\} \, dF(R, \tilde{\theta}) = 0. \tag{5.2}$$

Because entrepreneurs' expected profits are an increasing and convex function of R, high-θ types have a greater chance than low-θ types of receiving high returns, while limited liability protects the downside if they fail. That is, $\partial \pi(D, \tilde{\theta})/\partial \tilde{\theta} > 0$. Hence only those with $\theta \geq \tilde{\theta}$ will choose to undertake ventures; the rest eschew entrepreneurship. Differentiate (5.2) to obtain

$$\frac{d\tilde{\theta}}{dD} = \frac{\int_{D-B}^{\infty} dF(R, \tilde{\theta})}{\partial \pi(D, \tilde{\theta})/\partial \tilde{\theta}} > 0. \tag{5.3}$$

Thus as the interest rate is increased, the marginal venture becomes riskier, generating *adverse selection*. That is, a higher interest rate causes the entrepreneurial pool to be dominated by risky ventures.[9] The expected return to a bank is therefore a decreasing function of θ, since the bank gets $R^f = 0$ and hence makes a loss on a venture if it fails; and the incidence of failures increases as $\tilde{\theta}$ increases. This can be seen by writing banks' expected portfolio rate of return from lending at D as

$$\overline{\rho}(D) = \frac{\int_{\tilde{\theta}(D)}^{\infty} \rho(\theta, D) \, dG(\theta)}{1 - G(\tilde{\theta})}, \tag{5.4}$$

where $\rho(\theta, D) = D[1 - F(D - B, \theta)] < D$ is the expected rate of return to a venture characterised by (D, θ) given $R^f = 0$.[10] Write $\tilde{\rho} := \rho(\tilde{\theta}, D) > \overline{\rho} \equiv \overline{\rho}(D)$ and differentiate (5.4) to obtain

$$\frac{d\overline{\rho}}{dD} = -\frac{g(\tilde{\theta})}{1 - G(\tilde{\theta})}(\tilde{\rho} - \overline{\rho})\frac{d\tilde{\theta}}{dD} + \frac{\int_{\tilde{\theta}}^{\infty}[1 - F(D - B, \theta)] \, dG(\theta)}{1 - G(\tilde{\theta})}. \tag{5.5}$$

D has two effects on banks' expected portfolio rate of return. The second term of (5.5) is positive, capturing the positive effect of a higher interest rate on bank expected returns. But the first term is negative (by (5.3)), capturing an adverse selection effect. That is, a greater interest repayment increases the risk of banks' portfolios, leading to lower expected bank returns. If the first term outweighs the second, banks' expected returns $\overline{\rho}$ may eventually become a decreasing function of the interest rate D, as the pool of entrepreneurial ventures becomes dominated by risky types. This is illustrated in figure 5.2(a), where D_{cr}, termed the 'bank optimal' interest rate, is the rate that maximises bank expected profits and which therefore holds under competition.[11] In this case, by assumption A6 the supply of funds also becomes a decreasing function of D. This is illustrated in figure 5.2(b), which shows how credit rationing can occur if there is a 'high demand' for funds, and if $D_{cr} < D_m$, where D_m is the 'market-clearing' interest rate. Here banks deny credit to $L_1 - L^*$

Banks' expected portfolio rate of return, $\bar{\rho}$

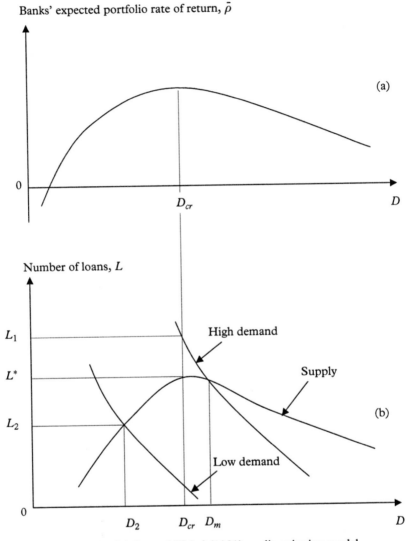

Figure 5.2 Stiglitz and Weiss' (1981) credit rationing model
(a) Banks' expected returns
(b) The market for returns

randomly chosen borrowers who are observationally indistinguishable from those who do receive loans. However, if there is a 'low demand' for funds, the market clears at (L_2, D_2) and credit rationing cannot occur.

A similar result can be obtained in a different model where all entrepreneurs are identical but can choose between a set of ventures that all offer the same expected return, yet which differ in terms of their risk. Then *moral hazard* may occur: entrepreneurs respond to an increase in the interest rate by choosing riskier ventures. Then, as in the adverse selection problem, banks' expected return function $\bar{\rho}$ may begin to decrease in D, yielding a bank-optimal interest rate $D_{cr} < D_m$. As before, banks may optimally ration credit rather than increase the interest rate to eliminate an excess demand for loanable funds.

Credit rationing is not the only possible market failure in SW's model. De Meza and Webb (1987, Proposition 5(A)) also showed that, irrespective of whether or not credit rationing occurs, there is bound to be under-investment in entrepreneurial ventures in SW's model as long as the supply of deposits is non-decreasing in ρ (as assumed in assumption A6). Thus there will be too few entrepreneurs for the social good, a problem exacerbated if credit rationing exists.[12] A subsidy on interest income can be recommended because it would increase both the equilibrium number of entrepreneurs and social efficiency.

A second source of possible market failure in SW's model is redlining.[13] To see this, suppose for expositional clarity that banks can distinguish between three distinct groups of entrepreneurs. The groups are indexed by θ, where θ can be good (g), bad (b) and 'OK' (o). Each group has an interior bank optimal interest rate, denoted by D_θ, and an expected return function $\rho_\theta(D)$. Let ρ^* denote the deposit rate, which must be unique in a competitive deposit market. As figure 5.3 shows, group g will be fully served, and so will some members of the marginal group o; but a group b generating returns of $\rho_b(D_b) < \rho^*$ cannot make a sufficient return to enable banks to compensate depositors *at any interest rate*. Hence *no member* of group b will obtain funds, even though these ventures may have above-average expected *social* returns. This group is redlined. The only solution to redlining is to somehow induce an outward shift in the supply of funds schedule, since that reduces ρ^*. One possibility is universal government lending (Ordover and Weiss, 1981). However, it does not necessarily follow that such a policy would be welfare-enhancing.

Although it has had an immense impact on the literature, SW's model is not immune from criticism. One problem is that SW assumed, rather than derived, debt to be optimal form of finance. Subsequent authors (Cho, 1986; de Meza and Webb, 1987) showed that equity is actually the optimal form of finance in the SW model. Furthermore, if all ventures are financed by equity, SW's competitive equilibrium is first best, without any credit rationing; and banks optimally randomise rather than fix interest rates as SW assumed (de Meza, 2002). It is therefore necessary to appeal to some factor outside the model that favours debt over equity finance if SW's results are to remain relevant in a strict sense. That could entail,

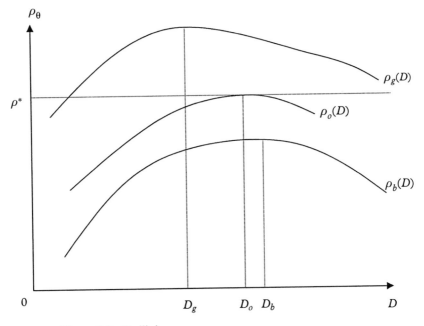

Figure 5.3 Redlining

for example, high costs of writing equity contracts. A second criticism of SW is that banks are assumed not to make use of other instruments that convey information about types. The interest rate does not work efficiently because of its indirect effects on the quality of loans; but other loan terms exist (such as collateral) that might circumvent the problem. This possibility is explored in subsection 5.1.3.

Other models of Type II credit rationing

Several other models have also generated Type II credit rationing outcomes by suggesting different ways of obtaining interior 'bank-optimal' interest rates that are lower than market-clearing ones. We list some interesting examples below:

1. Costly effort by entrepreneurs creates a 'hidden action' moral hazard problem (Watson, 1984). Entrepreneurs expend effort e on their ventures, which is unobserved by banks, at personal cost $c(e)$, where $c(\cdot)$ is a convex and increasing function. Generalise assumption A5 so that venture returns are now outcomes of a continuous random variable R. The distribution function of returns is $F(R, e)$: higher e implies higher

returns, so $F_e := \partial F/\partial e < 0$. Entrepreneurs repay D if $R > D$, otherwise they default and the bank seizes the outcome of R. Bank expected profits per loan at interest rate D (given effort e) is

$$\pi^B(D) = D[1 - F(D, e)] + \int_0^D R\, dF(R, e), \qquad (5.6)$$

which is increasing in e. Entrepreneurs choose

$$e^* = \operatorname{argmax} \left\{ \pi(D, e) = \int_D^\infty R\, dF(R, e) - D[1 - F(D, e)] - c(e) \right\},$$

from which it can be easily shown that $de^*/dD < 0$. Thus if the interest rate rises sufficiently, borrowers reduce effort. By (5.6), this may reduce banks' expected profits such that an interior bank-optimal interest rate $D_{cr} < D_m$ may emerge.

2. Free *ex post* observation of venture returns by entrepreneurs creates a 'hidden information' moral hazard problem (Williamson, 1986, 1987). Williamson assumed a continuum of venture return outcomes, $R \in [0, R_{max}]$. Unlike SW's model, entrepreneurs are assumed to enjoy no information advantage over banks about possible venture outcomes *ex ante*: both agents know only the density and distribution functions of returns $f(R)$ and $F(R)$. But unlike banks, entrepreneurs enjoy the advantage of costlessly observing the *ex post* outcome of R. In the usual way, banks optimally monitor *ex post* all and only ventures that declare default. Monitoring is assumed to cost $c > 0$ per loan but is perfectly effective. Bank expected profits are:

$$\pi^B(D) = \int_0^D R\, dF(R) + D[1 - F(D)] - cF(D). \qquad (5.7)$$

Differentiate (5.7) to obtain

$$\frac{\partial \pi^B(D)}{\partial D} = 1 - F(D) - cf(D).$$

Because $f(R) > 0 \,\forall R \in [0, R_{max}]$, it follows that $\{\partial \pi^B(D)/\partial D\}|_{D=R_{max}} < 0$. But if $c < 1/f(0)$, this implies that $\pi^B(D)$ reaches a maximum for $D < R_{max}$, which in turn implies a bank-optimal interest rate.[14]

Interestingly, Hillier and Worrall (1994) showed that in this model an excessive amount of monitoring is performed in equilibrium; the optimal policy response is to reduce monitoring by reducing the amount of lending. Hillier and Worrall considered several actual policies that could achieve this – including introducing credit rationing! However, Xu (2000) subsequently showed that this result is overturned if monitoring costs are endogenously determined.

3. In an adaptation of the Jaffee–Russell (1976) model discussed earlier, 'honest' entrepreneurs who resist the temptation to default opportunistically are the first to quit the loans market when the interest rate increases (Clemenz, 1986). This adverse selection may decrease the bank's expected profits such that an interior bank-optimal interest rate may emerge.

4. Type II credit rationing can facilitate efficient financial contracting under asymmetric information (Besanko and Thakor, 1987a). This idea is explained in subsection 5.1.3.

This is not meant to be an exhaustive list of models that generate Type II credit rationing. In fact, some additional ones, discussed in section 5.3, generate multiple sources of inefficiency, including the possibility of credit rationing. The fact that Type II credit rationing can be generated in a variety of ways might be taken as a sign of theoretical robustness. However, it should be stressed that credit rationing outcomes are not *bound* to occur even in these models. That is, there are plenty of sufficient but no necessary conditions for credit rationing to exist. For example, if adverse selection or moral hazard effects are very weak, then bank expected return functions will not deviate sufficiently from a monotonic increasing function to permit an interior bank optimal interest rate to arise. And, as we saw above, if there is a limited demand for funds, credit rationing might not occur even if there *is* a bank-optimal interest rate.

5.1.3   Arguments against the credit rationing hypothesis

The models outlined in the previous subsection are far from the only ones that treat the relationship between entrepreneurs and banks. It is a straightforward matter to propose plausible alternatives that generate only market-clearing outcomes (e.g. de Meza and Webb, 1987). Also, there are grounds for questioning how widespread credit rationing can be in practice when sources of finance other than debt contracts (e.g. trade credit, equity finance and leasing) are available. The argument in this subsection is that the theoretical case for credit rationing is not unassailable.

Below we describe a direct attack on the credit rationing hypothesis based on the idea that rationing can be eliminated by writing more sophisticated financial contracts that reveal the hidden information on which it depends. The key concept here is that agents have incentives to devise contracts that break equilibria in which good and bad risks are pooled together ('pooling equilibria'), replacing them with equilibria in which good credit risks separate themselves from bad risks and thereby obtain a lower interest rate ('separating equilibria'). For expositional ease, much of the discussion will work with just two entrepreneurial types, a good type g and a bad type b. The precise aspects that make them 'good' or 'bad'

Debt repayment, *D*

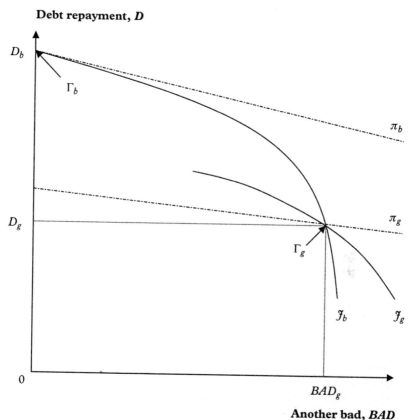

Another bad, *BAD*

Figure 5.4 The use of two-term contracts to separate hidden types

are unimportant here; it suffices merely to think of *g* being less prone to default than *b*. The population shares of the two types will be assumed fixed and known; it is the identities of each individual that cannot be observed by banks.

Consider figure 5.4 for the case of borrowers *b* and *g* and two contract terms: the gross interest rate, *D*, and another 'bad' (from borrowers' perspective), denoted *BAD*. It might help fix ideas to think of collateral posted by entrepreneurs at the bank's request as an example of *BAD*. Indifference curves $\mathcal{J}_b$ and $\mathcal{J}_g$ in (*D*, *BAD*) space show how the different borrowers are prepared to trade off one bad for another. Indifference curves closer to the origin are associated with higher borrower utility. The key point is that the different borrowers have differently sloped indifference curves. Good borrower types *g* have flatter indifference curves than bad types *b* because they are more likely to succeed and have to repay the bank D – and hence are more willing to endure more of BAD (e.g. risking more collateral) in return for a lower D. Conversely, bs are less willing to incur the cost of more BAD in return for a lower D because they are more likely to default and thereby avoid repaying D.[15] Crucially, if $\mathcal{J}_b$ and $\mathcal{J}_g$ cross only once (the so-called 'single-crossing property'), then contracts $\Gamma_b = (D_b, 0)$ and $\Gamma_g = (D_g, BAD_g)$ separate types and are consistent with banks' iso-profit lines π_b and π_g. That is, g would prefer a contract (D, BAD), just to the right of Γ_g along π_g, in preference to Γ_b; but b would prefer Γ_b to that contract. Hence if banks offer these two contracts – and under competition they *must* offer these contracts[16] – then each borrower type will self-select into the one that maximises their utility, so revealing their type. This equilibrium is incentive-compatible: each type does best under the contract that reveals their type. Masquerading as a different type will result in a lower payoff and so will not be chosen.

What this shows is that, in principle a richer contract than one based on interest rates alone can separate types. Type separation removes all information asymmetries and hence the possibility that asymmetric information-induced credit rationing can occur. This analysis readily generalises to more than two types. For example, with three types, three different (D, BAD) contracts can be offered that accomplish separation. However, with two or more dimensions of unobserved borrower heterogeneity, more than two *contract terms* are needed to separate types. For example, with two dimensions of heterogeneity (e.g. different entrepreneurial abilities and different venture risks), contracts might need to specify an interest rate, collateral, and a suboptimal loan size, say. But the principle remains essentially unchanged. In the limit, one can imagine banks enriching the menu of contracts with as many contract terms as it takes to reveal all the hidden information. In practice, of course, the environment may be too complicated for banks to effectively sort out the heterogeneous types – or they may run out of effective instruments. If so, some asymmetric information will remain, so the pooling of at least some types with the possibility of credit rationing is restored. But clearly, banks and the ablest entrepreneurs have incentives to search for new contract terms to reduce the occurrence of pooling, the former because of the dictates of competition, and the latter out of self-interest.

Several examples of BADs have been suggested in the literature:

- *Collateral.*[17] Collateral is an asset belonging to a borrower that can be seized by a bank if the borrower defaults. Unlike large established firms that can pledge company assets ('inside collateral'), most entrepreneurs can pledge only their own assets ('outside collateral'), typically their house. Most models of debt finance assume that banks automatically capture inside assets in the case of default, so their explicit analyses of collateral tend to be of the outside sort.

Collateral is widespread. Berger and Udell (1990) reported that nearly 70 per cent of all commercial and industrial loans in the USA are made on a secured basis, while Cressy (1993) found that 95 per cent of UK business overdrafts in excess of £20,000 were fully collateralised. However, collateral serves several possible purposes, not just as a screening device, as described above. It can also help persuade sceptical banks about the worth of ventures (Chan and Kanatos, 1985), and can encourage entrepreneurs to supply optimal effort (Boot, Thakor and Udell, 1991) or to operate a safer venture (Stiglitz and Weiss, 1992). In addition, it enables entrepreneurs to make credible promises about repayment (Hart and Moore, 1994, 1998; Hart, 1995), and enables banks to profitably re-negotiate debt when borrowers default (Bester, 1994).[18]

- *Unlimited liability.* Chamley (1983) explored a model in which individuals are risk averse (so relaxing assumption A2) and can choose between limited and unlimited liability debt contracts. Under symmetric information, risk-averse entrepreneurs would prefer limited liability because it provides insurance. But under asymmetric information high-ability entrepreneurs might be prepared to endure the *BAD* of unlimited liability in order to signal their higher ability to banks. These entrepreneurs obtain a lower interest rate to reflect their lower-venture risk, and so a partially separating equilibrium like the one in figure 5.4 can arise. If entrepreneurial ability was fairly homogeneous, the interest rate advantage might be insufficiently attractive, and every entrepreneur would choose limited liability. But in principle, a continuum of contracts specifying varying degrees of limited liability could be devised to perfectly separate all types and reveal the entire distribution of entrepreneurial abilities to banks.

- *A high initial interest rate in a multi-period setting* (Webb, 1991; Boot and Thakor, 1994). Webb (1991) proposed a two-period model in which higher ability translates into a higher probability of the venture being successful. Webb showed that even a single observation of entrepreneurs' performances provides information that can help banks separate types. Consider the following two contracts, whose arguments specify interest rates for the initial and subsequent periods, respectively: $\Gamma_1 = (D_0, D_0)$ and $\Gamma_2 = (D_1, (D_2|s_1)$ or $(D_0|f_1))$, where $(D_2|s_1) < D_0 < D_1$, and where $D_2|s_1$ and $D_0|f_1$, respectively, denote D_2 conditional on venture success in period 1 (s_1), and D_0 conditional on venture failure in period 1 (f_1). Webb showed that this set of contracts is sufficient to induce sorting of types, with gs choosing Γ_2 and bs choosing Γ_1.[19] The logic is that only gs are willing to pay a high first-period interest rate D_1. This is because unlike bs, the gs are genuinely confident about their chances of succeeding in the next period and so obtaining the low repayment D_2.

- *Joint liability under group lending* (Ghatak and Guinnane, 1999; Ghatak, 2000; Laffont and N'Guessan, 2000). Banks lend to groups of individuals who are made jointly liable for repayment. All group members are treated as being in default if any one member of the group does not repay their loan: the BAD is the default penalty levied on the group. Types match together in pairs because although both types prefer to match with gs, the joint benefits of so doing are greater for gs because they are more likely to succeed. Unlike bad types b, good types g are willing to accept a high BAD in return for low D. Thus joint liability acts like collateral even when borrowers lack 'formal' financial collateral.[20]

- *A sub-optimal loan size* (Bester, 1985b; Besanko and Thakor, 1987b; Milde and Riley, 1988; Innes, 1991, 1992; Schmidt-Mohr, 1997). Good types are more willing to waste resources by requesting inefficiently large (or small) loan sizes in order to signal their type.

5.1.4   Conclusion: evaluating the theoretical case for credit rationing

Proponents of credit rationing have responded to the objection that financial contracting can eliminate the pooling equilibria on which credit rationing depends by making the following observations:

1. Screening cannot work if extra contract terms are unavailable. For example, specifying BAD as collateral will be ineffective if borrowers have insufficient collateralisable wealth. Then pooling and credit rationing can emerge again. This may be an important point because it is known, for example that lack of collateral is one of the major reasons that banks refer borrowers to the UK's loan guarantee scheme.[21]

2. BAD contract terms might not be monotonically related to preferences, violating the single-crossing property underlying figure 5.4. Examples are plentiful. A simple one is if borrowers differ in their initial wealth and the richest are the least risk averse, since then both those with the safest (i.e. the rich) and those with the riskiest (i.e. the poor) ventures will offer collateral, muddying the signal (Stiglitz and Weiss, 1981; see also Stiglitz and Weiss, 1992, for another example). Collateral cannot effectively separate different types and the possibility of credit rationing emerges again.

3. If there is imperfect competition on the supply side of the market, banks can maximise surplus by means of pooling, rather than separating, contracts (Besanko and Thakor, 1987a).

4. If the number of high-risk types b is not too numerous, the benefits of screening different types might not compensate for the deadweight

costs of realising collateral. Banks can do better by offering pooling contracts than separating contracts, and the scope for collateral to serve as a screen disappears again (Mattesini, 1990).

5. Whether separating or pooling equilibria emerge also depends on the assumed nature of the game between entrepreneurs and banks, especially the timing of the moves of the game, and the definition of competitive equilibrium (Hellwig, 1987).

Even without running into these problems, it is possible to suggest credit rationing itself as a *BAD* that separates types! (Besanko and Thakor, 1987a; Smith and Stutzer, 1989; Gale, 1990a). Suppose entrepreneurs have no collateral, and that *BAD* is the probability that banks randomly ration borrowers. Then *g*s are willing to take the risk of being rationed in return for a lower interest rate, whereas *b*s care less about a lower interest rate and more about receiving a loan. In effect, credit rationing is the price that *g*s must pay to signal their types. However, this argument seems unrealistic. At the very least it is counter-intuitive that good risks are rationed, while bad risks are fully funded.[22]

In summary, a rich profusion of theoretical possibilities exists, enabling credit rationing to emerge in a number of different ways. To some extent, any effort to complicate contracts by opponents of credit rationing can be countered by the introduction of new dimensions of unobservable borrower heterogeneity by supporters of credit rationing. It would be desirable to take data to the various models to narrow the field of theoretical possibilities by discarding some models in favour of others. However, little progress on this front has been made to date. One obstacle is probably the maintained assumption that borrower and venture types are unobservable – which requires the researcher to obtain data on characteristics that are unobserved to banks. This point is important but is often overlooked. For example, consider the now pretty well-established evidence of a positive relationship between venture risk and collateral.[23] It might be thought that this refutes the screening model, which predicts that less risky types pledge more collateral than more risky types (recall figure 5.4). But that model assumes that screening based on observable characteristics *has already taken place*. In contrast, the above evidence relates to a pool of ventures with heterogeneous observable characteristics, in which the observably riskiest have to post the most collateral. Therefore this does not rule out the possibility that collateral does vary within observable groups in a manner consistent with the screening models. To convincingly reject the screening model, evidence would be needed of a positive correlation between risk and collateral among ventures that were *observably identical to banks*.

Regarding the criticisms of the credit rationing hypothesis based on efficient financial contracting, it is noteworthy that the available evidence suggests that actual lending rates are *not* explained by loan success (Cressy and Toïvanen, 1997). Also, banks do not appear to charge very different interest rates to even observably heterogeneous ventures.[24] This might be indicative of pooling in credit markets, in contrast to the separation implied by efficient contracting. Strictly speaking, however, that conclusion does not follow unless *every* loan term, not just the interest rate, is unrelated to loan success.[25]

It is certainly the case that credit rationing models are sensitive to changes in their assumptions. Some researchers apparently believe that this casts doubt on the relevance of the phenomenon (e.g. Hillier and Ibrahimo, 1993). On the other hand, as Clemenz (1986) has argued, it is very unlikely that necessary conditions for credit rationing can be found in any model that remains sufficiently general to be interesting. Furthermore, the number of possible mechanisms by which credit rationing can arise can perhaps be regarded as a strength not a weakness of the credit rationing hypothesis, because it expands the set of circumstances under which such rationing may occur. Elsewhere (Parker, 2002b), we concluded that the present state of the literature on credit rationing demonstrates the following points. (1) The *possibility* of credit rationing cannot be generally ruled out. (2) Credit rationing can emerge in a wide variety of lending environments. And (3) credit rationing models can invariably be generalised to include features that remove it. Further theoretical refinements of existing models are unlikely to change any of these points. Instead, the need is for empirical research to address directly the question of whether credit rationing exists, and if so, to what extent. This issue will be taken up in chapter 7.

5.2   Over-investment

Implicit in the models discussed so far is a presumption that financing problems are generally associated with too little entrepreneurship. This makes the contribution of de Meza and Webb (1987) (hereafter DW) especially interesting, because these authors proposed a model in which the opposite occurs: too much entrepreneurship.

DW utilised several similar assumptions to SW, including the pooling of heterogeneous types with a single contract. The main difference is the assumed structure of returns. DW assumed a continuum of entrepreneurs who differ by managerial ability, $\theta \equiv x$, where a greater ability x is associated with a greater *probability* that the venture succeeds, $p(x)$.[26] Ability is exogenous and unidimensional, with distribution function $G(x)$. As in SW, assume that the return in the failure state is $R^f = 0$. Each entrepreneur must invest all of their personal wealth B in the project to avoid transmitting an adverse signal about their type.[27] We can assume that this still leaves one unit of capital to be borrowed.

Now x chooses entrepreneurship if

$$p(x)(R^s - D) \geq \rho B, \tag{5.8}$$

i.e. otherwise they invest their assets B safely, ending with ρB. The marginal entrepreneur, for whom (5.8) holds with equality, is denoted by $\tilde{x}$. By inspection, a total of $1 - \hat{G}(\tilde{x})$ higher-ability individuals choose entrepreneurship. Importantly, the marginal entrepreneur $\tilde{x}$ is of low ability relative to other entrepreneurs. Denote the average success probability of entrepreneurs by $\bar{p}$, so $\bar{p} > p(\tilde{x})$ and $\bar{p}D > p(\tilde{x})D$.

Depositors receive a gross return ρ per dollar loaned, given by

$$\rho = \frac{D}{1 - \hat{G}(\tilde{x})} \int_{\tilde{x}}^{\infty} p(x) \, dG(x). \tag{5.9}$$

Social efficiency requires that all and only ventures are undertaken that satisfy the condition $p(x)R^s \geq \rho B$.

DW proved the following results:

1. A credit market equilibrium must be market clearing: there can be no credit rationing.[28]
2. In the competitive equilibrium more ventures are undertaken than is socially efficient.[29] This is DW's 'over-investment' result: resources would be more efficiently deployed if the least able entrepreneurs cancelled their ventures and became safe investors instead. The reason this does not happen is because under imperfect information the least able are cross-subsidised by the more able, who consequently find it privately worthwhile to undertake ventures that are socially inefficient.[30] DW went on to show that a tax on interest income could restore the economy to full efficiency. The rationale is that a higher tax increases the equilibrium interest rate and hence induces the least able entrepreneurs to exit. In subsequent papers, this policy was shown to be robust to the introduction of costly screening (de Meza and Webb, 1988); variable venture sizes (de Meza and Webb, 1989); and the addition of *ex ante* moral hazard à là SW (de Meza and Webb, 1999).
3. All entrepreneurs provide maximum self-finance and (if $R^f > 0$) debt is the optimal form of finance.[31]

The policy implications of the DW model are clear-cut. Subsidising credit reduces efficiency, a conclusion that is strengthened if there are agency and deadweight costs involved with such subsidies and if potential entrepreneurs are prone to unrealistic optimism (de Meza, 2002). Instead, the appropriate policy is to tax interest income as noted above, or to tax entrepreneurs' incomes while subsidising non-entrepreneurs. Such policies could even end up increasing the equilibrium number of entrepreneurs if they improved sufficiently the average quality of the borrower pool such that banks could reduce their interest rate and so lend to more entrepreneurs. However, subsequent work that generalises the basic DW model has challenged the purity of its predictions, finding potential roles for both credit rationing and under-investment. This work includes de Meza and Webb (1999) and the studies cited in section 5.3. We turn to these now.

5.3   Multiple sources of inefficiency in the credit market

Bernanke and Gertler (1990) added a prior stage to DW's model in which entrepreneurs must engage in costly search activity to locate a suitable venture. The information gathered is private information and good ventures are pooled with bad ventures at the second stage resulting in over-investment, as in DW. However, the pooling diminishes the return to finding a good venture, which diminishes the incentive to search, and promotes under-investment. Whether the net effect turns out to be under- or over-investment is ambiguous.

In a different vein, Hillier and Ibrahimo (1992) combined the SW and DW models by allowing individuals to operate ventures with heterogeneous risks *and* heterogeneous probabilities of success. These authors found that credit rationing, under-investment by some good types, and over-investment by some bad types can all occur individually or simultaneously. Also, the aggregate level of entrepreneurial investment can be greater than or less than what transpires in the 'first best' under symmetric information. The possible mixture of these various forms of inefficiency rules out interest taxes or income subsidies as corrective policies. Instead, Hillier and Ibrahimo (1992) proposed a progressive profit tax with full loss offset. But this policy can reduce work incentives, and in practice would require costly monitoring of venture returns by the tax authorities.

De Meza and Webb (2000) proposed another mixture model in which individuals have heterogeneous probabilities of success (as in DW, 1987) *and* can choose riskier ventures in response to an increase in the interest rate (as in SW's moral hazard problem). Then Type II credit rationing can coexist with over-investment. An appropriate policy instrument is to subsidise non-participation in entrepreneurship. This removes the least able entrepreneurs from the market and thereby increases banks' expected rate of return, and the supply of funds. Credit rationing diminishes, and social welfare and (paradoxically) aggregate participation by entrepreneurs in the loans market is increased.

In these models multiple sources of inefficiency are generated by assuming that venture returns are characterised by two kinds of entrepreneurial heterogeneity. A different approach allows expected returns inside and outside entrepreneurship to both be functions of hidden ability x, with expected return schedules that cross at least twice in (expected return, x) space. (This contrasts with DW's (5.8), where there is at most a single crossing.) As we saw in chapter 2, subsection 2.2.3, Parker (2003d) has a model with this property (see figure 2.1(c)). In this model, under-investment by some types, over-investment by other types and Type II credit rationing can all occur singly or jointly. The optimal corrective policy turns out to be a combination of differential (possibly non-linear) income taxes and an interest rate tax.[32] However, as with Hillier and Ibrahimo (1992) a practical limitation of this policy is that income taxes, unlike interest taxes, may create disincentives to labour supply that cause new forms of inefficiency to emerge.

5.4 Conclusion

Debt finance for new start-ups has an important bearing on entrepreneurship and policy towards it. From an entrepreneur's perspective, the availability and price of loans, and other contract terms such as collateral and the size of loans, are often of primary importance. The theoretical literature reviewed in this chapter showed that when entrepreneurs possess better information about their proposed ventures than banks do, it is possible for efficient contracting between banks and entrepreneurs to break down. Either too much or too little finance – and too few or too many entrepreneurial ventures – can occur from the standpoint of social efficiency.

The view of this author is that de Meza and Webb's (1987) model is an especially important contribution to the literature on financing new entrepreneurial ventures. That model challenges the widespread assumption that financing problems necessarily lead to too few entrepreneurs. De Meza and Webb showed that it is quite possible for there to be too many entrepreneurs in equilibrium, and that a suitable government policy for encouraging entrepreneurship might be to deter the least able from borrowing in the credit market. The importance of this point stems not from any claim that this outcome is bound to occur, but instead from its warning that policy makers should not automatically equate credit market imperfections with insufficient entrepreneurship, and should not immediately reach for instruments designed to draw marginal individuals into it.

The exposition of the theoretical models in this chapter included discussion of appropriate policy responses where they exist. These responses were diverse, reflecting the diversity of the models. One should certainly not take the policy recommendations too seriously. Many of the models generating them are rather fragile, in the sense that altering some of their assumptions can easily reverse the predicted forms of market failure and hence the policy conclusions. Also, the models are partial equilibrium in nature, and do not take into account broader effects that should be analysed in a general equilibrium setting (Hillier and Ibrahimo, 1993). However, these caveats have not prevented some policy makers from eagerly seizing some of these results, and using them to justify particular forms of intervention such as loan guarantee schemes (see chapter 10, section 10.1).

There would be a better basis for policy recommendations if one could sort through the various models and identify the ones with the greatest empirical relevance. As noted in subsection 5.1.4, empirical investigations along these lines would be valuable but probably fraught with difficulties. Unsurprisingly, therefore, the literature to date has not progressed very far in this direction. Attempting to reject models on the basis of their indirect predictions is also unlikely to be informative, for the simple reason that models can often be generalised in to better fit the stylised facts when they conflict with the original model.[33] This problem has also bedevilled efforts to measure the extent of Type I and Type II credit rationing – a topic we explore in chapter 7.

NOTES

1. We do not consider other implications of credit rationing, for example for the performance of the macro economy (see Blinder, 1989; Jaffee and Stiglitz, 1990, sec. 5; and Hillier and Ibrahimo, 1993, sec. 6).
2. As Jaffee and Stiglitz (1990) point out, the inability of individuals to borrow at the interest rate *they think is appropriate* is not a valid definition of credit rationing. Nor is the situation where borrowers can only obtain a small loan at their desired interest rate, with them having to pay more for a larger loan. Note that Definitions 8 and 9 are distinct because, unlike redlined ventures, rationed ventures are sufficiently productive to be capable of generating high enough returns for banks to at least break even.
3. Allen (1983) endogenised the default penalty by treating it as the present value of future borrowing opportunities, which are withdrawn from entrepreneurs who default. Type I rationing emerges again. Smith (1983) showed that the optimal policy in the Jaffee–Russell model is for the government to lend as much as is demanded at some appropriate interest rate.
4. For other criticisms of the Jaffee–Russell model, and a reply by its authors, see the exchange in the November 1984 issue of the *Quarterly Journal of Economics*.
5. Hillier (1998) clarified the nature of the requisite over-optimism, which is that entrepreneurs must over-estimate the payoffs in the successful state, rather than the probability of success itself.

6. Risk neutrality permits abstraction from insurance motives for borrowing. This is helpful when evaluating the efficiency of enterprises, though it proves to be informative to relax it below on occasions.

7. In the presence of costly state verification, it is efficient not to monitor non-defaulting ventures. This provides a rationale for debt to be the optimal contract. See, e.g., Townsend (1979), Diamond (1984) and Gale and Hellwig (1985).

8. This is sometimes referred to in the literature as the 'limited liability' assumption. In a legal sense, limited liability means that an entrepreneur whose company fails is liable only up to the value of the business assets, i.e. creditors cannot claim their personal wealth. Of course, under assumption A4 individuals who fail also lose their personal equity stake, B. Hence 'limited liability' here means that their losses are bounded at B.

9. Recall Adam Smith: 'the greater part of the money which was to be lent, would be lent to prodigals and profectors . . . Sober people, who will give for the use of money no more than a part of what they are likely to make by the use of it, would not venture into the competition' (1937). See also Wette (1983), who showed how adverse selection could also occur if banks varied collateral C while keeping D fixed. Analogous to (5.2), $\tilde{\theta}$ is defined as

$$\pi(C, \tilde{\theta} \mid D) = -C.F(D - C, \tilde{\theta}) + \int_{D-C}^{\infty} [R - D] \, dF(R, \tilde{\theta}) = 0,$$

since banks seize collateral C if entrepreneurs default. Total differentiation then yields

$$\frac{d\tilde{\theta}}{dC} = \frac{F(D - C, \tilde{\theta})}{\partial \pi(C, \tilde{\theta} \mid D)/\partial\tilde{\theta}} > 0,$$

i.e. an increase in collateral increases the risk of ventures that entrepreneurs must undertake to at least break even.

10. Note that banks' expected rate of return is equivalent to the deposit rate by assumptions A3 and A6. That is, to attract funds under competition from rivals, banks must transfer all supernormal profits to depositors.

11. If banks' expected return function has more than one mode, then SW showed that credit rationing is still possible if the highest mode occurs for an interest rate $\leq D_m$, where D_m is the market-clearing rate (see below). The other possibility is of two interest rates, where credit at the lower interest rate is rationed, but where all borrowers can obtain funds at the higher interest rate.

12. It is sometimes taken as axiomatic that credit rationing reduces the equilibrium number of entrepreneurs. But not all models have this property: see, e.g., Boadway et al. (1998) for one that does not.

13. For 'early' models of redlining in which the demand for loans was taken to be exogenous, see Hodgman (1960) and Freimer and Gordon (1965).

14. Hillier and Ibrahimo (1993) point out several advantages of Williamson's model over alternative ones, including SW's. It can explain several 'real-world' features of financial intermediation, and derives debt as the optimal contract. Also, Williamson's credit rationing result is robust to even perfect classification of borrowers into different risk categories.

15. For a formal proof in the context of collateral, see Bester (1985a).
16. The logic is simple. In a competitive equilibrium, a pooling contract, Γ_p say, must make zero expected profits. But this involves gs cross-subsidising bs. Hence gs will prefer Γ_g to Γ_p, and any bank not offering Γ_g will lose gs to rivals that do. With the departure of gs, the Γ_p contract becomes loss–making, and the only contract that can be offered to bs is Γ_b on which (like Γ_g) banks break even.
17. See Bester (1985a, 1987), Chan and Kanatos (1985), Clemenz (1986) and Besanko and Thakor (1987a). Coco (2000) surveys the literature.
18. On the latter, the value to the bank of bankrupt ventures' assets may be so low that banks do better re-negotiating debt rather than initiating bankruptcy proceedings. Knowing this, entrepreneurs have an incentive to default even when they are successful. But, crucially, banks can remove this incentive if they can seize defaulters' collateral. Then the benefits of debt re-negotiation can be realised by both entrepreneurs and banks.
19. In practice, multi-period lending contracts involve bank–borrower relationships. Evidence from Petersen and Rajan (1994), Harhoff and Korting (1998) and Berger and Udell (1995) shows that established borrowers benefit from lower interest rates and lower collateral requirements than new borrowers. This may reflect learning about the entrepreneur by the bank, or could be the outcome of an effort inducement device (Boot and Thakor, 1994).

    However, an issue that is sometimes overlooked in this literature (and which also pertains to other finite repeated games) is a dynamic inconsistency problem. Suppose an entrepreneur needs a stream of finance over several periods. If the borrowing relationship has a clear end, borrowers have an incentive to default in the final period. Anticipating that, banks will not lend in the final period, giving borrowers the incentive to default in the penultimate period. By backward induction, this continues until the mechanism unravels altogether – unless there is sufficient uncertainty about the end date, or if there is well-established progression from one loan tranche to the next.
20. In fact, the result does not depend on assortative matching of types in groups. Armendáriz de Aghion and Gollier (2000) showed that group lending still works when entrepreneurs are uninformed about each others' types and pair randomly.
21. Some 71 per cent of the respondents to a survey by KPMG (1999) cited lack of security as the main reason for using the scheme.
22. In a different vein, Stiglitz and Weiss (1983) proposed a multi-period model in which banks threaten to ration credit in later periods unless borrowers succeed in the first period. This induces good behaviour by borrowers and low default rates. But to be credible, banks must be seen to carry out their threat, so some credit must be rationed.
23. See, e.g., Leeth and Scott (1989) and Berger and Udell (1990, 1992, 1995). For example, Berger and Udell (1990) analysed data on a million US commercial loans over 1977–88. They measured loan risk in terms of above-average risk premia *ex ante*, and venture risk in terms of poor *ex post* performance. Both risk measures were positively and significantly associated with greater collateral. These findings are consistent with the 'collateral as incentive device'

model of Boot, Thakor and Udell (1991); with de Meza and Southey's (1996) model of over-optimistic entrepreneurs; with Coco's (1999) model where the most risk-averse types choose safe ventures and are less willing to post collateral; and with Bester's (1994) model of debt re-negotiation.

24. According to the Bank of England (1993), 80 (resp., 96) per cent of bank margins to small firms with turnover of less than £1 million in 1991–2 (resp., between £1 and 10 million) were between 0 and 4 percentage points (see also Keasy and Watson, 1995; Cowling, 1998). US evidence points to similar margins (Berger and Udell, 1992).

25. Black and de Meza (1990) showed that under pooling contracts the more able entrepreneurs operate safe ventures, depriving the less able in the risky venture of cross-subsidies and so leaving them potentially inactive. With only low-risk ventures funded in equilibrium, limited interest spreads emerge for this reason rather than because of pooling.

26. More generally, DW's results hold if entrepreneurs' returns can be ranked in terms of *first-order stochastic dominance*, rather than *second-order stochastic dominance* as in SW (recall Definitions 4 and 6 in chapter 2, subsection 2.2.1).

27. See also Leland and Pyle (1977), who showed that an entrepreneur's willingness to invest in his own venture is a favourable signal of venture quality – although the signal reduces the welfare of risk-averse borrowers who have to take larger stakes in their own firm than they would wish under the 'first-best' case of perfect information.

28. *Proof*: If there was an excess demand for funds, all banks could make profits by increasing D, since from (5.9), bank gross expected returns are unambiguously increasing in D (noting from (5.8) that the average probability of success must be an increasing function of D). There is no interior bank-optimal interest rate: increasing D to the market-clearing rate of D_m can always remove any excess demand for funds. Likewise, banks would be forced by competitive pressures to reduce D to D_m if there was an excess supply of funds.

29. *Proof*: The marginal entrepreneur $\tilde{x}$ generates an expected loss of $[\bar{p} - p(\tilde{x})]D$ to the bank, i.e. generates expected returns that are less than the opportunity cost of the funds used. This constitutes over-investment.

30. Subsequently, de Meza and Webb (1990) showed that their over-investment result is left intact by relaxing assumption A2 to allow entrepreneurs to be risk averse rather than risk neutral, as long as entrepreneurs are not 'too' risk averse. Sufficient risk aversion replaces the over-investment pooling equilibrium with a separating equilibrium in which the correct amount of investment occurs (but with an inefficient amount of risk-bearing). In contrast, over-investment is replaced by under-investment if assumption A6 is revoked to permit a backward-bending deposit supply curve.

31. *Proof*: The most able entrepreneurs are the least likely to fail. Therefore they can supply finance to themselves on better terms than they can obtain in the market, and prefer paying a fixed-debt repayment to sharing their returns with equity providers. Less able entrepreneurs must emulate them in these respects to avoid transmitting adverse signals about their true abilities that would separate them into less favourable contracts.

32. Another model with heterogeneous outside options is Chan and Thakor (1987). That model does not generate multiple sources of inefficiency, merely pricing out of the market the entrepreneurial types that have exclusive rights to a valuable outside option.

33. For example, de Meza and Webb's (1987) model predicts a negative relationship between personal wealth and entrepreneurship (see (5.8)) – in conflict with most evidence on the issue (see, e.g., chapter 7). But a subsequent paper published in 1999 by these two authors generalised the model by incorporating moral hazard, with the result that a positive relationship between wealth and entrepreneurship emerges.

6   Other sources of finance

Chapter 5 concentrated on issues relating to debt finance of entrepreneurial ventures. This broadly reflects the emphasis in the literature. Yet many start-ups obtain external finance through informal sources, such as loans from family and friends and credit co-operatives. A smaller number utilise equity finance (venture capital). Part of the interest in studying alternative sources of finance is that they might be able to fill any gaps created by credit rationing.

The structure of the chapter is as follows. Section 6.1 explains the economics of informal sources of finance, and section 6.2 treats aspects of equity finance that relate to typical entrepreneurial ventures. We will cite only selectively and sparingly from the extensive corporate finance literature on risk capital, most of which pertains to large firms. Section 6.3 concludes.

6.1   Informal sources of finance

6.1.1   Family finance

In his analysis of the 1992 CBO database, Bates (1997) showed that families are the most frequently used source of business loans in the USA after financial institutions (mainly banks). Bates reported that 26.8 per cent of non-minority-owned businesses used family finance, compared with 65.9 per cent who used loans from banks. Among some minority groups, however, family finance was used more extensively than bank finance. For immigrant Korean and Chinese business owners, family finance was used by 41.2 per cent, whereas bank finance was used by 37.4 per cent (see also Yoon, 1991). For all groups, family loans were of a smaller average size than bank loans, although family loans remained an important source of funds by value, being worth an average of $35,446 for non-minority owners compared with $56,784 for bank loans.

UK evidence tells a similar story. According to Curran and Blackburn (1993) and Metcalf, Modood and Virdee (1996), family loans account for between 15 and 20 per cent of start-up finance among ethnic-owned businesses in the UK, making it the largest source of funds after bank loans (see also Basu, 1998; Basu and Parker, 2001). Data from other countries tell a broadly similar story. Knight (1985) reported that the following sources of funds were used by high-tech Canadian firms at the pre-start-up stage: personal savings: 60 per cent, family/ friends: 13 per cent, bank loans: 12 per cent and trade credit: 6 per cent. The importance of families and friends for supplying start-up finance appears to be even stronger in developing countries.[1]

What motivates lending within families? Family members may have private information about borrowers that is unavailable to banks (Casson, 2003); and they may able to monitor and exert peer pressure on the borrower. For their part, family lenders may be trusted to behave sensitively if the entrepreneur encounters difficult borrowing conditions. Family lenders can also serve as loan guarantors to outside lenders (Jones et al., 1994).[2] Also, if the borrower stands to inherit the family lender's estate, then a family loan effectively becomes a mortgage on his own inheritance. In contrast, banks are usually unwilling to accept the prospect of inheritance as security for a loan (Casson, 2003).

Basu and Parker (2001) explored some of the theoretical issues by analysing a simple two-period model in which there are two family members – one borrower and one lender – and an entrepreneurial venture requiring external finance. Their model recognises some of the 'stylised facts' that most family loans tend to be interest-free (Light, 1972; Basu and Parker, 2001). Basu and Parker (2001) showed that family members are generally prepared to supply funds not only if they are altruistic towards the entrepreneur, but also if they are selfish. The selfish motive for lending at a zero interest rate arises if the loan entitles the lender to a sufficiently valuable option to 'call in the favour', and turn entrepreneur themselves at a later date. Using a sample of relatively affluent Asian immigrant entrepreneurs, Basu and Parker (2001) claimed to find evidence of both altruistic and selfish family lending motives. Also, they estimated that greater use of family finance was positively associated with an entrepreneur's age, the number of hours worked in their business and the employment of a spouse in the venture. Unsurprisingly, family finance was found to be a gross substitute for bank loans.

Other evidence suggests that family finance is not associated with successful enterprise, being correlated with low profitability and high failure rates in entrepreneurship (Yoon, 1991; Bates, 1997; Basu, 1998). The case for government intervention is in any case not clear-cut. And apart from the Dutch government, which offers tax exemptions for family finance, we know of few other policy initiatives in this area.

6.1.2   Micro-finance schemes

The term 'micro-finance' usually refers to small, often non-profit making, lending schemes, which are targeted at individuals who are unable to obtain funds from 'conventional' banks, usually because they are too poor to post collateral. Many such schemes are currently in operation around the world, mainly concentrated in developing countries with under-developed financial sectors. They include the Grameen Bank in Bangladesh, BancoSol in Bolivia and Bank Rayat in Indonesia.[3] Perhaps the most famous is the Grameen scheme, founded in 1976 by Muhammad Yunus, an economics professor. This scheme, which provides financing for non-agricultural self-employment activities, had served over 2 million borrowers by the end of 1994, of which 94 per cent were women.

Despite their differences, micro-finance schemes tend to share some common features, including direct monitoring of borrowers, stipulation of regular repayment schedules and the use of non-refinancing threats to generate high repayment rates from borrowers who would not otherwise receive credit (de Aghion and Morduch, 2000). Most of the economics literature on the subject has focused on group lending schemes (GLSs) with joint liability, whereby individuals form into groups and are jointly liable for penalties if one member of the group defaults. The nature of the penalty might be the denial of future credit to all group members if one member defaults (as in the Grameen scheme), or group liability for loans if a member defaults (as in the Bangladesh Rural Advancement Committee scheme).

The advantage of joint liability contracts is that they give entrepreneurs incentives to exploit local information and exert pressure to discipline members in a manner consistent with the interests of lenders (and, by releasing funds, thereby also the entrepreneurs). The particular mechanisms involved include:

1. *Mitigation of moral hazard.* Group members may be able to monitor each other in a manner unavailable to banks. For example, members may know or live near each other, and share information. Under joint liability each member's payoff depends on whether other members' ventures succeed, so all members have an incentive to monitor other members' behaviour, and to take remedial action against members who misuse their funds (Stiglitz, 1990). For example, group members might threaten others with social ostracism if they shirk in a manner that invites default, or if they invest in excessively risky ventures.

2. *Cheap state verification and repayment enforcement.* Group members may be in a better position than banks to learn about partners' venture

outcomes. Then joint liability can encourage them to exert peer pressure to deter partners from defaulting opportunistically in good states. Also, if group members have lower auditing costs than banks, a GLS may economise on state verification costs. Only if the whole group defaults will banks incur audit costs, so this arrangement reduces average auditing costs and enhances efficiency. Indeed, if bank audit costs are too high for banks to be able to offer *any* individual loan contract, a GLS could facilitate lending where none was possible before.

3. *Mitigation of adverse selection.* Rather than changing borrowers' behaviour, as above, joint liability can favourably alter the pool of borrowers. The way that this peer selection effect can promote efficient contracting was briefly discussed in chapter 5, subsection 5.1.3.

Some evidence confirms the usefulness of these three mechanisms. Wydick (1999) found from Guatemalan data that peer monitoring and a group's willingness to apply pressure on delinquent members were the salient factors explaining borrowing group performance. And using Costa Rican data, Wenner (1995) reported that repayment rates were highest among groups who actively screened their members via local reputations.

Micro-finance schemes promise several benefits. First, for the reasons outlined above, they can lead to improved repayment rates. The available evidence supports this claim.[4] Competitive (or non-profit making) banks can then recycle the benefit of higher repayment rates to borrowers in the form of lower interest rates and/or larger loan sizes. This may in turn further decrease the severity of asymmetric information problems such as adverse selection, as well as increasing borrower welfare directly. Second, ventures can be undertaken that would otherwise not be undertaken. This can be especially valuable in poor regions, where self-sufficient entrepreneurship promotes development and alleviates poverty – the so-called 'micro-finance promise'. Third, micro-finance schemes can carry in their train valuable social development programmes such as vocational training, civic information and information sharing to members. These have been found to add substantial value to participants' venture profitability rates (McKernan, 2002).

However, micro-finance schemes can also suffer from drawbacks. First, they can encourage excessive welfare-reducing monitoring by group members (Armehdáriz de Aghion, 1999); and the joint liability clause might encourage excessively cautious investment behaviour. Second, there is no guarantee that a scheme will break even, and subsidies may become necessary. Indeed, as Ghatak (2000) warned, joint liability contracts might drive out more 'conventional' single-liability contracts, undermining the viability of conventional loan markets. Third, the transfer of risk from banks to borrowers presumably reduces borrower welfare.

In some theoretical models, it can be shown that the benefits of micro-finance schemes outweigh the costs (e.g. Stiglitz, 1990). But this is not a general property and cannot be assumed to hold universally, notwith-standing some recent evidence of substantial benefits from Bangladeshi micro-finance schemes. On the latter, McKernan (2002) found that par-ticipation in such schemes increased monthly self-employment profits by 175 per cent on average. Pitt and Khandker (1998) discovered substan-tial gender differences in Bangladesh, with micro-finance credit having a significantly greater effect on households in which women rather than men were the scheme participants. Pitt and Khandker suggested that this might be indicative of how access to credit unleashes women's produc-tive skills that, unlike men's, are held in check by cultural and religious restrictions proscribing formal waged work.

6.1.3   Credit co-operatives, mutual guarantee schemes and trade credit

Credit co-operatives and Roscas

Credit co-operatives are voluntary groupings of individuals that obtain funds from, and allocate credit to, their members. Unlike GLSs, they re-semble banks in that they take deposits from their members as well as ex-tending loans; and the whole co-operative is liable for the debts of a single member. While the spread of liability dilutes the incentive to perform peer monitoring relative to GLSs, it does not eliminate it altogether (Banerjee, Besley and Guinnane, 1994).[5] Other features of co-operatives are similar to those of GLSs, including the threat of (possibly non-pecuniary) sanc-tions to discourage opportunistic behaviour by their members. However, given their larger group sizes, co-operatives are more vulnerable to co-variant risk, whereby large-scale shocks such as bad weather hit a region and result in mass default. The problem of size also makes banks wary of dealing with co-operatives that may be prone to collusion among their members who wish to perpetrate a fraud.

Rotating savings and credit associations (Roscas) play a similar role to credit co-operatives. Rosca members save on a regular basis and periodically allocate a pot of funds to particular members, either by lot or by bidding. These funds can be used to purchase an indivisible good. This process continues with past winners excluded until everyone has won the pot once (see Besley, Coate and Loury, 1993). While Roscas exist primarily to facilitate purchases of lumpy consumption goods by their members, they can also facilitate the accumulation of capital required for business entry.

GLSs, credit co-operatives and Roscas tend to be associated with low-income communities. Besley (1995) argued that these types of micro-finance schemes decline in importance as economic development occurs, or as the communities involved improve their access to formal credit markets.

Mutual Guarantee Schemes

Mutual Guarantee Schemes (MGSs) are private-sector versions of government-backed loan guarantee schemes (LGSs) (see chapter 10, subsection 10.1.1 for details of LGSs). Like a credit co-operative, a MGS is a voluntary grouping of individuals. But whereas credit co-operatives issue loans directly, a MGS merely guarantees a fraction of any loans made by banks to its members if the latter default. MGS members pay a fee or save in a fund that provides the scheme's capital. In practice, MGSs take a variety of organisational structures, though they share some features in common. They tend to be industry-based and located in distinct geographical areas, potentially enabling peer pressure to be exerted to encourage loan repayments.

MGSs are widespread in Europe, especially in Italy, where over 800 exist, with over 1 million member enterprises (Rossi, 1998). The values of guarantees vary from scheme to scheme, but according to Rossi (1998) the typical guarantee is for between 50 and 100 per cent of members' loans. MGSs are also common in Germany, where they are chartered as limited liability companies, with capital provided by the banking system, guilds and chambers of trade. Federal and state governments share the responsibility for guaranteeing up to 70 per cent of loans. The German MGSs claim to back loans with lower default rates than conventional bank loans (OECD, 1998). MGSs started to appear in the UK only in the 1990s, and their impact has been negligible to date; they are virtually unknown in the USA at the present time. It is currently unclear whether their existence owes more to underlying informational advantages or to mainly historical factors.

The value to banks of the loan guarantee is recycled in the form of lower interest rates charged to MGS members. As with GLSs, MGSs probably have an optimal size: small ones are best able to screen loan applications and exert peer pressure, but idiosyncratic risks are spread more widely in larger schemes.[6] In practice, MGSs often enhance their effectiveness by pre-screening loan applications, as well as by providing financial advice and encouraging valuable information sharing among members. A self-selection rationale for MGSs can also be proposed based on the analysis of subsection 5.1.3. The fee paid by members into the scheme can be thought of as a *BAD*, which 'safe' borrower types are more willing to pay than 'risky' types in return for a lower interest rate. Thus with a range of fees and savings requirements, MGSs can in principle separate types and facilitate efficient contracting.

Trade credit

Another potentially valuable source of 'inside' local information is trade credit. Trade credit comprises loans between firms that are used to purchase materials and goods in process. According to Acs, Carlsson and Karlsson (1999, table 1.5), the value of trade credit in the USA in 1995 was $233 billion, compared with $98 billion for bank loans.

Trade credit might be capable of mitigating credit rationing (Bopaiah, 1998). Its use can also convey a favourable signal of creditworthiness to banks, allowing entrepreneurs to leverage credit that might not otherwise have been forthcoming (Biais and Gollier, 1997).

6.2   Equity finance

6.2.1   Introduction

Another potential source of funds for some entrepreneurs is equity finance (EF). In contrast to a debt-finance contract, which stipulates in advance a given repayment due to a bank that is invariant to gross returns from the venture, an EF contract entitles a lender to a stake, or share, of a firm's profits. Much EF is provided by venture capitalists (VCs), who frequently manage several entrepreneurial ventures at any one time, and who are often actively involved in them to enhance their prospects of success.[7] VC profit shares are negotiated on a project-by-project basis, and tend to vary between 20 and 49.9 per cent (Bovaird, 1990). Most professional venture capital companies attract funds from outside investors, who are limited partners; VCs themselves are general partners. Outside equity investments typically last for between three and seven years. A VC's aim is usually to sell their stake at the end of this period, through an Initial Public Offering (IPO) or (more commonly) a trade sale.

There are both 'formal' and 'informal' private equity providers. Examples of the former include private independent venture funds, corporate subsidiaries, and special investment schemes. Among informal providers are 'business angels', who are high-net-worth individuals willing to invest risk capital in small unquoted companies. Business angels tend to concentrate on early-stage financing; their role usually declines at later stages when more substantial capital funds are needed.

6.2.2   *The scale of the equity finance market for entrepreneurs*

The USA has the largest formal VC market in the world. In 2001, for example, over $40 billion of VC funds were invested there, compared with only $12 billion in Europe (Bottazzi and da Rin, 2002). The US figure was down from its peak of $106 billion in 2000 – a figure that demonstrates the volatile pro-cyclicality of VC markets. The European market has grown dramatically since 1995, and is showing signs of convergence with the US market. Of particular interest is the growing importance of early-stage VC investments, which are arguably those most closely identified with individual entrepreneurship. Since the early 1990s about one-third of US VC investment has been in early-stage projects. In Europe in the early 1990s the fraction was one-tenth, but by 2001 it had also reached one-third (Bottazzi and da Rin, 2002).

Evidence on the size of the informal equity sector is less widely available. In the USA and UK it is thought to be about twice that of the formal equity sector, even though the individual deals are on a smaller scale. According to Mason and Harrison (2000), the UK's informal market for start-up and early-stage venture financing is broadly similar to the size of the formal market.[8] Wetzel (1987) estimated that there are around 250,000 business angels in the USA, of which around 100,000 are active in any given year. He also estimated that business angels finance over ten times as many ventures as professional VC firms. Wetzel emphasised a general problem of poor information about investment and investment opportunities that can cause poor matches between VCs and entrepreneurs and potentially inefficient investment. Business angels appear to have similar characteristics in the USA and UK, although UK investors tend to be less wealthy, investing about half of the sums of their US counterparts. UK business angels are also more likely to invest independently rather than in consortia, although similar to the USA eight times as many businesses raise finance from business angels than from institutional VC funds (Mason and Harrison, 2000).

EF accounts for only a small proportion of external finance for entrepreneurs in most countries. For example, Bates and Bradford (1992) reported that only 2.8 per cent of US small business start-ups obtained EF. Its receipt was found to be positively associated with owner education, age, the amount of self-finance, and a track record in business. A similar picture applies in the UK, where EF accounted for 1.3 per cent of total start-up finance by the end of the 1990s, down from 3 per cent at the start of the decade – despite the strong growth performance of the companies that used it (Bank of England, 2001). Indeed, several recent US studies claim to have detected various beneficial effects from venture capital. VCs' screening, monitoring and mentoring services lead to faster professionalisation (Hellmann and Puri, 2002), stronger innovation (Hellmann and Puri, 2000; Kortum and Lerner, 2000), higher growth (Jain and Kini, 1995) and possibly also employment creation (Belke, Fehr and Foster, 2002).

6.2.3   Factors affecting the availability of equity finance for entrepreneurs

It is natural to ask why EF accounts for such a small proportion of external finance for most entrepreneurs. The following reasons can be adduced:

1. *Financing costs.* There are fixed costs of issuing shares and listing on secondary markets where shares can be traded. Most enterprises never grow to a size where these costs are warranted, even for 'junior' stock markets such as the US NASDAQ, the UK Alternative Investment Market (AIM), or the European EASDAQ. Also, larger deals such as management buy-outs or buy-ins generate greater and more reliable fee income for VCs. Hence simple cost reasons restrict the viability and availability of EF for many entrepreneurs, especially those operating the newest and smallest ventures.

2. *Agency costs.* The involvement of outside financiers can cause conflicts of interest with entrepreneurs that reduce the latter's flexibility and impose costs on all of the contracting agents. This is probably true to some extent of all financial instruments, but it appears to be especially pronounced for EF. Entrepreneurs have incentives to take perquisites that reduce the outside value of the venture since, unlike debt finance, EF allows entrepreneurs to share the costs with VCs. In response, VCs monitor the entrepreneur, resulting in both a perceived 'loss of control' by the entrepreneurs, and agency costs that must be recouped in the form of greater VC equity stakes. If these stakes become sufficiently large, entrepreneurs can be discouraged from seeking EF altogether.

3. *Information costs.* Because entrepreneurs and financiers must co-operate closely once they enter a relationship, each side typically expends a costly search effort. High information-gathering costs can increase the price of funds beyond the willingness or ability of entrepreneurs to pay. Also, full disclosure conditions may compromise confidential information and encourage competitors to appear who bid away the superior returns of the venture being financed (Campbell, 1979). An additional problem occurs if entrepreneurs have more information about their ventures than lenders do. As was seen in chapter 5, if the least able entrepreneurs anticipate limited returns in good states, then they will prefer EF to debt finance since they have to share less with VCs if they succeed while avoiding a certain repayment in bad states. In contrast, abler entrepreneurs prefer debt finance, because they anticipate capturing greater upside returns. Attempting to sell equity therefore conveys a negative signal about an entrepreneur's ability, so entrepreneurs are dissuaded from signalling this by asking for an EF contract (Ross, 1977; Greenwald, Stiglitz and Weiss, 1984; de Meza and Webb, 1987; Innes, 1993).

For these reasons, entrepreneurs operating small firms often prefer to utilise debt finance, for which a cheap, well-established and relatively cost efficient market is available. It might be thought that the problem of costly EF can be circumvented if entrepreneurs approach informal financiers such as business angels for funds. But the supply of business angels may be limited; and imperfect information may frustrate high-quality matches between angels and entrepreneurs. Nor does the availability of informal EF change the predictions of the 'pecking-order' hypothesis, according to which entrepreneurs seek funds in an order that minimises external interference and ownership dilution (Myers and Majluf, 1984). This is internal finance followed by debt finance, with EF as a last resort.

6.2.4   Equity rationing, funding gaps and under-investment

It is sometimes claimed that there is a 'funding' or 'equity' gap for EF. The term 'equity gap' should be distinguished from 'equity rationing'. The former is commonly used to refer to a mismatch between entrepreneurs and VCs or business angels–for example, because fixed costs make VCs unwilling to supply the relatively small sums required by entrepreneurs. The latter refers to the problem, analogous to credit rationing, where there is a persistent excess demand for funds which even competitive VCs that face low costs are unwilling to satisfy.

It is reasonably straightforward to propose models of equity rationing that mirror the credit rationing models described in chapter 5. For example, Hellmann and Stiglitz (2000) modelled debt and equity providers who compete with each other to finance heterogeneous entrepreneurs who possess private information about both their project risks and returns. Hellmann and Stiglitz unified both the Stiglitz–Weiss (SW) and de Meza and Webb (DW) models outlined in chapter 5. Returns in the successful state are given by $\pi = \sigma\mu$, where the probability of success is $(1/\sigma)$, where σ measures risk. Suppose payoffs are zero in the failure state. Then expected returns are $(1/\sigma)\pi = \mu$. Entrepreneurs possess heterogeneous μ and σ values, known only to themselves. It is easy to show that both high-μ and high-σ individuals prefer debt finance to EF. Hellmann and Stiglitz (2000) assumed that lenders specialise in either debt finance or EF, and that entrepreneurs cannot use a mixture of both. They then showed that credit and equity rationing may occur individually or simultaneously. The usual culprit of lender return functions that decrease in their own price (chapter 5) accounts for the possibility of rationing in each individual market. As in SW, the mechanism is that lenders do not increase the price of funds to clear the market because good types may exit the market such that lenders' expected profits fall. Hellmann and Stiglitz (2000) also obtained the surprising result that competition between the two markets *may itself* generate the adverse selection that leads to rationing outcomes. The reason is that if many low-risk entrepreneurs switch between the debt and equity markets, competition induces lenders in one or both markets to reduce the price of funds below market-clearing levels in order to attract them – so rationing ensues. However, if only EF was offered, then credit rationing would disappear.

Hellmann and Stiglitz did not endogenise optimal contracts in their model, merely assuming coexistence of banks and VCs. Bracoud and Hillier (2000) studied the problem of optimal contracts in a generalisation of Hellman and Stiglitz's model, in which expected returns may vary among entrepreneurs. They showed that a variety of different optimal contracts is possible, depending on the form of the joint distribution of (μ, σ). A result of particular interest occurs in a two-type set-up, $\theta \in \Theta = \{b, g\}$, with probabilities of success p_g and $p_b < p_g$, returns if successful of $R_g^s < R_b^s$ and expected returns $E_b(R) > E_g(R)$. Bracoud and Hillier (2000) showed that gs will self-select into equity and bs into debt contracts, and that the equilibrium is first-best efficient. But this result disappears if $E_b(R) < E_g(R)$. Then the optimal contract pools the types together and whether it is in the form of equity or debt depends on the deposit rate, ρ.

Greenwald, Stiglitz and Weiss (1984) developed a model in which the least able entrepreneurs prefer EF and the ablest prefer debt finance (see above). Greenwald *et al* showed that the adverse signal transmitted by choosing EF can increase the cost of capital sufficiently to deter credit-rationed borrowers from availing themselves of EF altogether. This reinforces the potential importance of the SW credit rationing result, since it rebuts the argument that entrepreneurs who are rationed in the debt market can obtain funds elsewhere, e.g., in the form of EF.

Parallel to chapter 5, under-investment is also possible when EF contracts are used. There is a special result of interest despite its apparently limited applicability to small entrepreneurial ventures. Myers and Majluf (1984) analysed the problem of issuing new equity when a valuable investment opportunity appears. Managers of existing enterprises have more information about both the company's assets in place and the value of the new investment opportunity. Suppose that EF is used to finance the new investment; that managers act in the interests of their existing shareholders; and that shareholders do not actively rebalance their portfolios in response to what they learn from the firm's actions. Then Myers and

Majluf showed that a new share issue could reduce the share price by so much that managers might optimally pass up the new profitable opportunity, causing under-investment. In contrast, the use of internal funds or risk-free debt finance removes any under-investment, and does not reduce the share price – so is preferred to EF by managers. However, these results are sensitive to the objectives of managers of the enterprise and the behaviour of shareholders (see also Noe, 1988).

In short, the theoretical literature on equity rationing is inconclusive. On the empirical front, there is little hard evidence of equity rationing. For example, Dixon (1991) reported that 63 per cent of respondents in his UK VC survey claimed they had more available funds than attractive projects in which to invest. This is suggestive of an equity gap rather than equity rationing.

6.2.5   Policy recommendations

If it was desired to promote EF as a contractual arrangement, then one obvious policy recommendation would be to reduce new issue costs and secondary market transaction costs (Stoll, 1984). This might be accomplished by improving the efficiency of securities markets and by eliminating unnecessary regulations. But it is questionable how much scope exists for this in practice.

It might also be possible to increase the supply of VC funds by removing restrictions on the sources of investor finance, as happened in the case of pension funds in the USA at the end of the 1970s, for example. Governments might also be able to increase efficiency by subsidising agencies dedicated to improving information flows and matching between entrepreneurs and VCs. However, it is unclear why private sector firms could not perform this function. Indeed, we are beginning to see the emergence of internet-based matching services in the USA, the UK and other countries.

Governments might also affect the size of the VC industry via tax instruments. Reflecting the fact that VCs' rewards are primarily in the form of capital gains, rather than dividends or interest income, one such instrument is the capital gains tax (CGT). Poterba (1989a, 1989b) argued that because individuals who are liable to CGT provide relatively little risk capital, it is unlikely that changes in CGT will have much effect on the supply side of the market. Also, the impact of CGT on the demand side (i.e. entrepreneurs' demand for VC) is limited because entrepreneurs can defer their gains and so reduce the effective CGT rate below the statutory rate. In the light of these considerations, Poterba concluded that CGT is unlikely to have much impact on the size of the VC industry.[9] Also CGT is a blunt instrument, since the VC industry is just a small part of the CGT tax base. Hence CGT is probably unlikely to offer much potential for stimulating the use of EF.

In principle, other taxes might be used to encourage EF. Fuest, Huber and Nielsen (2002) studied the relative roles of corporation tax (CT) and income tax (IT). They argued that reducing CT below IT stimulates EF at the expense of debt finance, which is desirable *if* there is a socially excessive reliance on debt finance. Finally, Keuschnigg and Nielsen (2003) and Parker (2003c) studied the effects of taxes on VC financing behaviour. These authors showed that VCs are liable to provide too little valuable assistance to entrepreneurs, because by the nature of an EF contract VCs capture only a share of the returns to assistance while bearing all of the costs. Therefore a subsidy to assistance can be justified to restore the level of VC assistance to first-best levels.

6.3   Conclusion

Debt finance is not the only way that capital flows from lenders to entrepreneurs. Many other sources of finance are also available. We reviewed several of them in this chapter, grouped under the headings of informal sources of finance and equity finance.

Our treatment of alternative sources of finance has not been exhaustive or complete. For example, we did not discuss explicitly the role of credit cards, leasing arrangements or franchising – despite the possibility that these might have helped eliminate funding gaps caused by limited bank credit (Horvitz, 1984). Leasing can be more economical and less risky for small firms than debt finance, conferring tax advantages and being cheaper than buying capital that will not be utilised intensively (Bowlin, 1984). Likewise, franchisors have been able to finance expansion by requiring franchisees to furnish some or all of the necessary capital (Dant, 1995).

What emerges from our discussion of alternative sources of funding is the wide variety of different financing arrangements that are available to budding entrepreneurs. Academics and policy makers who express concern about credit rationing sometimes appear to overlook this. Even in countries where financial markets are poorly developed, and where aspiring entrepreneurs lack even nugatory amounts of collateral, micro-finance schemes have demonstrated the scope to expand financing activities, and to thereby facilitate new-venture creation.

However, it is premature to conclude that the existence of a rich array of financing instruments means that all entrepreneurs can and do avail themselves of them in practice. Data are needed to shed light on the extent to which entrepreneurs face borrowing constraints of one kind or another. That is the subject of chapter 7.

NOTES

1. See, e.g., Bell (1990) and Kochar (1997) for India, and Goedhuys and Sleuwaegen (2000) for Côte d'Ivoire.
2. Note that family ownership *per se* can also confer other advantages, including improved access to bank finance (see Bopaiah, 1998).
3. See Huppi and Feder (1990) and Morduch (1999) for reviews of the structure, rationale, costs and effects of various micro-finance schemes. These schemes are also being replicated in poorer rural and inner city areas of developed countries, e.g., Micro-Business International in the USA, the Calmedow Foundation in Canada and the ADIE Credit Project for Self-employment in France (Rahman, 1993).
4. According to Morduch (1999, table 3) the overdue rate on Grameen loans averaged 7.8 per cent over 1985–96, compared with much higher overdue rates, some exceeding 50 per cent, for conventional bank loans in comparable regions.
5. See Guinnane (1994) and Ghatak and Guinnane (1999, sec. 3.1) on the origins of credit co-operatives in Germany in the nineteenth century. Key features of the German system included screening of members (not all were admitted) and project proposals (not all were financed).
6. According to Hughes (1992), there is also a public good character to MGSs, because the founding firms pay the greatest cost in setting up the loan guarantee, which later members can benefit from at lower cost. However, this does not necessarily provide a case for public support as Hughes suggests, because there is nothing to prevent incumbents devising ways of forcing future members to share the costs.
7. VC involvement can take the form of advice and assistance, based on the VC's own experience and contacts, and access to investment bankers, lawyers, accountants and consultants. Some VCs take a seat on the board of directors, and retain control rights, including the ability to appoint managers and remove members of the entrepreneurial team.
8. Descriptions of the characteristics and investment practices of business angels appear in Wetzel (1987) and Gaston (1989) for the USA, and Mason and Harrison (1994, 2000) for the UK.
9. However, subsequent econometric evidence from Gompers and Lerner (1998) detected a significant negative impact on VC commitments from CGT rates, which those authors argued constituted evidence of demand-side effects.

7 Evidence of credit rationing

Chapter 5 set out the theoretical arguments for and against credit rationing, where rationing may be of loan sizes (Type I rationing) or the number of loans (Type II rationing). That chapter concluded that theory alone cannot determine whether credit rationing exists and how widespread it might be in practice. Empirical evidence on these issues comprises the content of the present chapter.

The chapter is divided into three parts. Section 7.1 chronicles tests of Type I credit rationing. After introducing the influential paper by Evans and Jovanovic (1989), we survey the empirical literature. Most of its contributions are predicated on econometric estimates of a relationship between self-employment participation and personal wealth. Section 7.2 provides a critique of this methodology. Section 7.3 treats the empirical literature on Type II credit rationing. As in chapter 5, we concentrate on tests of equilibrium credit rationing, not 'temporary' or disequilibrium credit rationing, arising from a temporary excess demand for credit while banks adjust their interest rates.[1] Reflecting the emphasis in published research to date, the evidence discussed below focuses on developed economies. The causes and effects of credit rationing in developing countries tend to be highly country-specific: see, e.g., Levy (1993) and Kochar (1997).

At the outset we reiterate a point made in chapter 1: that claims by survey respondents should be treated with great caution. In the present context, these are claims that they face credit rationing. For example, according to Blanchflower and Oswald (1998) and Blanchflower, Oswald and Stutzer (2001), half of employee survey respondents claiming to have seriously considered becoming self-employed in the past blamed insufficient capital as the reason for not making the switch. However, this does not necessarily mean that loans were unavailable to these respondents. Another survey approach asks business owners whether they regard themselves as credit rationed (see, e.g., Cosh and Hughes, 1994; Moore, 1994; Guiso, 1998). However, this approach is prone to self-serving bias whereby entrepreneurs might blame banks for inherent shortcomings in their loan applications. Asking entrepreneurs what the price of loans should be is uninformative in any case, since it does not necessarily reflect the genuine cost of funds.

For these reasons, the empirical tests described below will be based on observed behaviour rather than subjective beliefs. This introduces its own problems, because desired loan sizes (for Type I rationing) and observationally identical ventures from banks' perspective (for Type II rationing) are difficult or impossible to identify directly in practice. Consequently, actual tests of Type I and Type II credit rationing tend to be indirect in nature.

7.1   Tests of Type I rationing

7.1.1   The Evans and Jovanovic (1989) model

An influential paper by Evans and Jovanovic (1989) (hereafter, EJ) stimulated a wave of empirical research on Type I credit rationing. EJ assumed that entrepreneurs can borrow only up to a multiple $\gamma \geq 1$ of their initial assets, B, where γ is common to all individuals. Therefore entrepreneurs can operate only capital $k \in (0, \gamma B)$. This corresponds to the case of Type I credit rationing, since banks are willing to extend loans to everyone with some assets, up to some given asset-determined limit, irrespective of the interest rate entrepreneurs are prepared to pay.

EJ assumed that borrowing and production take place in a single period. Entrepreneurs' incomes y depend on k via the production function $y = xk^\alpha$, where x is managerial ability and $\alpha \in (0, 1)$ is a parameter. A constrained borrower enters entrepreneurship iff their earnings net of capital repayments $D = (1 + r)\gamma B$ (where $r > 0$ is the nominal interest rate) exceeds their earnings in paid employment, w. This occurs iff

$$x(\gamma B)^\alpha - (1 + r)\gamma B > w . \tag{7.1}$$

If a sample of individuals with given abilities are drawn at random from the population, then the probability that they are entrepreneurs is an increasing function of assets B, as can be verified by differentiating the LHS of (7.1). This is the first of two predictions:

1. There is a positive relationship between the probability of entering entrepreneurship, and assets prior to entering entrepreneurship.
2. Wealthier entrepreneurs will operate larger enterprises on average than poorer ones and so will receive higher incomes.

EJ estimated a simple probit model of entry into self-employment conditioned on assets (in levels and squared) – as well as wage experience, education, and assorted personal characteristics. They used NLS data on 1,500 white males over 1978–81 who were wage earners in 1976; and reported a positive and significant probit coefficient (p-value $= 0.02$) on initial assets. This supports prediction 1. Also, log self-employment incomes were also found to be significantly and positively related to log initial assets, supporting prediction 2.

EJ went on to estimate a structural model of occupational choice, borrowing constraints and a managerial ability–assets relationship. They estimated γ to be 1.44, and significantly greater than 1; a subsequent estimate by Xu (1998) based on more accurate data found $\hat{\gamma} = 2.01$. Also, EJ estimated that 94 per cent of individuals likely to start a business faced Type I credit rationing. They claimed that this prevented 1.3 per cent of Americans from trying entrepreneurship. These are large effects, which have encouraged subsequent researchers to explore their robustness.

7.1.2   Effects of assets on becoming or being self-employed

Following EJ, many researchers have used cross-sectional or longitudinal data to estimate a probit self-employment equation, including some measure of individuals' assets or asset windfalls among the explanatory variables. Others have used time-series data to estimate the effects of aggregate wealth on the average self-employment rate. Many of these studies have detected significant positive effects of personal wealth on self-employment propensities and rates (we will discuss below results relating to asset windfalls),[2] while a handful have detected insignificant effects (e.g., Taylor, 2001; Uusitalo, 2001). Taken at face value, these results appear to support EJ's claims about the importance of Type I credit rationing.

These results raise a number of questions. First, should researchers study the effects of wealth on the probability that individuals *are* self-employed, or the probability that they *become* self-employed? Arguably, the most precise effects are obtained by focusing on the latter since established entrepreneurs could not by definition have faced Type I credit rationing that was severe enough to have prevented their participation in entrepreneurship. Second, studying entry into self-employment avoids the charge of reverse causality, whereby the self-employed are wealthy because of previous success in self-employment. Indeed, it is now widely accepted that endogeneity problems render personal wealth variables of limited value in empirical investigations of Type I credit rationing.

In recognition of this point, several researchers have explored the role of financial variables that are arguably less prone to endogeneity. These include asset windfalls of some kind, such as inheritances, gifts, or lottery wins, that are presumably exogenous to the self-employment entry decision and that can potentially overcome any Type I credit rationing. Empirical studies have generally found positive, significant and substantial effects of windfalls on self-employment status and entry probabilities, with diminishing returns from higher windfall values.[3] We cite some 'typical' findings to give a flavour of the results. Blanchflower and Oswald (1998) reported that a Briton who received £5,000 in 1981 prices was twice as likely to be self-employed in 1981 as an otherwise comparable person who had received nothing. Holtz-Eakin, Joulfaiah and Rosen (1994a) reported that a $100,000 inheritance would increase the probability of a transition from paid employment to self-employment in the USA by 3.3 percentage points. Lindh and Ohlsson (1996) estimated that the probability of self-employment in Sweden would increase by 54 per cent if lottery winnings were received, and by 27 per cent on receipt of an average-sized inheritance.

Findings of a positive and significant role for windfalls appear to be robust to some obvious sources of bias. These include self-employed people being more willing to gamble on lotteries (the opposite appears to be the case according to Lindh and Ohlsson, 1996 and Uusitalo, 2001); to inheritances being anticipated or being in the form of family businesses; and to industry differences due to different required capital intensities (Bates, 1995). In fact, true effects from windfalls may be under-stated to the extent that researchers cannot always measure delayed entries into self-employment following the receipt of a windfall. Entry decisions may take several years to play out.

7.1.3   Effects of assets on firm survival

As well as facilitating start-ups, personal wealth might also enhance a new venture's survival prospects. As Holtz-Eakin, Joulfaian and Rosen (1994b) assert: 'if entrepreneurs cannot borrow to attain their profit-maximising levels of capital, then those entrepreneurs who have substantial personal financial resources will be more successful than those who do not' (1994b, p. 53). Holtz-Eakin, Joulfaian and Rosen argued that unexpected increases in wealth (such as inheritance) will make entrepreneurship more attractive if the alternative is a business operating with a suboptimal capital stock. But in the absence of credit rationing, entrepreneurs will presumably operate their optimal capital stocks, so inheritance may actually make outside options like paid-employment or tax sheltering more attractive, leading to voluntary exit. Hence Holtz-Eakin, Joulfaian and Rosen argued that if inheritance is positively associated with company survival this can be taken as relatively strong evidence of Type I credit rationing.

Holtz-Eakin (1994b) found that inheritances increase the probability that self-employed Americans remain in self-employment. Similar results have been obtained by other researchers using measures of personal wealth rather than windfalls (Bates, 1990; Black, de Meza and Jeffreys, 1996; Taylor, 1999; Quadrini, 1999; Bruce, Holz-Eakin and Quinn, 2000), though Taylor (2001) found no effect of inheritances on UK self-employment survival probabilities.

Human capital potentially complicates the argument. On one hand, greater human capital might increase the productivity of physical capital, increasing the desired capital stock and hence the severity of Type I rationing. On the other hand, if education and wealth are correlated, then any rationing constraint might be eased. Cressy (1996) claimed that failing to control for human capital endows personal (housing) wealth with spurious explanatory power in UK business survival regressions. However, US evidence does not support the general contention that financial inputs are unimportant for explaining survival once human capital is controlled for.

7.1.4 Effects of assets on investment decisions

Fazzari, Hubbard and Petersen (1988) reported evidence that investment by large US firms is closely related to cash flow, with greater sensitivity among firms that they considered to be most vulnerable to Type I credit rationing. Several authors have subsequently replicated these findings (see Hubbard, 1998, for a review). However, Kaplan and Zingales (1997) challenged the consensus, arguing that investment–cash flow sensitivity does not constitute a useful measure of such rationing.[4] There does appear to be a problem with the interpretation of credit rationing in this context. According to Hubbard (1998), firms desire a loan size L^* at the market interest rate r, but because of agency costs arising from imperfect information, banks are only willing to supply L^* at a higher interest rate than r. As Jaffee and Stiglitz (1990, p. 847) emphasise, this involves 'price rationing' rather than credit rationing, since firms could obtain L^* if they paid a higher interest rate.

7.2 Critique

While some of the evidence outlined in the previous section is consistent with Type I credit rationing in principle, other explanations are also possible:
• Inherently acquisitive individuals both build up assets and prefer entrepreneurship to paid-employment, whether or not capital constraints

exist. More generally, the wealthy (or those who receive gifts or inheritances) may for unmeasured reasons be intrinsically more likely to be entrepreneurs and to remain in entrepreneurship. Alternatively, entrepreneurship allows wealthier individuals to consume leisure more easily.

• Inheritances are left to those working hard at developing new businesses. Blanchflower and Oswald (1998) claim that there is little evidence that bequests more generally are related to recipients' incomes; but separate evidence exists of 'strategic bequest behaviour', whereby bequests are contingent on recipients' behaviour and characteristics (Bernheim, Shleifer and Summers, 1985).

• A positive relationship between the number of entrepreneurs and personal wealth can also be consistent with over-investment, rather than Type I credit rationing (de Meza and Webb, 1999).

• A positive association between start-ups and wealth (or windfalls such as inheritances and lottery winnings) might simply reflect the effects of decreasing absolute risk aversion (DARA, see Definition 2 of chapter 2, section 2.2), rather than borrowing constraints. Consider again the Kihlstrom and Laffont (1979) model outlined in chapter 2, subsection 2.2.4. Under DARA, an increase in the wealth of the marginal risk-averse individual makes them more willing to enter risky entrepreneurship, so increasing the aggregate rate of entrepreneurship (Cressy, 2000).

• Entrepreneurs prefer self-finance to external finance, perhaps because they regard the terms of the latter to be unreasonable. Consequently, these individuals wait until they have saved (or inherited) enough wealth to enter entrepreneurship without borrowing. Yet all the while banks may have been willing to lend all of the required funds to every loan applicant.

• On a related point, individuals propose ventures for financing that banks perceive to be unprofitable at the proposed scale of operation. Hence banks rationally deny as much credit as potential entrepreneurs request. The latter then delay entry until they have sufficient wealth.

• When wealth is plentiful, there is greater entry into entrepreneurship and the resulting competition discourages those with sufficient wealth yet poor investment projects – implying a higher average survival rate (Black, de Meza and Jeffreys, 1996).

• Distressed firms face higher interest rates and lower credit availability (Harhoff and Körting, 1998). An inheritance or windfall merely relaxes the entrepreneur's budget constraint and permits them to survive in business a little longer.

There are also reasons to believe that any Type I rationing that does exist will be limited in scope. According to Meyer (1990), 60 per cent of new entrepreneurs have no depreciable capital and so cannot be credit constrained. And entrepreneurs might not be passive victims of borrowing constraints, having incentives to seek escape routes such as saving (Parker, 2000). To see this, consider the following lifecycle consumption model. Entrepreneurs' incomes y are a concave function of capital $k \geq 0$: $y = q(k)$. Let wage income be w, so $\tilde{k} = q^{-1}(w)$ is the minimum capital needed to attract individuals into entrepreneurship. Financial assets B can be costlessly transformed into physical capital k; individuals have heterogeneous asset endowments. The optimal capital stock k^* is defined by the usual marginal productivity condition $(\partial q/\partial k)|_{k=k^*} = r + \alpha$, where $r > 0$ is the interest rate and $\alpha > 0$ the rate of depreciation of capital.

Suppose that banks constrain borrowing such that individuals with $B < \tilde{k}$ cannot enter entrepreneurship. Individuals with $\tilde{k} < B < k^*$ do become entrepreneurs but cannot attain k^* immediately. All individuals choose their occupation, physical investment path $\{dk(t)/dt\}$ and consumption path $\{\zeta(t)\}$ to maximise discounted lifetime utility, where $\delta > 0$ is the discount rate and $U(\zeta)$ is the (concave) instantaneous utility function. The Lagrangean for this state-space constrained optimal control problem is

$$\Lambda = U(\zeta)e^{-\delta t} + (\Lambda_B + \Omega_B)[rB + \max\{q(k), w\} - \zeta - dk/dt]$$
$$+(\Lambda_k + \Omega_k)[(dk/dt) - \alpha k], \qquad (7.2)$$

where $\Lambda_B > 0$ and $\Lambda_k > 0$ are co-state variables; and Ω_B and Ω_k are variables taking zero values if the credit rationing constraint and the $k \geq 0$ constraint, respectively, do not bind, and are positive otherwise. From (7.2), the first-order condition for consumption is

$$\frac{\partial U}{\partial \zeta} = e^{\delta t}(\Lambda_B + \Omega_B). \qquad (7.3)$$

Thus a rationed individual (with $\Omega_B > 0$) has higher marginal utility and hence lower consumption, than an unconstrained entrepreneur (with $\Omega_B = 0$) does. This implies that constrained entrepreneurs optimally invest their savings to build up physical capital, allowing them to either enter entrepreneurship or to attain k^* if they are already entrepreneurs. In contrast, unconstrained entrepreneurs have attained k^* and invest only to offset depreciation.

Some supportive evidence for savings as a means of building capital stocks comes from Quadrini's (1999) analysis of 1980s PSID data. Quadrini reported that American households with a self-employed head not only have greater wealth and higher wealth–income ratios on average, but also experience more upward mobility in the distributions of wealth and the wealth–income ratio than employee households do (see also

Knight and McKay, 2000, for UK evidence). However, the strategy of saving as an escape mechanism has its own limitations. Parker (2000) showed that some individuals will optimally choose to remain credit constrained forever, if they are so impatient that they prefer consuming when young to saving for the future. This implies that, in some cases, borrowing constraints should be regarded as voluntary, rather than involuntary. A second caveat to the escape mechanism is that some employees may earn too little (i.e. w is too low) to permit them to build up sufficient savings to enter self-employment. Also, at very low levels of income and consumption, reducing consumption in order to accumulate assets may not be optimal because it can seriously threaten health, production efficiency and longevity (Gersovitz, 1983). While this problem might not be widespread in developed economies, it might be more important in some poor developing countries.

It is now fairly well established that self-employment participation and survival rates are both positively related to personal wealth and financial windfalls. Furthermore, it has been convincingly demonstrated that these findings do not merely reflect superior wealth-creating opportunities in self-employment. However, these findings do not of themselves prove the existence of Type I credit rationing, since several alternative explanations are also consistent with them. One must conclude that given the present state of the literature we have not resolved the vexed question of whether Type I credit rationing exists, and if so, how widespread it is. Sharper tests of the Type I credit rationing hypothesis (possibly based on bank loan application micro-data matched with borrower surveys) are needed before any firmer conclusions can be reached.

7.3   Tests of Type II credit rationing

In the absence of Type II credit rationing, interest rates on commercial loans will adjust freely in response to changes in the supply of and demand for credit. But if credit rationing exists, that is no longer the case, and commercial loan rates will exhibit 'stickiness'. This, at least, can be expected to apply to non-commitment loans, where a commitment loan (CL) is a loan that a bank agrees to allocate to a firm over a specified period should the latter request it. Contractually, a CL cannot be rationed or withdrawn once it has been granted, so it can be regarded as a hedge against the future hazard of Type II credit rationing.

A problem with interpreting sticky loan rates as evidence of credit rationing is that alternative explanations for this phenomenon also exist. One is Fried and Howitt's (1980) implicit contract theory, whereby banks and borrowers agree to fix interest rates for long periods of time irrespective of economic conditions. Another is the 'distressed company' phenomenon, whereby banks prefer not to increase lending rates in line with base rates if this tips clients into bankruptcy and forces the lender to incur bankruptcy costs.[5]

Early studies used aggregate time-series data to test for loan rate stickiness (e.g. Goldfeld, 1966). More recent work along these lines by Slovin and Sushka (1983) and King (1986) provides mixed evidence on the loan rate stickiness issue. However, the highly aggregated nature of this research is a serious drawback, because it averages over heterogeneous loan types. Micro-data are to be preferred because of their greater detail and precision. Berger and Udell (1992), who proposed the following tests, conducted an especially thorough analysis of the credit rationing hypothesis using micro-data:

1. *The stickiness test.* Consider the following regression:

$$(r - \tilde{\rho})_i = \beta_1 \rho_i + \beta_2 \rho_i^2 + \gamma_1' X_{1i} + \gamma_2' X_{2i} + u_i \,, \qquad (7.4)$$

where ρ_i is the open-market (safe) interest rate for observation i; $\tilde{\rho}_i$ is the equivalent rate defined for the same term as the commercial loan rate r_i; X_{1i} is a vector of loan contract variables; X_{2i} is a vector of bank and macroeconomic variables; and u_i is a disturbance term. If there is loan rate stickiness of r, then a negative net effect from ρ_i should be observed, since an increase in ρ_i (and hence $\tilde{\rho}_i$) will reduce the loan premium on the LHS of (7.4) if r_i is sticky. The credit rationing hypothesis implies rate stickiness for non-CL cases, but not for CLs.

2. *The proportions test.* Consider the following regression:

$$\ln \left(\frac{p_c}{1 - p_c} \right)_i = \beta_1 \rho_i + \beta_2 \rho_i^2 + \gamma_1' X_{1i} + \gamma_2' X_{2i} + v_i \,, \qquad (7.5)$$

where p_c is the proportion of loans that are CLs. The Type II credit rationing hypothesis predicts that the proportion of CLs is an increasing function of ρ_i (or some other measure of credit market tightness). This is because Type II credit rationing reduces the number of non-CLs, while leaving the number of CLs unchanged (since they are contractually insulated from credit rationing) – so increasing p_c.[6]

Based on a sample of a million commercial loans in the USA between 1977 and 1988, Berger and Udell (1992) reported the following findings:

1. *The stickiness test*

   (a) The elasticity of the premium with respect to ρ was negative and significant (-0.19 and -0.34 for nominal and real ρ, respectively),[7] implying loan rate stickiness. However, CL rates were also sticky, suggesting that reasons other than Type II credit rationing must account for the observed stickiness.

(b) Less stickiness was observed during periods of 'credit crunch', contradicting the credit rationing hypothesis.

2. *The proportions test*
   (a) Doubling the nominal safe interest rate increased the probability of observing a CL in the sample by 1.7 per cent, supporting the Type II credit rationing hypothesis. However, opposite results were obtained when ρ was measured in real terms, so contradicting it.
   (b) In times of credit crunch or low loan-growth rates, the proportion of CLs was observed to decrease. The opposite would be expected to occur under credit rationing.

On the basis of this evidence, Berger and Udell (1992) concluded that 'information-based equilibrium credit rationing, if it exists, may be relatively small and economically insignificant' (1992, p. 1071). They went on to suggest that, even if some borrowers are rationed, others take their place and receive bank loans.

A direct upper bound estimate of the extent of Type II credit rationing can be proposed: the number of loans rejected by banks *for any reason*. If the loan rejection rate is very low, then credit rationing cannot be important. Using US data on small-company borrowing over 1987–8, Levenson and Willard (2000) estimated that only 2.14 per cent of small firms ultimately failed to obtain the funding they sought. Of course, the actual extent of credit rationing will be lower than this to the extent that some of these loans were observably non-creditworthy and so deserved to be rejected.[8]

In the light of these findings, claims of widespread credit rationing based on structural models (e.g. Perez, 1998) must surely be treated with scepticism. Other 'direct' evidence sheds further light on the Type II credit rationing phenomenon. Theories of rationing based on adverse selection suggest that bank managers deny credit in preference to raising interest rates, even if rationed borrowers are willing to pay higher rates (see chapter 5, section 5.1). National Economic Research Associates (NERA) (1990) obtained direct evidence of reluctance among bank managers to raise interest rates above the bank's 'standard' business rate for observably higher-risk projects. However, NERA found that this reluctance was motivated not by concerns about adverse selection or moral hazard, but by anxiety that public relations could be harmed by an image of the bank as a 'usurer'. It may be noted that the bank managers surveyed had no obvious motive for responding with self-serving bias.

It might be thought that there is an even simpler way to establish the existence of Type II credit rationing. This is to compare survival rates of entrepreneurial ventures funded with government-backed loans that would not have been granted without the government guarantee, with survival rates of ventures that were financed purely privately. If the two survival rates are similar, then it might seem possible to argue that the government intervention has alleviated credit rationing. In fact, although there is some evidence that Loan Guarantee Scheme (LGS)-backed start-ups do have similar survival rates as purely privately funded start-ups, this conclusion does not necessarily follow. The primary role of a LGS is to help fund entrepreneurs who lack collateral and/or a track record, and so are observably risky to finance. Banks refusing to finance ventures that they expect to be loss making cannot be construed as rationing credit. The whole point of a loan guarantee is to insure banks against most of the downside risk, turning some potentially loss making investments into profitable lending opportunities. The evidence does suggest that these are indeed the projects that banks typically put through LGSs (KPMG, 1999).

On the other hand, even if Type II credit rationing is empirically unimportant, the perception of it might discourage potential entrepreneurs from approaching banks in the first place. Some supporting evidence for this hypothesis comes from Levenson and Willard (2000), who estimated that 4.2 per cent of the individuals in their US sample were 'discouraged borrowers'. Cowling (1998) provides a similar estimate for the UK.

Overall, the evidence cited above does not provide much support for the notion that banks engage in Type II credit rationing. However, just as with Type I rationing, more research is needed before a clear conclusion can be reached. One interesting empirical avenue that might be worth pursuing is a detailed analysis of the characteristics of rejected loan applications. This could help tighten the upper-bound estimate of Type II credit rationing suggested by Levenson and Willard (2000), and might even rule out the phenomenon as having any empirical significance whatsoever.

NOTES

1. For empirical investigations of temporary credit rationing and references to the earlier literature, see e.g., Browne (1987) and Kugler (1987).
2. For cross-section studies, see Evans and Leighton (1989b), Bernhardt (1994), Bates (1995, 1997), Laferrère and McEntee (1995), van Praag and van Ophem (1995), Taylor (1996), Fairlie (1999), Quadrini (1999), Bruce, Holz-Eakin and Quinn (2000), Dunn and Holtz-Eakin (2000), and Johansson (2000). For time-series studies, see Robson (1991, 1996, 1998a, 1998b), Black, de Meza and Jeffreys (1996) and Cowling and Mitchell (1997).
3. See Holtz-Eakin, Joulfaian and Rosen (1994a, 1994b), Lindh and Ohlsson (1996), Blanchflower and Oswald (1998) and Taylor (2001).
4. See also the subsequent exchange between these authors in the May 2000 issue of the *Quarterly Journal of Economics*.

5. Both of these explanations can account for Berger and Udell's (1992) finding that up to 7 per cent of US commercial loans over 1977–88 charged interest rates at *below* the (safe) open-market rate.
6. An exception to this argument, noted by Berger and Udell (1992), could occur in the event of an increase in the demand for non-CLs only. Then credit rationing ensures that there will be no change in p_c despite greater credit market tightness.
7. Both these and all subsequent estimates quoted below were evaluated at sample means. Similar results were obtained using the growth of loan volumes as an inverse measure of credit market tightness.
8. Also, Levenson and Willard (2000) found the probability of loan denial to be negatively related to firm size, so the extent of credit rationing by value was even less than 2 per cent. UK evidence from Cosh and Hughes (1994) tells a similar story to Levenson and Willard (2000). From a sample of firms surveyed between 1987 and 1989, Cosh and Hughes (1994) reported that only 3.2 per cent of firms seeking external finance failed to obtain it.

Part III

Running and terminating an enterprise

8   Labour demand and supply

Considerable policy interest centres on entrepreneurship as a means of employment creation. This is one of two labour market-related topics explored in this chapter, the other being labour supply. Section 8.1 briefly outlines some evidence on employment by entrepreneurs, the factors that appear to affect it and the contribution made by small firms to aggregate job creation. Section 8.2 describes the nature of work performed by entrepreneurs, their labour supply, their changing participation rates as they age and their retirement behaviour.

8.1   Entrepreneurs as employers

8.1.1   Evidence about self-employed 'job creators'

In most countries only a minority of self-employed people hires other workers. For example, according to Bregger (1996), only 21 per cent of self-employed Americans hired any employees in 1995. Of these, a third had only one employee, and only one-seventh hired six or more. Of those who had held second jobs in which they were self-employed, only 7 per cent hired employees. Also, Kuhn and Schuetze (2001) found that only 32 per cent of male and 22 per cent of female self-employed owners of established Canadian businesses over 1982–98 hired any paid help. The story is similar in the UK, where the 1991 BHPS reveals that just over 30 per cent of self-employed people hired any other workers. According to Moralee (1998), employment-creating self-employment declined by about 7 per cent in the UK between 1992 and 1997. Lin, Picot Compton (2000) and Kuhn and Schuetze (2001) noticed a similar trend in Canada. The reasons behind these trends are unclear.

There are many reasons why only a minority of the self-employed employs others. They include the nature of the work (which is sometimes innately solo rather than team-based); high employee wage rates; government employment protection; and perhaps also borrowing constraints if employment is bundled with investment (Jefferson, 1997). In addition, some entrepreneurs seem to be intrinsically uninterested in growing their businesses;[1] and as small businesses expand and take on workers, they become likelier to incorporate, at which point the owners technically become employees of the incorporated firm rather than self-employed.

Curran and Burrows (1989) showed that British self-employed employers tend to have different characteristics to the own-account self-employed, being older, more likely to be full-time married males, better educated, from comfortable family backgrounds and working in 'distribution, hotels, catering and repairs'. In contrast, own-account self-employed males are heavily concentrated in construction. Curran and Burrows also observed that self-employed employers were more likely to own their home (89.3 per cent of males) than the own-account self-employed (75.6 per cent of males), who in turn were more likely to own their home than employees were (68.2 per cent of males). All of the above findings have received independent support in multivariate analyses of individual characteristics (see, e.g., Burke, Fitz-Roy and Nolan 2000 and Cowling and Taylor, 2001, for Britain; van Praag and Cramer, 2001, for the Netherlands; and Earle and Sakova, 2000, for Eastern Europe). The positive impact of education, parental education and parental self-employment on employer status also emerges clearly from these studies.

Can governments stimulate employment creation? Few of the covariates mentioned above are directly amenable to government control, but there is some evidence that self-employed hiring decisions are sensitive to personal income tax (IT) rates. Estimates by Carroll *et al.* (2000a) based on US IRS data suggest that a 10 per cent reduction in the marginal income tax rate increases the probability of the self-employed hiring workers by 12 per cent. The implied elasticity of 1.2 suggests that general income tax reductions might be a powerful way of stimulating employment creation. More research is needed in this area, however, before any firm conclusions can be reached.

8.1.2   Evidence about job creation by small firms

The publication of the influential Birch Report in the USA (Birch, 1979) stimulated a wave of research on the job creation performance of small firms. While small firms themselves are not the primary focus of interest in this book, many of them are owned and managed by entrepreneurs, so it seems appropriate to review this literature briefly. Our emphasis will be on facts about relative job creation performance, rather than on the determinants of employment growth in small firms, an issue that is treated in chapter 9.

Birch (1979) claimed that between 1969 and 1976, small firms employing fewer than twenty workers generated 66 per cent of all new US jobs, and firms with fewer than 100 employees accounted for 82 per cent of net job gains. The implication is that the small-firm sector is the primary engine of job creation. Subsequent researchers have confirmed these findings for the USA and other countries.[2] Strikingly, Acs and Audretsch (1993) highlighted a distinct and consistent shift away from employment in large firms and towards small enterprises in the 1980s in every major western economy.

Others have challenged these claims, however. An early rebuff came from Armington and Odle (1982), whose study of employment changes over 1978–80 revealed much smaller small-business job creation rates than Birch (1979). But as Kirchhoff and Greene (1998) pointed out, Armington and Odle's findings might have merely reflected the unusually subdued macroeconomic conditions prevailing between 1978 and 1980. Weightier criticisms of Birch's thesis came in the late 1980s and early 1990s. In particular, Davis and Haltiwanger (1992) and Davis, Haltiwanger and Schuh (1996a, 1996b) argued that 'conventional wisdom about the job-creating powers of small businesses rests on statistical fallacies and misleading interpretations of the data' (Davis, Haltiwanger and Schuh, 1996a, p. 57). These were said to include:

1. The 'size distribution fallacy', whereby static size distributions of numbers employed by employer size are used to draw inferences about dynamic changes in employment shares. Measures such as 'the net change in employment by small firms as a proportion of the net change in total employment' are biased when firms move between size categories. They can also be misleading if the denominator of this ratio is very small over a particular period, exaggerating the scale of employment growth by small firms.

2. The 'regression fallacy', whereby transitory size shocks bias the relationship between employment growth and firm size. To see this, let H_t^* be true employment size at time t, and H_t be observed size: $H_t = H_t^* + v_t$, where v_t is a measurement error with variance σ_v^2. Suppose $H_t^* = H_{t-1}^* + u_t$, where u_t is a transitory shock that is independent of v_t. Then the true average conditional change in employment size is zero:

$$E(\Delta H_t^* | H_{t-1}^*) = 0 .$$

However, were the conditional change in employment to be estimated using actual data, which are subject to measurement error and transitory shocks, one would erroneously find

$$E(\Delta H_t | H_{t-1}) = -\left[\sigma_v^2 / \left(\sigma_{H^*}^2 + \sigma_v^2 \right) \right] H_{t-1} < 0,$$

implying a spurious negative relationship between firm growth and size. This partly accounts for the importance of the next problem:

3. *Poor quality US micro-data,* distorting the true employment creation–firm size relationship.
4. *Confusion between net and gross job creation,* since small firms destroy many jobs as well as creating them.
5. *Sample selection bias,* whereby small firms with poor job creation records die and leave the sample, biasing upwards measured small firm job creation rates.[3]

While the researcher can do relatively little about low-quality data, it is possible to fix most of the other problems listed here. Most researchers now eschew simplistic static size distribution comparisons, and measure net, not gross, job creation rates. Many also circumvent the regression fallacy by measuring a firm's growth rate relative to a sample period average size rather than relative to initial size. Recognising these points, and using a panel of data on US manufacturing plants over 1972–88, Davis, Haltiwanger and Schuh claimed that, in contrast to Birch, *larger* plants and firms create (and destroy) most manufacturing jobs. In addition, Davis, Haltiwanger and Schuh found no clear relationship between rates of *net* job creation and employer size. However, despite some corroborative evidence from Wagner (1995), many other researchers have made similar corrections and reasserted a negative cross-section relationship between firm size and employment creation (see, e.g., Hall, 1987; Baldwin and Picot, 1995; Konings, 1995; Hart and Oulton, 1996; and Davidsson, Lindmark and Olofsson, 1998). Some of the disagreement may be attributable to the exclusion by Davis, Haltiwanger and Schuh and Wagner of service sector firms from their samples.

While the precise scale of the contribution by small firms to employment creation is still disputed, the OECD (1998) claimed that there is now 'general agreement' that the share of jobs accounted for by small firms has steadily increased since the early 1970s in most developed economies. It is also now known that a few firms with spectacular growth rates create a disproportionate number of jobs.[4] These firms, often called 'gazelles', commonly have over 100 employees but tend to be neither young nor small in terms of turnover or assets (OECD, 1998). Of course, there is no logical contradiction between a statement that small firms are the greatest source of net new jobs, and the statement that a small number of such firms creates a disproportionate number of jobs.

Finally, an issue that is arguably just as important as the rate of employment growth is the quality of the jobs created by new start-ups. The lower survival rates of new start-ups and the greater variance of their growth rates cast some doubt on the stability and durability of the new jobs created (Davis, Haltiwanger and Schuh, 1996a). Small firms also employ more part-time workers, freelancers and home-workers. Furthermore, their employees tend to be less well educated on average, receiving lower wages, fewer fringe benefits, lower levels of training and working longer hours with a greater risk of major injury[5] – while enjoying lower job tenure than their counterparts in larger firms (Brown, Hamilton and Medoff, 1990). Brown, Hamilton and Medoff (1990) in particular reported a substantial 'size-wage' premium, with workers in large companies earning over 30 per cent more on average than their counterparts in small firms. This finding appears to hold across industries and countries, too. Of course, small firms might also offer compensating benefits, such as a more flexible and informal working environment, greater employee involvement and more tangible commitment by the owners.

8.2   Entrepreneurs as suppliers of labour

8.2.1   Hours of work

Most self-employed Britons, Americans and Canadians work full-time rather than part-time (see, respectively, Casey and Creigh, 1988; Bregger, 1996; and Kuhn and Schuetze, 2001). Defining 'full-time' to be thirty or more hours per week, 80–90 per cent of male self-employed people work full-time, compared with about 50 per cent of their female counterparts. There is mixed evidence about whether the self-employed are more or less likely than employees to work part-time (Aronson, 1991; Bregger, 1996). But it is fairly well established that self-employed males work longer per week on average than employees do (Carrington, McCue and Pierce, 1996); and self-employed employers put in the greatest number of weekly hours of all (Curran and Burrows, 1989).[6] Self-employed Americans work a similar number of *weeks per year* as employees do, except in recessions, where the self-employed reduce their weekly work hours while employees reduce the number of weeks they work (Carrington, McCue and Pierce, 1996). According to these authors, annual work hours in the USA are no more cyclical for male self-employed workers than for male employees.

As with employees, average weekly self-employed work hours have been declining over time in most OECD countries, and the gap between the two groups of workers has also been narrowing in many of them (OECD, 1986; Aronson, 1991; Rees and Shah, 1994; Moralee, 1998). One possible reason is the growth in female self-employment, since as noted above a greater proportion of female than male self-employed work part-time. In the UK, part-time self-employment increased by 22 per cent between

1990 and 1997, while full-time self-employment decreased by 12 per cent (Moralee, 1998).

Explaining entrepreneurs' labour supply

There is now an extensive literature explaining the labour supply behaviour of employees (see Blundell and MaCurdy, 1999, for a review). That literature is partly concerned with measuring the impact of wages on hours worked. This has obvious policy relevance because income taxes reduce wages and hence may have important labour disincentive effects.

It is natural to seek to extend this analytical framework to entrepreneurs. However, only few studies have attempted this to date, taking entrepreneurs to be the self-employed. Part of the reason for the limited analysis of this issue is that sample sizes tend to be smaller for the self-employed than for employees. But there are also intrinsic difficulties involved in analysing labour supply for self-employed workers. First, many individuals are only self-employed temporarily, rendering lifecycle modelling of their behaviour problematic. Second, unlike employees who face a fixed wage, the self-employed 'wage' must be imputed from profits and work hours. As explained in chapter 1, section 1.5, measured wages are prone to under-reporting biases and compounding of returns to capital and labour; and if consumers' demand for self-employed labour is less than infinitely elastic, then the wage depends on the labour they supply – rendering the wage endogenous (Quinn, 1980).[7] Third, it can be difficult to separate labour supply decisions from labour demand considerations, if the self-employed hire outside labour. Fourth, there is a greater tendency for the self-employed to do multiple jobs than employees, which further complicates the modelling of their labour supply behaviour.[8]

Standard labour supply models decompose work-hour responses to wage changes into two components: a *substitution effect* and an *income effect*. The former describes how workers increase their work effort to exploit the higher return from working, holding income constant; the latter describes the effects of greater resources on the work–leisure choice. The former is positive in work–wage space; the latter is ambiguous in sign, but is negative if individuals demand more leisure as their income rises. If the substitution effect dominates, then labour supply is increasing in the wage rate (i.e. upward sloping in wage–hours space). But if the income effect becomes dominant at higher wage rates, then an individual's labour supply schedule can bend backwards, implying that work-hours eventually decline as wages rise.

There are two broad categories of labour supply model: static and lifecycle. An example of a static model of self-employed labour supply is

Wales (1973). Static models assume that individuals maximise a simple atemporal utility function $U(\zeta, h)$, where ζ is consumption and h is work-hours, subject to an atemporal budget constraint tying consumption to income, the latter being partly determined by h. Using such a model, Wales (1973) estimated that most self-employed Americans were located on a backward-bending segment of their labour supply schedule, implying that they would work *less* in response to a higher return to their labour. The predicted effects on work-hours of changes in marginal income tax rates were more muted. However, Wales addressed few of the practical problems pertaining to the modelling of self-employed labour supply noted above.

Static models have also been estimated for specific self-employed occupations, notably physicians, dentists and farmers. For example, Thornton (1998) estimated that the typical self-employed male physician was located on an upward sloping portion of their labour supply curve, although their labour supply was relatively insensitive to changes in hourly wage rates and non-practice income.[9] Thornton (1994) analysed the behaviour of self-employed farmers who can also choose to work off-farm in paid-employment. He reported a substantially greater responsiveness of farmer work-hours to the off-farm wage than to the on-farm (self-employed) wage (see also Lopez, 1984).

A problem with static labour supply models is that they ignore information from other time periods that can impact on individuals' current behaviour. For example, if an entrepreneur anticipates a future recession that will decrease the demand for his good, then he might work harder now than otherwise knowing that he can take more leisure later when it is cheaper. Lifecycle models incorporate information about future incomes in order to identify this kind of *intertemporal substitution*. Subject to the caveat that future incomes are difficult to predict for workers who are only temporarily self-employed, lifecycle models do at least enable policy-relevant labour supply elasticities to be estimated. This is because tax reforms typically impact on both current and future incomes (Blundell and MaCurdy, 1999, sec. 4.5).

Rees and Shah (1994) analysed the following lifecycle labour supply model. Let w and h_E represent the wage rate and hours of work in paid-employment, respectively. Hours in self-employment are denoted by $h_S \equiv h$, which together with managerial ability x are arguments of the self-employed production function: $q = q(h_S, x)$. Assets are given by B and consumption by ζ; r and δ are the rates of interest and intertemporal discounting, respectively; l denotes hours of leisure; and β is a vector of taste parameters. The output price is normalised to unity for simplicity. All variables are indexed by time t. The lifecycle problem can be written in discrete notation as:

$$\max_{\{\zeta_t, h_{St}, h_{Et}\}} \sum_t \left(\frac{1}{1+\delta}\right)^t U(\zeta_t, h_{Et}, h_{St}; \beta_t) \qquad (8.1)$$

$$\text{subject to} \quad 1 = h_{Et} + h_{St} + l_t \;\; ; \quad h_{Et}, h_{St}, l_t \geq 0 \quad \forall t \quad (8.2)$$

$$\text{and} \quad B_{t+1} = (1 + r_t)B_t + w_t h_{Et} + q(h_{St}, x) - \zeta_t. \qquad (8.3)$$

Equation (8.2) allows mixing of work between occupations, subject to available time being normalised to unity. Equation (8.3) is the intertemporal budget constraint describing the evolution of assets. The necessary conditions for a solution to this problem are:

$$U_{\zeta_t} = \tilde{\lambda}_t = \left(\frac{1+r_t}{1+\delta}\right) E_t(\tilde{\lambda}_{t+1})$$

$$-U_{h_{Et}} = \tilde{\lambda}_t w_t + \tilde{\omega}_{Et} \quad , \qquad -U_{h_{St}} = \tilde{\lambda}_t q_{h_{St}} + \omega_{St},$$

where $\tilde{\lambda}_t$ is the marginal utility of wealth, and the two $\tilde{\omega}_{jt}$ terms are Kuhn–Tucker multipliers required to ensure non-negative labour supplies. Assuming a particular separable form for the utility function, it is possible to derive, as an interior solution, a labour supply equation for each of the two occupations $j = \{S, E\}$, which has the semi-log form

$$h_{jt} = \beta_{0t} + \beta_1 \ln w_{jt} + \beta_2 \ln \tilde{\lambda}_t, \qquad (8.4)$$

where β_1 and β_2 are parameters, and β_{0t} is assumed to be related to personal characteristics.

A complete lifecycle model identifies $\tilde{\lambda}_t$ by forecasting future income profiles (Blundell and MaCurdy, 1999, sec. 4.4.4). Rees and Shah (1994) did not in fact do this, but simply estimated a version of (8.4) omitting $\tilde{\lambda}_t$ based on pooled cross-sections of UK GHS data from the 1970s and 1980s. Separate equations were estimated for employees and the self-employed. Their findings were as follows. First, for both groups, $\hat{\beta}_1$ was insignificant, implying that neither employees nor the self-employed significantly vary their hours of work in response to changes in the wage rate. Second, ill health was found not to significantly affect self-employed labour supply. Third, being married significantly increased self-employed labour supply (possibly because of having a spouse to help in the business), but having children under five years old significantly reduced it. Having older children made no difference to self-employed labour supply. Fourth, year dummies were negative and significant in the early 1980s. This probably reflects the limited opportunities for work in recession years, though it is also possible that the 'new' self-employed entrants to self-employment in these years may have been less inclined to work long hours. Either way, the negative sign of these dummies confounds the view that the much lauded 'enterprise culture' of the period translated into greater labour supply by the self-employed.

The omission by Rees and Shah (1994) of information on future incomes, which is required to estimate a complete lifecycle empirical model, may not be so serious if the results of Camerer *et al.* (1997) are generally applicable. These authors analysed daily variation in the work-hours and wages of self-employed taxi cab drivers in New York City. They argued that cab drivers find it easier to earn money quickly on some days than on others, because of exogenous factors like bad weather or train strikes. One might expect cab drivers to practise intertemporal substitution, working longer hours on high-wage days and taking time off on slack days. However, estimates from a simple double-log regression model $\ln h_{Si} = \beta_0 + \beta_1 \ln w_i + \beta_2' X_i + u_i$ (where X is a vector of exogenous variables) yielded exactly the opposite result. Drivers in the Camerer *et al.* sample responded to busier conditions (and hence higher hourly wages) by working *fewer* rather than longer hours. This is indicative of a backward-bending labour supply schedule. It is as though cab drivers take one day at a time, having a target income for each day, and stopping work as soon as they achieve it.

This behaviour might be explained by workers relying on simple heuristic rules in response to uncertainty. Perhaps surprisingly, uncertainty has not been extensively analysed in studies of self-employed labour supply. This is despite the possibility that it might help resolve the puzzle, alluded to at the end of chapter 1, subsection 1.5.1, of why the self-employed work longer hours on average than employees do, despite earning lower average wages. To see why, suppose that while employees can benefit from wage smoothing by their employers, receiving a constant w_E, the self-employed cannot diversify their risk, which takes the form of a wage shock ϱ where $E\varrho = 0$. Suppose that the self-employed indirect utility function is given by

$$V^* = U_1(w_S h^* + \varrho) + U_2(1 - h^*) + v, \qquad (8.5)$$

where $v > 0$ is a non-pecuniary advantage to self-employment, w_S is the self-employment wage and $U_1(\cdot)$ and $U_2(\cdot)$ are concave increasing and decreasing functions, respectively. Assume also that v is sufficiently great to ensure occupational equilibrium with $w_E > w_S$. The first-order condition determining optimal self-employed work-hours h^* is $w_S E \partial U_1/\partial h^* - \partial U_2/\partial h^* = 0$. Then it is known (Rothschild and Stiglitz, 1971) that a mean-preserving spread (MPS) in ϱ will increase or decrease

h^* as

$$\psi(\varrho) := w_S \partial U_1 / \partial h^* - \partial U_2 / \partial h^*$$

is convex or concave in ϱ. Differentiating twice with respect to ϱ yields

$$\frac{\partial^2 \psi(\varrho)}{\partial \varrho^2} = w_S \frac{\partial^3 U_1(\cdot)}{\partial y^3}, \tag{8.6}$$

where $y := w_S h^* + \varrho$. The RHS of (8.6) is positive if $\partial^3 U_1(\cdot)/\partial y^3 > 0$, in which case $\psi(\varrho)$ is convex, and labour supply increases with the degree of uncertainty. Since this condition on $U_1(\cdot)$ is satisfied by utility functions embodying decreasing absolute risk aversion (see Definition 2, chapter 2), this case seems a reasonable one. The self-employed effectively 'self-insure' by choosing a greater labour supply and thereby making the deterministic part of their income larger.

The foregoing provides a possible resolution of the self-employed labour supply puzzle, because it explains why the self-employed work harder in return for a lower wage than employees. The non-pecuniary benefit is necessary for anyone to choose self-employment at all, though it cannot of itself explain long work-hours in self-employment. However, the above result depends on risk affecting self-employment incomes additively. Were risk to impact on self-employment incomes in a multiplicative manner instead, then a MPS in ϱ would have ambiguously signed effects on self-employed labour supply. Naturally, other possible resolutions of the puzzle could also be proposed, such as unrealistic optimism by the self-employed, for example.

Finally, we note that further work remains to be done on improving our understanding of the labour supply of entrepreneurs. One aspect of this task might be to develop empirical specifications that are immune to self-employed income under-reporting biases. Another would be to model more explicitly non-pecuniary factors, in view of the findings of chapter 3, subsection 3.2.3 about their impact on the self-employed, together with Atrostic's (1982) evidence about their importance for explaining employees' labour supply behaviour.

Ageing and entrepreneurs' labour supply

At around the time of start-up, entrepreneurs often work very long hours in order to establish their enterprise. Once established, new enterprises often require somewhat less strenuous effort to maintain and manage. The implication is that younger entrepreneurs work harder than older ones do, since a greater proportion of the former implement start-ups than the latter, who have moved on to consolidate their earlier achievements. Certainly retired self-employed Americans work fewer hours on average than their non-retired counterparts (Fuchs, 1982; Honig and Hanoch, 1985). Younger entrepreneurs might also work longer hours than older ones because they have greater energy and stamina.

A further reason why entrepreneurs' labour supply may decline with age is that entrepreneurs' returns from expending costly effort decreases over time if effort reveals valuable information about innate ability. To see this, consider the following model proposed by Frank (1988). Consider an entrepreneur who works for a finite time span T. In each period he must choose whether to continue in entrepreneurship ($z_t = 1$) or to exit ($z_t = 0$). If $z_t = 1$, then he chooses labour supply, $h_t \in [0, \bar{h}]$. The disutility of supplying labour is given by $c(h_t)$, where $c(\cdot)$ is an increasing and convex function. The entrepreneur's revenue is $xh_t + \varrho_t$. Here x is ability, which is unknown to the entrepreneur at the time of entry in $t = 1$; his prior belief is that it is distributed with mean μ_1 and precision (defined as the reciprocal of the variance) v_1. Also, ϱ_t is a normally distributed random influence (e.g. 'luck'), distributed normally with mean zero and precision v_ϱ. Entrepreneurs perform Bayesian learning about x by observing successive realisations of $xh_t + \varrho_t$, which at time t is normally distributed with mean xh_t. Entrepreneurs' beliefs in $t + 1$ are characterised by a distribution with mean μ_{t+1} and precision v_{t+1}, where

$$\mu_{t+1} = \frac{v_t\mu_t + v_\varrho h_t(xh_t + \varrho_t)}{v_t + v_\varrho h_t^2} \tag{8.7}$$

$$v_{t+1} = v_t + v_\varrho h_t^2. \tag{8.8}$$

Evidently, if $h_t = 0$ then $\mu_{t+1} = \mu_t$ and $v_{t+1} = v_t$. Thus if the entrepreneur expends no effort, he obtains no new information about his entrepreneurial ability.

If $z_t = 0$, the individual takes an outside option (e.g. paid-employment) that yields utility w_t. Let U_t be the entrepreneur's discounted expected utility given that he entered initially and chooses all future z and h values optimally; $U_t \equiv 0$ for $t > T$. E_t is the expectations operator conditioned on the information available at time t, and $\beta = 1/(1 + \delta) \in (0, 1]$ is the discount factor. In each time period after entry at $t = 1$, we have

$$U_t = \max_{z_t, h_t} \left\{ w_t(1 - z_t) + [E_t(xh_t + \varrho_t) - c(h_t)]z_t + \beta E_t U_{t+1} \right\}$$
$$t = 2, 3, \ldots, T. \tag{8.9}$$

Proposition 7 (Frank, 1988). *Entrepreneurs optimally supply less labour as they age.*

Proof. We solve the model by backwards induction. At T, an entrepreneur remains in the industry (i.e. $z_T^* = 1$) if $w_T \leq \mu_T h_T^* - c(h_T^*)$, where h_T^* is optimal terminal effort, which satisfies $\mu_T = c_h(h_T^*)$. Given this solution, the period $T - 1$ problem is

$$U_{T-1} = \max_{z_{T-1}, h_{T-1}} \left\{ w_{T-1}(1 - z_{T-1}) + [E_{T-1}(xh_{T-1} + \varrho_{T-1}) \right.$$
$$\left. -c(h_{T-1})]z_{T-1} + \beta w_T(1 - z_{T-1}) + \beta E_{T-1} U_T^* z_{T-1} \right\}, \quad (8.10)$$

where U_T^* is the maximal payoff in T conditional on $z_{T-1} = 1$, and using an auxiliary result that entrepreneurs do not re-enter once they exit, so that $z_{T-1} = 0 \Rightarrow z_T = 0$. If the entrepreneur selects $z_{T-1} = 1$, then the maximising choice of h_{T-1}, namely h_{T-1}^*, satisfies the first-order condition

$$\mu_{T-1} - c_h(h_{T-1}) + \beta \frac{\partial [E_{T-1} U_T^*]}{\partial h_{T-1}} = 0, \quad (8.11)$$

where the derivative in this equation is obviously positive. Now for the presumed pattern of continuation to be optimal, we must have $\mu_{T-1} \leq \mu_T$. So even if $\mu_{T-1} = \mu_T$ it must follow that $h_{T-1}^* > h_T^*$. ∎

The logic behind Proposition 7 can be seen by comparing the period T objective with that for $T - 1$ (the latter is (8.10) in the proof). Only part of the payoff to supplying effort is the production of current output. Greater effort also generates returns in the form of valuable information about the future.[10] As the entrepreneur approaches retirement, the value of information about future returns in entrepreneurship declines to zero. Consequently, this gives the entrepreneur less incentive to supply costly effort as he ages.

For the reasons given earlier, a finding that entrepreneurs work fewer hours as they age can be attributed to several factors, not just declining information value from work. We now proceed to consider the specific issue of retirement and entrepreneurship in further detail.

8.2.2 Retirement

It is now well established in the UK and USA that among older workers, the self-employed are more likely to participate in the workforce than employees are.[11] In both countries, around one-third of the workforce aged over sixty-five is self-employed (Iams, 1987; Moralee, 1998; Bruce, Holz-Eakin and Quinn, 2000). This proportion appears to have been relatively stable over time. Among the very oldest segment of the workforce, self-employment rates are even higher (Fuchs, 1982). Several explanations of these phenomena can be proposed:

1. Older workers are from cohorts in which self-employment was once more common than it is now.

2. Employees are more likely to retire than the self-employed, perhaps because they face a statutory retirement age (as in, e.g., the UK), or early retirement incentives embodied in occupational pension rights. Neither factor is applicable to the self-employed. There might also be bias by employers against older workers, that encourages such workers to set up on their own if they wish to continue working. Some other individuals may work beyond the statutory retirement age because they have insufficient pension rights. And an entrepreneur who has devoted their life to creating and growing a business might also be unwilling to give it up altogether, perhaps choosing to work fewer hours rather than relinquishing control entirely.

3. Some employees switch into self-employment as they approach retirement.[12] This might occur because self-employment is an easier way for individuals to partially retire. For example, Quinn (1980) observed that the work hours of older self-employed individuals display markedly greater variation than do those of older employees. However, the extent of switching should not be over-stated: most self-employed Americans over sixty-five have been self-employed for many years rather than newly arrived from paid employment (Iams, 1987).

Despite this early work, there has been relatively little formal modelling of the self-employment retirement decision. One exception is Parker and Rougier (2001), who developed a simple continuous-time lifecycle model for this purpose. These authors estimated a two-equation model in which the (unobserved) probability of retirement, zr^*, and log lifetime wealth at age a, $\ln B_a$, are both endogenous variables for each individual i:

$$\ln B_{ai} = \gamma_1 zr_i^* + \beta_1' X_{1i} + u_{i1} \tag{8.12}$$

$$zr_i^* = \gamma_2 \ln B_{ai} + \beta_2' X_{2i} + u_{i2} \tag{8.13}$$

$$zr_i := \begin{cases} 1 & \text{if} \quad zr_i^* \geq 0 \\ 0 & \text{if} \quad zr_i^* < 0, \end{cases} \tag{8.14}$$

where X_1 and X_2 are non-identical vectors of exogenous variables, both of which include the self-employed wage, business wealth and several other personal characteristics. The model was estimated by full-information maximum likelihood using a sample of 197 self-employed individuals taken from the 1994 British *Retirement Survey*. The significant determinants of the probability of self-employed retirement were earned income at retirement (with a negative sign) and age. Unlike employees, for whom the probability of retirement has been found to be a strictly increasing function of age, the self-employed exhibited a quadratic pattern, with the probability of retirement increasing until age seventy-three, and decreasing thereafter. Those who were 'long-term' self-employed were significantly less likely to retire than those who had recently switched into self-employment. This may suggest that older employees who switch into self-employment regard self-employment as a transition towards full retirement. Strikingly, neither lifetime wealth nor poor health were significant determinants of retirement by the self-employed. This was despite both the relatively high levels of lifetime wealth and the greater incidence of poor health among the self-employed *Retirement Survey* respondents (Parker, 2003b) – and contrasts with previous findings about the impact of poor health on retirement among older American employed and self-employed workers (Quinn, 1980; Fuchs, 1982).[13]

Some commentators have contended that self-employment among older workers – so-called 'third-age entrepreneurship' – may be an important phenomenon. The institutional backdrop is that government policies in the USA and elsewhere since the 1980s have made continued work among older people an increasingly attractive option (Bruce, Holz-Eakin and Quinn, 2000). In addition, tax-based savings' incentives appear to be eagerly exploited by the self-employed (Power and Rider, 2002).[14] However, there is little evidence that third-age entrepreneurship is widespread. For example, questionnaire responses revealed that at most only 15 per cent of fifty–seventy-five-year-old Britons expressed any interest in self-employment (Curran and Blackburn, 2001). While acknowledging the limitations of survey claims about future anticipated behaviour, this figure is likely to be an upper-bound estimate of the true level of interest because no respondents have to bear immediately the costs of switching into entrepreneurship. Nor is it obvious that the importance of self-employment among older people is set to increase dramatically in the near future.

NOTES

1. For example, Hakim (1989b) reported that even in economically buoyant times, less than half of small firms in the UK see employment growth as an objective. Scase and Goffee (1982) claimed that some self-employed individuals do not hire workers if they suspect this will destroy a personal client-based service; if they believe that hired labour is unreliable; or if hiring entails spending one's time as a 'businessman' rather than as a 'craftsman'.
2. See Leonard (1986), Dunne, Roberts and Sammelson (1989a, 1989b), Brown, Hamilton and Medoff (1990), Acs and Audretsch (1993), OECD (1994a), Birch, Haggerty and Parsons (1997) and SBA (2001). According to SBA (2001), small firms account for about 75 per cent of net new jobs created each year in the USA. A similar proportion of new jobs were created in the self-employment sector in Canada in the 1990s (Lin, Picot and Compton, 2000).
3. However, job creation performance by small firms may be under-stated if growing firms undergo changes of ownership that subtract from employment growth

attributable to small firms by recording a false death, and adds to employment growth attributable to large firms by recording a false birth (Kirchhoff and Greene, 1998). Also, some small firms subcontract the manufacture and distribution of their products, which can create additional indirect employment that goes unrecorded – or is attributed to large firms that gain the manufacturing and distribution contracts. However, the latter effect is clearly offset by large firms that subcontract work to small firms.

4. In the context of the small firms literature, Storey (1994a) estimated that 5–10 per cent of manufacturing businesses that started in the 1970s provided 40–50 per cent of total employment in their cohort ten years later.

5. See Storey (1994a), who cited evidence that the likelihood of major injuries is 40 per cent higher for workers in firms with fewer than 50 employees than in larger firms.

6. Some interesting descriptive evidence on the characteristics of British self-employed people working more than eighty hours per week comes from Jones, McEvoy and Barrett (1993). They are concentrated in retailing; have low incomes and profits; are more reliant than other self-employed people on unpaid labour; are older; and are less likely to operate branches of their business.

7. In this case, the wage ought to be instrumented to avoid simultaneous equation bias, e.g., using a predicted wage imputed on the basis of exogenous characteristics.

8. The extent of multiple job holding is limited, however. For example, using the 1987–8 UK LFS, Hakim (1988) reported that only 5 per cent of the self-employed have second jobs, 60 per cent of which were also in self-employment. US evidence also points to a small and static role for multiple job holding in self-employment (Aronson, 1991).

9. See Thornton (1998) for more references to the physician labour supply literature. For studies relating to dentists, see Boulier (1979) and Scheffler and Rossiter (1983).

10. The term $\beta[\partial[\mathsf{E}_{T-1}U_T^*]]/[\partial h_{T-1}]$ in (8.11) can be interpreted as the marginal information value of an extra unit of effort.

11. For UK evidence, see Moralee (1998), and Parker (2003b); US evidence includes Quinn (1980), Fuchs (1982) and Iams (1987).

12. Nearly one-quarter of retired American employees who continue to work do so by switching into self-employment. Unlike career self-employed individuals, this is generally in different occupations and industries to their pre-retirement work (Iams, 1987). Fuchs (1982) estimated the relevant switching rate from paid employment to be around 2 per cent per annum for older male American employees.

13. These two studies found that personal wealth and eligibility for social security retirement benefits increase the probability that older self-employed Americans retire.

14. Power and Rider (2002) estimated the tax price elasticity of contributions to tax-deferred retirement savings plans by the self-employed to be –2.0. These incentives also significantly increase the probability that the self-employed contribute in the first place.

9   Growth, innovation and exit

In this chapter we investigate the growth, innovative performance and survival of new entrepreneurial ventures. Section 9.1 outlines an integrated theoretical model of firm entry, growth and exit by Jovanovic (1982). This model provides a useful framework for understanding why some small firms survive and grow, and why others die. It is also helpful for interpreting empirical results on these phenomena. Section 9.2 summarises evidence about the growth of small firms and innovation. Section 9.3 presents facts about the survival and exit of new small firms, and their determinants.

It is helpful to clarify at the outset what the chapter does not attempt to do. We do not cover the literature on dynamic industrial organisation that has developed since Jovanovic (1982) (see, e.g., Ericsson and Pakes, 1995). Nor do we analyse market entry by new firms, since many of these are not wholly new firms, but existing firms that have diversified into a new market, or that have re-positioned themselves from a different industrial sector (Storey, 1991). Nor will we repeat results about factors affecting market entry by entrepreneurs covered elsewhere in the book.

9.1   Jovanovic's (1982) dynamic selection model

In a highly influential paper, Jovanovic (1982) developed a model in which entrepreneurs have imperfect information about their innate abilities, which they can learn about only by trying entrepreneurship. The model shows that the ventures of able and/or lucky entrepreneurs survive and grow, while those of less able and/or unlucky entrepreneurs shrink and exit. It derives endogenously the entry and exit behaviour of new small-scale start-ups within an optimising framework. As will be seen later, the predictions of the model turn out to be consistent with a large body of empirical evidence about small firm dynamics.

The Jovanovic model shares some features in common with other economic models of entrepreneurship discussed in chapter 2, section 2.2. As in Lucas (1978), individuals have heterogeneous abilities in entrepreneurship; but unlike Lucas, entrepreneurs do not know their abilities when they start their ventures. As in the Kihlstrom and Laffont (1979) model, entrepreneurs face uncertainty; but unlike Kihlstrom and Laffont, all individuals are assumed to be risk neutral rather than risk averse. Finally, like Dixit and Rob (1994) and Parker (1996, 1997a), the Jovanovic model is dynamic. But in contrast to those models, there are no switching costs and entrepreneurs learn by doing.

For simplicity, Jovanovic assumed that entrepreneurs sell a homogeneous product, with a sequence of selling prices $\{P\}_0^\infty$ that is deterministic and known. Entrepreneurs are price takers and are too small to interact strategically with other firms. At time t each entrepreneur faces the cost function

$$c_t = c(q_t)\psi(x + \varrho_t),\qquad(9.1)$$

where q is the entrepreneur's output, $\psi(\cdot)$ is a continuous and increasing function, $c(\cdot)$ is a convex function, x is the entrepreneur's innate ability and $\varrho_t \sim N(0, \sigma_\varrho^2)$ is a random shock. Here x is an *inverse* measure of ability, since large x values index high-cost (inefficient) producers. Entrepreneurs know the distribution from which the shocks are drawn, and also the distribution from which abilities are drawn: $x \sim N(\bar{x}, \sigma_x^2)$.

Individuals all start with the same prior belief about their ability, $\bar{x}$. Hence no entrepreneur has a head start over others, and all enter at the same scale of operation. Entrepreneurs use a Bayesian updating rule to amend their beliefs about their ability as information comes in. They do this by observing the sequence of cost and profit outcomes from all previous periods in which they operated, and inverting the cost function (9.1) to obtain a new estimate of x.

This model differs in some important ways from the related model of Frank (1988), that was discussed in chapter 8, section 8.2. In Frank's model, entrants possessed heterogeneous beliefs about their own abilities, and entrepreneurs learned at different speeds depending on the effort they expended. The Jovanovic model abstracts from effort considerations; all entrepreneurs learn at the same speed.

Given the structure of the cost function in (9.1), low-x types are likely to receive low-cost outcomes and survive, while high-x types receive high-cost outcomes. However, this is not inevitable because of the presence of the stochastic term ϱ. For example, low-x types could receive an unlucky sequence of poor draws from ϱ, while high-x types might receive a lucky sequence of good draws. But as time goes on, random draws are likely to cancel out, and innate ability is increasingly likely to shine through.

In each period t, entrepreneurs choose output q_t to maximise expected profits $P_t q_t - Ec_t$. Note that $\partial q_t^*/\partial E\psi_t < 0$, where we define

$\psi_t := \psi(x + \varrho_t)$ for notational brevity. That is, individuals who perceive themselves to be low (resp., high) cost types increase (resp., decrease) output in the subsequent period: unusually high profits are followed by unusually high growth in the next period.

There is a common outside option (possibly wage-work) with a present value of w. There is also an unlimited number of potential entrepreneurs, who are indifferent between wage-work and entrepreneurship and who are assumed to choose wage-work. These individuals will enter the industry if the output price rises above the initial market equilibrium price P_0, and will therefore drive the price back down to P_0.[1] Hence in no period can the output price rise above P_0.

Entrepreneurs maximise their expected returns over an infinite horizon, with discount rate $\delta > 0$. Let a denote the length of time a firm has survived at time t, and define

$$\pi(P_t, \overline{\psi}) := P_t q(P_t|\overline{\psi}) - c[q(P_t|\overline{\psi})]\overline{\psi}$$

as expected profits maximised with respect to q, where $\overline{\psi} := \mathsf{E}\psi_t$. That is, $\overline{\psi}$ is an entrepreneur's expectation of his idiosyncratic cost term given his history of observing cost and profit outcomes. In order to determine whether to remain in the industry or to quit, entrepreneurs need to calculate the value of remaining. Let $V(\overline{\psi}, a, t; P)$ denote the expected value at t of a firm surviving a periods remaining in the industry at t and behaving optimally thereafter. This has two components, namely current profit and the discounted value of being able to operate in entrepreneurship subsequently:

$$V(\overline{\psi}, a, t; P) = \pi(P_t, \overline{\psi}) + \left\{ \frac{1}{1+\delta} \right.$$
$$\left. \int \max[w, V(z, a+1, t+1; P)]\ p(dz|\overline{\psi}, a) \right\}, \quad (9.2)$$

where $p(z|\overline{\psi}, a)$ is the probability that $\mathsf{E}\psi_{t+1} \leq z$ given that $\mathsf{E}\psi_t = \overline{\psi}$ and given that the firm has operated for a periods. Using a contraction mapping theorem, Jovanovic showed that a unique, bounded and continuous solution for V in (9.2) exists. He also showed that V is strictly decreasing in $\overline{\psi}$–i.e. the value of the firm is lower the higher is the entrepreneur's expectation about his costs.

Entrepreneurs are indifferent about remaining in business or exiting to take the outside option when

$$V(\overline{\psi}, a, t; P) = w. \quad (9.3)$$

Let $\overline{\psi}^*(a, t; P)$ be the level of $\mathsf{E}\psi_t$ at which the equality in (9.3) is satisfied. Because V is a decreasing function of $\overline{\psi}$, it follows that

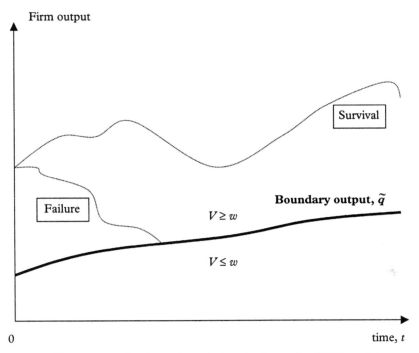

Figure 9.1   Selection and survival in the Jovanovic (1982) model

$\overline{\psi}^{*}(a, t; P)$ must be uniquely defined. Hence firms will exit at output of less than $\tilde{q} := q\,[P_t|\overline{\psi}^{*}(a, t; P)]$, and will remain in the industry otherwise. Figure 9.1 illustrates two examples of realisations of firms' outputs, together with this boundary. Below $\tilde{q}$ (the 'exit region') $V(\overline{\psi}, a, t; P) < w$ and above $\tilde{q}$ (the 'continuation region') $V(\overline{\psi}, a, t; P) > w$.

Jovanovic's model has the following implications for entrepreneurial ability, venture growth, exit, industry concentration, profits, and output:

J.1 Entrepreneurs who run young firms have had less time to accumulate information about their true abilities. Therefore the level and variability of growth rates are largest among younger and smaller firms. Growth rates are lower among mature surviving firms.

J.2 Firms that exit never return because they know that the output price cannot rise above the level at which they left; and an exiting entrepreneur never obtains any more information to change his terminal belief about his ability.

J.3 Results J.1 and J.2 imply that (cohort) industry concentration increases over time, since initially all firms of a given cohort were the same size, at which industrial concentration was at a minimum.

J.4 Entrepreneurs who remain in business indefinitely eventually learn their true ability, whereas entrepreneurs who exit tend to have relatively imprecise estimates of their true ability.

J.5 The last clause of J.4 implies that some entrepreneurs who exit might have true entrepreneurial abilities that exceed the marginal ability that would make entrepreneurship marginally attractive in the presence of perfect information. These entrepreneurs received unlucky draws from the distribution of shocks, and incorrectly (but understandably) interpreted these draws as evidence of low ability, prompting their withdrawal. The greater is the variance of shocks, σ_ϱ^2, the more of these 'efficient failures' there will be.

J.6 Surviving firms are larger and older than firms that failed, and they are also larger than new entrants.

J.7 Price is determined at the margin by smaller and younger firms. Larger, more efficient firms earn profits as a reward for their exceptional ability. For each cohort of firms, average profits increase as the industry matures. The distribution of profits resembles the distribution of ability. The more dispersed the latter, the more dispersed are firm sizes and profitability rates.

J.8 Let Q_t denote (deterministic) industry output at time t. If Q_t is non-decreasing in t, and $q(P|\overline{\psi})$ is a strictly concave function of $\overline{\psi}$, then the equilibrium price sequence is constant, and entry occurs at each t.

As will be seen in section 9.2, Jovanovic's predictions relating to firm growth rates (J.1) receive strong empirical support. However, at the risk of ending this section on a negative note, we shall conclude by mentioning two less satisfactory aspects of the model, and a caveat to the sharpness of its testable predictions.

It is debatable whether average cohort firm size and industrial concentration increase continually over time (in a first-order stochastic sense), as suggested by J.3 and J.6. One can think of many practical reasons, absent from Jovanovic's model, why firms might face barriers to growth, including regulatory and tax disincentives. Also, entrepreneurs have only finite attention to apportion between maintaining current projects and evaluating and adopting new projects. The opportunity cost of neglecting profitable current projects might deter firms from seeking growth and so place bounds on firms' sizes (Oi, 1983; Gifford, 1998). While some entrepreneurs might be able to release scarce resources to exploit profitable new opportunities by closing or transferring viable existing businesses to less able entrepreneurs (Holmes and Schmitz, 1990), this is not always feasible.

Another questionable result is that entrepreneurs who exit never return and 'try their luck again' (J.2). There is some evidence of 'repeat entrepreneurship', whereby failed entrepreneurs try again with new ventures, having learned valuable lessons from their previous failures (MacMillan, 1986). In fact, re-entry of failed entrepreneurs can be sustained in a modification of Jovanovic's model if the assumption of an inexhaustible supply of potential entrepreneurs is replaced with one stipulating a limited supply (Brock and Evans, 1986, pp. 60–3).

One caveat is that predictions J.1 through J.8 are not all unique to the Jovanovic model. For example, Frank (1988) and Segal and Spivak (1989) also predict that smaller firms will have higher and more variable growth rates. Frank's model was discussed in chapter 8, section 8.2; we briefly describe Segal and Spivak's model here. These authors considered an entrepreneur who chooses how much profit to take out of the firm and how much to re-invest in it. Re-investment of profits increases output, which is subject to random shocks.[2] The firm fails and closes if output reaches zero, perhaps following an unlucky sequence of successive adverse shocks. In that event, the owner pays an intangible dissolution cost – perhaps the loss of reputation. Now consider a new firm that enters the market with an output that is positive but sufficiently close to the zero boundary to make the prospect of failure a real possibility. Clearly, this firm owner has a stronger incentive to reinvest profits in order to decrease the risk of costly failure than the owner of a larger enterprise with output that is further from the boundary. It follows that small firms have higher output growth rates than larger firms, since reinvestment of profits promotes growth.

An interesting by-product of Segal and Spivak's model is the prediction that large firms have growth firms that converge to a constant. That result is consistent with Gibrat's Law, an important concept in the theory of firm growth. We discuss this next.

9.2 Growth and innovation

9.2.1 Gibrat's Law and extensions

Gibrat's 'Law of Proportionate Effect' (Gibrat, 1931) is a well-known benchmark model of firm growth. Gibrat's 'Law' states that if there is a fixed number of firms, and if firms' growth rates are independent of firm size and previous growth rates, then the distribution of firm sizes will be lognormal with a variance that increases over time. If q_{it} denotes a measure of size (e.g. number of employees, turnover or assets) of firm i at time t, then an econometric specification of Gibrat's Law is

$$\ln q_{i\,t+1} = \beta + \ln q_{it} + u_{i\,t+1}, \qquad (9.4)$$

where β is the mean firm growth rate, assumed the same for all i; and where $u_{i\,t+1}$ is a mean-zero stochastic disturbance term with a distribution that is identical across firms i. Early studies found some empirical support for lognormal firm-size distributions and firm-growth rates being roughly independent of firm size (see, e.g., Hart and Prais, 1956; Simon and Bonini, 1958).

Three assumptions underlying Gibrat's Law appear questionable. One is that the population of firms is fixed. In practice, of course, firms are born and die, so this assumption is not tenable. A second is that each firm faces a draw from a common distribution of random shocks. But recent evidence suggests that the variance of firm growth rates is higher for smaller firms (see below). Third, Gibrat's Law assumes that mean growth rates are the same for all firms. Again, recent evidence reviewed below refutes this claim, showing that smaller firms tend to have higher growth rates.

In the light of these problems several refinements to Gibrat's Law have been proposed (see Ijiri and Simon, 1977). Perhaps the most popular generalisation allows for heterogeneous growth rates, giving rise to the specification

$$\ln q_{i\,t+1} = \beta_i + \gamma \ln q_{it} + u_{i\,t+1}, \tag{9.5}$$

where β_i is the firm i-specific growth rate, and $\gamma < 1$ permits Galtonian *regression to the mean* in firm size: i.e. large firms have lower growth rates than small firms do. Clearly Gibrat's Law emerges as a special case of (9.5) when the β_i are the same for all i and when $\gamma = 1$.

A third, even more general, specification permits a direct test of the Jovanovic model described in chapter 9, section 9.1. This specification, suggested by Brock and Evans (1986, ch. 6), takes the form

$$\ln q_{i\,t+1} - \ln q_{it} = \beta + \gamma_1 \ln q_{it} + \gamma_2 [\ln q_{it}]^2 + \gamma_3 \ln a_{it} + \gamma_4 [\ln a_{it}]^2$$
$$+ \gamma_5 \ln q_{it} \ln a_{it} + u_{i\,t+1}, \tag{9.6}$$

where a_{it} is firm i's age at time t, and where β and the γs are parameters. The inclusion of both firm age a_{it} as well as firm size q_{it} on the RHS of (9.6) permits tests of prediction J.1 of the Jovanovic model. Of course, it is also possible to include firm- and owner-specific factors as additional explanatory variables in growth equations, in order to explore the effects of a broader range of possible growth determinants. We now turn to the empirical evidence on these issues.

9.2.2   Evidence on growth rates

Numerous empirical studies have sought to identify the determinants of small firm growth rates. While many disparate results have been published, one of the most important and widely verified is the following:

Firm growth rates are decreasing in firm size among firms of the same age; and are decreasing in firm age among firms of the same size.

Estimates of (9.5) reveal a tendency for smaller firms to grow faster than larger ones.[3] Results are similar if (9.6) is estimated.[4] Thus firm-growth rates generally decrease with firm size and age. In addition, the evidence shows that younger firms have more variable growth rates (Brock and Evans, 1986; Bates, 1990). These results all refute Gibratl's Law and provide broad support to Jovanovic's prediction J.1 – which has since been confirmed in many subsequent studies.[5]

Several other characteristics have also been associated with the growth of small firms. The contributions to this part of the literature have been numerous and diverse, so only a cursory overview is possible. In his survey of international studies, Storey (1994a) reported that the following factors were positively associated with firm growth: a low unemployment environment; education and previous managerial experience of the owner (Cooper, Gimeno-Gascon and Woo, 1994; Kangasharju and Pekkala, 2002); multiple founders;[6] rural location; and being a limited company. There is also some evidence that multiple-establishment (Variyam and Kraybill, 1992) and high-tech firms with access to multiple sources of finance (Westhead and Cowling, 1995) have higher growth rates than firms that do not. According to Storey (1994a), previous entrepreneurial experience in the same sector or in self-employment had mixed effects on firm growth rates; and family history, sources of finance, training and gender had few discernible effects.[7] The age of the owner-manager has been found in some studies to be negatively related to small-firm growth rates (Boswell, 1972; Barkham *et al.*, 1996) – though here again mixed results have been obtained. There are also mixed findings from studies that attempt to relate actual new-venture growth rates to entrepreneurs' declared ambitions to grow (e.g. compare Storey, 1994a, with Barkham, Hart and Hanvey, 1996). Reid (1993) found that growth is negatively affected by profitability. Watson (1990) emphasised the distinction between trading profits and retained profits – the difference between them comprising directors' remuneration and taxation. Watson reported a weak relationship between employment growth and trading profits, but a much stronger relationship with retained profits. This is consistent with the notion that retained profits are reinvested for expansion.

A common empirical finding is the irrelevance of many firm-specific and environmental factors for explaining small-firm growth rates. For example, Westhead and Cowling (1995) found that of sixty-seven potential explanatory variables (embracing personal and firm-specific characteristics, environmental factors and financial structure, *inter alia*), only a handful of them significantly explained firm growth.[8] This places obvious limitations on the scope to give policy advice aimed at promoting the growth of new ventures. One interesting exception relates to taxation. US evidence from Carroll *et al.* (2000b, 2001) showed that higher marginal income tax rates significantly and substantially decrease small-firm growth rates (measured in terms of business receipts) and investment expenditures.

9.2.3   Innovation

A feature of the growth of small firms that has not been mentioned so far is innovation, deemed by Schumpeter to be a central aspect of entrepreneurship.

Before turning to the evidence, we note that there are several reasons why small firms might possess an advantage over large firms at innovating. They are said to include:

- Bureaucratic inertia in large firms, which is not conducive to innovation (Link and Rees, 1990). Individuals located outside large firms might be able to develop innovative ideas untrammelled by conventional corporate thinking (Pavitt, Robson and Townsend, 1987).
- Shorter lines of communication in small firms (Fielden, Davidson and Makin, 2000).
- Greater responsiveness by small firms to changing demand and demography (Bannock, 1981).
- Greater ease of technology diffusion between small firms, especially when involved in networks and clusters that generate opportunities for cross-organisational learning (Morgan, 1997).
- Diminishing returns to R&D, which affect large firms more than small firms (Acs and Audretsch, 1991).
- Larger firms having greater demands on limited entrepreneurial attention for managing existing projects, and so facing a higher opportunity cost from innovating and thereby creating further demands on their attention (Gifford, 1998).
- Small firms having greater incentives to innovate if that helps them to overcome entry barriers and retaliatory conduct by incumbents (Acs and Audretsch, 1989).

On the latter point, innovation certainly seems to be associated with business entry, with several authors finding that industries with high rates of entry by small firms have higher rates of productivity growth and innovation (Geroski and Pomroy, 1990; Cosh, Hughes and Wood, 1999). Knowledge spillovers also appear to be important. According to SBA (2002b), a university's R&D expenditure leads to a significant increase in the number of new-firm formations in surrounding areas, for up to five years after the expenditure is made.

Several US studies lend support to the notion that smaller and younger firms have been relatively more innovative than larger and older firms.[9] According to Scherer (1991), in the 1980s 'small' US firms (i.e. those with fewer than 500 employees) created 322 innovations per million employees compared with 225 in large firms. Innovations in small firms seem to respond to different technological and environmental factors than those in large firms (Acs and Audretsch, 1987a, 1987b, 1988), being positively and significantly related to the presence of skilled labour. In contrast, large firms have a comparative innovative advantage in capital-intensive, concentrated and highly unionised industries producing differentiated goods supported by advertising. According to these authors, there was no measurable difference in the quality of innovations between small and large firms.

The UK evidence about innovation and firm size is more mixed. Pavitt, Robson and Townsend (1987) analysed the size distribution of innovating firms in the UK between 1945 and 1984, and concluded that small firms were more likely to introduce new innovations than large firms were. However, Tether, Smith and Thwaites (1997) challenged these findings, claiming that the largest firms have consistently been a disproportionately important source of innovation in the manufacturing sector of the UK. Also, Craggs and Jones (1998) reported that large firms were three times more likely to be *novel* innovators than their smaller competitors.

At the level of the individual entrepreneur, most start-ups are in noninnovative trades such as hairdressing and car-related businesses (Storey, 1994a). Real innovation appears to be confined to a handful of businesses run by a few skilled, visionary and determined entrepreneurs.

A problem with this whole strand of research is how to define innovation. A narrow definition uses the number of patents registered with national or international patent offices. However, the limitations of patent count measures are well known. On the other hand, broader definitions might include any method or marketing ploy that helps to create competitive advantage. Generally, the broader the definition, the higher the proportion of innovations attributable to small firms.

One way of trying to overcome these problems is to take a macro approach, regressing aggregate GDP growth rates (for example) on measures of entrepreneurial activity (Blanchflower, 2000; Reynolds *et al.*, 2001, 2002). However, this approach is almost certainly prone to severe problems of omitted variable bias, aggregation bias and endogeneity, while its reduced form nature prevents the interpretation of any of the estimated parameters.

Finally, we might ask whether free-market economies achieve the right balance between investment in innovation-generating research and entrepreneurs who bring innovations to market. Michelacchi (2003) studied this issue using a model with free occupational choice where rents to research and entrepreneurship are fixed exogenously by Nash bargaining. Michelacchi showed that, if rents to entrepreneurship are too low, then an economy could end up wasting research, with insufficient entrepreneurial skills to exploit the innovations produced by researchers. This might justify government intervention to promote entrepreneurship, though it should be noted that entrepreneurial over-investment is also possible. However, it is unclear whether Michelacchi's results are robust to an extension of his model in which rents are endogenously determined by the productivity of effort in each sector.

9.3   Exit

As explained above, the Jovanovic (1982) model makes several predictions about the types of firms that are likely to fail and leave the market, as well as about those that are likely to grow and prosper. This section focuses on the process of exit and its converse, survival. We first present, in subsection 9.3.1, some stylised facts about the survival rates of new ventures, the related issue of quits from self-employment, and the temporal distribution of new-firm failures. It is important to note at the outset that the continuation of an individual in self-employment is not necessary equivalent to survival of a business because an individual can remain self-employed while opening and closing successive businesses. Subsection 9.3.2 briefly describes two important econometric models of firm survival; and subsection 9.3.3 summarises the body of empirical results on firm-specific, owner-specific, and economy-wide factors associated with survival.

9.3.1   *Survival rates and their distribution*

It is now well known that new firms have low survival rates, and that many people who set up in self-employment do not remain self-employed for long. The evidence relating to self-employed exit rates points to broadly similar patterns in the USA and the UK. For example, Evans and Leighton (1989b) reported that a third of entrants to self-employment in the USA leave within three years. Daly (1991) provides similar figures for the UK. There is an intriguing possibility that exit rates have exhibited stability over very long time spans, with Nenadic (1990), for example, reporting that the three-year drop-out rate from self-employment in nineteenth-century Edinburgh was around 40 per cent.

Not surprisingly, even higher rates of exit from self-employment are observed during recessions. For example, using BHPS data over the recessionary period of 1991–5, Taylor (1999) reported that 40 per cent of ventures that had started since 1991 did not survive their first year in business. Interestingly, male respondents in this study claimed that the main reason for exit from self-employment was not bankruptcy (18 per cent), but a move to another job (48 per cent). Broadly similar reasons for exit were found for females, who generally had lower business survival rates than men (see also chapter 4, section 4.2). These bankruptcy figures may be downward biased if people wanted to avoid admitting personal failure to the survey interviewer, or if they sought other employment prior to an impending bankruptcy. But the figures are striking enough to debunk the popular belief that most individuals exit self-employment involuntarily, and also suggest that self-employment may be a transitional state between periods of employment, at least for some workers.[10]

Phillips and Kirchhoff (1989) disputed the 'prevailing wisdom' that '4 out of 5 new [American] firms fail in the first 5 years'. They found more favourable survival rates, with 40 per cent of new American firms surviving for at least six years. Survival and employment growth rates were highest among new manufacturing firms and lowest in construction, with firms in service industries being intermediate on both counts. New firm survival rates may be higher than this in other countries. For example, Pfeiffer and Reize (2000) reported one-year survival rates in Germany of around 90 per cent in the mid-1990s.[11]

Perhaps surprisingly, high-tech small firms appear to have higher survival rates than firms in more 'conventional' sectors (Cooper, 1986; Westhead and Cowling, 1995). This seems to contradict the popular view that high-tech firms are risky, although such a conclusion is not warranted without taking into account the extra measures that financiers take to screen these ventures and safeguard their investments.

The distribution of failure times of new start-ups is positively skewed and inverse U-shaped. Because it takes time for a firm to build up debts, and for creditors to perceive that a firm is financially troubled and to initiate bankruptcy proceedings, there is an initial 'honeymoon' period of a year or two in which business failures are relatively infrequent. Failures then peak at around two–four years, after which the frequency of failures decreases steadily with the length of time the firm has been trading. Mature businesses have low failure rates.[12] According to Cressy (1999), the distribution of failure times is temporally quite stable.

Several reasons might explain the inverse U-shaped skewed distribution of failure times. Frank (1988) proposed a particularly interesting idea. Similar to Jovanovic (1982), Frank developed a model in which entrepreneurs learn about their abilities over time by trying entrepreneurship. Unlike Jovanovic, entrepreneurs in Frank's model must pay a fixed entry cost that is sunk once they have entered the market. Rational entrepreneurs will therefore enter only if they expect to be of sufficiently high ability that they can recoup their costs. It follows that there will be an initial period with few exits, because even if some entrepreneurs receive poor outcomes in the marketplace, it takes time to disabuse such confident people of their initial beliefs. But after a while, even very confident individuals have to face reality, at which point they leave the market. Eventually, the frequency of exits tapers off, once most of the inefficient firms have left.[13]

9.3.2   Two useful econometric models of firm survival

Probit/logit models and hazard models are the most widely used techniques for quantifying the effects of individual- and firm-specific characteristics on the chances of survival in entrepreneurship.

Probit and logit models

Consider again the probit and logit models described in chapter 1, subsection 1.6.1. Those models regressed a binary variable z_i on a vector of explanatory variables, W_i, where i indexes an individual observation. One can define z_i as equal to one if individual i starts and remains in self-employment after some time interval has elapsed and zero if i has left self-employment by this time. Alternatively, in applications where i indexes a particular firm from a sample of firms, z_i can be defined as equal to one if the firm is still in business and zero if the firm has left the market. In both cases the marginal effects of an explanatory variable on the probability of survival are calculated using (1.11).

Hazard models

Hazard models provide a direct way of identifying the factors that determine *how long* (rather than whether) individuals remain in

self-employment, or how long firms remain in the market. For expositional clarity, consider for the moment the case of an individual remaining
in self-employment. At each discrete point in time t there is a probability
(or hazard) that individual i, who has been observed in self-employment
for a_i periods up to t, leaves self-employment. The Cox proportional
hazard model is described by

$$\mathcal{H}_i(t) = \mathcal{H}^0(t).\exp[\beta' X_i(t)],\tag{9.7}$$

where $\mathcal{H}^0(t)$ is the so-called 'baseline hazard' at t; X_i is a vector of characteristics for individual i; and β is a vector of parameters to be estimated.
This is called a 'single-risk' hazard model, because there is only a single
risk: that of leaving self-employment.

The single-risk model can be estimated without placing restrictions on
the form of the baseline hazard in (9.7). The probability of an individual
i's spell being completed by time $t + 1$ given that i was still self-employed
at t is

$$\mathcal{L}_i(t) = \Pr[a_i < t + 1 | a_i \geq t] = F[\gamma(t) + \beta' X_i(t)],$$

where $F[\cdot]$ is the cumulative distribution function of the Extreme Value
distribution; and $\gamma(t)$ is a set of dummy variables, one for each t, which
captures time dependence. To estimate the parameters $\gamma(t)$ and β, let
d_i be the observed duration of i in self-employment. This is either time
completed or time censored (by the end of the sample): define $\alpha_i = 1$ if
the time is completed and $\alpha_i = 0$ if it is censored. Then the log-likelihood
function is

$$\ln \mathcal{L} = \sum_{i=1}^{n} \left\{ \alpha_i \sum_{t=1}^{d_i-1} \ln[1 - \mathcal{L}_i(t)] + \alpha_i \ln \mathcal{L}_i(d_i) \right.$$

$$\left. + (1 - \alpha_i) \sum_{t=1}^{d_i} \ln[1 - \mathcal{L}_i(t)] \right\}.\tag{9.8}$$

Equation (9.8) is maximised with respect to β and the γs to obtain maximum likelihood estimates. The method is implemented on many standard
software packages. Note of course that a similar interpretation applies if
i indexes firms rather than self-employed individuals.

Failure may come from more than one source: for example, individuals may leave self-employment for either paid-employment or
unemployment. We might be interested to discover, for example, whether
self-employed individuals who exit into unemployment have different survival characteristics from those who exit into paid-employment. If so, a
'competing-risks' model is needed. Such a model posits a separate hazard function for each of the destinations, whose log-likelihoods are given

by (9.8) where $\alpha_i = 1$ now denotes exit into the given destination, and $\alpha_i = 0$ applies for other outcomes. The sum of the log-likelihoods over all possible destinations gives the total log-likelihood to be maximised, though in many applications, each destination hazard is estimated as a separate single-risk hazard where exit as a completed spell is defined only with respect to the given destination.

As an example of the potential practical importance of the distinction between single and competing risk formulations, consider the British study by Taylor (1999). In his competing-risk model, Taylor distinguished between voluntary exit into paid-employment and involuntary exit in the form of bankruptcy. This distinction turned out to be an important one, because while greater personal wealth was associated with a lower male bankruptcy rate in Britain, it had no effect either on voluntary exit or on exit for any reason.

9.3.3   Determinants of entrepreneurial survival and exit

There is an enormous body of research on the individual- and firm-specific determinants of entrepreneurial survival and exit. Rather than attempt to provide an exhaustive survey of every study, we summarise below the key determinants of survival in self-employment (for individuals) and business (for firms) in developed countries.[14]

- *Duration.* The evidence from hazard and probit models tells a consistent story across different countries. The probability of departures from self-employment decreases with duration in self-employment (Evans and Leighton, 1989b; Carrasco, 1999; Taylor, 1999; Lin, Picot and Compton, 2000), the age of the business, and the tenure of business managers (Westhead and Cowling, 1995; Holmes and Schmitz, 1996; Cressy, 1999; Taylor, 2001). These findings may reflect learning by self-employed business owners about their abilities and the external environment over time (see section 9.1).
- *Human capital of the entrepreneur.* The bulk of evidence points to a positive relationship between business survival and an entrepreneur's human capital.[15] In particular, previous experience in self-employment has been found to increase the probability of survival in a new spell of self-employment or business ownership (Holmes and Schmitz, 1996; Quadrini, 1999; Taylor, 1999). This may be indicative of entrepreneurial learning. In contrast, experience acquired in a managerial capacity prior to owning a business seems to have an insignificant impact on survival in self-employment (Bates, 1990; Boden and Nucci, 2000). Current occupational and business experience has stronger effects, with Taylor (1999) finding that professionals and skilled manual

workers had the lowest self-employment exit rates. In contrast, formal educational qualifications appear to have mixed effects on survival rates. For example, evidence from the competing-risks hazard model suggests that educational qualifications help predict exit by self-employed individuals to paid-employment, but not exit to bankruptcy (Taylor, 1999; and see also Nafziger and Terrell, 1996). Supporting evidence comes from the US study of Quadrini (1999), who found that the education of the head of household did not explain exit from self-employment. Kangasharju and Pekkala (2002) observed that more highly educated Finnish entrepreneurs had better survival prospects in recessions, but were more likely to leave self-employment (for paid-employment) in boom conditions.

Age also affects survival rates, which are higher on average for middle aged than for younger or older entrepreneurs (Bates, 1990; Holtz-Eakin, Joulfaian and Rosen, 1994b).[16] Cressy (1996) went so far as to claim that age rather than financial capital is the genuine determinant of survival, financial capital being merely correlated with human capital because borrowers with more human capital tend to request (and obtain) larger loans. However, several other studies have controlled for both human and financial capital and have found an important role for both (see, e.g., Bates, 1990; Reid, 1991).

- *Size of the enterprise.* Numerous studies have confirmed that the smallest firms have the highest birth and death rates, and that the youngest firms have the highest death rates – where birth and death rates are defined as the number of births and deaths within a given firm size class as a proportion of the total number of firms in that class.[17] These findings accord with prediction J.6 of the Jovanovic (1982) model outlined in section 9.1.[18]
- *Financial variables.* Most studies report a positive association between survival in business and access to capital. For example, according to Bates (1990, 1997), self-employed American males who started up firms between 1976 and 1982 with above-average amounts of finance were significantly more likely to survive than otherwise comparable American males (see also Cooper, Gimeno-Gascon and Woo, 1994). Similarly, Taylor's (1999) hazard model estimates predicted that survival was highest among British workers who had quitted their previous job and entered self-employment with some initial capital.[19] Self-finance appears to be more conducive to survival than debt finance does (Reid, 1991). This might be because self-finance is a positive indicator of venture quality (Repullo and Suarez, 2000) or because self-finance carries less risk exposure and lower debt-servicing costs.[20] According to Lin, Picot and Compton (2000), family finance is also

important: having a self-employed spouse reduced the likelihood of exits from self-employment in Canada through the provision of a steady stream of family income.

- *Innovation.* It might be thought that firms that choose to innovate improve their survival prospects relative to small firms that do not. However, the current body of evidence on this issue is mixed and inconclusive (e.g. contrast Audretsch, 1991; Agarwal, 1998, with Audretsch and Mahmood, 1995). The ambiguity of these results may be attributable to the use of aggregate measures of small-firm innovative activity in these studies. It might also be informative to disaggregate innovations by their type. For example, Cosh, Hughes and Wood (1999) found that in Britain product innovations significantly increased the probability that a small firm was acquired, while process innovations significantly decreased the probability of small-firm failure.

- *Marketing.* The size of the market in which small firms sell their products presumably also has an impact on survival. A limited amount of evidence suggests that the broader the market and product range, the greater the probability that small firms survive. For example, Reid (1991) estimated that that a 1 per cent increase in the product group range increased the probability that small Scottish owner-managed enterprises would stay in business by 0.34 per cent, all else equal. This result is consistent with diversification enhancing survival chances, for instance by facilitating market re-positioning when changing market conditions reveal profitable new niches (Holmes and Schmitz, 1990). And in an analysis based on German data, Brüderl, Preisendörfer and Ziegler (1992) reported that survival rates were higher for firms that aimed their products at a national rather than a local market.

- *Macroeconomic conditions*
  - **Unemployment.** It is now fairly well established that businesses that start up in conditions of high unemployment have worse survival prospects than firms that start up in more favourable economic conditions. For example, Audretsch and Mahmood (1995) found that in the USA new-firm hazard rates increase with the aggregate unemployment rate. And using a competing-risks hazard model estimated with British BHPS data, Taylor (1999) found that self-employed individuals who started businesses in times of high national unemployment were more likely to go bankrupt than otherwise comparable individuals who started up in more favourable national economic conditions. Corroborative evidence has also been reported using time-series data (Hudson, 1989).

    At an individual level, experience of unemployment also appears to worsen the survival prospects of businesses. For example, it has

been established that Spanish self-employed males who were unemployed prior to entering self-employment had hazard rates three
times greater than those who previously worked in paid-employment
(Carrasco, 1999; and see also Pfeiffer and Reize, 2000, for evidence
from Germany). Thus although the unemployed are more likely to
enter self-employment than others (see chapter 3, subsection 3.3.2),
many of them seem to be less suited to it in the long term, having
higher exit rates. The previously unemployed are more likely to have
rusty human capital, lower quality information about business opportunities and possibly also lower motivation.

– **Interest rates**. Time-series studies have consistently found that
higher (nominal) interest rates increase the aggregate rate of
bankruptcies in the UK.[21] The US evidence is less clear-cut (Hudson,
1989; Audretsch and Mahmood, 1995).[22] One reason for a positive
relationship between bankruptcies and interest rates might be higher
debt-servicing costs causing insolvency. Another is that interest rates
tend to be high in inflationary conditions, inflation being associated
with business uncertainty.

• *Industry organisation and ownership.* Mata and Portugal (1994) estimated
a proportional hazard model with Portuguese data, and reported that
survival prospects were higher in firms with multiple plants and in industries with high growth rates, and lower in industries with a greater
incidence of entry. These findings have since been corroborated by
Audretsch and Mahmood (1994) and Mata, Portugal and Guimaraes
(1995).

Bates (1998) asked whether franchisees were more likely to survive
relative to non-franchisees. Reasons for supposing they are include
their adoption of a proven business format or product, and benefits
from advertising and management training provided by the franchiser.
Using US CBO data of new-restaurant starts in 1986 and 1987, Bates
found that franchisees did indeed have higher survival rates than non-
franchisees, but lower survival rates if franchises owned by large corporations were excluded from the sample. Similar findings for the UK
have been obtained by Stanworth et al. (1998).

This completes our overview of the salient factors associated with the
demise of new entrepreneurial ventures and the departure of individuals
from self-employment. For the most part, the discussion has abstracted
from factors associated with entry into business. However, on a more
aggregated level, it is of interest to ask whether entry and exit rates are
related dynamically. We conclude by taking a brief look at this question.

Table 9.1 sets out several possible linkages between the aggregate birth
rate of new small firms in a region at time t, denoted FB_t, and the

Table 9.1 *Firm birth and death interactions*

| | Expected sign of each effect | | |
	Multiplier	Competition	Marshall
$\frac{\partial FB_{t+\Delta t}}{\partial FB_t}$	+	−	n.a.
$\frac{\partial FD_{t+\Delta t}}{\partial FD_t}$	+	−	n.a.
$\frac{\partial FB_{t+\Delta t}}{\partial FD_t}$	−	+	n.a.
$\frac{\partial FD_{t+\Delta t}}{\partial FB_t}$	−	+	+

Notes: n.a. = Not applicable.

corresponding death rate, FD_t. Depending on the nature of the firms that enter the market, and the market itself, births at t could either promote more or less births and deaths at a future time $t + \Delta t$, where $\Delta t > 0$. The same ambiguities also apply to the effects of firms dying at t on births and deaths at $t + \Delta t$. For example, births could promote future births (and retard future deaths), in the case of a new innovative product that spawns imitators and spin-offs, and so increases the survival prospects of existing firms. This is called a 'multiplier' effect in Table 9.1. Alternatively, births could decrease the opportunity for future births and cause the eventual demise of rivals because of increased competition. This is called a 'competition' effect.[23] In addition, as Marshall pointed out in his graphic 'trees of the forest' analogy of small firm longevity, 'sooner or later age tells on them all' (1930, p. 263). Since (barring takeover) death inevitably follows birth, this is termed the 'Marshall' effect.

It is possible to estimate the structure of birth–death interdependence using the following reduced form econometric model:

$$\Delta FB_{it} = \sum_{\Delta t=1}^{m} \alpha_{1\Delta t} \Delta FB_{i,t-\Delta t} + \sum_{\Delta t=1}^{m} \beta_{1\Delta t} \Delta FD_{i,t-\Delta t}$$
$$+ \sum_{\Delta t=1}^{m} \gamma_{1\Delta t} \Delta X_{i,t-\Delta t} + u_{it} \tag{9.9}$$

$$\Delta FD_{it} = \sum_{\Delta t=1}^{m} \alpha_{2\Delta t} \Delta FB_{i,t-\Delta t} + \sum_{\Delta t=1}^{m} \beta_{2\Delta t} \Delta FD_{i,t-\Delta t}$$
$$+ \sum_{\Delta t=1}^{m} \gamma_{2\Delta t} \Delta X_{i,t-\Delta t} + v_{1t}, \tag{9.10}$$

where i denotes a region, t is a time period, m is the number of lags through which birth–death interdependence manifests itself, the αs, βs and γs are parameters to be estimated, the u_{it} and v_{it} are disturbances and X is a vector of macroeconomic variables that potentially affect births and deaths (see, e.g., Highfield and Smiley, 1987; Yamawaki, 1990). Longitudinal data are needed to estimate (9.9) and (9.10).

Johnson and Parker (1994) estimated a version of (9.9) and (9.10) without macroeconomic control variables. Their data came from ten years of annual British VAT registration and deregistration data in the retailing industry between 1980 and 1990. Each year contained information for each of sixty counties. These authors reported rich interdependencies between births and deaths, with lags of up to five years being statistically significant. Multiplier effects dominated in the case of deaths (i.e. fewer deaths today are associated with fewer deaths and more births in the future) and competition effects dominated in the case of births (i.e. more births today cause more deaths and fewer births in the future). While the deep factors underlying this asymmetry are not explained, these findings may suggest that researchers should avoid treating firm entry and exit separately when using aggregated data.[24]

9.4   Conclusion

This chapter focused on entrepreneurship in ventures that have passed the start-up stage and are making their way in the competitive marketplace. At the risk of drawing a caricature, the basic facts can be summarised as follows. Typically, new firms established by entrepreneurs are small. The entrepreneurs who own these firms learn rapidly about their abilities to succeed in business and the majority soon become aware that they are unable to compete as successfully as they had anticipated. Most of these entrepreneurs leave the market between two and four years after entry. Generally, firms that exit are not just young, but also small. In contrast, surviving new firms tend to have higher and more variable growth rates, with rates of growth that often exceed those experienced by larger enterprises – especially if they are small, run by an experienced and educated entrepreneur and formed in a low-unemployment environment. Eventually, surviving firms settle down into maturity. A few of them – and it is only a small proportion – experience protracted rapid growth and a fraction of these ultimately become the large enterprises of the future.

The model of Jovanovic (1982) formed the theoretical centrepiece of the chapter. Jovanovic emphasised the importance of dynamics, with entrepreneurs learning about their abilities to compete and survive in the market post-entry. His model provided a useful platform for organising the plethora of empirical results that have emerged from the burgeoning literature on small-firm growth and survival rates. Instead of recapping or summarising that material here, we shall instead consider some of the broader implications that follow from them.

It is tempting to seek policy recommendations from the findings outlined in this chapter. While this is perhaps understandable, a few cautionary words are in order. First, as Paul Geroski has pointed out, 'entry appears to be relatively easy, but survival is not' (Geroski, 1995, p. 23). Much of the policy debate about encouraging enterprise and small businesses focuses on encouraging entry by, for example, removing or relaxing borrowing constraints or information-related impediments to start-up (see chapter 10). But in view of high small-firm failure rates, this effort may be misguided. It might be more productive to investigate whether government can and should intervene to help improve survival rates – or even whether resources could be allocated more efficiently by discouraging some start-ups altogether. There are echoes here of some of the proposed cures for 'over-investment' suggested in the small-firm finance literature, and discussed in chapter 5.

However, even here practical policy recommendations tend to be vague. As Holtz-Eakin (2000) points out, the literature currently lacks a notion of what the optimal rate of business failure is, making the role of government policy towards survival rates unclear. But even if we had that knowledge, it still does not follow that government intervention is automatically justified. As a careful reading of the literature makes clear, academic researchers have achieved only limited success in identifying the factors that conduce to business survival and growth. While some general findings are now fairly well established, substantial amounts of variation in survival and growth rates remain unexplained. And while it is one thing to use some form of multivariate analysis to identify the characteristics of high-growth businesses once growth has been achieved, it is quite another to identify high-growth firms in advance. On a case-by-case basis, we are evidently still a long way from being able to 'pick winners'; nor is it obviously a good idea to target support on 'high-flyers' that are presumably best placed to thrive without it. It is anyway asking a lot of government to acquire the necessary information to implement accurate policies, even supposing that it can always be relied upon to always act effectively when dispensing selective assistance.

Another problem is that government policies designed to promote growth and survival may have perverse effects. Even well-intended policies could encourage non-targeted firms to change their behaviour in order to exploit any assistance on offer, or to dilute their incentive to succeed in the marketplace on their own merits. An example of this in the context of exit is changes to English bankruptcy law, which is currently being reformed to make it more forgiving of business failure. There is a perception that the law has in the past prevented failed entrepreneurs from re-entering the market and exploiting the valuable experience they have acquired from failing the first time round (Gladstone and Lane-Lee, 1995). In fact, English bankruptcy law does not compare too unfavourably in this respect with that prevailing in many other OECD countries (OECD, 2000b). According to Fan and White (2002), a more lenient treatment of bankruptcies does stimulate entrepreneurship and increase the average level of business experience of active entrepreneurs. But it can also give systematically over-optimistic individuals greater opportunities to repeatedly waste scarce resources in ultimately unviable business propositions. Unscrupulous operators forming temporary enterprises designed to cheat the public could also abuse laxer bankruptcy laws.

Perhaps general policies that enhance the stock of human capital, and increase the incentives to innovate, are more promising ways of promoting entrepreneurship and growth. After all, more educated entrepreneurs tend to run firms that grow faster (though not ones that necessarily survive for longer). Also, promoting high-tech enterprise might increase overall survival rates, to the extent that these firms have better survival prospects than 'conventional' firms. Examples of possible policies include tax breaks for innovative start-ups and R&D; government funding of university innovation-based research; and investment in basic education and skills. Even if the policies do not 'work' directly in generating higher levels of entrepreneurial activity, they might still be justified in terms of their positive impact on the economy's human capital stock. Of course, many countries have policies designed to foster innovation and entrepreneurship; but a question mark hangs over the true 'additionality' of these policies. More research needs to be undertaken on this issue specifically, and on the micro-level relationships between innovation, survival, growth and government policy more generally.

NOTES

1. See Brock and Evans (1986, pp. 60–3) for a relaxation of this assumption.
2. Reinvestment of profits may promote growth by enabling small firms to attain the industry's minimum efficient scale (Audretsch, 1991) or to circumvent borrowing constraints (Parker, 2000).
3. See Hall (1987), Reid (1993) and Hart and Oulton (1996). A very small number of small firms enjoy dramatic growth rates (Reid, 1993; Storey, 1994a; DTI, 1999). For example, the DTI (1999) estimated that only about 1 per cent of new business start-ups in the UK eventually achieve a turnover in excess of £1 million.

4. For example, using data on 8,300 small US firms over 1976–82, measuring firm size in terms of employment, and controlling for industry and regional factors, Brock and Evans (1986) reported the following estimates of (9.6): $\hat{\gamma}_1 = -2.25$, $\hat{\gamma}_2 = -0.35$, $\hat{\gamma}_3 = -3.02$ and $\hat{\gamma}_5 = 0.98$. All these estimates were significantly different from zero, and were robust to sample-selection bias caused by surviving firms having higher growth rates. However, a caveat is that there may be a lag before growth occurs. According to Phillips and Kirchhoff (1989), only 10 per cent of new firms between 1976 and 1986 grew in employment terms in the first four years, but over half had grown within eight years.

5. See Evans (1987a, 1987b), Cooper, Woo and Dunkelberg (1989), Dunne, Roberts and Sammelson (1989a), Audretsch (1991), Davis and Haltiwanger (1992), Variyam and Kraybill (1992), Mata (1994), Barkham, Hart and Hanvey (1996) and Goedhuys and Sleuwaegen (2000). Geroski (1995) and Sutton (1997) review the literature.

6. See Cooper and Bruno (1977), Johnson and Rodger (1983), Roberts (1991), Cooper, Gimeno-Gascon and Woo (1994) and Barkham, Hart and Hanvey (1996). Multiple founders have a broader base of skills and experience and may give each other psychological support.

7. For US evidence of insignificant effects from gender on gross business earnings growth rates, see Kalleberg and Leicht (1991). Cooper, Eimeno-Gascon and Woo (1994) reported positive and significant effects on growth from starting capital.

8. These included firm size, the owner's education and multiple sources of funding.

9. See Scherer (1980, pp. 407–38, 1991), Acs and Audretsch (1988), Audretsch (1991), Cohen and Klepper (1996) and Klepper (1996). These findings refute Schumpeter's prediction of ever-increasing concentration of innovation in large firms.

10. See also Lin, Picot and Compton (2000), who showed that a much higher proportion of Canadians who left self-employment departed the labour force altogether, than Canadians who left paid-employment.

11. See also Fuest, Huber and Nielsen (2002), who cited OECD data from the late 1980s displaying marked cross-country variations in entrants' business survival rates. According to these data, between 30 and 50 per cent of new entrants survive for seven years. The highest survival rates were observed in France and Portugal; the lowest in Finland and the UK.

12. See Altman (1983) and Hudson (1989) for US evidence and Hudson (1987b) and Cressy (1999) for UK evidence.

13. One implication, noted by Frank (1988), is that failing entrepreneurs remain in the market not because they mistakenly believe that they should condition their behaviour on sunk costs, but because of their strongly held prior belief that they are intrinsically able (but unlucky). For rational decision makers sunk costs are bygones; and 'bygones are bygones in love, war and economics.'

14. Applications to developing countries are less common, though see Nziramasanga and Lee (2001). Bates (1999) analysed the duration of self-employment among Asian immigrants into the USA.

15. See Brock and Evans (1986), Bates (1990, 1997), Brüderl, Preisendörfer and Ziegler (1992), Cooper, Gimeno-Gascon and Woo (1994), Cressy (1996, 1999), Gimeno *et al.* (1997), Brüderl and Preisendörfer (1998), Taylor (1999), Boden and Nucci (2000) and Kangasharju and Pekkala (2002). This finding appears to hold for males and females of all ethnic groups, though failure rates tend to be higher for women, blacks and non-founders than for non-minority male founders (Holmes and Schmitz, 1996).

16. However, the effects of age on survival in self-employment may be unstable through time (Holtz-Eakin, Joulfaian and Rosen 1994b; Cressy, 1996; Taylor, 1999), reflecting the state of the business cycle.

17. UK studies include Dunne and Hughes (1994), Storey (1994a), Westhead and Cowling (1995) and Hart and Oulton (1996). US studies include Brock and Evans (1986) Evans (1987a, 1987b), Cooper, Woo and Dunkelberg (1989), Dunne, Woo and Dunkelberg (1989a), Audretsch (1991), Audretsch and Mahmood (1995) and Gimeno *et al.* (1997). For evidence on Portugal and Germany, see Mata and Portugal (1994), Brüderl, Preisendörfer and Ziegler (1992), and Brüderl and Preisendorfer (1998), respectively.

18. There are limitations to the generality of this result, however. According to Agarwal and Audretsch (2001), this relationship does not hold for mature stages of the product lifecycle, or for technologically intensive products. Also, firm size must be viewed as relative to the minimum efficient scale in the industry of which the firm is a member. New-firm survival is lower in industries where scale economies are important (Audretsch, 1991; Audretsch and Mahmood, 1995).

19. See also Hall (1992), whose survey of reports from the British Official Receiver showed that about one-quarter of insolvencies were attributable to under-capitalisation and the poor management of debt by the former owners.

20. However, *exclusively* self-financed firms might be expected to have lower probabilities of survival, because banks that refuse to lend to the riskiest venture proposals must therefore depend entirely on self-finance (de Meza and Webb, 1988). Also, the most unrealistically over-optimistic entrepreneurs would naturally prefer to use their own funds than to borrow at a higher interest rate from banks (de Meza and Southey, 1996).

21. See Wadhwani (1986), Reid and Jacobson (1988), Storey *et al.* (1987) and Hudson and Cuthbertson (1993). A dissenting view is found in Simmons (1989), although see Keeble, Walker and Robson (1993) for a critique of Simmons' work.

22. Many of these studies may be sensitive to the spurious regression problem outlined in chapter 1, subsection 1.6.4. Other macroeconomic variables have also been linked with exit in aggregate studies. See, e.g., Audretsch and Mahmood (1995), who found a greater hazard for US manufacturing firms facing higher wages, and Cressy (1999), who found that GDP growth positively impacted on small British firms' survival probabilities.

23. This concept is related to, but distinct from, that of the 'seedbed', according to which some small firms will go on to grow and become the successful large job-creators of the future, displacing older incumbents. Beesley and Hamilton (1984) defined 'seedbed' industries as those with high birth and

death rates. They identified such industries in terms of the degree of 'turbulence', commonly defined as the ratio of the sum of birth and death rates to the existing stock of businesses. Reynolds (1999) showed that a variety of job and establishment turbulence measures were significantly correlated with annual regional job growth in the USA, which he interpreted as evidence of creative destruction.

24. Subsequently Kangasharju and Moisio (1998) broadly replicated these findings, using Finnish data and a more efficient instrumental variables estimator. One difference was their finding that deaths had a major impact on future births and deaths in Finland, whereas births made relatively little difference to the dynamics. However, Johnson and Parker (1996) found that the inclusion of macroeconomic variables in (9.9) and (9.10) eliminated some of the lagged birth/death effects – something that Kangasharju and Moisio (1998) did not take account of.

Part IV

Government policy

10 Government policy: issues and evidence

Government interventions in market economies can impact heavily on both the welfare of entrepreneurs and the size of the entrepreneurship sector. Government intervention is often motivated by a belief that entrepreneurs generate important positive social and economic externalities, such as new ideas, new products, new employment and enhanced competitiveness. If entrepreneurs are unable to appropriate all of these benefits themselves, there may be too little private investment for the social good, making a case for government intervention.

Many governments also see entrepreneurship as a route out of poverty and dependence on state benefits, and as a means of achieving self-reliance. At the same time, though, governments often evince concern about the living and working conditions of the poorest and most vulnerable workers, who are often found in entrepreneurship, either as self-employed business owners or as employees of the self-employed.

In most developed economies, the main channels of government intervention are through the credit market, the tax system and expenditure on assistance and advice. Government regulation can also affect the performance of entrepreneurial ventures. This chapter provides an overview of both the theory and evidence relating to government intervention in these areas.

The chapter is organised as follows. Section 10.1 describes and analyses government interventions in the credit market. Sections 10.2 and 10.3 develop the theory of taxation and entrepreneurship, with regard to the income tax system and tax evasion and avoidance. Section 10.4 presents evidence about the effects of taxation on entrepreneurship, including issues related to tax evasion and under-reporting of self-employment incomes to the tax authorities. Section 10.5 briefly surveys various forms of direct government assistance to entrepreneurs, and the impact of regulations on small firms. Section 10.6 concludes.

10.1   Credit market interventions

Chapter 5 reviewed the theoretical case for credit rationing and under-investment in entrepreneurial ventures. This case has received substantial attention in policy circles and has motivated various kinds of government intervention, especially loan guarantee schemes (LGSs). In this section, we first describe such schemes, before evaluating their appropriateness in terms of theoretical models of credit rationing. Then evidence on their actual performance in the UK and USA is reviewed. Finally, we briefly discuss other forms of government intervention in credit markets.

10.1.1   Loan Guarantee Schemes

Organisation

LGSs provide a government-backed guarantee to encourage banks and other financial institutions to lend to small firms who are unable to raise conventional finance because of a lack of security or an established track record. LGSs are widespread, with versions operating in the USA, the UK, France, Germany and Canada and several other countries.

Although the details vary between countries – and within given countries depending on the type of loan[1] – the basic principles of a LGS are the same. A LGS typically guarantees finance for both new start-ups and going concerns. Only borrowers unable to secure a conventional loan from a bank, and in non-proscribed industrial sectors,[2] may apply for a loan guarantee. A bank nominates ventures for approval by the government and administers the loans. Conditional on approval by the government, the bank takes the usual repayment if the venture succeeds. If it fails, the bank is liable only for a fraction of the loss, with the rest borne by the government. In the USA, the Small Business Administration (SBA) underwrites between 75 and 80 per cent of loans; in the UK, the British government underwrites between 70 and 85 per cent. Borrowers are charged an arrangement fee, and pay the usual market rate plus a small premium. Operational costs can be substantial (see table 10.1 for details on this and other aspects of LGSs in several countries).

Theoretical perspectives

Can governments without access to inside information about entrepreneurs' ventures use a LGS to improve on the competitive equilibrium under asymmetric information? If financial markets were efficient, one would expect all loans involving reasonable degrees of risk and promising reasonable rates of return on capital to be made by private-sector lenders. Any rejected loan applications would reflect exceptional

Table 10.1   *Features of LGSs in the UK, the USA, France, Germany and Canada*

Terms	UK	USA	France	Germany	Canada
Maximum guarantee	70–85%	75–80%[a]	50–65%[b]	80%	85%
Arrangement fee	1% of loan	2–3.875% of guarantee	None	0.75% of guarantee	2% of loan
Loan premium	1.5% of loan	0.5% of credit	0.6% of credit	0.8–1% of credit	1.25% of credit
Loan term	2–10 years	7–25 years	2–15 years	15–23 years	0–10 years
Number of guarantees	6,942 (1996–7)	45,300 (1997)	5,000 (1996)	6,850 (1996)	30,765 (1997)
Net cost of scheme	£46million (1997–8)	£95million (1998)	£36million (1996)	n.a.	£42.5m (1997)

Notes: [a] 70 per cent for start-ups; 85 per cent for firms with at least two years' trading history.
[b] 65 per cent for start-ups. n.a. = Not available.
Source: KPMG (1999, table 4.1).

levels of risk; and any government-backed lending to facilitate such ventures would therefore be expected to result in high default rates. However, if the financial market for small-firm lending is inefficient – a possibility explored in chapter 5 – then the case for government intervention in credit markets may be stronger. A few studies have addressed this issue directly, the most notable being a pair of papers by William Gale.

Using a simple model with two types of agent, one high-risk (b), and one low-risk (g), Gale (1990a) showed how a LGS can actually be self-defeating. In line with the analysis of chapter 5, banks would ideally prefer to fund gs to bs, but under asymmetric information they cannot observe these types directly from the pool of loan applicants. All agents are assumed to have socially efficient ventures, so if there is any credit rationing it entails an efficiency loss. A crucial assumption made by Gale is that it is costly for banks to seize collateral C when ventures fail, so any policy that discourages the use of collateral will increase efficiency in this respect. There are two possibilities: (a) collateral is plentiful, and (b) collateral is limited.

Consider (a) first. When collateral is available, the analysis of subsection 5.1.3 can be applied. In terms of figure 5.4, C is the BAD, and a separating equilibrium exists, in which gs choose a low-D, high-C contract Γ_g (where D is the interest repayment) to differentiate themselves from bs who choose a high-D, low-C contract, Γ_b. There is no credit rationing. Now the introduction of a LGS targeted only at g-type ventures would make the Γ_g contract more attractive because competitive banks would have to pass on the benefit of lower default penalties to their customers. So to restore separation of types under incentive compatibility, gs would have to post *greater* C than before, reducing efficiency. Here is one example of how a LGS can actually be counter-productive. But if the LGS applied to b-type contracts only, or to both contracts simultaneously, the effect is to decrease the relative attractiveness of Γ_g to bs, so that gs can separate themselves by posting less collateral. Under the assumption of costly collateral realisation, this yields a clear efficiency and welfare gain.

Case (b), with limited collateral, is more interesting, for two reasons. First, it is the situation that most frequently motivates the use of LGSs in practice (Bates, 1984; KPMG, 1999). Second, the policy implications are striking: Gale showed that banks *might respond to a LGS by rationing credit further*. To see this, note that because collateral can no longer be used to separate types, some other device must be sought. Following the analysis of subsection 5.1.3, random rationing of credit in the Γ_g contract will serve the purpose. Thus we start with a separating equilibrium where, in terms of figure 5.4, BAD is the probability of being credit rationed. In equilibrium, bs select $\Gamma_b^1 =$ (high-D, 'zero-credit rationing') contracts, and gs choose $\Gamma_g^1 =$ (low-D, 'positive probability of credit rationing') contracts. A LGS targeted on the rationed gs increases the probability that a rationed borrower obtains a loan under Γ_g^1, i.e., it reduces BAD so that bs may now covet Γ_g^1. To preserve separation, banks have to counteract the LGS policy by restricting credit further. Thus the government's policy is frustrated by the reactions of private-sector agents, and overall welfare decreases. The only way of increasing efficiency and welfare in this scenario is to target LGS-backed loans on the unrationed high-risk group, i.e., the bs; but because governments usually try to target assistance on rationed loan applicants, this policy seems somewhat counter-intuitive.[3]

Although interesting, Gale's analysis seems of limited relevance for real-world applications of LGSs. There is no credit rationing in scenario (a) of Gale's (1990a) model. Everyone obtains a loan; the only rationale for introducing a LGS is to reduce the use of inefficient collateral. But this is contrary to the real-world LGS rationale of increasing the volume of lending. While this rationale is applicable in scenario (b), where there is initially credit rationing, it seems unrealistic that the good risks are credit rationed (see subsection 5.1.3). And in both scenarios, the realism of a model without any pooling of entrepreneurial types seems limited.

Different results are obtained from Gale's second model (1990b), which is arguably more realistic. Gale started with a set-up based on the Stiglitz and Weiss (1981) (SW) model, with two identifiable sets of borrowers: general, and targeted. Among the targeted borrowers there may be multiple observable groups (as in SW and Riley, 1987). Initially, the economy may be characterised by market-clearing, redlining or credit rationing equilibria. Gale derived four key results. First, unsubsidised government interventions merely substitute publicly provided credit for privately provided credit, and so are ineffective. A subsidy element is needed to improve on the competitive equilibrium – which explains why government credit programmes tend to lose money in practice, as shown in table 10.1. Second, if credit rationing exists in the initial equilibrium, a subsidised loan guarantee is more effective than an interest subsidy. Third, with multiple target groups subject to rationing or redlining, a subsidy to one group may increase banks' expected returns by so much that other, initially non-rationed, groups may become rationed or redlined.[4] Fourth, interest subsidies funded by lump-sum taxes can increase social efficiency by mitigating adverse selection, as in SW.

Innes (1991) analysed an asymmetric information model in which under- or over-investment (though not credit rationing) can occur. Heterogeneous entrepreneurs can choose loan sizes, and there is scope for high-ability entrepreneurs to signal their types by asking for loans that are larger than the socially efficient level. Innes showed that a LGS is an ineffective means of intervention. The reason is instructive. The government's absorption of some of the default costs provides a positive incentive for entrepreneurs to make inefficient investment choices. Large maximum guarantee levels simply exacerbate over-investment by entrepreneurs, with the complicity of banks whose downside risks are covered by the government.

Evaluation

In practice, as table 10.1 shows, the charge to the government of failed guaranteed ventures can be high, so it is important to evaluate the effectiveness of these schemes.[5] The success of a LGS is limited by several factors. One possibility is that some borrowers would have received a loan in the absence of the LGS. That is, the ventures financed under the scheme are not truly 'additional', imposing a deadweight cost. A second is that a LGS encourages self-selection of the riskiest ventures, while reducing the bank's incentive to evaluate thoroughly the viability of investment proposals (Rhyne, 1988). The severity of this problem can be expected to increase in line with the loan guarantee fraction. This requires careful screening by bureaucrats; but they may be poorly equipped to make such judgements. Third, successful start-ups financed by a LGS may displace existing enterprises. This is thought to be a particular problem in retailing, catering and motor vehicle maintenance in the UK, for example.[6]

Another limiting factor is that the scale of LGSs is often small in relation to the rest of the market. Guaranteed loans in the UK and the USA comprise only about 1 per cent of all small and medium-sized enterprise (SME) on-lending by value, making it a marginal source of lending to the SME sector.[7]

Bosworth, Carron and Rhyne (1987) conducted a thorough evaluation of the SBA's LGS. Bosworth, Carron and Rhyne started with an 'optimistic' estimate that around 20 per cent of SBA-backed loans were non-additional. Applying an empirically-based 23 per cent default rate for the whole portfolio, this means that only 60 per cent of SBA loans could generate benefits to offset the costs of the scheme, requiring a net subsidy of 8.7 per cent. Thus the economic benefits required for the scheme to break even were 14.5 (=8.7/0.6) per cent of the loan amount – over and above the mandated loan repayments.[8] Bosworth, Carron and Rhyne and Rhyne (1988) doubted whether the economic benefits would be as great as this.

Some detailed evaluation evidence has also been compiled for the UK's Small Firm Loan Guarantee Scheme (SFLGS). Survey work by KPMG (1999) estimated that around 70 per cent of SFLGS-supported firms were 'finance-additional' (i.e. would not have been financed without the involvement of the LGS), and leveraged £161 million of additional private finance between 1993 and 1998. However, survey results identified high displacement rates of between 76 and 86 per cent. This limited the employment creation contribution of guaranteed ventures to between 0.3 and 0.6 jobs per firm in the eighteen months following the loan, amounting to under 10,000 net additional jobs in total. The net additional cost per job charged to the government was estimated at between £9,500 and £16,600.

Naturally, there might be other supply-side benefits from LGSs that are hard to quantify, such as greater competitiveness caused by the creation of LGS-backed ventures, and the benefit of keeping initially struggling businesses afloat that might develop profitably and grow in the future. Early evidence pointed to high failure rates of LGS-backed businesses (Bosworth, Carron and Rhyne, 1987; Rhyne, 1988); but since then the UK and US LGSs have been made more stringent with lower guarantee fractions. This is reflected in more recent UK evidence that LGS-funded businesses do not have higher failure rates on average than non-LGS-funded businesses (KPMG, 1999). In addition, Cowling and Mitchell (1997) provided some econometric evidence that the SFLGS had a positive if modest effect on the aggregate UK self-employment rate. But all this evidence is only mildly supportive of LGS programmes. While they do not do much obvious harm, they do not appear to do very much good either.

10.1.2   Other interventions

The US Federal government issues direct loans to small businesses, mainly in rural sectors (Gale, 1990b). Total disbursements under the SBA's Small Business Investment Companies and Minority Investment Companies programmes reached $680 million by 1987. However, the scale of direct US Federal lending has declined over time, with a move towards guarantees rather than loans.[9] State governments, which either provide loans directly or in conjunction with private lenders, have taken up some of the slack. Some states also provide venture capital in the form of equity investments, either directly or indirectly via state-subsidised venture capital companies (Smith and Stutzer, 1989). In the UK, direct government lending is less common than grants from local or regional agencies, although centrally funded grants and equity investment schemes have been implemented, including SMART for innovative ventures in new and small firms, the Business Expansion Scheme and the Enterprise Investment Scheme (see, e.g., Deakins, 1999, chapter 8, for details).

Using a simple model of credit rationing as a screening device (see subsection 5.1.3 and the discussion above), Smith and Stutzer (1989) analysed the effects of government loans on the extent of credit rationing and efficiency. The analysis is essentially the same as for Gale's (1990a) model with limited collateral, discussed above. In response to loans that reduce credit rationing of g borrowers, banks ration credit further to restore efficient contracting. Thus in this model a policy of using loans to reduce credit rationing is counter-productive because it works against the wishes of private-sector agents, who counteract its effects.

Government grants and loans might be expected to have a positive impact on employment, unless there is crowding out via displacement. Wren (1998) calculated the effects on employment among English manufacturing firms of government capital grants and rent assistance. Wren reported that grants had greater long-term employment effects on new small firms than on their older and larger rivals – despite the lower survival rates of the former relative to the latter. However, the absolute numbers of jobs created were quite small. For example, even before accounting for displacement and opportunity costs of funds, Wren estimated that capital grants generated just 0.082 job per £1,000 after five years, with an implied gross direct cost per job to the exchequer of £12,195 (=1,000/0.082). The corresponding figure for large firms was 0.004, which was insignificantly different from zero. Wren conjectured that the (slightly) greater effect for small firms reflected their higher marginal cost of external funds, which made them more responsive to assistance.

10.2   Taxation, subsidies and entrepreneurship: theory

The material in this section builds on that of chapter 2, section 2.2, which analysed models of occupational choice and participation in entrepreneurship. Those models did not incorporate government activities, an omission that is rectified below.

One reason why governments might seek to alter occupational choices relates to risk. Entrepreneurship is commonly regarded as a risky activity, so with missing or incomplete markets for risk sharing, private risk-averse agents might undertake insufficient risk taking from society's perspective. Even developed economies tend to lack insurance markets that smooth entrepreneurial incomes over time or between risky and safe occupations. The absence of such markets may be attributable to moral hazard problems, for instance where entrepreneurs would supply less effort in response to having income insurance. Also, capital indivisibilities, fixed set-up costs and signalling considerations may prevent entrepreneurs from diversifying their risk by operating several ventures concurrently. While partnerships can be used to share some risks in principle, they can rarely diversify all risk and tend to be used by only a minority of entrepreneurs in any case. There might therefore be a case for government intervention to favour risky activities.

Set against this, the elimination of risk can be costly, and governments might not have a cost advantage over the market (Black and de Meza, 1997). And if there is over-investment in entrepreneurial activities, then entrepreneurship should be discouraged, rather than encouraged (de Meza, 2002). Also, tax-favouring small firms but not large ones presumably involves withdrawing the subsidy as firms grow – which can act as a perverse tax on growth (Holtz-Eakin, 2000).

In principle, the government has at its disposal several policy instruments for affecting occupational choice between 'risky' and 'safe' occupations. The discussion below will focus specifically on the personal income tax (IT) system. We will not consider interest taxes or subsidies, whose effects on occupational allocations under asymmetric information have already been analysed in chapter 5. In addition we will not analyse corporate taxes because only a minority of entrepreneurs run incorporated businesses that are liable to them.[10]

The relationship between income taxation and entrepreneurship is complex in all but the very simplest cases, an example of which is afforded by the Lucas (1978) model described in chapter 2, subsection 2.2.3. In Lucas' model, individuals have heterogeneous entrepreneurial abilities x; a cut-off level of ability $\tilde{x}$ separates those who become entrepreneurs (with $x \geq \tilde{x}$) from those who become employees (with $x < \tilde{x}$). The cut-off ability is defined implicitly by the condition $\pi(\tilde{x}) = w$, where entrepreneurial profit π is an increasing function of ability, and where w is the employee wage. A flat-rate (or excess profit) tax $\tau \in (0, 1)$ on entrepreneurs' profits changes the cut-off ability to $\tilde{\tilde{x}}$, defined by $[1 - \tau]\pi(\tilde{\tilde{x}}) = w$. Evidently $\tilde{\tilde{x}} > \tilde{x}$, so entrepreneurs with abilities in the range $x \in [\tilde{x}, \tilde{\tilde{x}})$ close down their firms and switch to paid-employment. The extra supply of labour decreases the employee wage, while the smaller number of firms implies excess demand for their goods, so increasing their prices. Thus larger firms gain from the tax at the expense of smaller ones, and may actually become better off on net. The simple message that follows is summarised by the following quotation from the UK Employment Department, when reviewing the impact of UK income tax cuts in the 1980s: 'A more beneficial tax regime has been an important factor in stimulating enterprise' (1989, p. 16).

Part of the reason for the clear-cut policy advice just enunciated is that it came from a model that abstracted from risk. More complicated and subtle results emerge from models that recognise the risk-bearing role of entrepreneurship. A key model that provides a good entry point to the theoretical literature on risk taking, IT and entrepreneurship is Kanbur (1981). Kanbur's model has the following features. A single good is produced by entrepreneurs using a strictly concave stochastic production function $q(H, \varrho)$, where H is the number of paid-employees hired by each entrepreneur, and ϱ is a random variable from which firms receive independent draws. Here as in all the other models discussed below, the size of the workforce is normalised to unity. Employees receive a safe competitive wage w which adjusts to clear the labour market. Identical risk-averse individuals have a concave (risk-averse) utility function $U(\cdot)$ and choose between becoming an entrepreneur entitled to risky residual profits or a worker earning w with certainty. Labour supply is exogenously fixed. Price flexibility ensures full employment.

Consider a policy of differential income taxation, under which a proportional subsidy rate $\varsigma > 0$ is applied to wage income, financed by a proportional tax rate $\tau > 0$ levied on risky entrepreneurial profit income, $\pi := q(H, \varrho) - wH$. Individuals are indifferent between the two occupations when

$$V(\tau, w) := \max_{H} \mathsf{E} U\left[(1 - \tau)\pi\right] = U\left[(1 + \varsigma)w\right] . \tag{10.1}$$

This tax system has three offsetting effects: (1) Taxation reduces post-tax incomes in entrepreneurship, making entrepreneurship less attractive. (2) Taxation smooths entrepreneurs' incomes over different states, providing insurance that makes entrepreneurship more attractive. And (3) this benefit of risk pooling increases the demand for labour, pushing up wages relative to profits (Kihlstrom and Laffont, 1983b).

By the normalisation rule, the proportion of the workforce in entrepreneurship is $n_S = [1 + H(\tau, w)]^{-1}$, where $H(\tau, w) := \text{argmax}$ $V(\tau, w)$. The government's objective is to maximise a utilitarian social welfare function, Ω, defined on post-tax utilities:

$$\Omega := n_S V(\tau, w) + [1 - n_S] U [(1 + \varsigma)w] . \qquad (10.2)$$

Maximising Ω with respect to τ, and evaluating the result from a position of no government intervention gives the result

$$\left. \frac{d\Omega}{d\tau} \right|_{\tau=\varsigma=0} = \frac{\mathsf{E}(\pi)\mathsf{E}(U_\pi) - \mathsf{E}(\pi U_\pi)}{H\mathsf{E}(U_\pi) + U_w} . U_w > 0 .$$

That is, government should tax the risky occupation and subsidise the safe one. The reason is that the gain made by each employee more than offsets the loss incurred by each entrepreneur, whose losses are in any case mitigated by the income smoothing provided by the tax.

Under assumption 1 of chapter 2, subsection 2.2.1, i.e., decreasing absolute risk aversion, Kanbur also showed that positive taxation of entrepreneurs' profits decreases the equilibrium number of entrepreneurs relative to the no-tax outcome.[11] Kanbur interpreted this to mean that there are too many entrepreneurs in the market equilibrium relative to this higher welfare equilibrium.

It should be noted that lump-sum taxes or subsidies alone would be ineffective in this model because they would not reduce the variance of entrepreneurs' profits. In contrast, a proportional income tax applied to both occupations with a lump-sum component *is* effective – and has ambiguous effects on the equilibrium number of entrepreneurs. Let $\tau := 1 - \beta$ be the uniform marginal tax rate and let γ be the lump-sum component of the linear tax system. The case of $\beta = 1$ corresponds to the free-market solution and $\beta = 0$ to the case of 100 per cent taxation and redistribution. It is assumed that the tax system raises zero net revenue, so γ is determined endogenously by β. Individuals are indifferent between the two occupations when

$$\max_H EU \{\gamma + \beta[q(H, \varrho) - wH]\} = U (\gamma + \beta w) . \qquad (10.3)$$

As β goes to zero, risk is completely pooled, incomes are equalised, and social welfare (10.2) approaches its maximum. However, and in contrast to the earlier results, the effect on the equilibrium number of entrepreneurs is ambiguous. Not even assumption 1 of subsection 2.2.1 provides enough structure in this general case to sign the overall effect. Even further complications arise if the tax decreases the optimal capital stock of enterprises, since with any given distribution of personal wealth, business entry becomes easier and so the equilibrium number of entrepreneurs can actually increase (Kihlstrom and Laffont, 1982).

Boadway, Marchand and Pestieau (1991) showed that Kanbur's social welfare result is robust to extensions where abilities and risk attitudes are heterogeneous, but not to non-pecuniary returns that differ between occupations. In the latter case, the optimal β is less than 1, reflecting a trade-off between equity, efficiency and insurance considerations. However, in other models, stronger results can be obtained. Using a two-sector general equilibrium model, Black and de Meza (1997) showed that a subsidy to the risky sector (entrepreneurship) paid for by taxing the safe sector (paid-employment) can actually benefit all parties, implying a Pareto improvement. Entrepreneurs gain from income smoothing and the subsidy, leading to net entry into entrepreneurship; but this promotes competition that decreases the price of the risky-sector good consumed by employees. That benefit can outweigh the cost of the subsidy that employees provide.

The analysis so far has considered a linear IT system. In contrast, the tax schedules in most countries are non-linear functions of income, usually piecewise linear and progressive. If entrepreneurs' profits are uncertain, a progressive tax system acts as an income smoothing device, which can be expected to encourage participation in entrepreneurship.[12] Kanbur (1982) used this reasoning to refute the popular assertion that 'entrepreneurial' societies tend to be unequal ones. If individuals are risk averse and if measured inequality depends in part on the inequality of entrepreneurs' incomes, then an increase in entrepreneurs' income inequality can increase overall inequality while decreasing the number of entrepreneurs.

In practice, most IT systems tend to treat entrepreneurs and employees more or less equally. Exceptions to equal treatment include special taxes levied on the self-employed (e.g. the self-employment SECA tax in the USA: see Joulfaian and Rider, 1998); lower social security entitlements for the self-employed reflected in lower mandated social security contributions (as is common in many countries: OECD, 1994b); and greater opportunities for legal tax deductibility and illegal tax evasion in self-employment. Examples of legal deductions include business expenses (in most countries), private pension contributions (e.g. Keogh plans in the USA), and capital gains exemptions (as in the USA: see Holtz-Eakin, 2000). There is also a difference in inheritance tax treatment in some countries, where favourable provisions can facilitate intergenerational transfers of small businesses (OECD, 1998).

An interesting policy question is whether entrepreneurs *ought* to face the same IT schedule as employees. This issue has been analysed by Pestieau and Possen (1992) and Parker (1999a). For example, Parker calibrated a simple model of occupational choice using data from the UK economy in the mid-1990s. He solved for the optimal linear differential IT rates that maximised utilitarian and inequality-averse social welfare functions. The key finding was that governments should tax entrepreneurs at a *lower* marginal rate than employees. This policy encourages entry into entrepreneurship because that occupation has generated higher incomes than paid-employment on average, despite bearing greater risk (see also Parker, 2001). One way of implementing a differential tax is to adjust the parameters of counter-evasion policies to tolerate a desired amount of tax evasion by the self-employed (see below for more on this). However, the applicability of Parker's optimal policy may be limited, because the self-employed appear to be less productive than employees in some other countries (see chapter 1, subsection 1.5.1). Also, an optimal linear differential tax might be dominated by non-linear differential taxes – about which little is known at present.[13]

To conclude, the theoretical literature does not provide clear-cut predictions about the effects of income taxes on either the equilibrium number of entrepreneurs or social welfare. The reason is that when entrepreneurs are heterogeneous, risk averse and vulnerable to uncertainty, income taxation impacts on the attractiveness of entrepreneurship and social welfare in diverse ways. One effect is on efficiency, for example if taxes are distortionary. A second effect is on equity, because tax systems redistribute incomes. Another effect is on risk sharing because income taxes can effectively insure entrepreneurs. These effects may all offset each other; and even strong restrictions on preferences and technology cannot be guaranteed to simplify matters enough to deliver straightforward predictions. The inescapable conclusion is that theory itself is unlikely to resolve the issue, and that data are needed to identify the salient effects. That is the subject of section 10.4.

10.3   Tax evasion and avoidance: theory

There are two principal reasons why entrepreneurs might pay different amounts of tax than employees with the same pre-tax incomes:

(1) Allowable cost deductions in self-employment (such as business expenses), and the leeway to draw up accounts to practice intertemporal tax-shifting;[14] and (2) Differing effectiveness of tax enforcement by income source, resulting in different incentives for income under-reporting and tax evasion by the self-employed. Unlike entrepreneurs' profits, wage and salary incomes usually offer little or no scope for tax evasion, because of third-party reporting and tax withholding by employers.

There is a large literature on the economics of tax evasion, but we focus below only on the following issues: (1) How the number of entrepreneurs is affected by taxation when tax evasion opportunities exist, and (2) Appropriate tax-penalty policies when individuals can choose freely between entrepreneurship and paid-employment.

Key theoretical studies that address the issue of tax evasion and the number of entrepreneurs include Watson (1985) and Jung, Snow and Trandel (1994). For example, Jung, Snow and Trandel analysed a model of an economy comprising two occupations. Tax evasion is possible in one occupation (self-employment, S) but not in the other (paid-employment, E). A proportional tax rate $\tau = 1 - \beta$ is applied to pre-tax income in each occupation, $y_j = y_j(n_S)$ ($j = \{E, S\}$), where income in each occupation is a function of n_S, the proportion of individuals choosing S. Reflecting diminishing marginal returns to labour in each occupation, $dy_S/dn_S < 0$ and $dy_E/dn_S > 0$. Each self-employed person chooses how much income Y to conceal from the tax authorities and which occupation to join; labour is inelastically supplied irrespective of occupation. The probability of being audited by the tax authority is Π: if an individual is caught, they must pay a penalty which is a multiple $\kappa > 0$ of the evaded tax, τY. With all individuals possessing identical utility functions $U(\cdot)$, the optimal amount of income concealed, Y^*, is

$$Y^* = \quad \text{argmax} \left\{ (1 - \Pi)U[y_S\beta + Y(1 - \beta)] + \Pi.U[y_S\beta - \kappa Y(1 - \beta)] \right\}.$$

Labour market equilibrium occurs when individuals are indifferent between E and S:

$$U(\alpha) = [1 - \Pi].U(\vartheta) + \Pi.U(\gamma),$$

where

$$\alpha := y_E(n_S^*)\beta, \quad \vartheta := y_S(n_S^*)\beta + Y^*(1 - \beta),$$
$$\gamma := y_S(n_S^*)\beta - \kappa Y^*(1 - \beta),$$

where n_S^* is the equilibrium number of individuals choosing self-employment. It is easily shown that n_S^* is decreasing in Π (see also Watson, 1985).

Using the implicit function theorem,

$$\frac{\partial n_S^*}{\partial \tau} = \frac{U_\alpha y_E - \{[1 - \Pi].U_\beta + \Pi.U_\gamma\} y_S}{\Delta},$$

where subscripts on U denote derivatives, and where we define

$$\Delta := \beta \left\{ U_\alpha \frac{dy_E}{dn_S^*} - [(1 - \Pi).U_\beta + \Pi.U_\gamma] \frac{dy_S}{dn_S^*} \right\} > 0.$$

Manipulating this expression, it is possible to prove the following proposition:

Proposition 8 (Jung, Snow and Trandel, 1994). *When tax evasion is endogenously chosen, an increase in the marginal income tax rate τ will increase (leave unchanged) (decrease) the equilibrium number of self-employed if individuals have increasing (constant) (decreasing) relative risk aversion.*

The logic of this proposition is as follows. An increase in the tax rate increases the expected benefit of evasion, though this may be offset by a shift in risk, since tax evasion induces uncertainty and the extent of risk aversion depends on post-tax income which has been reduced by the tax. But under increasing relative risk aversion, the individual becomes less risk averse after the tax so the expected benefits to self-employment are positive. Given the generally accepted nature of assumption 1 of subsection 2.2.1, which posits *non*-increasing relative risk aversion, Proposition 8 provides a basis for expecting the number of self-employed to be negatively related to average and marginal income tax rates. However, this result – and indeed all the results discussed in this and the previous section – is clearly sensitive to the assumption that workers do not respond to income taxation by working and producing less. Although this issue is well researched in labour and public economics, it has yet to command much attention from researchers in entrepreneurship, perhaps because of the intrinsic difficulties involved with modelling (continuous) labour supply adjustments jointly with (discrete) occupational choice (Kanbur, 1981; Parker, 2001).[15]

A different question is what income taxes and enforcement policies the government *should* choose in the presence of tax evasion. Pestieau and Possen (1991) studied this problem using a model in which only the self-employed can evade tax, and where its control (e.g. by greater auditing of the self-employed) discourages risk taking. Auditing is costly both for the government and for individuals who must prepare their tax records for inspection: these costs impose deadweight losses on the economy. Therefore governments concerned purely with efficiency should do no auditing at all. However, inequality-averse governments want to raise tax to redistribute incomes and must audit in order to protect the tax base. The government chooses the probability Π that individuals are audited; Pestieau and Possen (1991) further assumed that tax evaders who are caught are fined an exogenous amount that renders them *ex post* the poorest of all individuals. For sufficient degrees of inequality aversion, Pestieau and Possen (1991) showed that the optimal Π* rises to the point where tax evasion is deterred completely. The reason is that under extreme inequality aversion, the welfare of the poorest individuals should be maximised – but because these are assumed to be detected tax evaders, tax evasion itself should be completely discouraged. With this policy in place, everyone is encouraged to become self-employed, on the assumption that self-employment is the most productive occupation. Clearly, Pestieau and Possen's (1991) results are very sensitive to their assumptions. In practice, many governments impose less stringent penalties on detected tax evaders (Smith, 1986).

10.4   Taxation, tax evasion and entrepreneurship: evidence

As the previous two sections have shown, the theoretical literature does not predict a simple or unambiguous relationship between the extent of entrepreneurship and the structure of the IT system. Therefore the form of that relationship has to be determined empirically. Before turning to econometric investigations of this issue, we briefly describe in subsection 10.4.1 evidence about the extent of income under-reporting and excessive business expensing by the self-employed. Subsection 10.4.2 presents econometric evidence about the effects of IT and tax evasion opportunities in self-employment on the occupational choice decision. We argue that most existing evidence is vitiated by various methodological problems, and conclude by presenting some new results that cast doubt on the thesis that tax and tax evasion opportunities affect occupational choices for the majority of self-employed people.

10.4.1   *Income under-reporting by the self-employed*

Direct evidence about the extent of income under-reporting and tax evasion by the self-employed is available from data provided by the US Internal Revenue Service's (IRS's) Taxpayer Compliance Measurement Program (TCMP). The TCMP data are compiled by teams of auditors who analyse thoroughly the tax affairs of samples of employee and self-employed taxpayers on a case-by-case basis. These data have been utilised by numerous researchers to estimate rates of income under-reporting. The TCMP has been running since the 1960s and it tells a reasonably consistent story over time. A typical result, cited by Kesselman (1989) and based on a 1983 TCMP report, estimated that whereas 97–99 per cent of employee income was reported to the IRS, non-farm proprietors reported on average only 78.7 per cent of their gross incomes.[16] A similar estimate was obtained from 1969 TCMP data reported by Clotfelter (1983). The sums involved are not trivial either. Carson (1984) estimated that the self-employed are collectively responsible for one-quarter of total unreported income in the USA.

Rates of self-employed income under-reporting to the tax authorities of around 20 per cent have also been found in the UK, although these are based on less comprehensive data (Macafee, 1982, p. 155). Smith (1986) proposed a slightly lower self-employed income under-reporting rate of 14 per cent, and suggested that preventative policy actions in the construction sector in particular have reduced under-reporting rates.

A slightly different question, but one that is directly relevant for empirical research, is the extent to which self-employed people under-report incomes to survey interviewers, despite assurances by the latter to interviewees that all data are treated in strict confidence and cannot be divulged to any government department. Several indirect methods for estimating this kind of under-reporting have been proposed, based on comparisons between respondents' reported incomes and expenditures. It is not sufficient to identify as under-reporters households that spend more than they earn, because some households may genuinely dissave and not under-report, while others may under-report and not dissave (Dilnot and Morris, 1981). A more reliable approach proposed by Pissarides and Weber (1989) estimates expenditure equations for the self-employed and employees, and then inverts them to estimate 'true' incomes. Three assumptions underlie this approach: (i) All occupational groups report expenditures correctly to the survey interviewers;[17] (ii) employees report incomes correctly; and (iii) the income elasticity of consumption is the same for members of all occupations with the same characteristics. Let ζ_i denote the expenditure of household i, X_i a vector of the household's characteristics, y_i the household's reported income and z_i a dummy variable equal to unity if the household is headed by a self-employed person, and zero otherwise. Pissarides and Weber estimated the following regression using data on a sample of n households:

$$\ln \zeta_i = \alpha' X_i + (\beta_1 + \beta_2 z_i) \ln y_i + \gamma z_i + u_i \qquad i = 1, \ldots, n, \qquad (10.4)$$

where u_i is a white-noise disturbance term. The γ coefficient is expected to be positive in the presence of income under-reporting by the self-employed.

In the following, an overbar denotes an average value, and a † a true value of a variable. (10.4) implies that average consumption for a self-employed household is

$$\overline{\ln \zeta_i} = \alpha' \overline{X_i} + (\beta_1 + \beta_2)\overline{\ln y_i} + \gamma + u_i \qquad i \in S. \tag{10.5}$$

But assumption (iii) above implies that

$$\overline{\ln \zeta_i} = \alpha' \overline{X_i} + \beta_1 \overline{\ln y_i^\dagger} + u_i. \tag{10.6}$$

Equating (10.5) and (10.6) and re-arranging yields the percentage under-reporting rate of self-employment incomes as:

$$\overline{\ln y_i^\dagger} - \overline{\ln y_i} = (\gamma + \beta_2 \overline{\ln y_i})/\beta_1 \qquad i \in S. \tag{10.7}$$

Using 1982 UK FES data, Pissarides and Weber (1989) calculated the RHS of (10.7) and estimated the self-employment income under-reporting rate to be 55 per cent.[18] It was estimated that blue-collar workers concealed a slightly higher proportion of their income, of between 51 and 64 per cent, compared with 28–54 per cent for white-collar workers. Subsequent work by Baker (1993), based on the same methodology, generated slightly lower self-employed income under-reporting rates of between 20 and 50 per cent based on UK FES data over 1978–91. Under-reporting rates were found to differ across occupational and industry groups, with *lower* under-reporting rates among blue-collar than white-collar self-employed workers – in contrast to Pissarides and Weber (1989). According to Baker, under-reporting rates have exhibited no discernible patterns over time.

10.4.2 Tax, tax evasion and occupational choice: econometric evidence

Previous researchers have attempted to measure the tax incentive to being self-employed, by regressing the probability of being self-employed (or the self-employment rate in the case of time-series studies) on tax-related and other explanatory variables. As usual, suppose there are two occupations, self-employment S and paid-employment E, indexed by j: $j = \{S, E\}$. In a cross-section sample of individuals indexed by i, the basic model of the probability of being self-employed, z_i^*, is

$$z_i^* = \alpha' X_i + \beta T_i + u_i, \tag{10.8}$$

where X_i is a design matrix containing k personal characteristics or environmental control variables, and T_i is a variable designed to capture the tax incentive effect. Alternatively, in a time-series application, i denotes a time period, and z_i^* must be interpreted as the fraction of the workforce that is self-employed.

A number of different variables have been suggested as candidates for T_i:

1. Tax liabilities in E, denoted T_{iE} (Long, 1982a, 1982b), with the possible addition of payroll taxes in E (Moore, 1983a). The rationale is that the costs of evasion in S (e.g. fines or imprisonment) are worth bearing only when taxes are high. Both Long and Moore estimated β to be significant and positive using cross-section samples of US data.[19]

2. Average and/or marginal tax rates on all incomes liable to tax, denoted by ART_i and/or MRT_i. The rationale is similar to that given above; the evidence is mixed.[20] Both Blau (1987) and Schuetze (2000) reported decomposition results suggesting that tax rate variables explained a greater proportion of changes in North American self-employment rates than any other macroeconomic or demographic explanatory variable.[21] Robson and Wren (1999) argued that marginal and average tax rates capture different effects, the former labour supply incentives and the latter evasion incentives – so both variables should be included in (10.8).

3. Average or marginal tax rates in S relative to E, denoted by $\Delta_j ART_i$ or $\Delta_j MRT_i$ (Bruce, 2000), where

$$\Delta_j ART_i := A\hat{R}T_{iE} - A\hat{R}T_{iS} \quad \text{and} \quad \Delta_j MRT_i := M\hat{R}T_{iE} - M\hat{R}T_{iS},$$

where ˆ denotes an actual value if $i \in j$ and a predicted value if $i \notin j$. This recognises that tax liabilities in both occupations matter. Bruce (2000) obtained mixed evidence in his application based on US data.

In short, the evidence obtained to date paints a mixed picture about the role of tax and tax evasion opportunities for explaining occupational choice. However, many of these studies fail to condition on relative income, which is surprising given their apparent implicit belief that pecuniary factors affect occupational choice. It is therefore hard to evaluate the genuine effect of personal taxes on entrepreneurship from these studies.

It possible to address this problem by extending the structural probit model of occupational choice described in chapter 1, subsection 1.6.2. As in that model, assume that z_i^* is a function of i's net earnings differential $y_{iS}^n - y_{iE}^n$ (where y_{ij}^n denotes net income), as well as a set of other explanatory variables, X_i. Let γ denote a scalar and ω a vector of estimable parameters, and let u_i be a stochastic normally distributed disturbance term. Then

$$z_i^* = \gamma \left[\ln y_{iS}^n - \ln y_{iE}^n \right] + \omega' X_i + u_i, \tag{10.9}$$

where one expects $\gamma > 0$. Predicted net incomes received in unobserved occupations can be obtained by estimating selectivity corrected gross earnings functions (see chapter 1, subsection 1.5.3) and applying the rules of the IT code. Now suppose individuals avoid a proportion $\kappa \in (0, 1]$ of their tax liability in occupation S.[22] Then, provided the applicable tax rate for predicted incomes is the same for individuals in both occupations (as tends to be the case when income tax bands are broad), it can be shown (Parker, 2003a) that (10.9) can be re-written as

$$z_i^* = \gamma \left[\ln \hat{y}_{iS}^n + \kappa . T(\hat{y}_{iS}; y_{io}, W_i) - \ln \hat{y}_{iE}^n \right] + \omega' X_i + u_i, \quad (10.10)$$

where $\hat{y}_{iS}^n$ is predicted net self-employment income in the absence of tax evasion, and where $T(\hat{y}_{iS}; y_{io}, W_i)$ are tax liabilities conditional on pre-tax self-employment income y_{iS}, other pre-tax taxable income y_{io} and tax-relevant personal characteristics W_i.

Equation (10.10) is a non-linear 'structural probit' equation. Arguably, $\kappa . T(\hat{y}_{iS}; y_{io}, \tilde{W}_i)$ measures the correct incentive to be self-employed, since it captures directly the amount of tax that can be avoided if one becomes self-employed, while taking into account also the earnings differential between the two occupations. Parker (2003a) estimated (10.10) using three British micro-data sets and could find no evidence to reject the hypothesis that $\kappa = 0$. It is important to be clear about what this result does and does not tell us. It does *not* mean that the self-employed do not evade or avoid tax. Instead, it suggests that these activities do not appear to impact significantly on occupational choice behaviour for most self-employed Britons (i.e. this is why κ cannot be identified precisely). Nor could it be robustly established that relative incomes themselves had any clear impact on occupational choice – in line with other findings based on the linear structural probit model summarised in chapter 3, section 3.1. Thus, it is possible that no tax incentive effect exists *because pecuniary factors generally do not appear to be significant determinants of the decision to be self-employed*. If so, then the policy implications are clear: any efforts to promote entrepreneurship through the income tax system will be ineffective.

10.5   Direct government assistance and regulation

10.5.1   Entrepreneurship schemes targeted at the unemployed

Governments in several countries have set up schemes to encourage the unemployed to become self-employed. Government objectives as far as these schemes are concerned include unemployment reduction, job creation and the fostering of enterprise, as well as generation of other benefits such as self-sufficiency of participants, economic development of high-unemployment areas and the provision of opportunities for socially excluded groups (OECD, 1998).

The largest schemes have operated in the UK, France, Spain, Germany and Denmark; to date, they have not been adopted in the USA. Most schemes share a number of features in common. Rather than attempt to describe them all, I will just briefly describe the UK's Enterprise Allowance Scheme (EAS).[23] The EAS was established in 1982, offering income support of £40 per week to unemployed people with £1,000 to invest in a new business for up to the whole of the first year in self-employment. The idea was to partially compensate individuals for the loss of state benefits entailed by becoming self-employed. Individuals were offered advice on running a small business, but were not screened for eligibility to join the scheme. At its peak in 1987–8, 106,000 people were on the EAS, with take-up rates declining continuously thereafter before the scheme was transferred to the Training & Enterprise Councils (TECs) in 1991–92.[24] In most years, the number of EAS recipients comprised a small fraction of the annual unemployment flow, although they accounted for up to 30 per cent of new UK business starts (Bendick and Egan, 1987). Most EAS businesses were concentrated in services, construction and retail commerce. They typically involved limited amounts of investment, and were on a small scale – possibly because of limited market opportunities in areas of high unemployment where many recipients were located. Enterprises endowed with the most physical and human capital tended to have the highest survival rates.

The cost-effectiveness of EAS-type schemes is a key issue for its government sponsors. These schemes can be expected to involve a substantial deadweight cost, since a number of new businesses would probably have started even in the absence of the scheme. Also, an EAS may support inefficient businesses, displace viable competitors and fail to help the long-term unemployed.[25] Furthermore, as Bendick and Egan (1987) pointed out, EAS participants are a self-selected group of unemployed people, being disproportionately young, male and having been unemployed for less than six months prior to commencing in the EAS.

The evidence on these issues is stark. According to Bendick and Egan (1987), 50 per cent of UK EAS-sponsored businesses would have started anyway; 50 per cent of those that did start displaced other businesses; about 50 per cent of the assisted firms survived for less than three years; and those that did start created a fraction of one job in addition to the job of the proprietor. There is in fact mixed evidence about the quality of EAS-supported businesses, as measured by their survival rates.[26] The self-employment incomes of EAS recipients have been estimated to be similar to the incomes they could have obtained in alternative occupations, although it is possible that the experience of self-employment under the EAS enhanced participants' future earnings (Bendick and Egan, 1987).

Taking account of deadweight costs, displacement effects and the cost of administering the scheme, relative to the benefits generated by the new start-ups, Storey (1994a) estimated that after taking account of the fact that the government would have paid unemployment benefits anyway, the EAS was essentially cost-effective, even though its effects on job creation and unemployment reduction were slight.[27] There is a more general point to be made here about the precise objectives of EAS-type schemes. Schemes targeted at the unemployed face a trade-off between economic objectives (e.g. high survival rates, profitability and employment creation) and social objectives (e.g. putting to work the hardest to employ). On this point Bendick and Egan (1987) concluded: 'The programmes in these countries [France and Britain] have succeeded in turning less than one per cent of transfer payment recipients into entrepreneurs, and an even smaller proportion into successful ones. They cannot be said to have contributed greatly to solving either social *or* economic problems, let alone both' (1987, p. 540).[28] Storey (1994a) concluded that the EAS probably had a greater political than economic effect.

The evidence for countries other than the UK is similar. Pfeiffer and Reize (2000) investigated the effects of bridging allowances to unemployed Germans on firm survival and employment growth rates. They found that survival rates in West Germany were not significantly different for those starting up with bridging allowances; but survival rates were 6 per cent lower in East Germany for those with bridging allowances. Having a bridging allowance made no discernible difference to employment growth rates, leading Pfeiffer and Reize (2000) to conclude that Germany's enterprise allowance scheme does not appear to have had a job creation impact. Together with the British evidence cited above, one is led to conclude that, despite favourable publicity, schemes designed to promote enterprise among the unemployed have had only a very limited impact in practice.

10.5.2   Information-based support for start-ups

Governments in many countries subsidise or operate agencies that provide support to entrepreneurs, either for new start-ups, existing small firms, or both. Private-sector institutions are also involved in this process. The oft-cited rationale for support to start-ups is straightforward: potential entrepreneurs often lack information about what it is like to start a business, how to develop a business idea and obtain finance, how to identify customers and how regulations and state benefits affect them. They might also be naïve, proposing poorly thought-out business plans that convey an inadvertently negative impression of their business idea. Even worse, they may be unaware of deficiencies in their own business skills. These problems may cause inefficiency and excessive exit rates of otherwise viable businesses. Hence there is a case, at least in principle, for government involvement in improving the access to information.

Support for start-ups often involves not only the provision of information, but also mentoring, training and advisory services, via public-sector providers and subsidised advisers and consultants. Many programmes combine these types of assistance in packages for target groups. For brevity, and to convey the basic ideas, we describe below only a few features of the UK institutional set-up, which is quite extensive and well established. Indeed, it is possible to criticise the proliferation of small-business support programmes for engendering confusion among entrepreneurs. In the UK the public-sector organisations involved in delivering these programmes include Business Links, Enterprise Agencies (EAs), local authorities, Regional Development Agencies (RDAs), the Department for Trade and Industry (DTI), the Department for Education and Skills (DES), Learning and Skills Councils, non-governmental organisations (NGOs) (such as the Princes Trust), business associations and networks and universities and colleges. Rather than provide an account of what each of these organisations do, we shall describe just a couple of the more prominent ones.

In 1992 the British government established the Business Link (BL) scheme. BL's purpose is to bring together various sources of support available to entrepreneurs and small firm owners. Via a network of local business advice centres, the (publicly funded) BL scheme aims to provide local information; marketing, training and planning support; advice; and consultancy support for SMEs.[29] Initially BL focused its support on SMEs with high-growth potential that employed between 10 and 200 staff. A key part of the process was the role of personal business advisors, who conducted free 'health checks' on businesses that requested it. More recently, however, BL has begun to work with businesses of all sizes, including start-ups. Their work is complemented by Enterprise Agencies (EAs) (Enterprise Trusts in Scotland) and TECs. TECs are fundholders of enterprise support and training, on which many EAs are dependent for funding. The delivery of business services varies from agency to agency, with considerable geographical diversity.

The Princes Trust is a form of support directed towards young people. It provides them with cheap small loans packaged with advice, mentoring and government-provided income support. While it has been credited with effective job creation, the mentoring aspect of this programme makes it resource-intensive and therefore necessarily limited in scope.

The effectiveness of government intervention to help start-ups in the UK has been critically evaluated by Reid and Jacobsen (1988), Casson (1990), Bennett, Wicks and McCoshan (1994), Storey (1994a) and Bennett and Robson (1999), among others. Bennett, Wicks and McCoshan (1994) concluded that greater empowerment is needed to make TECs more effective in their relations with small firms. Reid and Jacobsen (1988) found that Enterprise Trusts were bracketed with bank managers and accountants as among the most valuable sources of advice to new small entrepreneurial firms. Bennett and Robson (1999) also highlighted the importance of accountants and lawyers as sources of advice, while noting that 27 per cent of their survey respondents had also used BL. This is a higher take-up rate for a public support service than has been found by other researchers. Storey (1994a) in particular pointed out the difficulties of linking assistance to improvements in performance by the recipients. In his words, 'a substantial "unproven" verdict hangs over the policies in this area.' (1994a, p. 295). Set against this, Bendick and Egan (1987) cited evidence that French support services were generally associated with higher rates of business survival. Also Marshall et al. (1993) reported a positive impact of government-assisted management and training development on the performance of participating firms in Britain. However, an area where perhaps more could be done is in raising awareness at the pre-start stage of entrepreneurship. As several researchers have noted, both public and private sectors appear to be less equipped to offer support at the pre-start stage than at or just after the time of start-up (Smallbone and Lyon, 2001).

10.5.3   Regulation and other interventions

This subsection mentions briefly three other examples of government intervention in the small-business sector. They are procurement, social protection and regulation. Procurement and regulation are usually framed at the level of the firm, rather than the entrepreneur. Our interest will be in their impact on small firms, since these are probably most closely identified with entrepreneurs.

Procurement is an important way that government can aid small businesses. For instance, since 1942, the US Federal government has systematically allocated a share of its purchases to small businesses. According to SBA (2001), small businesses received $69.3 billion in fiscal year 1999 in Federal government contracts. This amounted to 35.6 per cent of total federal procurement. The construction sector received most procurement money. On top of this, state governments in the USA also provide large sums of procurement money to the small-business sector.

A second channel of government involvement is social protection. This tends to be less extensive for the self-employed than for employees. For example, although the self-employed are eligible for social security pensions in almost all countries, they are usually ineligible for accident, sickness and unemployment insurance. In contrast, employees are usually eligible for all of these benefits. Some commentators contend that the differential treatment is an 'accidental' feature of early legislation. Originally, many welfare policies were conceived for full-time workers in regular employment: the self-employed were effectively 'left out' (see Aronson, 1991). However, governments are also no doubt aware of the potential moral hazard problems entailed by extending accident, sickness and unemployment insurance to the self-employed. Working for themselves, the self-employed would presumably find it easier to slack and spuriously claim benefits. On a more positive note, the self-employed in several countries are eligible for tax relief on some services that they have to purchase privately, e.g., private pensions (via Keogh plans in the USA, for example). In the UK, social security ('National Insurance') contributions are nominally set at a lower level for the self-employed, reflecting the lower level of benefit coverage the state offers them.

Finally, governments also regulate businesses, often for health and safety reasons. They also issue licences and exempt small businesses from some regulations and taxes. We shall not attempt to review regulation exemptions for small firms: several examples from the USA are described in Brock and Evans (1986) and Aronson (1991, pp. 104–5).

Brock and Evans (1986) (hereafter, BE) conducted one of the most thorough investigations into the effects of government regulation on small firms. BE commenced by documenting the general increase in government regulations since the 1970s. They observed that regulations are widely believed to put small firms at a disadvantage because they impose fixed costs (such as administrative compliance costs) that larger firms are able to spread over greater output, reducing their average impact compared with small firms. After an exhaustive analysis of the extant evidence, BE concluded that economies of scale do indeed exist for some forms of regulation. This is especially true of paperwork-based regulations, e.g., relating to banking and pensions. BE estimated compliance costs to be some ten times greater for small firms compared with their larger counterparts.[30] Also, regulations can harm small firms simply because they are more likely to engage in the proscribed activity (e.g. small mines involve proportionately more accidents than large mines).

However, substantial economies of scale were not found to exist with respect to environmental regulations.

It is instructive to trace out the impact of regulation on small firms in a general competitive equilibrium, in which they compete with larger firms. Suppose, for example, that firms' costs are increasing in output q and decreasing in heterogeneous ability, $x-$, e.g. costs are given by $c = c(q)/x$, where $c_q > 0$. There is an outside wage of w, so entrepreneurs with ability greater than or equal to a cut-off ability $\tilde{x}$ become entrepreneurs, with the rest becoming employees. Firms hire employees: the most able run the largest firms, and the least able run the smallest (see chapter 2, subsection 2.2.3). Now it is easy to see that the imposition of a regulatory fixed cost will cause $\tilde{x}$ to increase. The smallest firms exit, and their owners become workers, increasing the supply of labour and so driving down w. At the same time, the smaller number of firms reduces the supply of output, increasing the price level. Surviving (i.e. larger) firms increase output to mop up the excess demand for their goods. The effects on small firms are clearly negative; but, notably, large firms can gain from the regulation if the increase in price and decrease in the wage rate outweigh the higher regulatory costs they face. Thus large firms can have an incentive to apply political pressure for greater regulation, which can end up artificially capping entrepreneurship (see also Baumol, 1983).

Clearly, then, it is possible for regulation to reduce social welfare. But this does not mean that the optimal amount of regulation is zero. For example, if all firms generate a negative externality, such as pollution, then some regulation may be socially desirable. The question is how much regulation is optimal, and which firms should be regulated. BE analysed this issue in the context of the simplified model described above, for the case where the regulatory compliance cost faced by firms is non-decreasing in the tax rate and tax burden imposed on firms. Taxation is required to provide firms with incentives to produce more socially efficient levels of output. The key finding from BE's theoretical analysis was that the optimal regulatory tax schedule consists of a tax rate that is generally positive but may be zero below some firm-size threshold, together with a licence fee to discourage the formation of inefficient firms.

This solution is interesting, because the zero tax threshold corresponds to the kind of 'tiering' of regulations that are observed in many countries. Tiering refers to granting lighter regulatory burdens, or complete exemption, to small firms, in recognition of regulations' potentially adverse effects on competition discussed above.[31] However, there are potential pitfalls with tiering regulations as well. Tiering may preserve inefficient firms in the market, and encourage larger, more efficient, firms to become smaller in order to qualify for a lighter regulatory touch.

Brock and Evans (1986) concluded that there is little evidence that regulation has disproportionately harmed small firms. Of course, this could simply reflect the success of tiering in protecting small firms from the worst excesses of government interference in their businesses. In recognition of the regulatory damage that governments can inadvertently inflict on small business, the US legislature passed the Regulatory Flexibility Act. This instrument forces US government agencies to undertake a thorough analysis of the economic impact of their proposed regulations, and to consider alternatives that are less likely to harm small firms (SBA, 2001).

10.6   Conclusion

This chapter has critically evaluated the existing state of theoretical and empirical knowledge about the impact of government intervention on entrepreneurship in general and the self-employed in particular. We discussed interventions to promote new start-ups by making finance easier to obtain, via loan guarantee schemes and direct assistance to the unemployed; the theory of taxation and occupational choice when incomes in entrepreneurship are uncertain; theory and evidence about tax evasion and self-employment; evidence about the effects of the personal income tax system on self-employment and occupational choice; government-sponsored advice and assistance to entrepreneurs; and the effects of regulation. It is no easy matter to draw conclusions from such a diverse body of work. But a few general principles and findings stand out.

First, regarding interventions designed to promote new start-ups, governments in several countries expend substantial resources on LGSs and schemes to encourage the unemployed to become self-employed. Evaluation studies have not produced a ringing endorsement of these schemes. While they do not appear to misallocate resources badly, there is little evidence that they improve efficiency much either. If governments are to be persuaded to enlarge the scope and extent of these schemes, researchers should provide more convincing evidence that small businesses generate substantial social and economic benefits that are being impeded by some kind of market failure.

A second general conclusion is that the rich theoretical literature on income taxation and occupational choice presents an array of conflicting predictions and policy recommendations. Even the class of models that restricts attention to uniform linear income tax systems are unable to answer unambiguously such basic questions as 'Will higher income tax rates increase or decrease the equilibrium number of entrepreneurs?' and 'What are the effects of income tax on the welfare of entrepreneurs, and on social welfare more generally?' Naturally, generalising these simple models to take account of other factors, including tax evasion, differential income taxation, non-linear (progressive) taxation, non-pecuniary aspects of work and social inequality aversion can be expected to enlarge further the set of theoretical predictions. To date, the literature has not paid much attention to the effects of switching costs (economic or psychic) on the potency of fiscal interventions. But that could be a useful ingredient in future work if it restricts the set of possible outcomes in a realistic way and so increases the stability of the theoretical results.

Another practical suggestion for increasing the policy relevance of the models is to embed them in a simulation-based framework. As well as being amenable to numerical sensitivity analysis, simulation methods would enable researchers to extend the scope of their theoretical enquiries, and to incorporate several useful 'real-world' features of labour markets that have been relatively neglected in occupational-choice models. These include, but are not confined to, the joint modelling of labour supply and occupational choice.

A third conclusion from this chapter is unambiguous: as a group, the self-employed systematically and regularly under-report their incomes and over-claim their business expenses to the tax authorities. Evidence from the UK and the USA suggests that the self-employed under-report their incomes by between 20 and 50 per cent compared with just 1–3 per cent for employees. However, it cannot be established that pecuniary factors generally make individuals likelier to choose self-employment, let alone tax evasion opportunities specifically.

Finally, an area where there might be greater potential for effective government involvement is in the provision of information and advice to entrepreneurs. There appears to be a case, at least in principle, for governments to subsidise improved information flows to help the market function more efficiently; and economies of scale can be achieved in this area by concentrating provision in a few well-publicised advisory bodies. In fact, the problem in some countries seems to be not the absence of these agencies, but their proliferation and the sparse use made of them by entrepreneurs. Evidence from a survey of new US start-ups bears this out. Reynolds and White (1997) concluded that government policies and programmes have very little direct effect on the start-up process: few 'nascent' entrepreneurs were aware of the large number of available programmes, reflected in take-up rates of less than 10 per cent. Here too, governments need to spend public money wisely. Assistance directed towards enhancing general competitiveness and growth is likely to be more socially productive than trying to give individual firms an advantage over their close rivals. That might accelerate the competitive race without increasing the number of winners; there is little point after all in helping some participants to play more cunningly a zero-sum game.

NOTES

1. For example, the US variants of the basic scheme include the Certified Lender Program (which promises banks a three-day approval time) and the Preferred Lender Program (under which loans can be made without prior approval by the Small Business Administration (SBA), at the price of a smaller guarantee). According to Smith and Stutzer (1989), about one-third of state governments in the USA also guarantee loans, with guarantee percentages varying within and between states. The US SBA LGS dates back to 1953 – (see Rhyne, 1988, for a review of the historical and political context). The UK Small Firms LGS (SFLGS) dates back to 1981: see Cowling and Clay (1995) for a full background to this scheme, operational details, and an econometric model of take-up rates by entrepreneurs. Bates (1984) describes the Economic Opportunity Loan program.
2. These include banking, real estate development and publishing in the USA; and retailing, catering and motor vehicle maintenance in the UK. One reason for excluding support in certain sectors is to reduce business displacement (see below).
3. See also Smith and Stutzer (1989), who proposed a similar mechanism and outcome.
4. In terms of figure 5.3, a LGS targeted on group b increases b's expected rate of return schedule above ρ^* in that diagram if the scheme is sufficiently generous. But ρ^* also increases, reflecting the greater overall profitability of private loans – possibly leading to redlining of the non-targeted group o, who were not initially redlined. These perverse crowding-out effects may serve to generate pressure for further subsidies. In Gale's words: 'Credit subsidies create demand for more credit subsidies' (1990b, p. 190).
5. If financial markets are characterised by credit rationing, then the quality of the rationed ventures should be high, and LGS programmes should not make much of a loss. If they do make losses, can this be taken as evidence that credit rationing does not exist, and that private lenders were right to reject the ventures? Not necessarily: losses could also be caused by high programme administrative costs (Rhyne, 1988).
6. The UK's SFLGS was amended in 1989 and 1996 for precisely this reason, restricting loans to sectors with low displacement rates.
7. The small scale of the UK's SFLGS has prompted some commentators to argue that the principal role of the scheme was as a temporary 'demonstration effect': i.e. to demonstrate to banks profitable opportunities for unsecured lending in the small business sector (Storey, 1994a).
8. Furthermore, Rhyne (1988) estimated that in order to cover programme costs, each successful SBA-backed loan would have had to generate additional benefits over the lifetime of the loan of between 17 and 29 per cent above the return necessary to stay in business.

9. The rationale has been two-fold. First, loan guarantees facilitate bank-borrower relationships, unlike direct Federal loans; and they also reduce undesirable competition between the SBA and banks (Rhyne, 1988). More recent data from the SBA (2001) indicate that between 1991 and 2000 the SBA backed a total of $95 billion in loans to small businesses.

10. Corporate taxes tend to be flat-rate taxes, whereas IT tends to be progressive, with marginal tax rates that rise with income. This raises the issue of optimal incorporation choice by the self-employed, since high-income self-employed individuals have a tax incentive to reclassify their earnings as corporate rather than personal (Fuest, Huber and Nielsen, 2002). According to Gordon (1998), this tax differential has declined from high levels in the 1950s and 1960s to very low levels at the time of writing. See Gordon (1998) for further details and references to the literature.

11. Obviously, entrepreneurship also becomes unambiguously less attractive if just entrepreneurs are taxed without a subsidy being given to employees and with the tax receipts being spent on an 'outside' good. Likewise, Kihlstrom and Laffont (1983b) showed that a tax on wages only (with receipts spent on an outside good) increases the number of entrepreneurs under assumption 1.

12. See Kanbur (1979), and Yuengert (1995) for affirmative evidence. Gentry and Hubbard (2000) found the opposite result, but that reflects an unfavourable differential tax to self-employment caused by imperfect loss offsets, that outweighs insurance or tax evasion advantages to entrepreneurship (see also Cullen and Gordon, 2002). That is, profits are subject to a higher tax rate than the rate against which any losses can be deducted, making risky entrepreneurship less attractive.

13. The only paper we know of in this area is by Moresi (1998), who extended Mirrlees' classic optimal tax analysis to the realm of entrepreneurship. Moresi studied the general properties of optimal non-linear differential taxes when entrepreneurs have heterogeneous exogenous abilities and workers receive a common wage. Few firm predictions emerge from the general form of this model.

14. For Canadian evidence on intertemporal tax-shifting by the self-employed, see Sillamaa and Veall (2001).

15. In a simplified model with labour supply choice, Robson and Wren (1999) showed how higher marginal tax rates can decrease the self-employment rate if gross incomes are more sensitive to labour supply in self-employment than in paid-employment.

16. The corresponding figure for net incomes, which includes both understatement of receipts and over-statement of expenses, was 50.3 per cent. Kesselman (1989) also reported wide industry variations in under-reporting rates, with taxicab drivers being the most likely to under-report. According to Clotfelter (1983), self-employed income under-reporting is positively associated with high net incomes and high marginal tax rates, though subsequent evidence by Kesselman (1989) cast doubt on these results. Joulfaian and Rider (1996) estimated that income under-reporting is significantly negatively associated with the tax audit rate, with an elasticity of approximately −0.70.

17. A good example is food expenditure. The self-employed have no incentive to under-report food expenditure to the survey interviewers, since it raises no tax or business deductibility issues.

18. Since the self-employed accounted for around 10 per cent of UK GDP, this implies that the size of the 'black economy' in the UK was about 5.5 per cent of GDP in 1982.

19. In fact, payroll taxes can have complicated effects on occupational choice. They might induce employers to substitute self-employed contract labour for regular employees, implying a positive relationship between employer payroll taxes and the incidence of self-employment. But they might also discourage employees from choosing self-employment if they expect to become employers.

20. For positive β estimates see Blau (1987), Yuengert (1995), Parker (1996), Robson (1998b) and Schuetze (2000). For a negative β estimate see Fölster (2002). Cowling and Mitchell (1997), Robson and Wren (1999), Parker and Robson (2000) and Bruce (2002) reported insignificant or mixed effects.

21. For example, Blau (1987) estimated that the reduction in marginal tax rates (MRT) at the bottom of the US income distribution and the rise in MRT at the top accounted for between about a half and two-thirds of the observed increase in self-employment between 1973 and 1982. This was despite Blau's puzzling finding of conflicting impacts on self-employment rates from MRT measured at different income levels.

22. In accordance with the evidence cited earlier, there is little or no evasion in E, so there is no need to introduce a corresponding term for E. In (10.10) below, κ is treated as an unknown parameter to be estimated.

23. For a detailed summary of self-employment schemes for the unemployed in Germany, France, the UK and Denmark, see Meager (1993, 1994).

24. The EAS was later renamed as the Business Start Up Scheme and then became part of various Single Regeneration Budgets, under more flexible terms than those stipulated at its inception, and with a greater emphasis on targeted support.

25. Meager (1994) suggested that grant-based schemes are superior to allowance-based schemes (such as the UK's EAS) by enabling new ventures to overcome entry barriers in some industries, so reducing displacement effects.

26. Storey (1994a) reported that around 14 per cent of EAS entrants failed in the first year of operation, during which the EAS subsidy was received. Taylor (1999) cited a UK Department of Employment report that two-thirds of individuals completing their first year of the EAS were still in business two years later. These are higher survival rates than Taylor found for British self-employed workers overall.

27. In particular, all non-proprietor jobs were created by 20 per cent of surviving firms (Bendick and Egan, 1987). More than 60 per cent of the jobs created in surviving firms after three years under the EAS were in 4 per cent of the businesses originally created (Storey, 1994a).

28. Consistent with this, time-series econometric evidence from Parker (1996) suggests that the EAS increased UK self-employment rates only modestly

and in the short run only. See Meager (1993, 1994) for time-series regression results for Germany.

29. BL was reformed during 2000–1 by the UK government to be part of the Small Business Service, in order to replicate aspects of the US SBA. Chiefly, this involves adding a new role for BL as a 'voice for SMEs'.

30. See also Sandford (1981), who estimated that compliance costs related to sales taxes were forty times higher as a proportion of turnover for UK firms with turnover of less than £10,000 than for firms with a turnover of over £1m.

31. More generally, 'tiering may occur in any of the major aspects of a regulatory program: in the substantive requirements; in reporting and record keeping requirements; or in enforcement and monitoring efforts. Tiering may entail less frequent inspections, lighter fines for non-compliance, exemptions, waivers, reduced requirements, or simpler reporting requirements for certain types of firms' (Brock and Evans, 1986, p. 74).

11   Conclusions

11.1   Summary

Self-employment and entrepreneurship are important economic phenomena. Self-employment is widespread throughout the world and small firms are the principal vehicles for the organisation of production. Far from self-employment being an occupation in irrevocable decline, the evidence outlined in chapter 1 showed that numbers of self-employed people are holding up strongly in many countries. While it is true that declining transportation and communications costs, more capital-intensive methods of production, and industry consolidation do not favour many small-scale enterprises (White, 1984), these changes may be less pervasive in many service industries. And some of these changes might be amenable to exploitation by entrepreneurs who can discern in them profitable opportunities.

Our review of the theories and evidence about entrepreneurship in chapters 2 and 3 revealed that economists regard entrepreneurial ability and willingness to take risks as key factors determining who becomes an entrepreneur. While more work remains to be done on estimating structural models to identify the empirical importance of these factors, we now know a fair amount about the specific characteristics of entrepreneurs. They often come from families with a tradition of self-employment or business ownership; they are on average older, reasonably well educated and more likely to be married, and are generally over-optimistic about their prospects of success. On the balance of evidence, non-pecuniary factors appear to be more important than pecuniary factors in explaining why people choose to be entrepreneurs.

Self-employed people in most OECD countries tend to be predominantly white, male and middle aged. This is changing, however. Increasing numbers of females are turning to self-employment, while many ethnic minority groups have participation rates in self-employment that are both higher and growing more rapidly than those of indigenous groups. Although it is still unclear why females and members of some

266

ethnic groups are under-represented in self-employment, the research reviewed in chapter 4 found little evidence of discrimination against them, either in the product or the capital markets. An ongoing puzzle is why black Britons and Americans have such low self-employment rates, in contrast to Asians in these two countries. There is clearly a need for further research on these topics.

In principle, limited access to finance might be one cause of low black self-employment rates in the UK and the USA, though the evidence here is not clear-cut. In fact, it is not well established that there is a shortage of debt finance for *any* new start-ups. Just because banks deny credit to some loan applicants does not necessarily mean that they ration credit. Even if bank loans are unavailable, other sources of credit often exist, such as personal and family finance, trade credit, franchising, and sometimes even equity finance. The scale and potential contribution of these sources of finance were reviewed in chapter 6. In the case of equity finance, it seems that the low anticipated returns and high risk of proposed ventures, rather than unavailability of funds, explains the limited use of this source of finance in practice.

The theoretical literature reviewed in chapters 5 and 6 is unable to answer definitively the question about whether finance is rationed, and whether there is too little or too much investment by entrepreneurs. Consequently, governments should probably not take any of the academic policy recommendations emanating from this literature too seriously. The most pressing need is for direct evidence about the nature of any inefficiency in the market for start-up finance. Chapter 7 reviewed the evidence about borrowing constraints, including studies finding a positive relationship between personal wealth and windfalls, and participation and survival in self-employment. We argued that such correlations do not constitute evidence of borrowing constraints, and concluded that direct evidence from bank loan rejections suggest that credit rationing, if it exists at all, can be only very limited in practice. On the other hand, the perception of borrowing constraints among entrepreneurs might discourage them from applying for funds from banks and other lenders. It is unclear how prevalent this 'discouraged borrower' syndrome is.

In the light of these findings, it is therefore interesting that governments in several major economies continue to back private bank loans to new ventures. The reason is presumably a joint belief in credit rationing and the importance of entrepreneurship, perhaps because of its job creating promise. In fact, as shown in chapter 8, although small firms appear to create a disproportionate number of new jobs on net in the OECD, most self-employed people in most countries do not hire any employees. Instead, they rely on supplying long work hours of their own. A puzzle is why the self-employed work relatively long hours for relatively low returns. One reason might be greater income variability in self-employment, combined with non-pecuniary factors, leading self-employees to 'self-insure' by working harder. Self-employed jobs can be pleasurable in their own right, especially if they involve the excitement of successfully establishing and maintaining one's own enterprise. An unwillingness to see one's life work disappear might also account for why so many self-employed people continue to work well into their seventies and sometimes even their eighties.

Having launched a new enterprise, what happens to it next? Chapter 9 showed that most new ventures are small and remain so, if they survive at all. Survivors tend to have higher and more variable growth rates, and tend to be run by experienced owners located in areas of low unemployment. Only very few new enterprises grow sufficiently to eventually become large firms. Models of entrepreneurial learning appear to explain most of these stylised facts well. We suggest that promotion of sustainable entrepreneurship might be better served by trying to forestall exit, rather than encouraging entry. But government efforts to 'pick winners' are unlikely to be successful; and it is unclear what specific government policies are best suited to boost survival rates. This will no doubt be an ongoing topic of interest in future entrepreneurship research.

Several specific forms of government intervention designed to promote entrepreneurship were analysed in chapter 10. Because of the policy importance of this issue, we devote the remainder of this chapter to it.

11.2   Implications for policy-makers

Many economists would argue that government intervention in markets is usually justified only in order to correct for some kind of market failure. Examples of market failures in the context of this book include the unavailability (or too easy availability) of new venture finance due to asymmetric information problems; positive social externalities from entrepreneurship; and spillovers from entrepreneurs' innovations that are not realised because they cannot be fully captured by the entrepreneurs themselves. One useful way of thinking about these issues is in terms of the supply of and demand for entrepreneurs. In an economy with flexible prices and wages and no market failures there is no reason to expect any persistent imbalance between the supply of and demand for entrepreneurs. In such an economy there would be no obvious rationale for government involvement in entrepreneurship. Therefore the key question is whether any market failures exist in practice, that inhibit the supply of or demand for effective entrepreneurship, and cause more or less entrepreneurship than is socially desirable. Note by the way that the recognition of scope for welfare-improving government intervention does not automatically justify such intervention. Intervention invariably incurs direct costs, in addition to the opportunity cost of public funds; and bureaucrats cannot always be trusted to allocate public money wisely. Our evaluation in chapter 10 of loan guarantee schemes and income support schemes targeted at the unemployed concluded that these schemes are relatively small in scope and generate benefits that do not obviously outweigh their costs.

It is quite understandable that government policies towards entrepreneurship err on the side of modesty rather than extravagance. Governments invariably face conflicting aspirations and objectives. They want to target resources to achieve focus but are unable to pick winners; they want to make assistance selective to control budgetary costs but wish also to both remain inclusive and avoid spreading resources too thinly; and they want policies to make a big impact for political reasons while minimising costs and programme deadweight losses. These trade-offs are deep-rooted and probably inescapable.

We believe that there are several major problems with the way that governments around the world currently conduct policy with regard to entrepreneurship. What follows are personal views based on a distillation of the literature encompassed in this book.

First, it is unclear why governments wish to promote entrepreneurship in the first place. One is led to suspect that their involvement is motivated by ideology rather than by a pragmatic evaluation of the costs and benefits. Many governments apparently believe that entrepreneurs create jobs and that higher levels of enterprise promote economic growth. There is certainly no shortage of small-business practitioners and academics that have vested interests in encouraging these beliefs, despite the limited evidence we have found in this book to support them (see in particular chapters 8 and 9). It rarely seems to be acknowledged in these circles that entrepreneurial ventures might also possess drawbacks. For example, small firms do less training and pay lower wages than large firms, so a policy of encouraging small firms at the expense of large ones might actually damage the national skill base.

Second, there has been an explosion of policy initiatives in many countries, that now resemble 'a patchwork quilt of complexity and idiosyncracy' (Curran, 2000, p. 36).[1] This has generated confusion among the intended beneficiaries, which might help explain why take-up rates for information-based support services have been so low, rarely exceeding 10 per cent even for programmes like training support that are open to all small firms. Another problem is that a plethora of policy initiatives complicates the task of evaluating specific policies, because policies tend to work jointly rather than in isolation. This problem adds to other difficulties of evaluating government policies towards entrepreneurship, that are chiefly attributable to a paucity of rigorous cost-benefit analyses.

Third, from the viewpoint of many entrepreneurs, governments have an undoubted tendency to regulate too much. Some regulation is necessary and welfare-improving (e.g. clean air legislation), and can create entrepreneurial opportunities as well as constraints. But governments seem to find it just too tempting to over-regulate. By its very nature, regulation – and the mindset that accompanies it – is the antithesis of entrepreneurship; and bureaucrats, the handmaidens of regulation, have vested interests in proliferating it. The dangers of regulation are twofold. First, it can make it costly for individuals to set up new businesses (Djankow *et al.*, 2002). Second, and probably more importantly, the need to master, and comply with, complex government statutes crowds out entrepreneurs' valuable time and resources from more productive activities. As the burden of red tape grows year on year, one is led to wonder whether governments are merely paying lip service to entrepreneurship rather than genuinely seeking to promote it.

To conclude, this author believes that governments can improve matters by being clearer about their objectives. Instead of formulating policies to boost employment creation and growth, they should address only specific and demonstrable market failures. Most importantly they should do less, funding fewer but better publicised initiatives, and regulating less. One practical suggestion in this regard is for the UK and European governments to emulate the US Regulatory Flexibility Act, which forces government agencies to consider the impact of proposed regulations on small businesses, and to consider alternatives that are likely to harm small firms less. Governments should also be reluctant to use tax policy actively to promote entrepreneurship, since the theoretical results on this topic are ambiguous, and the empirical results are mixed, precluding any clear recommendations. Future research might fruitfully apply micro-simulation methods to evaluate policies that take account of labour supply and occupational adjustments in the presence of tax evasion, risk aversion, and non-pecuniary factors.

Finally, governments should set aside their prejudice that there is always too little entrepreneurship, and at least consider the possibility that there can be too much of it. This is especially important because policies designed to help entrepreneurs can exacerbate the incidence of any overinvestment. For example, consider a policy of giving entrepreneurs a tax advantage that reduces the pre-tax rate of return they require to launch a new venture. Such a policy risks encouraging investment in inefficient projects, since rational investors might forsake investments with higher (pre-tax) rates of return in favour of the less productive tax-favoured investments (Holtz-Eakin, 2000). It is therefore incumbent on policy-makers and supporters of entrepreneurship to take into account private-sector reactions to their policies, and to identify clearly the social benefits motivating them. At present there is only limited evidence about these alleged benefits. As with policies in other areas, too, governments should legislate and intervene only when there is hard evidence that the benefits of their actions outweigh the costs.

NOTE

1. Curran (2000) cited a report by Gavron *et al.* (1998) that examined no fewer than 200 UK government entrepreneurship initiatives, whose total cost amounted to £632m throughout 1995–6 alone. Fuest, Huber and Nielsen (2002) cited research identifying over 500 programmes to promote entre-preneurial entry in Germany.

References

Acs, Z. J. and D. B. Audretsch (1987a). Innovation in large and small firms, *Economics Letters*, 23, pp. 109–12

(1987b). Innovation, market structure, and firm size, *Review of Economics and Statistics*, 49, pp. 567–74

(1988). Innovation in large and small firms: an empirical analysis, *American Economic Review*, 78, pp. 678–90

(1989). Small firm entry in manufacturing, *Economica*, 56, pp. 255–65

(1991). R&D, firm size and innovative activity, in Z. J. Acs and D. B. Audretsch (eds.), *Innovation and Technological Change*, Ann Arbor, University of Michigan Press, pp. 39–59

(1993). *Small Firms and Entrepreneurship: An East–West Perspective*, Cambridge, Cambridge University Press

Acs, Z. J., D. B. Audretsch and D. S. Evans (1994). Why does the self-employment rate vary across countries and over time?, Discussion Paper, 871, London, CEPR

Acs, Z. J., B. Carlsson and C. Karlsson (1999). The linkages among entrepreneurship, SMEs and the macroeconomy, in Z. J. Acs, B. Carlsson and C. Karlsson (eds.), *Entrepreneurship, Small and Medium Sized Enterprises and the Macroeconomy*, Cambridge, Cambridge University Press, pp. 3–42

Agarwal, R. (1998). Small firm survival and technological activity, *Small Business Economics*, 11, pp. 215–24

Agarwal, R. and D. B. Audretsch (2001). Does entry size matter? The impact of the life cycle and technology on firm survival, *Journal of Industrial Economics*, 49, pp. 21–43

Aldrich, H., J. Cater, T. Jones, D. McEvoy and P. Velleman (1985). Ethnic residential concentration and the protected market hypothesis, *Social Forces*, 63, pp. 996–1009

Aldrich, H. and R. Waldinger (1990). Trends in ethnic businesses in the United States, in R. Waldinger, H. Aldrich and R. Ward (eds.), *Ethnic Entrepreneurs*, Newbury Park, CA, Sage

Allen, F. (1983). Credit rationing and payment incentives, *Review of Economic Studies*, 50, pp. 639–46

Altman, E. (1983). *Corporate Financial Distress*, New York, Wiley-Interscience

Amit, R., L. Glosten and E. Muller (1993). Challenges to theory development in entrepreneurship research, *Journal of Mathematical Sociology*, 30, pp. 815–34

Amit, R., E. Muller and I. Cockburn (1995). Opportunity costs and entrepreneurial activity, *Journal of Business Venturing*, 10, pp. 95–106

Appelbaum, E. and E. Katz (1986). Measures of risk aversion and comparative statics of industry equilibrium, *American Economic Review*, 76, pp. 524–29

Appelbaum, E. and C. Lim (1982). Long-run industry equilibrium with uncertainty, *Economics Letters*, 9, pp. 139–45

Arabsheibani, G., D. de Meza, J. Maloney and B. Pearson (2000). And a vision appeared unto them of a great profit: evidence of self-deception among the self-employed, *Economics Letters*, 67, pp. 35–41

Armendáriz de Aghion, B. (1999). On the design of a credit agreement with peer monitoring, *Journal of Development Economics*, 60, pp. 79–104

Armendáriz de Aghion, B. and C. Gollier (2000). Peer group formation in an adverse selection model, *Economic Journal*, 110, pp. 632–43

Armington, C. and M. Odle (1982). Small business: how many jobs?, *Brookings Review*, Winter, 14–17

Aronson, R. L. (1991). *Self Employment: A Labour Market Perspective*, Ithaca, NY, ILR Press

Atrostic, B. K. (1982). The demand for leisure and non-pecuniary job characteristics, *American Economic Review*, 72, pp. 428–40

Audretsch, D. B. (1991). New-firm survival and the technological regime, *Review of Economics and Statistics*, 73, pp. 441–50

Audretsch, D. B. (1995). *Innovation and Industry Evolution*, MIT Press, Cambridge MA

Audretsch, D. B. and Z. J. Acs (1994). New firm start-ups, technology and macroeconomic fluctuations, *Small Business Economics*, 6, pp. 439–49

Audretsch, D. B. and T. Mahmood (1994). The rate of hazard confronting new firms and plants in US manufacturing, *Review of Industrial Organisation*, 9, pp. 41–56

(1995). New firm survival: new results using a hazard function, *Review of Economics and Statistics*, 77, pp. 97–103

Audretsch, D. B. and M. Vivarelli (1997). Determinants of new firm start-ups in Italy, *Empirica*, 23, pp. 91–105

Baker, P. (1993). Taxpayer compliance for the self-employed: estimates from household spending data, Working Paper, W93/14, London, Institute for Fiscal Studies

Baldwin, J. and G. Picot (1995). Employment generation by small producers in the Canadian manufacturing sector, *Small Business Economics*, 7, pp. 317–31

Baltensperger, E. (1978). Credit rationing: issues and questions, *Journal of Money, Credit, and Banking*, 10, pp. 170–83

Banerjee, A. V., T. Besley and T. W. Guinnane (1994). Thy neighbour's keeper: the design of a credit co-operative with theory and a test, *Quarterly Journal of Economics*, 109, pp. 491–515

Banerjee, A. V. and A. F. Newman (1993). Occupational choice and the process of development, *Journal of Political Economy*, 101, pp. 274–98

Bank of England (1993). *Bank Lending to Smaller Businesses*, London, Bank of England

(1999). *The Financing of Ethnic Minority Firms in the United Kingdom*, London, Bank of England

(2001). *Finance for Small Firms*: Eighth Report, London, Bank of England

Bannock, G. (1981). *The Economics of Small Firms: Return from the Wilderness*, Oxford, Basil Blackwell

Bannock, G. and A. Peacock (1989). *Government and Small Business*, London, Paul Chapman Publishing

Barkham, R., M. Hart and E. Hanvey (1996). Growth in small manufacturing firms: an empirical analysis, in R. Blackburn and P. Jennings (eds.), *Small Firms' Contribution to Economic Regeneration*, London, Paul Chapman Publishing, pp. 112–25

Barreto, H. (1989). *The Entrepreneur in Microeconomic Theory: Disappearance and Explanation*, London, Routledge

Barro, R. J. (1976). The loan market, collateral, and rates of interest, *Journal of Money, Credit, and Banking*, 8, pp. 439–56

Barzel, Y. (1987). The entrepreneur's reward for self-policing, *Economic Inquiry*, 25, pp. 103–16

Basu, A. (1998). An exploration of entrepreneurial activity among Asian small businesses in Britain, *Small Business Economics*, 10, pp. 313–26

Basu, A. and S. C. Parker (2001). Family finance and new business start-ups, *Oxford Bulletin of Economics and Statistics*, 63, pp. 333–58

Bates, T. (1984). A review of the Small Business Administration's major loan programs, in P. M. Horvitz and R. R. Pettit (eds.), *Small Business Finance: Sources of Financing for Small Business, Part B*, Greenwich, CT, JAI Press, pp. 211–39

(1985). Entrepreneur human capital endowments and minority business viability, *Journal of Human Resources*, 20, pp. 540–54

(1990). Entrepreneur human capital inputs and small business longevity, *Review of Economics and Statistics*, 72, pp. 551–9

(1991). Commercial bank finance in white and black owned small business start ups, *Quarterly Review of Economics and Business*, 31, pp. 64–80

(1994). Firms started as franchises have lower survival rates than independent small business startups, Discussion Paper, Center for Economic Studies, US Census Bureau, Washington DC

(1995). Self-employment entry across industry groups, *Journal of Business Venturing*, 10, pp. 143–56

(1997). *Race, Self-Employment and Upward Mobility: An Illusive American Dream*, Baltimore, Johns Hopkins University Press

(1998). Survival patterns among newcomers to franchising, *Journal of Business Venturing*, 13, pp. 113–30

(1999). Exiting self-employment: an analysis of Asian immigrant-owned small businesses, *Small Business Economics*, 13, pp. 171–83

Bates, T. and W. D. Bradford (1992). Factors affecting new firm success and their use in venture capital financing, *Journal of Small Business Finance*, 2, pp. 23–38

Baumol, W. J. (1968). Entrepreneurship in economic theory, *American Economic Review, Papers and Proceedings*, 58, pp. 64–71

(1983). Toward operational models of entrepreneurship, in J. Ronen (ed.), *Entrepreneurship*, Lexington, MA, D.C. Heath, pp. 29–48

(1990). Entrepreneurship: productive, unproductive, and destructive, *Journal of Political Economy*, 98, pp. 893–921

(1993). *Entrepreneurship, Management and Structure of Payoffs*, Cambridge, MA, MIT Press

Bearse, P. J. (1984). An econometric analysis of black entrepreneurship, *Review of Black Political Economy*, 12, pp. 117–34

Becker, E. (1984). Self-employed workers: an update to 1983, *Monthly Labor Review*, 107, pp. 14–18

Beesley, M. E. and R. T. Hamilton (1984). Small firms' seedbed role and the concept of turbulence, *Journal of Industrial Economics*, 33, pp. 217–29

Belke, A., R. Fehn and N. Foster (2002). VC investment and labour market performance: a panel data analysis, Paper presented to the CESifo Conference on Venture Capital, Entrepreneurship, and Public Policy, Munich, November

Bell, C. (1990). Interactions between institutional and informal credit agencies in rural India, *World Bank Economic Review*, 4, pp. 297–327

Bendick, M. and M. L. Egan (1987). Transfer payment diversion for small business development: British and French experience, *Industrial and Labor Relations Review*, 40, pp. 528–42

Bennett, R. J. and P. J. A. Robson (1999). The use of external business advice by SMEs in Britain, *Entrepreneurship and Regional Development*, 11, pp. 155–80

Bennett, R. J., P. J. Wicks and A. McCoshan (1994). *Local Empowerment and Business Services: Britain's Experiment with TECs*, London, UCL Press

Berger, A. N. and G. F. Udell (1990). Collateral, loan quality and bank risk, *Journal of Monetary Economics*, 25, pp. 21–42

(1992). Some evidence on the empirical significance of credit rationing, *Journal of Political Economy*, 100, pp. 1047–77

(1995). Relationship lending and lines of credit in small firm finance, *Journal of Business*, 68, pp. 351–81

Bernanke, B. and M. Gertler (1990). Financial fragility and economic performance, *Quarterly Journal of Economics*, 105, pp. 87–114

Bernardo, A. E. and I. Welch (2001). On the evolution of overconfidence and entrepreneurs, *Journal of Economics and Management Strategy*, 10, pp. 301–30

Bernhardt, D. (2000). Credit rationing?, *American Economic Review*, 90, pp. 235–9

Bernhardt, I. (1994). Competitive advantage in self-employment and paid work, *Canadian Journal of Economics*, 27, pp. 273–89

Bernheim, B. D., A. Shleifer and L. H. Summers (1985). The strategic bequest motive, *Journal of Political Economy*, 93, pp. 1045–76

Bertrand, T. and L. Squire (1980). The relevance of the dual economy model: a case study of Thailand, *Oxford Economic Papers*, 32, pp. 480–511

Besanko, D. and A. V. Thakor (1987a). Collateral and rationing: sorting equilibria in monopolistic and competitive credit markets, *International Economic Review*, 28, pp. 671–89

(1987b). Competitive equilibrium in the credit market under asymmetric information, *Journal of Economic Theory*, 42, pp. 167–82

Besley, T. (1995). Nonmarket institutions for credit and risk sharing in low-income countries, *Journal of Economic Perspectives*, 9, pp. 115–27

Besley, T., S. Coate and G. Loury (1993). The economics of rotating savings and credit associations, *American Economic Review*, 83, pp. 792–810

Bester, H. (1985a). Screening vs. rationing in credit markets with imperfect information, *American Economic Review*, 75, pp. 850–55

(1985b). The level of investment in credit markets with imperfect information, *Journal of Institutional and Theoretical Economics*, 141, pp. 503–15

(1987). The role of collateral in credit markets with imperfect information, *European Economic Review*, 31, pp. 887–99

(1994). The role of collateral in a model of debt renegotiation, *Journal of Money, Credit, and Banking*, 26, pp. 72–86

Biais, B. and C. Gollier (1997). Trade credit and credit rationing, *Review of Financial Studies*, 10, pp. 903–37

Binks, M. and A. Jennings (1986). Small firms as a source of economic rejuvenation, in J. Curran *et al.* (eds.), *The Survival of the Small Firm*, 1, Aldershot, Gower, pp. 19–37

Binks, M. and P. Vale (1990). *Entrepreneurship and Economic Change*, London, McGraw-Hill

Birch, D. L. (1979). *The Job Generation Process*, MIT Programme on Neighbourhood and Regional Change, Cambridge, MA, MIT

Birch, D. L., A. Haggerty and W. Parsons (1997). *Who's Creating Jobs?*, Cambridge, MA, Cognetics Inc.,

Black, J. and D. de Meza (1990). On giving credit where it is due, Discussion Paper, 9008, Department of Economics, University of Exeter

(1997). Everyone may benefit from subsidising entry to risky occupations, *Journal of Public Economics*, 66, pp. 409–24

Black, J., D. de Meza and D. Jeffreys (1996). House prices, the supply of collateral and the enterprise economy, *Economic Journal*, 106, pp. 60–75

Blackburn, R. A. (1992). Small firms and subcontracting: what is it and where?, in P. Leighton and A. Felstead (eds.), *The New Entrepreneurs: Self-Employment and Small Business in Europe*, London, Kogan Page, pp. 305–21

Blanchflower, D. G. (1997). The attitudinal legacy of communist labour relations, *Industrial and Labor Relations Review*, 50, pp. 438–59

(2000). Self-employment in OECD countries, *Labour Economics*, 7, pp. 471–505

Blanchflower, D. G. and R. B. Freeman (1994). Did the Thatcher reforms change British labour market performance?, in R. Barrell (ed.), *The UK Labour Market*, Cambridge, Cambridge University Press, pp. 51–92

Blanchflower, D. G. and B. D. Meyer (1994). A longitudinal analysis of the young self-employed in Australia and the United States, *Small Business Economics*, 6, pp. 1–19

Blanchflower, D. G. and A. Oswald (1990). Self-employment and the enterprise culture, in R. Jowell, S. Witherspoon and L. Brook (eds.), *British Social Attitudes: The 1990 Report*, London, Gower

(1998). What makes an entrepreneur?, *Journal of Labour Economics*, 16, pp. 26–60

Blanchflower, D. G., A. Oswald and A. Stutzer (2001). Latent entrepreneurship across nations, *European Economic Review*, 45, pp. 680–91

Bland, R., B. Elliott and F. Bechhofer (1978). Social mobility in the petite bourgeoisie, *Acta Sociologica*, 21, pp. 229–48

Blau, D. M. (1985). Self-employment and self-selection in developing country labour markets, *Southern Economic Journal*, 52, pp. 351–63

(1986). Self-employment, earnings and mobility in peninsular Malaysia, *World Development*, 14, pp. 839–52

(1987). A time-series analysis of self-employment in the United States, *Journal of Political Economy*, 95, pp. 445–67

Blinder, A. S. (1989). *Macroeconomics Under Debate*, Ann Arbor, University of Michigan Press

Blundell, R. and T. MaCurdy (1999). Labour supply: a review of alternative approaches, in O. Ashenfelter and D. Card (eds.), *Handbook of Labour Economics, 3A*, Amsterdam, Elsevier, pp. 1559–1695

Boadway, R., M. Marchand and P. Pestieau (1991). Optimal linear income taxation in models with occupational choice, *Journal of Public Economics*, 46, pp. 133–62

Boadway, R. N. Marceau, M. Marchand and M. Vigneault (1998). Entrepreneurship, asymmetric information and unemployment, *International Tax and Public Finance*, 5, pp. 307–27

Boden, R. J. (1996). Gender and self-employment selection: an empirical assessment, *Journal of Socioeconomics*, 25, pp. 671–82

Boden, R. J. and A. R. Nucci (1997). Counting the self-employed using household and business sample data, *Small Business Economics*, 9, pp. 427–36

(2000). On the survival prospects of men's and women's new business ventures, *Journal of Business Venturing*, 15, pp. 347–62

Bögenhold, D. and U. Staber (1991). The decline and rise of self-employment, *Work Employment and Society*, 5, pp. 223–39

Bond, E. W. (1986). Entrepreneurial ability, income distribution and international trade, *Journal of International Economics*, 20, pp. 343–56

Boot, A. W. A. and A. V. Thakor (1994). Moral hazard and secured lending in an infinitely repeated credit market game, *International Economic Review*, 35, pp. 899–920

Boot, A. W. A., A. V. Thakor and G. F. Udell (1991). Secured lending and default risk: equilibrium analysis, policy implications and empirical results, *Economic Journal*, 101, pp. 458–72

Bopaiah, C. (1998). Availability of credit to family businesses, *Small Business Economics*, 11, pp. 75–86

Borjas, G. J. (1986). The self-employment experience of immigrants, *Journal of Human Resources*, 21, pp. 485–506

Borjas, G. J. and S. G. Bronars (1989). Consumer discrimination and self-employment, *Journal of Political Economy*, 97, pp. 581–605

Borooah, V. K. and M. Hart (1999). Factors affecting self-employment among Indian and black Caribbean men in Britain, *Small Business Economics*, 13, pp. 111–29

Boswell, J. (1972). *The Rise and Decline of Small Firms*, London, Allen & Unwin

Bosworth, B. P., A. S. Carron and E. Rhyne (1987). *The Economics of Government Credit*, Washington, DC, Brookings Institution

Bottazzi, L. and M. da Rin (2002). Financing entrepreneurial firms in Europe: facts, issues, and research agenda, Paper presented to the CESifo Conference on Venture Capital, Entrepreneurship, and Public Policy, Munich, November

Boulier, B. L. (1979). Supply decisions of self-employed professionals: the case of dentists, *Southern Economic Journal*, 45, pp. 892–902

Bovaird, C. (1990). *Introduction to Venture Capital Finance*, London, Pitman

Bowlin, O. D. (1984). Lease financing: an attractive method of financing for small firms, in P. M. Horvitz and R. R. Pettit (eds.), *Small Business Finance: Sources of Financing for Small Business, Part B*, Greenwich, CT, JAI Press, pp. 155–62

Boyd, D. P. (1984). Type A behaviour, financial performance and organisational growth in small business firms, *Journal of Occupational Psychology*, 57, pp. 137–40

Boyd, R. L. (1990). Black and Asian self-employment in large metropolitan areas: a comparative analysis, *Social Problems*, 37, pp. 258–69

Bracoud, F. and B. Hillier (2000). Equity or debt? Contracts in markets with asymmetric information, *Manchester School*, 68, pp. 1–23

Bregger, J. E. (1996). Measuring self-employment in the United States, *Monthly Labor Review*, 119, pp. 3–9

Brock, W. A., and D. S. Evans (1986). *The Economics of Small Businesses: Their Role and Regulation in the US Economy*, New York, Holmes & Meier

Brockhaus, R. H. (1980). Risk taking propensity of entrepreneurs, *Academy of Management Journal*, 23, pp. 509–20

(1982). The psychology of the entrepreneur, in C. Kent, D. Sexton and K. Vesper (eds.), *The Encyclopaedia of Entrepreneurship*, Englewood Cliffs, NJ, Prentice-Hall

Brown, C., J. Hamilton and J. Medoff (1990). *Employers Large and Small*, Cambridge, MA, Harvard University Press

Brown, S. and J. G. Sessions (1998). Education, employment status and earnings: a comparative test of the strong screening hypothesis, *Scottish Journal of Political Economy*, 45, pp. 586–91

(1999). Education and employment status: a test of the strong screening hypothesis in Italy, *Economics of Education Review*, 18, pp. 397–404

Browne, F. X. (1987). Sluggish quantity adjustment in a non-clearing market – a disequilibrium application to the loan market, *Journal of Applied Econometrics*, 2, pp. 335–49

Bruce, D. (1999). Do husbands matter? Married women entering self-employment, *Small Business Economics*, 13, pp. 317–29

(2000). Effects of the United States tax system on transitions into self-employment, *Labour Economics*, 7, pp. 545–74

(2002). Taxes and entrepreneurial endurance: evidence from the self-employed, *National Tax Journal*, 55, pp. 5–24

Bruce, D., D. Holtz-Eakin and J. Quinn (2000). Self-employment and labour market transitions at older ages, Working Paper, CRR WP 2000–13, Boston College

Brüderl, J. and P. Preisendörfer (1998). Network support and the success of newly founded businesses, *Small Business Economics*, 10, pp. 213–25

Brüderl, J., P. Preisendörfer and R. Ziegler (1992). Survival chances of newly founded business organisations, *American Sociological Review*, 57, pp. 227–42

Brusch, C. G. (1992). Research on women business owners: past trends, a new perspective and future directions, *Entrepreneurship Theory and Practice*, 4, pp. 5–30

Bruyat, C. A. and P. A. Julien (2001). Defining the field of research in entrepreneurship, *Journal of Business Venturing*, 16, pp. 165–80

Burke, A. E., F. R. Fitz-Roy and M. A. Nolan (2000). When less is more: distinguishing between entrepreneurial choice and performance, *Oxford Bulletin of Economics and Statistics*, 62, pp. 565–87

Calvo, G. and S. Wellisz (1980). Technology, entrepreneurs, and firm size, *Quarterly Journal of Economics*, 95, pp. 663–77

Camerer, C. and Lovallo, D. (1999). Overconfidence and excess entry: an experimental approach, *American Economic Review*, 89, pp. 306–18

Camerer, C., L. Babcock, G. Loewenstein and R. Thaler (1997). Labour supply of New York City cabdrivers: one day at a time, *Quarterly Journal of Economics*, 112, pp. 407–41

Campbell, M. and M. Daly (1992). Self-employment: into the 1990s, *Employment Gazette*, 100, pp. 269–92

Campbell, T. S. (1979). Optimal investment financing decisions and the value of confidentiality, *Journal of Financial and Quantitative Analysis*, 14, pp. 913–24

Cantillon, R. (1755). *Essai Sur la Nature du Commerce en Général*, 1931 edn., ed. and tran. by H. Higgs, London, Macmillan

Caputo, R. K. and A. Dolinsky (1998). Women's choice to pursue self-employment: the role of financial and human capital of household members, *Journal of Small Business Management*, 36, pp. 8–17

Carlsson, B. (1989). Flexibility and the theory of the firm, *International Journal of Industrial Organization*, 7, pp. 179–203

(1992). Management of flexible manufacturing – an international comparison, *Omega*, 20, 11–22

Carlsson, B., D. B. Andretsch and Z. J. Acs (1994). Flexible technology and plant size – United States manufacturing and metalworking industries, *International Journal of Industrial Organization*, 12, pp. 359–72

Carr, D. (1996). Two paths to self-employment? Women's and men's self-employment in the United States, 1980, *Work and Occupations*, 23, 26–53

Carrasco, R. (1999). Transitions to and from self-employment in Spain: an empirical analysis, *Oxford Bulletin of Economics and Statistics*, 61, pp. 315–41

Carrington, W. J., K. McCue and B. Pierce (1996). The role of employer/employee interactions in labour market cycles: evidence from the self-employed, *Journal of Labour Economics*, 14, pp. 571–602

Carroll, G. R. and E. Mosakowski (1987). The career dynamics of self-employment, *Administrative Sciences Quarterly*, 32, pp. 570–89

Carroll, R., D. Holtz-Eakin, M. Rider and H. S. Rosen (2000a). Income taxes and entrepreneurs' use of labour, *Journal of Labour Economics*, 18, pp. 324–51

(2000b). Entrepreneurs, income taxes and investment, in J. B. Slemrod (ed.), *Does Atlas Shrug? The Economic Consequences of Taxing the Rich*, New York, Russell Sage pp. 427–55

(2001). Personal income taxes and the growth of small firms, in J. Poterba (ed.), *Tax Policy and the Economy*, 15, Cambridge, MA, MIT Press, pp. 121–47

Carson, C. S. (1984). The underground economy: an introduction, *Survey of Current Business*, 64, pp. 21–37

Carter, N. M., M. Williams and P. D. Reynolds (1997). Discontinuance among new firms in retail: the influence of initial resources, strategy and gender, *Journal of Business Venturing*, 12, pp. 125–45

Carter, S. and T. Cannon (1992). *Women as Entrepreneurs*, London, Harcourt-Brace Jovanovich

Casey, B. and S. Creigh (1988). Self-employment in Great Britain: its definition in the LFS, in tax and social security law and in labour law, *Work Employment and Society*, 2, pp. 381–91

Casson, M. (ed.) (1990). *Entrepreneurship*, London, Edward Elgar

(1999). Entrepreneurship and the theory of the firm, in Z. J. Acs, B. Carlsson and C. Karlsson (eds.), *Entrepreneurship, Small and Medium Sized Enterprises and the Macroeconomy*, Cambridge, Cambridge University Press, pp. 45–781

(2003). *The Entrepreneur: An Economic Theory*, 2nd edn. Cheltenham, Edward Elgar

Chamley, C. (1983). Entrepreneurial abilities and liabilities in a model of self-selection, *Bell Journal of Economics*, 14, pp. 70–80

Chan, Y.-S. and G. Kanatos (1985). Asymmetric valuations and the role of collateral in loan agreements, *Journal of Money, Credit, and Banking*, 17, pp. 84–95

Chan, Y.-S. and A. V. Thakor (1987). Collateral and competitive equilibria with moral hazard and private information, *Journal of Finance*, 42, pp. 345–63

Chell, E., C. Haworth and S. Brearley (1991). *The Entrepreneurial Personality: Concepts, Cases and Categories*, London, Routledge

Chiswick, B. R. (1978). The effect of Americanisation on the earnings of foreign-born men, *Journal of Political Economy*, 86, pp. 897–921

Chiswick, C. U. (1976). On estimating earnings functions for LDCs, *Journal of Development Economics*, 3, pp. 67–78

Cho, Y. (1986). Inefficiencies from financial liberalisation in the absence of well-functioning equity markets, *Journal of Money, Credit, and Banking*, 18, pp. 191–9

Christiansen, L. R. (1971). Entrepreneurial income: how does it measure up?, *American Economic Review*, 71, pp. 575–85

Clark, K. and S. Drinkwater (1998). Ethnicity and self-employment in Britain, *Oxford Bulletin of Economics and Statistics*, 60, pp. 383–407

(2000). Pushed out or pulled in? Self-employment among ethnic minorities in England and Wales, *Labour Economics*, 7, pp. 603–28

(2002). Enclaves, neighbourhood effects and employment outcomes: ethnic minorities in England and Wales, *Journal of Population Economics*, 15, pp. 5–29

Clark, K., S. Drinkwater and D. Leslie (1998). Ethnicity and self-employment earnings in Britain 1973–95, *Applied Economics Letters*, 5, pp. 631–34

Clemenz, G. (1986). *Credit Markets with Asymmetric Information*, Lecture Notes in Economics and Mathematical Systems, 272, Berlin, Springer-Verlag

Clotfelter, C. T. (1983). Tax evasion and tax rates: an analysis of individual returns, *Review of Economics and Statistics*, 65, pp. 363–73

Coate, S. and S. Tennyson (1992). Labour market discrimination, imperfect information and self-employment, *Oxford Economic Papers*, 44, pp. 272–88

Coco, G. (1999). Collateral, heterogeneity in risk attitude and the credit market equilibrium, *European Economic Review*, 43, pp. 559–74

(2000). On the use of collateral, *Journal of Economic Surveys*, 14, pp. 191–214

Cohen, W. M. and S. Klepper (1996). A reprise of size and R&D, *Economic Journal*, 106, pp. 925–51

Connelly, R. (1992). Self-employment and providing child care, *Demography*, 29, pp. 17–29

Cooper, A. C. (1986). Entrepreneurship and high tech, in D. Sexton and R. Smilor (eds.), *The Art and Science of Entrepreneurship*, Cambridge, MA, Ballinger, pp. 153–68

Cooper, A. C. and A. V. Bruno (1977). Success among high-technology firms, *Business Horizons*, 2, pp. 16–22

Cooper, A. C., F. J. Gimeno-Gascon and C. Y. Woo (1994). Initial human and financial capital as predictors of new venture performance, *Journal of Business Venturing*, 9, pp. 371–95

Cooper, A. C., C. Y. Woo and W. C. Dunkelberg (1988). Entrepreneurs' perceived chances for success, *Journal of Business Venturing*, 3, pp. 97–108

(1989). Entrepreneurship and the initial size of firms, *Journal of Business Venturing*, 4, pp. 317–22

Copulsky, W. and H. McNulty (1974). *Entrepreneurship and the Corporation*, New York, AMACOM

Cosh, A. D. and A. Hughes (1994). Size, financial structure and profitability: UK companies in the 1980s, in A. Hughes and D. Storey (eds.), *Finance and the Small Firm*, London, Routledge, pp. 18–63

Cosh, A. D., A. Hughes and E. Wood (1999). Innovation in UK SMEs: causes and consequences for firm failure and acquisition, in Z. J. Acs and B. Carlsson (eds.), *Entrepreneurship, Small and Medium Sized Enterprises and the Macro Economy*, Cambridge, Cambridge University Press

Covick, O. (1983). Self-employment growth in Australia, in R. Blandy and O. Covick (eds.), *Understanding Labour Markets in Australia*, Sydney, Allen & Unwin, pp. 84–110

Cowling, M. (1998). Regional determinants of small firm loans under the UK Loan Guarantee Scheme, *Small Business Economics*, 11, pp. 155–67

(2000). Are entrepreneurs different across countries?, *Applied Economics Letters*, 7, pp. 785–89

Cowling, M. and N. Clay (1995). Factors influencing take-up rates on the Loan Guarantee Scheme, *Small Business Economics*, 7, pp. 141–52

Cowling, M. and P. Mitchell (1997). The evolution of UK self-employment: a study of government policy and the role of the macroeconomy, *Manchester School*, 65, pp. 427–42

Cowling, M. and M. Taylor (2001). Entrepreneurial women and men: two different species?, *Small Business Economics*, 16, pp. 167–75

Craggs, P. and P. Jones (1998). UK results from the Community Innovation Survey, *Economic Trends*, 539, London, HMSO

Cramer, J. S., J. Hartog, N. Jonker and C. M. van Praag (2002). Low risk aversion encourages the choice for entrepreneurship: an empirical test of a truism, *Journal of Economic Behaviour and Organization*, 48, pp. 29–36

Creedy, J. and P. S. Johnson (1983). Firm formation in manufacturing industry, *Applied Economics*, 15, pp. 177–85

Cressy, R. C. (1993). *The Startup Tracking Exercise: Third Year Report*, National Westminster Bank of Great Britain, November

   (1996). Are business start-ups debt-rationed?, *Economic Journal*, 106, pp. 1253–70

   (1999). Small business failure: failure to fund or failure to learn?, in Z. J. Acs, B. Carlsson and C. Karlsson (eds.), *Entrepreneurship, Small and Medium Sized Enterprises and the Macroeconomy*, Cambridge, Cambridge University Press, pp. 161–85

   (2000). Credit rationing or entrepreneurial risk aversion? An alternative explanation for the Evans and Jovanovic finding, *Economics Letters*, 66, pp. 235–40

Cressy, R. C. and O. Toïvanen (1997). Is there adverse selection in the credit market? Warwick Business School, mimeo

Cromie, S. (1987). Motivations of aspiring male and female entrepreneurs, *Journal of Occupational Behaviour*, 8, pp. 251–61

Cukierman, A. (1978). The horizontal integration of the banking firm: credit rationing and monetary policy, *Review of Economic Studies*, 45, pp. 165–78

Cullen, J. B. and R. H. Gordon (2002). Taxes and entrepreneurial activity: theory and evidence for the US, NBER Working Paper, 9015, National Bureau of Economic Research

Curran, J. (2000). What is small business policy in the UK for? Evaluation and assessing small business policy, *International Small Business Journal*, 18, pp. 36–50

Curran, J., and R. A. Blackburn (1993). *Ethnic Enterprise and the High Street Bank*, Kingston University (UK), Small Business Research Centre

   (2001). Older people and the enterprise society: age and self-employment propensities, *Work Employment and Society*, 15, pp. 889–902

Curran, J. and R. Burrows (1989). National profiles of the self-employed, *Employment Gazette*, 97, pp. 376–85

   (eds.) (1991). *Paths of Enterprise*, London, Routledge

Curran, J., R. Burrows and M. Evandrou (1987). *Small Business Owners and the Self-Employed in Britain: An Analysis of the GHS Data*, London, Small Business Research Trust

Daly, M. (1991). The 1980s – a decade of growth in enterprise, *Employment Gazette*, 99, pp. 109–34

   et al. (1991). Job creation 1987–1989: the contributions of large and small firms, *Employment Gazette*, 99, pp. 109–34

Dant, R. P. (1995). Motivation for franchising: rhetoric versus reality, *International Small Business Journal*, 14, pp. 10–32

Davidsson, P., L. Lindmark and C. Olofsson (1998). The extent of overestimation of small firm job creation – an empirical examination of the regression bias, *Small Business Economics*, 11, pp. 87–100

Davis, S. J. and J. C. Haltiwanger (1992). Gross job creation, gross job destruction and employment reallocation, *Quarterly Journal of Economics*, 107, pp. 819–63

Davis, S. J., J. C. Haltiwanger and S. Schuh (1996a). *Job Creation and Destruction*, Cambridge, MA, MIT Press

(1996b). Small business and job creation: dissecting the myth and reassessing the facts, *Small Business Economics*, 8, pp. 297–315

de Aghion, B. A. and J. Morduch (2000). Microfinance beyond group lending, *Economics of Transition*, 8, pp. 401–20

de Meza, D. (2002). Overlending? *Economic Journal*, 112, pp. F17–F31

de Meza, D. and C. Southey (1996). The borrower's curse: optimism, finance and entrepreneurship, *Economic Journal*, 106, pp. 375–86

de Meza, D. and D. C. Webb (1987). Too much investment: a problem of asymmetric information, *Quarterly Journal of Economics*, 102, pp. 281–92

(1988). Credit market efficiency and tax policy in the presence of screening costs, *Journal of Public Economics*, 36, pp. 1–22

(1989). The role of interest rate taxes in credit markets with divisible projects and asymmetric information, *Journal of Public Economics*, 39, pp. 33–44

(1990). Risk, adverse selection and capital market failure, *Economic Journal*, 100, pp. 206–14

(1992). Efficient credit rationing, *European Economic Review*, 36, pp. 1277–90

(1999). Wealth, enterprise and credit policy, *Economic Journal*, 109, pp. 153–63

(2000). Does credit rationing imply insufficient lending?, *Journal of Public Economics*, 78, pp. 215–34

Deakins, D. (1999). *Entrepreneurship and Small Firms*, 2nd edn., London, McGraw-Hill

Denison, E. F. (1967). *Why Growth Rates Differ: Postwar Experience in Nine Western Countries*, Washington, DC, Broowings Institution

Dennis, W. J. (1996). Self-employment: when nothing else is available?, *Journal of Labour Research*, 17, pp. 645–61

(DTI) (1999). *The Small Business Service: A Public Consultation Document*, London, Department of Trade and Industry

Devine, T. J. (1994a). Characteristics of self-employed women in the United States, *Monthly Labor Review*, 117, pp. 20–34

(1994b). Changes in wage-and-salary returns to skill and the recent rise in female self-employment, *American Economic Review, Papers and Proceedings*, 84, pp. 108–113

(1995). CPS earnings data for the self-employed: words of caution for use and interpretation, *Journal of Economic and Social Measurement*, 21, pp. 213–51

Devine, T. J. and T. Mlakar (1993). Inter-industry variations in the determinants of self-employment, Pennsylvania State University, mimeo

Diamond, D. (1984). Financial intermediation and delegated monitoring, *Review of Economic Studies*, 51, pp. 393–414

Dilnot, A. W. and C. N. Morris (1981). What do we know about the black economy?, *Fiscal Studies*, 2, pp. 58–73

Dixit, A. and R. Rob (1994). Switching costs and sectoral adjustments in general equilibrium with uninsured risk, *Journal of Economic Theory*, 62, pp. 48–69

Dixon, R. (1991). Venture capital and the appraisal of investments, *Omega*, 19, pp. 333–44

Djankow, S., R. La Porta, F. Lopez-de-Silanes and A. Shleifer (2002). The regulation of entry, *Quarterly Journal of Economics*, 117, pp. 1–37

Dolton, P. J. and G. H. Makepeace (1990). Self-employment among graduates, *Bulletin of Economic Research*, 42, pp. 35–53

Dosi, G. (1988). Sources, procedures, and microeconomic effects of innovation, *Journal of Economic Literature*, 26, pp. 1120–71

Du Rietz, A. and M. Henrekson (2000). Testing the female underperformance hypothesis, *Small Business Economics*, 14, pp. 1–10

Dunn, T. and D. Holtz-Eakin (2000). Financial capital, human capital and the transition to self-employment: evidence from intergenerational links, *Journal of Labour Economics*, 18, pp. 282–305

Dunne, P. and A. Hughes (1994). Age, size, growth and survival – UK companies in the 1980s, *Journal of Industrial Economics*, 42, pp. 115–40

Dunne, T, M. Roberts and L. Sammelson (1989a). The growth and failure of US manufacturing plants, *Quarterly Journal of Economics*, 104, pp. 495–515

  (1989b). Plant turnover and gross employment flows in the US manufacturing sector, *Journal of Labour Economics*, 7, pp. 48–71

Dutz, M. A., J. A. Ordover and R. D. Willig (2000). Entrepreneurship, access policy and economic development: lessons from industrial organisation, *European Economic Review*, 44, pp. 739–47

Earle, J. S. and Z. Sakova (2000). Business start-ups or disguised unemployment? Evidence on the character of self-employment from transition economies, *Labour Economics*, 7, pp. 575–601

Eden, D. (1975). Organisational membership versus self-employment: another blow to the American Dream, *Organisational Behaviour and Human Performance*, 13, pp. 79–94

Edwards, L. N. and E. Field-Hendrey (2002). Home-based work and women's labour force decisions, *Journal of Labour Economics*, 20, pp. 170–200

Elkan, W. (1988). Entrepreneurs and entrepreneurship in Africa, *World Bank Research Observer*, 3, 171–85

Employment Department (1989). *Small Firms in Britain*, London, HMSO

Ericsson, R. and A. Pakes (1995). Markov perfect industry dynamics: a framework for empirical work, *Review of Economic Studies*, 62, pp. 53–82

Evans, D. S. (1987a). The relationship between firm growth, size and age: estimates for 100 manufacturing industries, *Journal of Industrial Economics*, 35, pp. 567–81

  (1987b). Tests of alternative theories of firm growth, *Journal of Political Economy*, 95, pp. 657–74

Evans, D. S. and B. Jovanovic (1989). An estimated model of entrepreneurial choice under liquidity constraints, *Journal of Political Economy*, 97, pp. 808–27

Evans, D. S. and L. S. Leighton (1989a). The determinants of changes in US self-employment, 1968–1987, *Small Business Economics*, 1, pp. 111–19

(1989b). Some empirical aspects of entrepreneurship, *American Economic Review*, 79, pp. 519–35

Evans, M. D. R. (1989). Immigrant entrepreneurship: effects of ethnic market size and isolated labour pool, *American Sociological Review*, 54, pp. 950–62

Fain, T. S. (1980). Self-employed Americans: their number has increased, *Monthly Labor Review*, 103, pp. 3–8

Fairlie, R. W. (1999). The absence of the African-American owned business: an analysis of the dynamics of self-employment, *Journal of Labour Economics*, 17, pp. 80–108

(2002). Drug dealing and legitimate self-employment, *Journal of Labor Economics*, 20, 538–67

Fairlie, R. W. and B. D. Meyer (1996). Ethnic and racial self-employment: differences and possible explanations, *Journal of Human Resources*, 31, pp. 757–93

(2000). Trends in self-employment among white and black men during the twentieth century, *Journal of Human Resources*, 35, pp. 643–69

Fan, W. and M. J. White (2002). Personal bankruptcy and the level of entrepreneurial activity, NBER Working Paper, 9340, National Bureau of Economic Research

Farber, H. S. (1999). Alternative and part-time employment arrangements as a response to job loss, *Journal of Labour Economics*, 17, pp. S142–S169

Fazzari, S., R. Hubbard and B. Petersen (1988). Financing constraints and corporate investment, *Brookings Papers on Economic Activity*, 2, pp. 141–95

Federal Reserve System (1958). *Financing Small Business. Report to the Committees for Banking and Currency and the Select Committees on Small Business*, US Congress, Washington, DC, US Government Printing Office

Felstead, A. (1992). Franchising, self-employment and the 'enterprise culture': a UK perspective, in P. Leighton and A. Felstead (eds.), *The New Entrepreneurs: Self-Employment and Small Business in Europe*, London, Kogan Page, pp. 237–65

Ferber, M. A. and J. Waldfogel (1998). The long-term consequences of nontraditional employment, *Monthly Labor Review*, 121, pp. 3–12

Fielden, S. L., M. J. Davidson and P. J. Makin (2000). Barriers encountered during micro and small business start-up in North West England, *Journal of Small Business and Enterprise Development*, 7, pp. 295–304

Flota, C. and M. T. Mora (2001). The earnings of self-employed Mexican-Americans along the US–Mexico border, *Annals of Regional Science*, 35, 483–99

Fölster, S. (2002). Do lower taxes stimulate self-employment?, *Small Business Economics*, 19, pp. 135–45

Foreman-Peck, J. (1985). Seedcorn or chaff? New firm formation and the performance of the inter-war economy, *Economic History Review*, 38, pp. 402–22

Form, W. H. (1985). *Divided We Stand: Working Class Stratification in America*, Urbana, IL, University of Illinois Press

Foti, A. and M. Vivarelli (1994). An econometric test of the self-employment model: the case of Italy, *Small Business Economics*, 6, pp. 81–93

Frank, M. Z. (1988). An intertemporal model of industrial exit, *Quarterly Journal of Economics*, 103, pp. 333–44

Fredland, J. E. and R. D. Little (1981). Self-employed workers: returns to education and training, *Economics of Education Review*, 1, pp. 315–37

Freimer, M. and M. J. Gordon (1965). Why bankers ration credit, *Quarterly Journal of Economics*, 79, pp. 397–416

Frey, B. S. and M. Benz (2002). Being independent is a great thing: subjective evaluations of self-employment and hierarchy, Institute for Empirical Research in Economics, Working Paper, 135, University of Zürich

Fried, J. and P. Howitt (1980). Credit rationing and implicit contract theory, *Journal of Money, Credit, and Banking*, 12, pp. 471–87

Friedman, M. (1953). *The Methodology of Positive Economics*, Chicago, University of Chicago Press

Fuchs, V. R. (1982). Self-employment and labour-force participation of older males, *Journal of Human Resources*, 17, pp. 339–57

Fuest, C., B. Huber and S. B. Nielsen (2002). Why is the corporation tax lower than the personal tax rate? The role of small firms, *Journal of Public Economics*, 87, pp. 157–74

Fujii, E. T. and C. B. Hawley (1991). Empirical aspects of self-employment, *Economics Letters*, 36, pp. 323–9

Gale, D. and M. Hellwig (1985). Incentive-compatible debt contracts: the one-period problem, *Review of Economic Studies*, 52, pp. 647–63

Gale, W. G. (1990a). Collateral, rationing, and government intervention in credit markets, in R. Glenn Hubbard (eds.), *Asymmetric Information, Corporate Finance, and Investment* Chicago, University of Chicago Press, pp. 43–61

(1990b). Federal lending and the market for credit, *Journal of Public Economics*, 42, pp. 177–93

Gaston, R. J. (1989). The scale of informal capital markets, *Small Business Economics*, 1, pp. 223–30

Gavron, R., M. Cowling, G. Holtham and A. Westall (1998). *The Entrepreneurial Society*, London, IPPR

Gentry, W. M. and R. G. Hubbard (2000). Tax policy and entrepreneurial entry, *American Economic Review*, 90, pp. 283–87

(2001). Entrepreneurship and household saving, NBER Working Paper, 7894, National Bureau of Economic Research

Georgellis, Y. and H. J. Wall (2000). What makes a region entrepreneurial? Evidence from Britain, *Annals of Regional Science*, 34, pp. 385–403

Geroski, P. A. (1995). What do we know about entry?, *International Journal of Industrial Organization*, 13, pp. 450–56

Geroski, P. A. and R. Pomroy (1990). Innovation and the evolution of market structure, *Journal of Industrial Economics*, 38, pp. 299–314

Gersovitz, M. (1983). Savings and nutrition at low incomes, *Journal of Political Economy*, 91, pp. 841–55

Ghatak, M. (2000). Screening by the company you keep: joint liability lending and the peer selection effect, *Economic Journal*, 110, pp. 601–31

Ghatak, M. and T. W. Guinnane (1999). The economics of lending with joint liability: theory and practice, *Journal of Development Economics*, 60, pp. 195–228

Gibrat, R. (1931). *Les Inégalités Economique*, Paris, Siley

Gifford, S. (1998). *The Allocation of Limited Entrepreneurial Attention*, Boston, MA, Kluwer

Gill, A. M. (1988). Choice of employment status and the wages of employees and the self-employed: some further evidence, *Journal of Applied Econometrics*, 3, pp. 229–34

Gimeno, J., T. B. Folta, A. C. Cooper and C. Y. Woo (1997). Survival of the fittest? Entrepreneurial human capital and the persistence of underperforming firms, *Administrative Science Quarterly*, 42, pp. 750–83

Gladstone, R. and J. Lane-Lee (1995). The operation of the insolvency system in the UK. Some implications for entrepreneurialism, *Small Business Economics*, 7, pp. 55–67

Glaeser, E. L., D. Laibson and B. Sacerdote (2000). The economic approach to social capital?, NBER Working Paper, 7728, National Bureau of Economic Research

Goedhuys, M. and L. Sleuwaegen (2000). Entrepreneurship and growth of entrepreneurial firms in Côte d'Ivoire, *Journal of Development Studies*, 36, pp. 122–45

Goldfeld, S. M. (1966). *Commercial Bank Behaviour and Economic Activity: A Structural Study of Monetary Policy in the Post War United States*, Amsterdam North-Holland

Gomez, R. and E. Santor (2001). Membership has its privileges: the effect of social capital and neighbourhood characteristics on the earnings of microfinance borrowers, *Canadian Journal of Economics*, 34, pp. 943–66

Gompers, P. A. and J. Lerner (1998). What drives venture capital fundraising?, *Brookings Papers on Economic Activity*, pp. 149–92

Goodman, A. and S. Webb (1994). For richer, for poorer: the changing distribution of income in the UK, 1961–91, *Fiscal Studies*, 15, pp. 29–62

Gordon, R. H. (1998). Can high personal tax rates encourage entrepreneurial activity?, *IMF Staff Papers*, 45, pp. 49–80

Gordus, J. P., P. Jarley and L. A. Ferman (1981). *Plant Closings and Economic Dislocation*, Kalamazoo, MI, W. E. Upjohn Institute for Employment Research

Gray, J. A. and Y. Wu (1995). On equilibrium credit rationing and interest rates, *Journal of Macroeconomics*, 17, pp. 405–20

Greenwald, B., J. E. Stiglitz and A. Weiss (1984). Informational imperfections in the capital market and macroeconomic fluctuations, *American Economic Review*, 74, pp. 194–9

Gromb, D. and D. Scharfstein (2002). Entrepreneurship in equilibrium, NBER Working Paper, 9001, National Bureau of Economic Research

Grossman, G. M. (1984). International trade, foreign investment, and the formation of the entrepreneurial class, *American Economic Review*, 74, pp. 605–14

Gruber, J. and J. Poterba (1994). Tax incentives and the decision to purchase health insurance: evidence from the self-employed, *Quarterly Journal of Economics*, 109, pp. 701–33

Guinnane, T. (1994). A failed institutional transplant: Raiffeisen's credit cooperatives in Ireland, 1894–1914, *Explorations in Economic History*, 31, pp. 38–61

Guiso, L. (1998). High-tech firms and credit rationing, *Journal of Economic Behaviour and Organization*, 35, pp. 39–59

Haber, S. E., E. J. Lamas and J. Lichtenstein (1987). On their own: the self-employed and others in private business, *Monthly Labor Review*, 110, pp. 17–23

Hakim, C. (1988). Self-employment in Britain: recent trends and current issues, *Work, Employment and Society*, 2, pp. 421–50

(1989a). New recruits to self-employment in the 1980s, *Employment Gazette*, 97, pp. 286–97

(1989b). Workforce restructuring, social insurance coverage and the black economy, *Journal of Social Policy*, 18, pp. 471–503

Hall, B. H. (1987). The relationship between firm size and firm growth in the US manufacturing sector, *Journal of Industrial Economics*, 35, pp. 583–606

Hall, G. (1992). Reasons for insolvency amongst small firms – a review and fresh evidence, *Small Business Economics*, 4, pp. 237–50

Hamermesh, D. S. (1993). *Labour Demand*, Princeton, Princeton University Press

Hamilton, B. H. (2000). Does entrepreneurship pay? An empirical analysis of the returns to self-employment, *Journal of Political Economy*, 108, pp. 604–31

Hamilton, R. T. (1989). Unemployment and business formation rates: reconciling time series and cross-section evidence, *Environment and Planning C*, 21, pp. 249–55

Harhoff, D. and T. Körting (1998). Lending relationships in Germany – empirical evidence from survey data, *Journal of Banking and Finance*, 22, pp. 1317–53

Harper, D. A. (1996). *Entrepreneurship and the Market Process: An Enquiry into the Growth of Knowledge*, London, Routledge

Harris, J. R. and M. P. Todaro (1970). Migration, unemployment and development: a two-sector analysis, *American Economic Review*, 60, pp. 126–42

Harris, R. I. D. and R. Sollis (2003). *Applied Time-Series Modelling and Forecasting*, Chichester, John Wiley

Harrison, R. T. and M. Hart (1983). Factors influencing new business formation: a case study of Northern Ireland, *Environment and Planning*, 15, pp. 1395–1412

Hart, O. (1995). *Firms, Contracts and Financial Structure*, Oxford, Clarendon Press

Hart, O. and J. Moore (1994). A theory of debt based on inalienability of human capital, *Quarterly Journal of Economics*, 109, pp. 841–79

(1998). Default and renegotiation: a dynamic model of debt, *Quarterly Journal of Economics*, 113, pp. 1–26

Hart, P. E. and N. Oulton (1996). Growth and size of firms, *Economic Journal*, 106, pp. 1242–52

Hart, P. E. and P. E. Prais (1956). The analysis of business concentration: a statistical approach, *Journal of the Royal Statistical Society*, 119, pp. 150–91

Harvey, M. (1995). Towards the insecurity society: the tax trap of self-employment, London, The Institute of Employment Rights

Hawley, F. B. (1907). *Enterprise and the Productive Process*, New York, Putnam

Headen, A. E. (1990). Wage returns to ownership, and fee responses to physician supply, *Review of Economics and Statistics*, 72, pp. 30–7

Hébert, R. F. and A. N. Link (1988). *The Entrepreneur – Mainstream Views and Radical Critiques*, 2nd edn., New York, Praeger

Heckman, J. J. (1979). Sample selection bias as a specification error, *Econometrica*, 47, pp. 475–92

Hellmann, T. and M. Puri (2000). The interaction between product market and financing strategy: the role of venture capital, *Review of Financial Studies*, 13, pp. 959–84

  (2002). Venture capital and the professionalisation of start-ups: empirical evidence, *Journal of Finance*, 57, pp. 169–97

Hellmann, T. and J. Stiglitz (2000). Credit and equity rationing in markets with adverse selection, *European Economic Review*, 44, pp. 281–304

Hellwig, M. (1987). Some recent developments in the theory of competitive markets with adverse selection, *European Economic Review*, 31, pp. 319–25

Highfield, R. and R. Smiley (1987). New business starts and economic activity: an empirical investigation, *International Journal of Industrial Organization*, 5, pp. 51–66

Hillier, B. (1998). The borrower's curse: comment, *Economic Journal*, 108, pp. 1772–74

Hillier, B. and M. V. Ibrahimo (1992). The performance of credit markets under asymmetric information about projects means and variances, *Journal of Economic Studies*, 19, pp. 3–17

  (1993). Asymmetric information and models of credit rationing, *Bulletin of Economic Research*, 45, pp. 271–304

Hillier, B. and T. Worrall (1994). The welfare implications of costly monitoring in the credit market, *Economic Journal*, 104, pp. 350–62

HMSO (1971). *Report on the Committee of Inquiry on Small Firms* (Bolton Report), Cmnd 4811, London, HMSO

  (1979). *Interim Report on the Financing of Small Firms* (Wilson Report), Cmnd 7503, London, HMSO

  (1991). *Constraints on the Growth of Small Firms*, London, HMSO

Hodgman, D. (1960). Credit risk and credit rationing, *Quarterly Journal of Economics*, 74, pp. 258–78

Holmes, T. J. and J. A. Schmitz (1990). A theory of entrepreneurship and its application to the study of business transfers, *Journal of Political Economy*, 98, pp. 265–94

  (1996). Managerial tenure, business age, and small business turnover, *Journal of Labour Economics*, 14, pp. 79–99

Holtz-Eakin, D. (2000). Public policy toward entrepreneurship, *Small Business Economics*, 15, pp. 283–91

Holtz-Eakin, D., D. Joulfaian and H. S. Rosen (1994a). Entrepreneurial decisions and liquidity constraints, *Rand Journal of Economics*, 25, pp. 334–47

(1994b). Sticking it out: entrepreneurial survival and liquidity constraints, *Journal of Political Economy*, 102, pp. 53–75

Holtz-Eakin, D., J. Penrod and H. S. Rosen (1996). Health insurance and the supply of entrepreneurs, *Journal of Public Economics*, 62, pp. 209–35

Holtz-Eakin, D., H. S. Rosen and R. Weathers (2000). Horatio Alger meets the mobility tables, *Small Business Economics*, 14, pp. 243–74

Honig, M. and G. Hanoch (1985). Partial retirement as a separate mode of retirement behaviour, *Journal of Human Resources*, 20, pp. 21–46

Horvitz, P. M. (1984). Problems in the financing of small business: introduction and summary, in P. M. Horvitz and R. R. Pettit (eds.), *Small Business Finance: Sources of Financing for Small Business, Part B* Greenwich, CT, JAI Press, pp. 3–18

House, W. J., G. K. Ikiara and D. McCormick (1993). Urban self-employment in Kenya: panacea or viable strategy?, *World Development*, 21, pp. 1205–23

Hout, M. and H. S. Rosen (2000). Self-employment, family background, and race, *Journal of Human Resources*, 35, pp. 670–92

Hubbard, R. G. (1998). Capital-market imperfections and investment, *Journal of Economic Literature*, 36, pp. 193–225

Hudson, J. (1987a). Company births in Great Britain and the institutional environment, *International Small Business Journal*, 6, pp. 57–69

(1987b). The age, regional and industrial structure of company liquidations, *Journal of Banking, Finance and Accounting*, 14, pp. 199–213

(1989). The birth and death of firms, *Quarterly Review of Economics and Business*, 29, pp. 68–86

Hudson, J. and K. Cuthbertson (1993). The determinants of bankruptcies in the UK: 1971–1988, *Manchester School*, 61, pp. 65–81

Hughes, A. (1992). The problems of finance for smaller businesses, in N. Dimsdale and M. Prevezer (eds.), *Capital Markets and Company Success*, Oxford, Oxford University Press

Hundley, G. (2001a). Why women earn less than men in self-employment, *Journal of Labour Research*, 22, pp. 817–29

(2001b). Why and when are the self-employed more satisfied with their work?, *Industrial Relations*, 40, pp. 293–317

Huppi, M. and G. Feder (1990). The role of groups and credit co-operatives in rural lending, *The World Bank Research Observer*, 5, pp. 187–204

Iams, H. M. (1987). Jobs of persons working after receiving retired worker benefits, *Social Security Bulletin*, 50, pp. 4–19

Ijiri, Y. and H. A. Simon (1977). *Skew Distributions and the Sizes of Business Firms*, Amsterdam, North-Holland

Innes, R. (1991). Investment and government intervention in credit markets when there is asymmetric information, *Journal of Public Economics*, 46, pp. 347–81

(1992). Adverse selection, investment, and profit taxation, *European Economic Review*, 36, pp. 1427–52

(1993). Financial contracting under risk neutrality, limited liability and *ex ante* asymmetric information, *Economica*, 60, pp. 27–40

Iyigun, M. F. and A. L. Owen (1999). Entrepreneurs, professionals and growth, *Journal of Economic Growth*, 4, pp. 213–32

Jaffee, D. and F. Modigliani (1969). A theory and test of credit rationing, *American Economic Review*, 59, pp. 850–72

Jaffee, D. and T. Russell (1976). Imperfect information, uncertainty, and credit rationing, *Quarterly Journal of Economics*, 90, pp. 651–66

Jaffee, D. and J. E. Stiglitz (1990). Credit rationing, in B. M. Friedman and F. H. Hahn (eds.), *The Handbook of Monetary Economics, II*, Amsterdam, North-Holland, pp. 838–88

Jain, B. and O. Kini (1995). Venture capital participation and the post-issue operating performance of IPO firms, *Managerial and Decision Economics*, 16, pp. 593–606

Jefferson, P. N.(1997). Unemployment and financial constraints faced by small firms, *Economic Inquiry*, 35, pp. 108–19

Jenkins, S. P. (1995). Accounting for income inequality trends: decomposition analyses for the UK, 1971–1986, *Economica*, 62, pp. 29–63

Johansson, E. (2000). Self-employment and liquidity constraints: evidence from Finland, *Scandinavian Journal of Economics*, 102, pp. 123–34

Johnson, D. G. (1954). The functional distribution of income in the United States, 1950–1952, *Review of Economics and Statistics*, 36, pp. 175–82

Johnson, P. (1981). Unemployment and self-employment: a survey, *Industrial Relations Journal*, 12, pp. 5–15

Johnson, P. and S. Parker (1994). The interrelationships between births and deaths, *Small Business Economics*, 6, pp. 283–90

(1996). Spatial variations in the determinants and effects of firm births and deaths, *Regional Studies*, 30, pp. 679–88

Johnson, P. and J. Rodger (1983). From redundancy to self-employment, *Employment Gazette*, 91, pp. 260–64

Jones, T., D. McEvoy and G. Barrett (1993). Labour intensive practices in the ethnic minority firm, in J. Atkinson and D. Storey (eds.), *Employment, The Small Firm and the Labour Market*, London, Routledge, pp. 172–205

(1994). Raising capital for the ethnic minority small firm, in A. Hughes and D. Storey (eds.), *Finance and the Small Firm*, Routledge, London, pp. 145–81

Joulfaian, D. and M. Rider (1996). Tax evasion in the presence of negative income tax rates, *National Tax Journal*, 49, pp. 553–70

(1998). Differential taxation and tax evasion by small business, *National Tax Journal*, 51, pp. 675–87

Jovanovic, B. (1982). Selection and the evolution of industry, *Econometrica*, 50, pp. 649–70

(1994). Firm formation with heterogeneous management and labour skills, *Small Business Economics*, 6, pp. 185–91

Jung, Y. H., A. Snow and G. A. Trandel (1994). Tax evasion and the size of the underground economy, *Journal of Public Economics*, 54, pp. 391–402

Kalleberg, A. L. and K. T. Leicht (1991). Gender and organisational performance: determinants of small business survival and success, *Academy of Management Journal*, 34, pp. 136–61

Kanbur, S. M. (1979). Of risk taking and the personal distribution of income, *Journal of Political Economy*, 87, pp. 769–97

(1980). A note on risk taking, entrepreneurship, and Schumpeter, *History of Political Economy*, 12, pp. 489–98

(1981). Risk taking and taxation: an alternative perspective, *Journal of Public Economics*, 15, pp. 163–84

(1982). Entrepreneurial risk taking, inequality and public policy: an application of inequality decomposition analysis to the general equilibrium effects of progressive taxation, *Journal of Political Economy*, 90, pp. 1–21

Kangasharju, A. and A. Moisio (1998). Births–deaths nexus of firms: estimating VAR with panel data, *Small Business Economics*, 11, pp. 303–13

Kangasharju, A. and S. Pekkala (2002). The role of education in self-employment success in Finland, *Growth and Change*, 33, pp. 216–37

Kaplan, S. N. and L. Zingales (1997). Do investment–cash flow sensitivities provide useful measures of financing constraints?, *Quarterly Journal of Economics*, 112, pp. 169–215

Katz, J. A. (1990). Longitudinal analysis of self-employment follow-through, *Entrepreneurship and Regional Development*, 2, pp. 15–25

Kaufmann, P. J. and R. P. Dant (1998). Franchising and the domain of entrepreneurship research, *Journal of Business Venturing*, 14, pp. 5–16

Kaufmann, P. J. and F. Lafontaine (1994). Costs of control: the source of economic rents for McDonald's franchisees, *Journal of Law and Economics*, 37, pp. 417–53

Kawaguchi, D. (2003). Human capital accumulation of salaried and self-employed workers, *Labour Economics*, 10, pp. 55–71

Keasy, K. and R. Watson (1995). The pricing of small firm bank finance: evidence from the UK, *Applied Economics Letters*, 2, pp. 208–10

Keeble, D., S. Walker and M. Robson (1993). *New Firm Formation and Small Business Growth: Spatial and Temporal Variations and Determinants in the United Kingdom*, Employment Department Research Series, 15, London, HMSO

Keeton, W. R. (1979). *Equilibrium Credit Rationing*, New York, Garland Publishing

Kent, C. A. and F. W. Rushing (1999). Coverage of entrepreneurship in principles of economics textbooks: an update, *Journal of Economic Education*, 30, pp. 184–8

Kesselman, J. R. (1989). Income tax evasion: an inter-sectoral analysis, *Journal of Public Economics*, 38, pp. 137–82

Kets de Vries, M. F. R. (1977). The entrepreneurial personality: a person at the crossroads, *Journal of Mathematical Sociology*, 14, pp. 34–57

Keuschnigg, C. and S. B. Nielsen (2003). Tax policy, venture capital and entrepreneurship, *Journal of Public Economics*, 87, pp. 175–203

Kidd, M. P. (1993). Immigrant wage differentials and the role of self-employment in Australia, *Australian Economic Papers*, 32, pp. 92–115

Kihlstrom, R. E. and J. J. Laffont (1979). A general equilibrium entrepreneurial theory of firm formation based on risk aversion, *Journal of Political Economy*, 87, pp. 719–49

(1982). A competitive entrepreneurial model of the stock market, in J. McCall (ed.), *The Economics of Information and Uncertainty*, Chicago, University of Chicago Press

(1983a). Implicit labour contracts and free entry, *Quarterly Journal of Economics Supplement*, 98, pp. 55–105

(1983b). Taxation and risk taking in general equilibrium models with free entry, *Journal of Public Economics*, 21, pp. 159–81

Kilby, P. (1983). An entrepreneurial problem, *American Economic Review, Papers and Proceedings*, 73, pp. 107–11

King, R. G. and R. Levine (1993). Finance, entrepreneurship and growth, *Journal of Monetary Economics*, 32, pp. 513–42

King, S. R. (1986). Monetary transmission: through bank loans or bank liabilities?, *Journal of Money, Credit, and Banking*, 18, pp. 290–303

Kirchhoff, B. A. (1991). Entrepreneurship's contribution to economics, *Entrepreneurship Theory and Practice*, 16, pp. 93–112

Kirchhoff, B. A. and P. G. Greene (1998). Understanding the theoretical and empirical content of critiques of US job creation research, *Small Business Economics*, 10, pp. 153–69

Kirzner, I. (1973). *Competition and Entrepreneurship*, Chicago, University of Chicago Press

(1985). *Discovery and the Capitalist Process*, Chicago, University of Chicago Press

Klepper, S. (1996). Entry, exit, growth and innovation over the product life cycle, *American Economic Review*, 86, pp. 562–83

Knight, F. H. (1921). *Risk, Uncertainty and Profit*, New York, Houghton-Mifflin

Knight, G. and S. McKay (2000). Lifetime experiences of self-employment, *Labour Market Trends*, 108, pp. 470–72

Knight, K. E. and T. Dorsey (1976). Capital problems in minority business development: a critical analysis, *American Economic Review, Papers and Proceedings*, 66, pp. 328–31

Knight, R. M. (1985). The financing of small high-technology firms in Canada, *Journal of Small Business and Entrepreneurship*, 3, pp. 5–17

Kochar, A. (1997). An empirical investigation of rationing constraints in rural credit markets in India, *Journal of Development Economics*, 53, pp. 339–71

Konings, J. (1995). Gross job flows and the evolution of size in UK establishments, *Small Business Economics*, 7, pp. 213–20

Kortum, S. and J. Lerner (2000). Assessing the contribution of venture capital to innovation, *Rand Journal of Economics*, 31, pp. 674–92

Koskela, E. (1983). Credit rationing and non-price loan terms: a re-examination, *Journal of Banking and Finance*, 7, pp. 405–16

KPMG (1999). *An Evaluation of the Small Firms Loan Guarantee Scheme*, London, HMSO

Kravis, I. B. (1959). Relative income shares in fact and theory, *American Economic Review*, 49, pp. 917–49

Kugler, P. (1987). Credit rationing and the adjustment of the loan rate: an empirical investigation, *Journal of Macroeconomics*, 9, pp. 505–25

Kuhn, P. J. and H. J. Schuetze (2001). Self-employment dynamics and self-employment trends: a study of Canadian men and women, 1982–1998, *Canadian Journal of Economics*, 34, pp. 760–84

Kuznets, S. (1966). *Modern Economic Growth: Rate Structure and Spread*, New Haven, CT, Yale University Press

Laband, D. N. and B. F. Lentz (1983). Like father, like son: toward an economic theory of occupational following, *Southern Economic Journal*, 50, pp. 474–93

Laferrère, A. and P. McEntee (1995). Self-employment and intergenerational transfers of physical and human capital: an empirical analysis of French data, *Economic and Social Review*, 27, pp. 43–54

Laffont, J.-J. and T. N'Guessan (2000). Group lending with adverse selection, *European Economic Review*, 44, pp. 773–84

Lazear, E. P. (2002). Entrepreneurship, NBER Working Paper, 9109, National Bureau of Economic Research

Lazear, E. P. and R. L. Moore (1984). Incentives, productivity, and labour contracts, *Quarterly Journal of Economics*, 99, pp. 275–96

Le, A. T. (1999). Empirical studies of self-employment, *Journal of Economic Surveys*, 13, pp. 381–416

(2000). The determinants of immigrant self-employment in Australia, *International Migration Review*, 34, pp. 183–214

Lebergott, S. (1964). Factor shares in the long term: some theoretical and statistical aspects, in The behaviour of income shares: selected theoretical and empirical issues, *NBER Studies in Income and Wealth*, 27, Princeton

Lee, M. A. and M. S. Rendall (2001). Self-employment disadvantage in the working lives of blacks and females, *Population Research and Policy Review*, 20, pp. 291–320

Lee, R. M. (1985). The entry to self-employment of redundant steelworkers, *Industrial Relations Journal*, 16, pp. 42–9

Leeth, J. D. and J. A. Scott (1989). The incidence of secured debt – evidence from the small business community, *Journal of Financial and Quantitative Analysis*, 24, pp. 379–94

Leff, N. H. (1979). Entrepreneurship and economic development: the problem revisited, *Journal of Economic Literature*, 17, pp. 46–64

Leibenstein, H. (1968). Entrepreneurship and development, *American Economic Review*, 58, pp. 72–83

Leighton, P. (1982). Employment contracts: a choice of relationships, *Employment Gazette*, 90, pp. 433–39

(1983). Employment and self-employment: some problems of law and practice, *Employment Gazette*, 91, pp. 197–203

Leland, H. E. and D. H. Pyle (1977). Informational asymmetries, financial structure and financial intermediation, *Journal of Finance*, 32, pp. 371–87

Lentz, B. F. and D. N. Laband (1990). Entrepreneurial success and occupational inheritance among proprietors, *Canadian Journal of Economics*, 23, pp. 563–79

Leonard, J. S. (1986). On the size distribution of employment and establishments, NBER Working Paper, 1951, National Bureau of Economic Research

LeRoy, S. F. and L. D. Singell (1987). Knight on risk and uncertainty, *Journal of Political Economy*, 95, pp. 394–406

Levenson, A. R. and K. L. Willard (2000). Do firms get the financing they want? Measuring credit rationing experienced by small businesses in the US, *Small Business Economics*, 14, pp. 83–94

Levy, B. (1993). Obstacles to developing indigenous small and medium enterprises: an empirical assessment, *World Bank Economic Review*, 7, pp. 65–83

Lewis, W. A. (1955). *The Theory of Economic Growth*, London, Allen & Unwin

Light, I. (1972). *Ethnic Entrepreneurs in America*, Berkeley, CA, University of California Press

(1984). Immigrant and ethnic enterprise in North America, *Ethnic and Racial Studies*, 7, pp. 195–216

Light, I. and E. Bonacich (1988). *Immigrant Entrepreneurs: Koreans in Los Angeles 1965–1982*, Berkeley, CA, University of California Press

Light, I. and C. Rosenstein (1995). *Race, Ethnicity and Entrepreneurship in Urban America*, New York, Aldine de Gruyter

Lin, Z., G. Picot and J. Compton (2000). The entry and exit dynamics of self-employment in Canada, *Small Business Economics*, 15, pp. 105–25

Lindh, T. and H. Ohlsson (1996). Self-employment and windfall gains: evidence from the Swedish lottery, *Economic Journal*, 106, pp. 1515–26

Link, A. N. and C. Rees (1990). Firm size, university research and the returns to R&D, *Small Business Economics*, 2, pp. 25–33

Lofstrom, M. (2002). Labour market assimilation and the self-employment decision of immigrant entrepreneurs, *Journal of Population Economics*, 15, pp. 83–114

Long, J. E. (1982a). The income tax and self-employment, *National Tax Journal*, 35, pp. 31–42

(1982b). Income taxation and the allocation of market labour, *Journal of Labour Research*, 3, pp. 259–76

Lopez, R. (1984). Estimating labour supply and production decisions of self-employed farm producers, *European Economic Review*, 24, pp. 61–82

Loscocco, K. A. (1997). Work–family linkages among self-employed women and men, *Journal of Vocational Behaviour*, 50, pp. 204–26

Loufti, M. F. (1992). An overview of self-employment in Europe: nature, trends and policy issues, in P. Leighton and A. Felstead (eds.), *The New Entrepreneurs: Self-Employment and Small Business in Europe*, London, Kogan Page, pp. 41–68

Lucas, R. E. (1978). On the size distribution of business firms, *Bell Journal of Economics*, 9, pp. 508–23

Luthans, F., A. Stajkovic and E. Ibrayeva (2000). Environmental and psychological challenges facing entrepreneurial development in transitional economies, *Journal of World Business*, 35, pp. 95–100

Macafee, K. (1982). A glimpse of the hidden economy in the national accounts of the United Kingdom, in V. Tanzi, (ed.), *The Underground Economy in the United States and Abroad*, Lexington, MA, Lexington Books, pp. 147–61

MacDonald R. and F. Coffield (1991). *Risky Business? Youth and the Enterprise Culture*, London, Falmer Press

MacMillan, I. C. (1986). To really learn about entrepreneurship, let's study habitual entrepreneurs, *Journal of Business Venturing*, 1, pp. 241–3

Macpherson, D. A. (1988). Self-employment and married women, *Economics Letters*, 28, pp. 281–4

Maddala, G. S. (1983). *Limited-Dependent and Qualitative Variables in Econometrics*, Cambridge, Cambridge University Press

Maddison, A. (1991). *Dynamic Forces in Capital Development*, Oxford, Oxford University Press

Manove, M. (2000). Entrepreneurs, optimism and the competitive edge, Boston University, Mimeo

Manser, M. E. and G. Picot (2000). The role of self-employment in US and Canadian job growth, *Monthly Labor Review*, 123, pp. 10–25

Marsh, A., P. Heady and J. Matheson (1981). *Labour Mobility in the Construction Industry*, London, HMSO

Marshall, A. (1930). *Principles of Economics*, London, Macmillan

Marshall, J. N., N. Alderman, C. Wong and A. Thwaites (1993). The impact of government-assisted management training and development on small and medium-sized enterprises in Britain, *Environment and Planning C*, 11, pp. 331–48

Mason, C. M. and R. T. Harrison (1994). Informal venture capital in the UK, in A. Hughes and D. J. Storey (eds.), *Finance and the Small Firm*, London, Routledge, pp. 64–111

    (2000). The size of the informal venture capital market in the United Kingdom, *Small Business Economics*, 15, pp. 137–48

Mata, J. (1994). Firm growth during infancy, *Small Business Economics*, 6, pp. 27–39

Mata, J. and P. Portugal (1994). Life duration of new firms, *Journal of Industrial Economics*, 42, pp. 227–45

Mata, J., P. Portugal and P. Guimaraes (1995). The survival of new plants: start-up conditions and post-entry evolution, *International Journal of Industrial Organization*, 13, pp. 459–81

Mattesini, F. (1990). Screening in the credit market, *European Journal of Political Economy*, 6, pp. 1–22

Maxim, P. S. (1992). Immigrants, visible minorities, and self-employment, *Demography* 29, pp. 181–98

Mayer, A. (1975). The lower middle class as historical problem, *Journal of Modern History*, 47, pp. 409–36

Mazumdar, D. (1981). *The Urban Labour Market and Income Distribution – A Study of Malaysia*, New York, Oxford University Press

McClelland, D. C. (1961). *The Achieving Society*, Princeton, Van Nostrand

McKernan, S. M. (2002). The impact of microcredit programs on self-employment profits: do noncredit program aspects matter?, *Review of Economics and Statistics*, 84, pp. 93–115

Meager, N. (1992a). Does unemployment lead to self-employment?, *Small Business Economics*, 4, pp. 87–103

(1992b). The characteristics of the self-employed: some Anglo-German comparisons, in P. Leighton and A. Felstead (eds.), *The New Entrepreneurs: Self-employment and Small Business in Europe*, London, Kogan Page, pp. 69–99

(1993). From unemployment to self-employment in the European Community, in F. Chittenden, *et al.* (eds.), *Small Firms: Recession and Recovery*, London, Paul Chapman Publishing, pp. 27–53

(1994). Self-employment schemes for the unemployed in the European Community, in G. Schmid (ed.), *Labour Market Institutions in Europe*, New York, M. E. Sharpe, pp. 183–242

Meager, N., G. Court and J. Moralee (1994). *Self-Employment and the Distribution of Income*, Brighton, The Institute for Manpower Studies

(1996). Self-employment and the distribution of income, in J. Hills (ed.), *New Inequalities*, Cambridge, Cambridge University Press

Meredith, G. G., R. E. Nelson and P. A. Neck (1982). *The Practice of Entrepreneurship*, Geneva, ILO

Metcalf, H., T. Modood and S. Virdee (1996). *Asian Self-Employment: The Interaction of Culture and Economics*, London, Policy Studies Institute

Meyer, B. (1990). Why are there so few black entrepreneurs?, NBER Working Paper, 3537, National Bureau of Economic Research

Michelacchi, C. (2003). Low returns in R&D due to the lack of entrepreneurial skills, *Economic Journal*, 113, pp. 207–25

Milde, H. and J. G. Riley (1988). Signaling in credit markets, *Quarterly Journal of Economics*, 103, pp. 101–29

Miller, R. A. (1984). Job matching and occupational choice, *Journal of Political Economy*, 92, pp. 1086–1120

Moore, B. (1994). Financial constraints to the growth and development of small high technology firms, in A. Hughes and D. Storey (eds.), *Finance and the Small Firm*, London, Routledge, pp. 112–44

Moore, C. S. and R. E. Mueller (2002). The transition from paid to self-employment in Canada: the importance of push factors, *Applied Economics*, 34, pp. 791–801

Moore, R. L. (1983a). Self-employment and the incidence of the payroll tax, *National Tax Journal*, 36, pp. 491–501

(1983b). Employer discrimination: evidence from self-employed workers, *Review of Economics and Statistics*, 65, pp. 496–501

Moralee, L. (1998). Self-employment in the 1990s, *Labour Market Trends*, 106, pp. 121–30

Morduch, J. (1999). The microfinance promise, *Journal of Economic Literature*, 37, pp. 1569–1614

Moresi, S. (1998). Optimal taxation and firm formation: a model of asymmetric information, *European Economic Review*, 42, pp. 1525–51

Morgan, K. (1997). The learning region: institutions, innovation and regional renewal, *Regional Studies*, 31, pp. 491–503

Moskowitz, T. J. and A. Vissing-Jørgensen (2002). The returns to entrepreneurial investment: a private equity premium puzzle?, *American Economic Review*, 92, pp. 745–78

Myers, S. C. and N. S. Majluf (1984). Corporate financing and investment decisions when firms have information that investors do not have, *Journal of Financial Economics*, 13, pp. 187–221

Myrdal, G. (1944). *An American Dilemma: The Negro Problem and Modern Democracy*, New York, Harper

Nafziger, E. W. and D. Terrell (1996). Entrepreneurial human capital and the long run survival of firms in India, *World Development*, 24, pp. 689–96

National Economic Research Associates (NERA) (1990). *An Evaluation of the Loan Guarantee Scheme*, Department of Employment Research Paper, 74, London, HMSO

Nenadic, S. (1990). The life cycle of firms in nineteenth century Britain, in P. Jobert and M. Mors (eds.), *The Birth and Death of Companies: An Historical Perspective*, Lancaster, Parthenon

Nisjen, A. (1988). Self-employment in the Netherlands, *International Small Business Journal*, 7, pp. 52–60

Noe, T. H. (1988). Capital structure and signalling game equilibria, *Review of Financial Studies*, 1, pp. 331–55

Norton, W. I. and W. T. Moore (2002). Entrepreneurial risk: have we been asking the wrong question?, *Small Business Economics*, 18, pp. 281–7

Nziramasanga, M. and M. Lee (2001). Duration of self-employment in developing countries: evidence from small enterprises in Zimbabwe, *Small Business Economics*, 17, pp. 239–53

OECD (1986, 1994a). *Employment Outlook*, Paris, OECD Publications
  (1994b). *Taxation and Small Businesses*, Paris, OECD Publications
  (1998). *Fostering Entrepreneurship*, Paris, OECD Publications
  (2000a). The partial renaissance of self-employment, in *Employment Outlook*, Paris, OECD Publications
  (2000b). *OECD SME Outlook*, Paris, OECD Publications

O'Farrell, P. N. and A. R. Pickles (1989). Entrepreneurial behaviour within male work histories: a sector-specific analysis, *Environment and Planning*, 21, pp. 311–31

Oi, W. Y. (1983). Heterogeneous firms and the organisation of production, *Economic Inquiry*, 21, pp. 147–71

Olekalns, N. and H. Sibly (1992). Credit rationing, implicit contracts, risk aversion and the variability of interest rates, *Journal of Macroeconomics*, 14, pp. 337–47

Ordover, J. and A. Weiss (1981). Information and the law: evaluating legal restrictions on competitive contracts, *American Economic Review, Papers and Proceedings*, 71, pp. 399–404

Otani, K. (1996). A human capital approach to entrepreneurial capacity, *Economica*, 63, pp. 273–89

Palich, L. E. and D. R. Bagby (1995). Using cognitive theory to explain entrepreneurial risk-taking: challenging conventional wisdom, *Journal of Business Venturing*, 10, pp. 425–38

Parasuraman, S. and C. A. Simmers (2001). Type of employment, work–family conflict and well-being: a comparative study, *Journal of Occupational Behaviour*, 22, pp. 551–68

Parker, S. C. (1996). A time series model of self-employment under uncertainty, *Economica*, 63, pp. 459–75

(1997a). The effects of risk on self-employment, *Small Business Economics*, 9, pp. 515–22

(1997b). The distribution of self-employment income in the United Kingdom, 1976–1991, *Economic Journal*, 107, pp. 455–66

(1999a). The optimal linear taxation of employment and self-employment incomes, *Journal of Public Economics*, 73, pp. 107–23

(1999b). The inequality of employment and self-employment incomes: a decomposition analysis for the UK, *Review of Income and Wealth*, 45, pp. 263–74

(2000). Saving to overcome borrowing constraints: implications for small business entry and exit, *Small Business Economics*, 15, pp. 223–32

(2001). Risk, self-employment and differential income taxation, *Manchester School*, 69, pp. 1–15

(2002a). On the dimensionality and composition of entrepreneurship, Barclays Centre for Entrepreneurship Discussion Paper, 1, Durham Business School; forthcoming, *Academy of Entrepreneurship Journal*

(2002b). Do banks ration credit to new enterprises? And should governments intervene?, *Scottish Journal of Political Economy*, 49, pp. 162–95

(2003a). Does tax evasion affect occupational choice?, *Oxford Bulletin of Economics and Statistics*, 65, 379–94

(2003b). The distribution of wealth among older self-employed Britons, *Fiscal Studies*, 24, pp. 23–43

(2003c). 'There's something about sharing': using public policy to promote efficient venture capital investment, Paper presented to the 59th Congress of the International Institute of Public Finance, Prague

(2003d). Asymmetric information, occupational choice and government policy, *Economic Journal*, forthcoming

Parker, S. C. and M. T. Robson (2000). Explaining international variations in self-employment: evidence from a panel of OECD countries, Working Paper, No. 2008, Department of Economics and Finance, University of Durham

Parker, S. C. and J. Rougier (2001). An econometric analysis of the retirement behaviour of the self-employed, Paper presented to the 2001 Econometric Society European Meetings, University of Lausanne

Pavitt, K., M. Robson and J. Townsend (1987). Technological accumulation, diversification and organisation in UK companies, 1945–1983, *Manchester School*, 35, pp. 81–99

Perez, S. J. (1998). Testing for credit rationing: an application of disequilibrium econometrics, *Journal of Macroeconomics*, 20, pp. 721–39

Pestieau, P. and U. M. Possen (1991). Tax evasion and occupational choice, *Journal of Public Economics*, 45, pp. 107–25

(1992). How do taxes affect occupational choice?, *Public Finance*, 47, pp. 108–19

Petersen, M. A. and R. G. Rajan (1994). The benefits of lending relationships: evidence from small firm business data, *Journal of Finance*, 49, pp. 3–37

Pfeiffer, F. and F. Reize (2000). Business start-ups by the unemployed – an econometric analysis based on firm data, *Labour Economics*, 7, pp. 629–63

Phillips, B. D. and B. A. Kirchhoff (1989). Formation, growth and survival: small firm dynamics in the US economy, *Small Business Economics*, 1, pp. 65–74

Phillips, J. D. (1962). *The Self-employed in the United States*, Urbana, IL, University of Illinois Press

Phillips, P. C. B. (1986). Understanding spurious regressions in econometrics, *Journal of Econometrics*, 33, pp. 311–40

Pickles, A. R. and P. N. O'Farrell (1987). An analysis of entrepreneurial behaviour from male work histories, *Regional Studies*, 21, pp. 425–44

Piore, M. J. and C. F. Sabel (1984). *The Second Industrial Divide: Possibilities for Prosperity*, New York, Basic Books

Pissarides, C. A. and G. Weber (1989). An expenditure-based estimate of Britain's black economy, *Journal of Public Economics*, 39, pp. 17–32

Pitt, M. M. and S. R. Khandker (1998). The impact of group-based credit programs on poor households in Bangladesh: does the gender of participants matter?, *Journal of Political Economy*, 98, pp. 106, 958–96

Pollert, A. (1988). The 'flexible firm': fixation or fact?, *Work, Employment and Society*, 2, pp. 281–316

Portes, A. and M. Zhou (1996). Self-employment and the earnings of immigrants, *American Sociological Review*, 61, pp. 219–30

Poterba, J. M. (1989a). Venture capital and capital gains taxation, in L. H. Summers (ed.), *Tax Policy and the Economy*, Cambridge, MA, MIT Press, pp. 47–67

(1989b). Capital gains tax policy towards entrepreneurship, *National Tax Journal*, 42, pp. 375–89

Power, L. and M. Rider (2002). The effect of tax-based savings incentives on the self-employed, *Journal of Public Economics*, 85, pp. 33–52

Praag, C. M. van (1999). Some classic views on entrepreneurship, *De Economist*, 147, pp. 311–35

Praag, C. M. van and J. S. Cramer (2001). The roots of entrepreneurship and labor demand: individual ability and low risk aversion, *Economica*, 68, pp. 45–62

Praag, C. M. van, J. S. Cramer and J. Hartog (2002). Low risk aversion encourages the choice for entrepreneurship: an empirical test of a truism, *Journal of Economic Behavior and Organization*, 48, pp. 29–36

Praag, C. M. van and H. van Ophem (1995). Determinants of willingness and opportunity to start as an entrepreneur, *Kyklos*, 48, pp. 513–40

Quadrini, V. (1999). The importance of entrepreneurship for wealth concentration and mobility, *Review of Income and Wealth*, 45, pp. 1–19

Quinn, J. F. (1980). Labour-force participation patterns of older self-employed workers, *Social Security Bulletin*, 43, pp. 17–28

Rafiq, M. (1992). Ethnicity and enterprise: a comparison of Muslim and non-Muslim owned Asian businesses in Britain, *New Community*, 19, pp. 43–60

Rahman, A. (1993). The general replicability of the Grameen Bank model, in A. N. M. Wahid (ed.), *The Grameen Bank: Poverty Relief in Bangladesh*, Boulder, CO, Westview Press, pp. 209–22

Ray, R. N. (1975). Self-employed Americans in 1973, *Monthly Labor Review*, 98, pp. 49–54

Razin, E. and A. Langlois (1996). Metropolitan characteristics and entrepreneurship among immigrants and ethnic groups in Canada, *International Migration Review*, 30, pp. 703–27

Rees, H. and A. Shah (1986). An empirical analysis of self-employment in the UK, *Journal of Applied Econometrics*, 1, pp. 95–108

(1994). The characteristics of the self-employed: the supply of labour, in J. Atkinson and D. J. Storey (eds.), *Employment, the Small Firm and the Labour Market*, London, Routledge, pp. 317–27

Reid, G. C. (1991). Staying in business, *International Journal of Industrial Organization*, 9, pp. 545–56

(1993). *Small Business Enterprise: An Economic Analysis*, London, Routledge

(1999). Capital structure at inception and the short-run performance of micro-firms, in Z. J. Acs, B. Carlsson and C. Karlsson (eds.), *Entrepreneurship, Small and Medium Sized Enterprises and the Macroeconomy*, Cambridge, Cambridge University Press, pp. 186–205

Reid, G. C. and L. R. Jacobsen (1988). *The Small Entrepreneurial Firm*, David Hume Institute, Aberdeen, Aberdeen University Press

Repullo, R. and J. Suarez (2000). Entrepreneurial moral hazard and bank monitoring: a model of the credit channel, *European Economic Review*, 44, pp. 1931–50

Reynolds, P. D. (1999). Creative destruction: source or symptom of economic growth?, in Z. J. Acs, B. Carlsson and C. Karlsson (eds.), *Entrepreneurship, Small and Medium Sized Enterprises and the Macroeconomy*, Cambridge, Cambridge University Press, 97–136

Reynolds, P. D., D. J. Storey, and P. Westhead (1994). Cross-national comparisons of the variation in new firm formation rates, *Regional Studies*, 28, pp. 443–56

Reynolds, P. D. and S. B. White (1997). *The Entrepreneurial Process: Economic Growth, Men, Women and Minorities*, Westport, CT, Quorum Books

Reynolds, P. D. et al. (2001, 2002). *Global Entrepreneurship Monitor Executive Reports*, www.gemconsortium.com

Rhyne, E. H. (1988). *Small Business, Banks and SBA Loan Guarantees*, New York, Quorum Books

Riley, J. (1979). Testing the educational screening hypothesis, *Journal of Political Economy*, 87, pp. S227–S252

(1987). Credit rationing: a further remark, *American Economic Review*, 77, pp. 224–27

Roberts, E. B. (1991). *Entrepreneurs in High Technology*, Oxford, Oxford University Press

Robinson, P. B. and E. A. Sexton (1994). The effect of education and experience on self-employment success, *Journal of Business Venturing*, 9, pp. 141–56

Robson, M. T. (1991). Self-employment and new firm formation, *Scottish Journal of Political Economy*, 38, pp. 352–68

(1996). Macroeconomic factors in the birth and death of UK firms: evidence from quarterly VAT registrations, *Manchester School*, 64, pp. 170–88

(1997). The relative earnings from self and paid employment: a time series analysis for the UK, *Scottish Journal of Political Economy*, 44, pp. 502–18

(1998a). Self-employment in the UK regions, *Applied Economics*, 30, pp. 313–22

(1998b). The rise in self-employment amongst UK males, *Small Business Economics*, 10, pp. 199–212

Robson, M. T. and C. Wren (1999). Marginal and average tax rates and the incentive for self-employment, *Southern Economic Journal*, 65, pp. 757–73

Rosa, P., S. Carter and D. Hamilton (1996). Gender as a determinant of small business performance: insights from a British study, *Small Business Economics*, 8, pp. 463–78

Rosen, S. (1981). The economics of superstars, *American Economic Review*, 71, pp. 845–58

(1997). Austrian and neoclassical economics: any gains from trade?, *Journal of Economic Perspectives*, 11(4), pp. 139–52

Ross, S. A. (1977). The determination of financial structure: the incentive-signalling approach, *Bell Journal of Economics*, 8, pp. 23–40

Rossi, S. E. (1998). Credit guarantee schemes: the case of Italy, in D. J. Storey (ed.), *Small Business: Critical Perspectives of Business and Management, I–IV*, London, Routledge, 2000, pp. 693–710

Rothschild, M. and J. E. Stiglitz (1971). Increasing risk: II. Its consequences, *Journal of Economic Theory*, 3, pp. 66–84

Rotter, J. B. (1982). *The Development and Applications of Social Learning Theory: Selected Papers*, Praeger, New York

Rubery, J., J. Earnshaw and B. Burchell (1993). *New Forms and Patterns of Employment: The Role of Self-Employment in Britain*, Baden-Baden, Nomos Verlagsgesellschaft

Sanders, J. M. and V. Nee (1996). Immigrant self-employment: the family as social capital and the value of human capital, *American Sociological Review*, 61, pp. 231–49

Sandford, C. (1981). *Costs and Benefits of VAT*, London, Heinemann

Say, J. B. (1828). *Cours Complet d'Economie Politique Practique*, Paris

Scase, R. and R. Goffee (1982). *The Entrepreneurial Middle Class*, London, Croom Helm

Schaffner, J. A. (1993). Rising incomes and the shift from self-employment to firm-based production, *Economics Letters*, 41, pp. 435–40

Scheffler, R. M. and L. F. Rossiter (1983). Compensation schemes and the labour supply of dentists, *Quarterly Review of Economics and Business*, 23, pp. 29–43

Schere, J. C. (1982). Tolerance of ambiguity as a discriminating variable between entrepreneurs and managers, *Academy of Management Proceedings*, pp. 404–8

Scherer, F. M. (1980). *Industrial Market Structure and Economic Performance*, Chicago, Rand McNally College Publishing

(1991). Changing perspectives on the firm size problem, in Z. J. Acs and D. B. Audretsch (eds.), *Innovation and Technological Change*, Ann Arbor, University of Michigan Press, pp. 24–38

Scheutze, H. J. (2000). Taxes, economic conditions and recent trends in male self-employment: a Canada–US comparison, *Labour Economics*, 7, pp. 507–44

Schiller, B. R. and P. E. Crewson (1997). Entrepreneurial origins: a longitudinal inquiry, *Economic Inquiry*, 35, pp. 523–31

Schmidt-Mohr, U. (1997). Rationing versus collateralisation in competitive and monopolistic credit markets with asymmetric information, *European Economic Review*, 41, pp. 1321–42

Schmitz, J. A. (1989). Imitation, entrepreneurship and long-run growth, *Journal of Political Economy*, 97, pp. 721–39

Schultz, T. P. (1990). Women's changing participation in the labour force: a world perspective, *Economic Development and Cultural Change*, 38, pp. 457–88

Schultz, T. W. (1980). Investment in entrepreneurial ability, *Scandinavian Journal of Economics*, 82, pp. 437–48

Schumpeter, J. A. (1934). *The Theory of Economic Development*, Cambridge, MA, Harvard University Press

(1939). *Business Cycles*, New York, McGraw-Hill

(1947). The creative response in economic history, *Journal of Economic History*, 7, pp. 149–59

Segal, U. and A. Spivak (1989). Firm size and optimal growth rates, *European Economic Review*, 33, pp. 159–67

Selden, J. (1999), Small and medium enterprises: their role in the economy, *Labour Market Trends*, 107, pp. 543–50

Sexton, D. L. and N. Bowman (1985). The entrepreneur: a capable executive and more, *Journal of Business Venturing*, 1, pp. 29–40

Shane, S. (1996). Explaining variation in rates of entrepreneurship in the United States: 1899–1988, *Journal of Management*, 22, pp. 747–81

Shapero, A. (1975). The displaced uncomfortable entrepreneur, *Psychology Today*, pp. 83–8

Sheshinski, E. and J. Drèze (1976). Demand fluctuations, capacity utilisation, and costs, *American Economic Review*, 66, pp. 731–42

Shorrocks, A. F. (1988). Wealth holdings and entrepreneurial activity, in D. Kessler and A. Masson (eds.), *Modelling the Accumulation and Distribution of Wealth*, Oxford, Clarendon Press, pp. 241–56

Sillamaa, M.-A. and M. R. Veall (2001). The effect of marginal tax rates on taxable income: a panel study of the 1988 tax flattening in Canada, *Journal of Public Economics*, 80, pp. 341–56

Simmons, P. (1989). Bad luck and fixed costs in bankruptcy, *Economic Journal*, 99, pp. 92–107

Simon, H. A. and C. P. Bonini (1958). The size distribution of business firms, *American Economic Review*, 48, pp. 607–17

Slovin, M B. and M. E. Sushka (1983). A model of the commercial loan rate, *Journal of Finance*, 38, pp. 1583–96

van der Sluis, J., C. M. van Praag and W. Vijverberg (2003). Entrepreneurship selection and performance: a meta-analysis of the impact of education in industrialised countries, University of Amsterdam, Mimeo

Small Business Administration (SBA) (1986, 2001). *The State of Small Business*, Washington, DC, Office of Advocacy

(1996). *White Paper on the Financing of Small Business*, Washington, DC, Office of Advocacy

304   References

(2002a). Small business's share of economic growth, Research Summary, 211, Washington, DC

(2002b). The influence of R&D expenditures on new firm formation and economic growth, Research Summary, 222, Washington, DC

Smallbone, D. and F. Lyon (2001). Policy support for new business start-ups: a review, Middlesex University, Mimeo

Smallbone, D. and F. Welter (2001). The distinctiveness of entrepreneurship in transition economies, *Small Business Economics*, 16, pp. 249–62

Smith, A. (1937). *The Wealth of Nations*, New York, Random House

Smith, B. (1983). Limited information, credit rationing, and optimal government lending policy, *American Economic Review*, 73, pp. 305–18

Smith, B. D. and M. J. Stutzer (1989). Credit rationing and government loan programs: a welfare analysis, *AREUEA Journal*, 17, pp. 177–93

Smith, S. (1986). *Britain's Shadow Economy*, Oxford, Clarendon Press

Sowell, T. (1981). *Markets and Minorities*, New York, Basic Books

Spear, R. (1992). The co-operative spirit: some UK evidence, in P. Leighton and A. Felstead (eds.), *The New Entrepreneurs: Self-Employment and Small Business in Europe*, London, Kogan Page, pp. 325–41

Spilling, O. R. (1996). Regional variation of new firm formation: the Norwegian case, *Entrepreneurship and Regional Development*, 8, pp. 217–43

Staber, U. and D. Bogenhold (1993). Self-employment: a study of seventeen OECD countries, *Industrial Relations Journal*, 24, pp. 126–37

Stanworth, J., D. Purdy, S. Price and N. Zafiris (1998). Franchise versus conventional small business failure rates in the US and UK: more similarities than differences, *International Small Business Journal*, 16, pp. 56–69

Steinmetz, G. and E. O. Wright (1989). The fall and rise of the petty bourgeoisie: changing patterns of self-employment in the postwar United States, *American Journal of Sociology*, 94, pp. 973–1018

Stiglitz, J. (1970). The effects of income, wealth and capital gains taxation on risk taking, *Quarterly Journal of Economics*, 83, pp. 263–83

(1990). Peer monitoring and credit markets, *World Bank Economic Review*, 4, pp. 351–66

Stiglitz, J. and A. Weiss (1981). Credit rationing in markets with imperfect information, *American Economic Review*, 71, pp. 393–410

(1983). Incentive effects of terminations: applications to the credit and labor markets, *American Economic Review*, 73, pp. 912–27

(1987). Credit rationing: reply, *American Economic Review*, 77, pp. 228–31

(1992). Asymmetric information in credit markets and its implications for macro-economics, *Oxford Economic Papers*, 44, pp. 694–724

Stoll, H. R. (1984). Small firms' access to public equity financing, in P. M. Horvitz and R. R. Pettit (eds.), *Small Business Finance: Sources of Financing for Small Business, Part A* Greenwich, CT, JAI Press, pp. 177–238

Storey, D. J. (1982). *Entrepreneurship and the New Firm*, London, Croom Helm

(1991). The birth of new firms – does unemployment matter? A review of the evidence, *Small Business Economics*, 3, pp. 167–78

(1994a). *Understanding the Small Business Sector*, London, Routledge

(1994b). The role of legal status in influencing bank financing and new firm growth, *Applied Economics*, 26, pp. 129–36

(ed.) (2000). *Small Business: Critical Perspectives on Business and Management*, I–IV, London, Routledge

Storey, D. J. and A. M. Jones (1987). New firm formation – a labour market approach to industrial entry, *Scottish Journal of Political Economy*, 34, pp. 37–51

Storey, D. J., K. Keasey, R. Watson and P. Wynarczyk (1987). *The Performance of Small Firms*, London, Croom Helm

Sumner, D. A. (1981). Wage functions and occupational selection in a rural less developed country setting, *Review of Economics and Statistics*, 63, pp. 513–19

Sutton, J. (1997). Gibrat's legacy, *Journal of Economic Literature*, 35, pp. 40–59

Tassel, E. van (1999). Group lending under asymmetric information, *Journal of Development Economics*, 60, pp. 3–25

Taylor, M. P. (1996). Earnings, independence or unemployment: why become self-employed?, *Oxford Bulletin of Economics and Statistics*, 58, pp. 253–66

(1999). Survival of the fittest? An analysis of self-employment duration in Britain, *Economic Journal*, 109, pp. C140–C155

(2001). Self-employment and windfall gains in Britain: evidence from panel data, *Economica*, 68, pp. 539–65

Teilhet-Waldorf, S. and W. H. Waldorf (1983). Earnings of self-employed in an informal sector: a case study of Bangkok, *Economic Development and Cultural Change*, 31, pp. 587–607

Tether, B. S., I. J. Smith and A. T. Thwaites (1997). Smaller enterprises and innovation in the UK: the SPRU Innovations Database revisited, *Research Policy* 2, pp. 19–32

Thakor, A. (1996). Capital requirements, monetary policy, and aggregate bank lending: theory and empirical evidence, *Journal of Finance*, 51, pp. 279–324

Thakor, A. and R. Calloway (1983). Costly information production equilibria in the bank credit market with applications to credit rationing, *Journal of Financial and Quantitative Analysis*, 18, pp. 229–56

Thornton, J. (1994). Estimating the choice behaviour of self-employed business proprietors: an application to dairy farmers, *Southern Economic Journal*, 60, pp. 579–95

(1998). The labour supply behaviour of self-employed solo practice physicians, *Applied Economics*, 30, pp. 85–94

Timmons, J. A. (1976). Characteristics and role demands of entrepreneurship, *American Journal of Small Business*, 3, pp. 5–17

Townsend, R. (1979). Optimal contracts and competitive markets with costly state verification, *Journal of Economic Theory*, 21, pp. 417–25

Tucker, I. B. (1988). Entrepreneurs and public-sector employees: the role of achievement motivation and risk in occupational choice, *Journal of Economic Education*, 19, pp. 259–68

(1990). Employer seniority discrimination: evidence from entrepreneurial occupational choice, *Economics Letters*, 32, pp. 85–89

Tyson, L. d'Andrea, T. Petrin and H. Rogers (1994). Promoting entrepreneurship in Eastern Europe, *Small Business Economics*, 6, pp. 165–84

Uusitalo, R. (2001). Homo entreprenaurus?, *Applied Economics*, 33, pp. 1631–38

Variyam, J. N. and D. S. Kraybill (1992). Empirical evidence on determinants of firm growth, *Economics Letters*, 38, pp. 31–6

Vijverberg, W. P. M. (1986). Consistent estimates of the wage equation when individuals choose among income-earning activities, *Southern Economic Journal*, 52, pp. 1028–42

Wadhwani, S. B. (1986). Inflation, bankruptcy, default premia and the stock market, *Economic Journal*, 96, pp. 120–38

Wagner, J. (1995). Firm size and job creation in Germany, *Small Business Economics*, 7, pp. 469–74

Wales, T. J. (1973). Estimation of a labour supply curve for self-employed business proprietors, *International Economic Review*, 14, pp. 69–80

Watkins, J. M. and D. S. Watkins (1984). The female entrepreneur: her background and determinants of business choice – some British data, *Frontiers of Entrepreneurship Research*, Wellesley, MA, Babson College

Watson, H. (1984). Credit markets and borrower effort, *Southern Economic Journal*, 50, pp. 802–13

  (1985). Tax evasion and labour markets, *Journal of Public Economics*, 27, pp. 231–46

Watson, R. (1990). Employment change, profits and directors' remuneration in small and closely-held UK companies, *Scottish Journal of Political Economy*, 37, pp. 259–74

Webb, D. C. (1991). Long-term financial contracts can mitigate the adverse selection problem in project financing, *International Economic Review*, 32, pp. 305–20

Weber, M. (1930). *The Protestant Ethic and the Spirit of Capitalism*, New York, Scribner

Wellington, A. J. (2001). Health insurance coverage and entrepreneurship, *Contemporary Economic Policy*, 19, pp. 465–78

Wennekers, S. and R. Thurik (1999). Linking entrepreneurship and economic growth, *Small Business Economics*, 13, pp. 27–55

Wenner, M. D. (1995). Group credit: a means to improve information transfer and loan repayment performance, *Journal of Development Studies*, 32, pp. 263–81

Westhead, P. and M. Cowling (1995). Employment change in independent owner-managed high-technology firms in Great Britain, *Small Business Economics*, 7, pp. 111–40

Wette, H. (1983). Collateral in credit rationing in markets with imperfect information: note, *American Economic Review*, 73, pp. 442–5

Wetzel, W. E. (1987). The informal venture capital market: aspects of scale and market efficiency, *Journal of Business Venturing*, 2, pp. 299–313

White, L. J. (1982). The determinants of the relative importance of small business, *Review of Economics and Statistics*, 64, pp. 42–9

  (1984). The role of small business in the US economy, in P. M. Horvitz and R. R. Pettit (eds.), *Small Business Finance: Sources of Financing for Small Business, Part A*, Greenwich, CT, JAI Press, pp. 19–49

Whittington, R. C. (1984). Regional bias in new firm formation in the UK, *Regional Studies*, 18, pp. 253–56

Williams, D. L. (2001). Why do entrepreneurs become franchisees? An empirical analysis of organisational choice, *Journal of Business Venturing*, 14, pp. 103–24

Williams, D. R. (2000). Consequences of self-employment for women and men in the United States, *Labour Economics*, 7, pp. 665–87

Williamson, O. E. (1985). *The Economic Institutions of Capitalism*, New York, Free Press

Williamson, S. D. (1986). Costly monitoring, financial intermediation and equilibrium credit rationing, *Journal of Monetary Economics*, 18, pp. 159–79

(1987). Costly monitoring, loan contracts and equilibrium credit rationing, *Quarterly Journal of Economics*, 102, pp. 135–45

Wit, G. de (1993). Models of self-employment in a competitive market, *Journal of Economic Surveys*, 7, pp. 367–97

Wit, G. de and van Winden, F. (1989). An empirical analysis of self-employment in the Netherlands, *Small Business Economics*, 1, pp. 263–72

(1990). An empirical analysis of self-employment in the Netherlands, *Economics Letters*, 32, pp. 97–100

(1991). An M-sector, N-group behavioural model of self-employment, *Small Business Economics*, 3, pp. 49–66

Wolpin, K. I. (1977). Education and screening, *American Economic Review*, 67, pp. 949–58

Wren, C. (1998). Subsidies for job creation: is small best?, *Small Business Economics*, 10, pp. 273–81

Wydick, B. (1999). Can social cohesion be harnessed to repair market failures? Evidence from group lending in Guatemala, *Economic Journal*, 109, pp. 463–75

Xu, B. (1998). A re-estimation of the Evans–Jovanovic entrepreneurial choice model, *Economics Letters*, 58, pp. 91–5

(2000). The welfare implications of costly monitoring in the credit market: a note, *Economic Journal*, 110, pp. 576–80

Yamawaki, H. (1990). The effects of business conditions on net entry: evidence from Japan, in P. A. Geroski and J. Schwalbach (eds.), *Entry and Market Contestability: An International Comparison*, Oxford, Basil Blackwell

Yoon, I. J. (1991). The changing significance of ethnic and class resources in immigrant business, *International Migration Review*, 25, pp. 303–31

Yuengert, A. M. (1995). Testing hypotheses of immigrant self-employment, *Journal of Human Resources*, 30, pp. 194–204

Author index

Subject index